THE PRINCIPLES OF HINDU ETHICS

THE PRINCIPLES OF HINDU ETHICS

By
Maganlal A. Buch

BHARATIYA KALA PRAKASHAN
DELHI (INDIA)

First Edition : 1921 India
New Type Setting and Revised Edition : 2003
Edition : 2024

Published by C.P. Gautam *for*
BHARATIYA KALA PRAKASHAN
3480/1, Ground Floor, Narang Colony,
Tri Nagar, Delhi - 110035,
Phone No. : 011 71522860, 9811642997, 8595139625,
E-mail : info@bkpbooks.com; sales.bkpbooks@gmail.com
Website: www.bkpbooks.com

ISBN : 978-81-8090-006-8

Laser Type Setting
Creative Graphics

Printed by :
G.S. Offset Printers
Delhi

उत्तिष्ठत जाग्रत प्राप्य वरान्निबोधत।

Kath. Up.

उद्धरेदात्मनात्मानं नात्मानमवसादयेत्।
आत्मैवह्यात्मनो बंधुरात्मैव रिपुरात्मनः॥

Gita

सत्यान्न प्रमदितव्यं धर्मान्न प्रमदितव्यं।
कुशलान्न प्रमदितव्यं भूत्यै न प्रमदितव्यं॥

Ta. Up.

यान्यवद्यानि कर्माणि। तानि सेवितव्यानि। नो इतराणि।

Ta. Up.

न जातु कामान्नभयान्न लोभाद्धर्मं त्यजेन्जीवितस्यापि हेतोः।
धर्मो नित्यः सुखदुःखेत्वनित्ये जीवो नित्यो हेतुरस्यत्वनित्यः॥

Mahabharata

CONTENTS

PREFACE

I have ventured in this small volume to take a systematic survey of the Hindu ideas on morality. The wealth of ethical reflexions scattered all over the ancient sacred writings of the Hindus always proved a tempting field to my humble ambitions; and I have here endeavoured to present them in a connected form. So far as I know very few writers have cultivated this field. Scholars are generally attracted by high metaphysical ideas on the one hand and political thought on the other hand; but the unpretentious and yet all too precious work of the Hindu Rishis on subjects of morality remained largely unexplored. I have tried to trace out the ethical thought of the ancient Hindus from the early Rig-Vedic period down to the age of the Mahabharata and the Dharma-shastras. The period covered here witness indeed the rise and fall of Hindu culture, its very interesting evolution in successive periods under diverse historical conditions. Yet while there is a rich diversity of moral ideals, presented to us during these periods of Hindu history, a clear thread of unity runs through all these. At no period can we say that there is a sudden break or charm in the continuity of our civilization; and an unmistakeable attempt was made at every new turn to trace the changes of thought or practice to some old authority. The Hindu ethical theory has therefore an organic coherence about it; its childhood, its period of adolescence, and its old age were all definitely connected with each other. The Hindu sages always tried to unite reason with experience; and while they continuously introduced new modifications necessitated by changes in environment, they never thought they were departing from the ancient Vedic practice. Thus the unchanging East went on perpetually changing; and yet at every step forward it cast a constant glance at the past and thus preserved the unity of the Hindu social organism. The Hindu of today, though differing widely from the Vedic Aryan in almost every incident or accident of his position, still claims to be–and not quite unjustly,–the heir of all the ages,– the child of that great race which was the pioneer of a mighty civilization in the world.

This long evolution has a manifold interest for us. To a Hindu, it is almost a necessity of his position to understand the precise significance of his culture. The greatest task of the present age in the East is the discovery of the soul of Asia. The whole Asia is struggling to discover the fundamentals of its position–the bed-rock of its culture,–the unity of thought and experience behind all apparent diversities,–to find its own Self in the midst of all accidents or *Upadhis*. India is similarly challenged by the outside world to give expression to its own soul. The world is waiting to listen to the right word from the people who say they represent what was once a unique civilization. Has India any message for the world? It is the earnest attempt of the greatest geniuses of our age to help India to utter the right word. Dr. Tagore the great Asiatic poet-laureate.– Shrijuta Arabinda Ghose, the great Asiatic scholar and philosopher, Mahatma Gandhi, the *Karma-yogin*, the arch-exponent of the creed of the East–the perfect non-violence in thought, word, and deed;–all are engaged in this supreme work of the interpretation of the East. It is for the humbler workers to do their little bit in this task of tasks.

I also hope that a systematic study of the Hindu ethical thought will have an interest of its own for foreign scholars. It will help them to formulate a precise ethical theory comprehensive enough to meet all possible facts. Every people has an ethics of its own; its precise presentation is necessary in a vast, inductive study of ethical ideas of all times and all ages. Ethics may be either idealistic, presenting the standards of action, the various ideals dominating various people; or empirical, presenting ethical facts,–virtues and vices. A systematic study of Hindu ethics in the way done here is above all a contribution to sociological literature. Morality has an important bearing on the relations of man and man in society; and a study of ancient Hindu society from this standpoint is not without its own value in the science of society.

No one can be more conscious of the limitations of the work than the author himself. Hindu ethics is a vast subject : its satisfactory, all-round treatment will be the work of many minds. The present volume is merely a beginning in this hitherto not much–explored field. Persons of greater equipment may take up the work and attack it from various points of view. There are a dozen books on Christian Ethics; why should we not have a dozen books on Hindu ethics? I intend here to make a descriptive survey; and avoid the work of interpretation as far as possible. I have therefore tried to avoid my own comments. An accurate rendering of the ideas of the ancient Rishis requires that they should be presented in their own words. It is the ethics of the ancient thinkers I have to explain; and in the interests of impartial exposition, the author's personality should be in the background. The precise force of the sentiments cannot be brought out except by a reproduction of the passages. The exposition becomes more concrete, more vigorous, more picturesque, as more accurate and faithful if the original texts are allowed to point their own moral in their own way.

Colligation, interpretation, systematisation : such is the work of the application of the scientific method to the data presented before us in the ancient Scriptures. Passages recur continuously emphasizing the importance of truthfulness; passages also recur where exceptions to it are pointed. It is in such cases that the work of systematisation is so interesting and fruitful. The doctrine of *Ahimsa* emphasises the morality of love and forbearance; but what are the limitations to this fundamental principle? In this way it becomes more easy to find out the ultimate principles of the science of morality. If ever a subject gained by systematic co-ordination it was the subject of ethical thought of the Hindus. Variety of reflections is the characteristic of every Hindu moral position : conflicting ethical judgments are delivered on every occasion. However, it is quite clear that there is a perfect order, harmony, system in all these. A little reflection serves to bring out this.

A work of this type has both theoretical and practical value. Its value from the point of view of thought is sufficiently clear. It has interest for the student of Hindu thought, for the student of ethics, for the student of sociology. Its practical value lies in the fact that it enables the statesmen and people of other countries as well as of India to understand the Hindu mind, to measure its strength and limitations, to judge properly its mental attitude. But above all, it enables social reformers to strike out proper lines of social evolution. Every society must build upon its past : its progress to be sound and permanent must be evolved from its own national temperament. A comparative study of the Hindu thought and practice of different ages serves to show that the Hindu thought had a wonderful principle of development within itself. Its most striking characteristic was elasticity. Its adapatability enabled it to stem every new tide and to conquer every attack from within and without. The greatest upheaval from within was the great Buddhist awakening; yet Hinduism showed wonderful vitality by absorbing all the best elements of Buddhism and thus enriching itself in the end. Similarly it proved victorious over various rival alternatives, Islam or Christianity. Its social organization of caste and its religious tolerance enabled it to assimilate the best in every system of thought. Buddha was accepted as an incarnation : Kapila who denied Godhead was himself made an incarnation of God; and who knows whether Mahomet would not have been worshipped by the Hindus, had he been born in India? If such was the case with the past Hinduism, will Hinduism fail to show the same elasticity in the face of the portentous phenomenon of modern civilization? It is fervently hoped that the reconstruction of Hindu beliefs and practices may take place in near future, which discarding its agelong excrescences may re-establish in all their pristine strength some of the best ideas of the ancient Rishis. For such a reconstruction, a strictly scientific study of our past is an indispensable prerequisite. An impartial weighing and balancing both sides of every question in the dry light of reason is, I believe, one of the features of the present attempt. Facts are not studied with a view to support any *a priori* theory or preconceived view of the author. The personal bias is kept apart as far as possible : the interests of truth are considered paramount. And the result is a system of morality as rich, as varied, as full of complexities as life itself. There is no reason why we should be ashamed of any part of this ancient legacy. Kalidas expresses the idea of a true scientific spirit in a pointed way : "All that is old is not necessarily good; nor all that is new, faultless. The wise therefore accept one or the other on a proper examination of both."

It remains for me to acknowledge my obligations to a few kind and liberal friends. My thanks are due to the Divan Sahib for his blessings on of my humble work and acceptance of my dedication. I hope the readers and critics of this book will kindly excuse the unfortunate typographic errors which have crept into the book owing to the hurry with which the book has been printed.

–M.A. Buch

ABBREVIATIONS

Rg.	Rig-veda
Av.	Atharva-veda
Yj.	Yajur-veda
Tai. S.	Taittiriya Samhita
Vaj. S.	Vajasneyi Samhita
Mai. S.	Maitrayani Samhita
S. Br. , Sh. Br.	Shatapatha Brahmana
Ai. Br.	Aitareya Brahmana
Kaus. Br.	Kaushitaki Brahmana
Up.	Upanishad
Tait.	Taittiriya
Br.	Brihadaranyaka
Ai.	Aitareya
Ch.	Chandogya
Mu.	Mundaka
Pr.	Prashna
Ish.	Isha
G. Gr. S.	Gobhila Grihya Sutras
A. Gr. S.	Ashwalayana Grihya Sutras
S. Gr. S.	Shankhayana Grihya Sutras
Ap. Gr. S.	Apastamba Grihya Sutras
M. Gr. S.	Manava Grihya Sutras
H. Gr. S.	Hiranyakeshi Grihya Sutras
Ka. S.	Kaushitaki Sutras
Apastamba	Apastamba Dharma-Sutras Apastamba Dharma-Shastra
M.	Manu-Smriti
Bg.	Bhagwad-Gita
Y. or. Yaj.	Yajnavalkya-Smriti

R.	Ramayana
S.N.	Shukra-Niti
Mahabharata	Bombay Edition-Nirnaya-Sagar Press.
Dharma-Shastras	M.N. Dutt.
Mk. P.	Markandeya Purana
Sh.	Shakuntala
S.B.	Shankara-Bhashya
C. Com.	Shankara's Commentary

Chapter - I

THE HINDU VIEW OF LIFE

What is the Hindu view of Life?

There is a remarkable agreement as well as divergence between various ideals of life evolved by various peoples. Ethical systems of the world may be grouped in various ways. There are systems like the Greek ethics, for example, which look upon the perfection of earthly life as the goal of man. There are other systems like the ethics of early Christianity, which look upon life Beyond as the main purpose of our life here. Thus there is naturalistic ethics and there is supranaturalistic ethics; the former revelling in the affirmation of our worldly life, the latter glorying in its denial. Now here the Hindu attitude is peculiar. The perfection of the natural man is a valuable ideal for a Hindu, but it is not an end in itself. Eternal life has far greater claims upon man here than the transitory three day's existence of ours on earth. But eternal life is not allowed to swallow up our sojourn here. Marriage, pursuit of wealth, acquisition of fame, success in war and peace, family prosperity : those are held highly desirable things, when they are enjoyed in a righteous spirit. No man can repose in peace as long as he has not made his own contribution to the building up and furthering of the secular civilization. But while it is enjoined on all persons to fulfil to the best of their capacity their worldly ambitions summed up in वित्तैषणा, लोकैष्णा, and पुत्रैषणा, it was clearly perceived that these were not highly important ends, but mere means for the gratification of the inner propensities. Man, if he wants to save himself, must rise to a higher level and transcend altogether the power of these earthly longings. The perfection of the natural man must ultimately give way to the perfection of the spiritual man. Life here and now must be a moment in the Life Eternal.

Here the Hindu view decidedly parts company with the Graeco-Persian view of life. No important religious systems of life perhaps attach to our earthly stay so much value and weight as the Zoroastrian and the Greek systems. These were the systems of the child-man. The sunlit spirit of man had in it no misgivings, no suspicions of the dark shadows of life. There was perfect healthiness of outlook, the natural man unhesitatingly went forth to give an objective shape to his inner thought. Objectivity was the predominant note of this type of mind. A natural confidence in human powers to deal with all situations, and a consequent optimism characterised the Greek and the Persian mind. A free indulgence in all the natural desires of man, a strong love of all the earthly powers and goods, an intense passion for physical and intellectual perfection were the normal marks of the unsophisticated soul of the natural man. Such institutions as celibacy and fasting and renunciation were considered abnormal. Here we may remark that the early Vedic view was exactly of this type. An enormous fondness for life itself and all the numberless ways in which it delights to affirm itself was a common characteristic of the Vedic, the Gothic and the Greek ages.

But the Hindu consciousness soon underwent a great change. It passed from the stage of objectivity into the stage of subjectivity. Doubt began to enter the soul of man. From the natural man was gradually born the spiritual man. Here the Hindu theory has some resemblances with the Christian view. A tendency to deny the values of earthly life, to look to the transcendental realities began to assert itself. A life of poverty, meekness, renunciation began to grow in favour with the *Rishis*. Self-control, self-denial, self-effacement took the place of self-assertion and self-fulfilment. Hard discipline of monastic life became crystallised into an institution. A difference between time and eternity, one and many, changeful and changeless, material and spiritual made itself felt. Man's mind took a vaster and deeper view of existence and its problems, and found its only refuge from life's miseries and sorrows in the Eternal and Changeless.

Here the Hindu view of morality comes in contact with the Buddhistic system. If ever an ethical system was so completely overshadowed by metaphysics it is the Buddhistic system. Christ realised acutely the contrast between nature and spirit, between this world and the world beyond the grave. However, he addressed himself to the ethical problems of his age and not to problems of metaphysics. Recognition of the spirit of man, emphasis on the equality and fraternity of human beings, concentration on love as the panacea for all ills : were his main contributions to the problem of Life. But there was not a vast metaphysical background to his system. It was a simple creed–the creed of love of Man and God. The whole teaching of the New Testament was characteristically Eastern–Eastern in its emphatic assertion of the triumph of spirit over matter, Eastern in its gospel of humility and self-denial, Eastern in its overwhelming emphasis on love as the one supreme principle of all life. But the Hindu and Buddhistic systems were, above all, metaphysical systems. The problem of existence was with them fundamental; the problem of conduct was quite secondary. Moral life was a mere preparation for the higher life of the soul; it was a mere scaffolding, mere ladder to be kicked away when man gets emancipation. It touched mere surface of life, its roots were not deep. The Buddhistic view traced the roots of all evils to *Trishna* or desire or will to live, which in turn owed its origin to ignorance. The Hindu view ultimately traced all evil to error or illusion. The ultimate solution in both cases was intellectual, not volitional; knowledge was more fundamental than action, insight than efforts. Men fled to Philosophy not to morality as a refuge from all the ills of the world.

It is, therefore, one of the differences between systems of

morality like the Jewish, Islamic, Christian and Zoroastrian on the one hand, and the Hindu, Jain, and Buddhistic systems on the other that while the former glorify a life of action, of striving and willing and energising, the latter place above everything else a life of mystic illumination, of perfect gnosis, of the highest realisation. The Greeks also identified knowledge with virtue and vice with ignorance. Never was a nation so fond of contemplation as the Greeks. It was the ideal life of philosophers; it filled them with raptures. The reply of Anaxagoras to a question as to what he had been born for, was the reply of the whole Greek nation : "For the contemplation of the sun, and moon, and heaven, and the order governing the entire universe". The whole force and energy of the Islamic and Jewish and Zoroastrian faith is directed to showing that life is a battle between opposing forces, between powers of Light and Darkness. All men figure as soldiers ranged on one side or the other. The Greeks thought of Life not as a battle of mighty forces, not as a theatre of epic actions, but as a riddle, a problem, an intellectual treat. The Hindus pictured life as a conflict between *Maya* and *Brahman*, between appearance and reality, between ignorance and knowledge. Their whole aim was "to go from nonexistence to existence, from darkness to light."

It must be said, however, to the credit of the Hindus that far from making all morality a mere subjective fancy, a private illusion, they made it the one central thing in this life. Morality or *Karma* is the one Law dominating all life human and infra-human; but it is the special characteristic, the very prerogative of human beings. No being can transcend its limits : once launched into existence or *Samsara*, its operation was inexorable. The Hindu view lays deep the foundations of moral life in the very heart of the universe : it is as objective, as real as the whole world itself. The whole universe comes into existence and vanishes solely under the influence of the Law of *Karma*. Another point which is connected with this position is the objective validity of freedom of the will in the Hindu theory.

Man's belief in himself as a centre of fresh actions is not altogether an illusion. Man's self-consciousness becomes the basis of his whole life; and this self-consciousness has as much reality as the objective world.

The fact is that the Hindu theory is able to make a paradoxical combination of two opposing theories owing to its distinction between empirical and transcendental points of view. The empirical world is real, and so is the transcendental world. No one is more emphatic than *Shankara* in repudiating the theory that the entire world is an illusion. The outer world is no more an illusion than the inner world; the reality of objects is equal to the reality of ideas. But both the outer and inner worlds have partial reality; apart from the Self, they are abstractions. Hence the necessity of absolute reality of the Self. From the point of view of the Self or *Brahman*, the empirical world appears to be an illusion, because it is not free from the limitations of time, space and causality which hedge in our view. Hence the so called self-consciousness (अहंकार), with the whole moral life based on it shrinks into unreality, from the point of view of the higher self of man. But for all practical purposes, the self is real, the world is real and the action of the self upon the world, whether it be moral or immoral, is real.

Now it can be easily understood why the Hindus are not puzzled by the Problem of Evil. Evil, indeed, has as much reality as the good-so far the Hindu view is quite logical. But to make of the Evil the central thing in our theory and to create a *Satan* or *Ahriman* out of it is not possible to the Hindu. The Hindu solves the knot by his theory of *Maya*. God is the supreme Reality—above good, above evil, essentially super-moral, super-rational, super-personal. The whole existence, as we view it ordinarily, has the taint of imperfection about it— including in it both moral saintliness and moral depravity—and is called evil from the metaphysical stand-point. All limitation is evil; all ignorance is evil; all belief in abstractions as realities is evil. Man is essentially a transcendental being, capable of overcoming the distinctions of good and evil. Morality is, after all, a provincialism of our planet; its whole existence is rooted in our belief in our narrow egos. Once the narrow egoism disappears, the whole structure of ethics collapses.

The Hindu theory of life runs through three great ages. The first is the Vedic Age—the age of affirmation. The second is the age of the *Upanishads*—the age of denial of the world and affirmation of the spirit. The third is the age of synthesis when the values of the world are re-affirmed in the light of the spirit. This was the age of the *Gita.* It was in this way that the Hindu theory gains such a depth and complexity. Its development was spread over centuries; it came under the profound influence of metaphysical ideals; it was based upon vast and varied experience of a great race. The Buddhistic system was born in the second period; it was strong in its metaphysics; but it loses sight of proper perspective when it becomes a gospel for the world. The Hindu theory is almost unique in the way in which it reconciles the positive and the negative factors, the empirical and the transcendental elements of morality. The world is affirmed, denied, and re-affirmed. It is possible to satisfy here the claims of various types of men, those who would fain become the purest idealists and those who would become giant men of deeds. It is possible here to reconcile the claims of victorious war and of disposition to peace. Buddhism is not so favourable to active virtues; *Islam* and Parsism are not so favourable to the self-denying virtues of a *Sannyasin.* We believe it is the singular excellence of Hinduism that it is the most comprehensive faith, doing justice to life in all its phases and aspects.

Very few systems of morality have done sufficient justice to the fact of existing varieties and differences of talents, team peraments, characters and circumstances, amon men. Whether we look to the theology of the Hindus or its system of life–we find this to be the most remarkable fact about it–its capacity to accommodate itself to persons of all possible grades of development and culture. The Buddhist religion is more suited to monks and nuns-persons who like self-renunciation above everything else. The average man, full of worldly ambitions, thirsting to do right and avoid wrong is more satisfied with the simple, stern, logical systems of the Parses and Moslems. But if we want a system as wide, as comprehensive, as elastic, as diversified as life itself, we must go to this great historical faith. It is called *Sanatana Dharma*–containing principles which are true for all time, and it fully justified this title.

There are various reasons which enable the Hindu theory to meet all possible requirements. The first is its synthesis of matter and spirit, *Maya* and *Brahman,* of the empirical and transcendental points of view. The second is the fact that it is based not upon the teaching of one man-however great he may be, but of a series of men. It is an impersonal faith. The strain of doing justice to all possible developments upon one historical person is too great. The Hindu teaching believes in the infallibility of the Vedas, but by the Vedas they mean no book, no set, rigid revelation, but revelations to the *Rishis* of all times of the eternal truths which regulate all life. Otherwise what is the meaning of saying that the Vedas are the causes of the origin of gods and men and the whole existence? The Hindu faith is, therefore, protected from a narrow-mindedness, from local or national prejudices, from the limitations due to a particular historical age. It has in it a wonderful principle of development; it never precludes the possibility of new seers, new prophets, who may receive the revelation freshly and carry on the work of readjusting old morality to new situations. Thirdly, the Hindu belief in *Avataras* or incarnations enables it to reconcile the demands of those who want 'universal religion, and those who want 'specific' religion. All the possibilities of a religion believing in the personality of God or historic personalities of either the son of God or prophets and *Mahdis* are conserved in Hinduism; and yet there is the religion of pure *Brahman* for those who can devote themselves to the Absolute. Fourthly the Hindu belief in the unity of God and diversity of His manifestations is favourable to all types of worships, the worship of pure *Brahman*, of personal god, of local deities, and of great men. Very few religions are so capable of appreciating the ideas that God is the same in all faiths, and that all its prophets are correct prophets more or less, that all beings embody the same *Atman*, as Hindu faith. Hence the Hindu is full of forbearance for all possible varieties in creed and practice. Fifthly, there is the institution of *Varnashrama*–making provision for both quietistic, and activistic longing of man, for age and youth and childhood, for those who worship ideas, and those who worship facts, for those who are capable of hand-work and for those who are fitted for brain-work, for war and peace, for trade and commerce, for culture and character, for all possible interests of societies, for all posible types of men, for all possible varieties of situations.

The greatest asset of the Hindu view is its belief in the Oneness of Atman—the same heart beating in all creation—in man, and God, and nature. The Islamic faith is great because of the equality it bestows on all Moslems, without distinction of caste or creed of colour. But the Hindu view emphasizes the fact that men are not outwardly equal, but inwardly equal, that true democracy is spiritual. The Hindu believes that the fact of caste is not peculiar to the Hindus, but common to all humanity. It is the difference between the *Gunas* or qualities and *Karma* or actions which accounts for castes. As long as men differ in these adjuncts, caste will survive in one form or another. The difference between nation and nation may go; the difference between race and race may go, but the difference between the qualities and actions of man and man will not go, so long as the empirical world survives. The Hindus recognised this fact and tried to express it in the outer structure of society. But fundamentally—the Hindus were never ambiguous—all men, all beings are one. Here was the true philosophic basis for that brotherhood of man so eloquently preached by Jesus, for the love for all beings human as well as sub-human, so well practised by Buddha. The Aryan humanity was broad and extensive including within its range all the animal creation, and even the vegetable kingdom; above all, it was supplied with a true spiritual foundation in the doctrine of the unity of souls and their identity with *Brahman.*

The highest word of Hindu ethics is the ideal of disinterested action—of *Asanga Karma.* The true renunciation is the renunciation of narrow egoism of ours. A life of strenuous endeavours, of philanthropic efforts, of humanitarian deeds was the highest of all types of life. But for action to be the one best thing for man, it must cast off its vulgar character, its narrow outlook, its passion for consequences. It is the consciousness behind an action that gives it all the colour that it has. It is here that a revolution is so necessary. The stand-point must be changed, the vision must be broadened, the horizon must be expanded. All the limitations, all the accidents, incidental to one's position here must gradually vanish. Man must move, not as an isolated point, an atomic self, but as a centre for the divine, an organ for the Infinite, a messenger of God. Man is nothing if not the highest. Man must, therefore, die as a member of this world, to be reborn into the kingdom of God. The kingdom of God is within us. The Self is the innermost fact about us. To find this Self is the whole task of our education, our culture. Such is the message of the Hindu sages; and a lofty message it is.

Chapter - II

CRITERIA OF MORALITY

(1)

Nothing impressed the naive, wondering mind of the primeval *Vedic Rishis* as the striking uniformities of co-existence and succession which they saw in nature. It was one of the greatest and most important truths which dawned upon these ancient people. They laid the foundations of science when they noticed the fact that nature every-where works according to fixed laws. But they did not halt here. Their bright imagination soon saw striking identities between the realm of causes and the realm of ends, between the natural order and the moral order. If the reign of law was a dominant fact of the outer universe, it must be equally dominant in human affairs. Law, order, regularity must be found everywhere; and sin crept in when these were disobeyed by human weakness or perversity. The gods were the guardians of the natural order and they became the guardians of the moral order too; they helped and strengthened those who conformed to laws, while their punishment would certainly fall upon those who neglected or defied these standards of action.

The questioning of the sages were : "Where is the ancient law divine? What is its new diffuser now? Ye gods who yonder have home in the three lucid realms of heaven, that count ye truth, and what untruth? What is your firm support of Law?"[1] Men may be crooked in their ways, owing to malice and weakness, but there was no such cause in the case of the forces of nature. Hence they manifested the operation of fixed laws. "Ne'er may the earth and heaven which know not malice, nor the fixed hills be bowed by sage devices."[2] "Splendid by Law! declaring Law, truth-speaking, truthful in thy works (*Some*)"[3]. The sun is produced for the maintenance of Law[4]; and he spreads the reign of Law by diffusing light everywhere.5 "About the Holy Law toils *Savitar,* the God : the horn of holy Law hath he spread far and wide."[6] "This Savitar, God, is my chief joy and pleasure, who breaketh not the universal statute."[7] I *(Indra)* as a God, ne'er violate the statutes of Gods, of *Vasus, Rudras, Adityas.*"[8] The whole universe is supported by these laws, and gods owe their power and position to their obedience to these laws. "Radiant, as high Truth, cherished best at winning strength, Truth based upon the statute that supports the heavens."[9] The sun was raised to heaven by ever-lasting laws.[10] Indra says : "The Holy Law's commandments make me mighty."[11] "*Mitra* and *Varuna*, through Law, lovers and cherishers of Law, Have ye obtained your mighty power."[12] Conformity to Law is the source of all virtue and power to the mortals; and gods help those who try to follow this path. All the rest are the wicked persons. "True to Law, born in Law, the strengtheners of Law, terrible, haters of false, in their felicity which gives the best defence may our men and princes dwell."[13] "Lead us beyond all pain and grief along the path of holy Law,"[14] *Agni* is a "kind friend to men who keep the holy Law."[15] "From these (rays) the eyeless and deaf have turned aside; the wicked travel not the pathway of the Law."[16]

From the earliest times there exists the strongest conviction about the supremacy of the moral law in the world; but as regards the exact nature and contents of the moral law there can never be unanimity of opinion. The Hindu sages were strongly impressed by the mysterious nature of the ultimate basis of the categorical imperative with us. कर्मणो गहना गतिः। "The fruits of virtuous acts ordained in the Vedas, as also of all transgressions, the origin and destruction of acts are mysteries even to the gods! These are not known to anybody and everbody. Those regenerate ones that have destroyed all aspirations, that have built all their hopes on vows and asceticism, that have burnt all their sins and have acquired minds where quiet and peace and holiness dwell understand all these."[17] Morality is often very subtle; its nature becomes inscrutable to all except the very best and wisest. "What pathway leadeth to the Gods? Who knoweth this of a truth and who will now declare it?"[18] "It is difficult to find out the reasons on which duties stand even as it is difficult to find out the legs of a snake. As a hunter of beasts discovers the track of a shaft-struck deer by observing spots of blood on the ground, even so one should seek to discover the reasons of duties."[19] "As the dust that lies on the Earth, if pounded between two stones, becomes finer and finer, even so questions of morality, the more they are reflected upon and discussed, become finer and finer."[20] "As no one can mark the track of birds in the sky or of fish in the water, similarly the track of persons whose souls have been cleansed by knowledge cannot be marked by any."[21]

Various tests, however, are laid down to distinguish the moral actions from the immoral ones. The scriptural authority is often deemed sufficient for the guidance of ordinary persons. The *Shrutis* are based upon the direct revelation of truth to the seers and hence they possess absolute authority for all orthodox persons. "Having observed all the Shastras, allied with the Vedas with the eye of knowledge, the erudite one shall perform the duties (peculiar to his order) in conformity with the proofs of the Shruti."[22] "The Veda is called the *Shruti* ; and the *Dharma-shastra* is called the *Smriti*; their teachings should not be put to the test of logic (should not be misconstrued by sophistry'–Kulluka), for virtue has emanated from these two... In the case of two conflicting Shrutis, both of which are equally authoritative, the wise have called both of them sources of equal authority."[23] "What was not revealed in the Vedas is revealed in the Smritis. That revealed truth which is not to be found in both is sung in the *Puranas*."[24]. Shankaracharya says : "The holy writ is the ground of discriminating between right and wrong. 'This is duty', 'this is immorality'–all this can be known only by means of Scriptures, because the nature of virtue and vice is transcendental and depends upon time, place and circumstance. What is virtue in one situation becomes vice in another. Hence the Shastras alone constitute our basis of moral knowledge."[25] The Gita says : "He who having cast aside the ordinances of the Scriptures, followeth the promptings of desire attaineth not to perfection, nor happiness, nor the highest goal. Therefore, let the Scriptures by thy authority, in determining what ought to be done, or what ought not to be done. Knowing what hath been declared by the ordinances of the Scriptures, thou oughtest to work in the world."[26]

An independent and unfettered use of reason in deciding all questions of morality is to be condemned. Morality is too subtle to be fully scrutinised by the unaided light of reason. "In the universe are seen creatures consisting of the five elements. Men endeavour to ascertain their proportions by exercising their reason. Those matters, however, that are beyond the grasp of understanding should never be sought to be solved by it. That which is above nature is a mark of inconceivable."[27] Persons who make morality too much a matter of reasoning are apt to be led into sophistries; and it is the spirit of sophistry which is deprecated. "The Brahmin, who by dint of logic, tries to bring these Shastras into contempt, shall be excommunicated from the society, as a heretical calumniator of the Vedas."[28] But the right use of private judgment is not denied. It should be constructive, desirous of finding out truth with all possible help, and not destructive, merely aiming at criticism and mischief. "He who wishes to know the ture principle of virtue must know all the sciences which are based on positive observation, inference, and the teachings of Vedas. He who discusses the ethical teachings of the Vedas and of the *Smritis* based on them, by processes of reasoning not hostile to their tenets, is alone enabled to know the right principle of virtue and no one else."[29] "In days of old, *Ushanas* said unto the *Daityas* this truth, which should remove all doubts, that Scriptures are no Scriptures if they cannot stand the test of reason."[30] A full grasp of all the details of a situation is necessary before any correct judgment can be arrived at as regards any course of action in it. A narrow, pedantic application of the dicta of the Shastras will only lead to awkward failure. "The duties of a king can never be discharged by rules drawn from a morality that is one-sided...........Righteousness sometimes takes the shape of unrighteousness and *vice versa.* He who does not know this, becomes confounded when confronted by an actual instance of the kind. Before the occasion comes, one should comprehend the circumstances under which righteousness and its reverse become confused. Having acquired this knowledge, a wise king should, when the occasion comes, act accordingly, aided by his judgment."[31] In fact, an unbridled use of reason is as much to be avoided as a blind adherence to the holy texts. "The truths herein disclosed are incapable of being understood by the aid of inference alone or by that of mere study of the Scriptures. One must understand it oneself by the aid of faith.[32]

Example is said to be better than precept; and it is certainly more accessible to the intelligence of the ordinary people than the latter. The average, untutored intelligence of the masses cannot be expected to grasp the meaning of the holy texts, nor can it strike out its own paths in matters of morality by a full use of its own intelligence. For all people at this level of culture, the greatest source of guidance as well as inspiration was the conduct of the great and the good. Tradition, history and all such means were utilised for getting a proper insigth into the practice of the ancient as well as respectable people. "Go forth, go forth upon the ancient pathways whereon our sires of old have gone before us."[33] "Lead us not from our fathers' and from Manu's path into the distance far away."[34] "They that are good constitute the way."[35] "Argument leads to no certain conclusion; the Shrutis are different from one another; there is not even one *Rishi* whose opinion can be accepted as infallible; the truth about religion and duty is hid in caves; therefore, that alone is the path which the great have trod."[36] "In virtue of conflicting authority, let him take to the path adopted by his fathers and grandfathers; by adopting that path, he will not incurenmity of any man."[37]

Hegal once wrote that the wisest of us should follow the ethos of our own country. Manu also thinks that the actual ways of living of the best people in a society should be the standard of morality in that society. A capacity for forming sound moral judgments does not require in a person very high intellectual calibre or learning, but high character. Conduct is indeed the three-fourths of life; and the right judgments are to be drawn from the conduct of the best men, and not so much from their intellectual lucubrations. "The tract of country, which lies between the Saraswati and the Drishadwati, the two celestial rivers, that god-built country is called Brahma-vartam. The conduct of life, as it obtains from generation to generation in that country among twice-born and the mixed castes, is called *Sadachar* (good conduct)."[38] The essence of morality is well understood to be more in practice than in theory; and so we find धर्म or duty defined as आचार or conduct. "Through (observing) good conduct one acquires a long life, through good conduct one acquires a desirable progeny; through conduct one acquires decayless wealth, and good conduct kills all the inauspicious (bodily) traits of a person."[39] "The theory of religion and morals is very complicated, hence people should practise the rules of Shruti, Smriti, and *Puranas* which have been followed by good men."[40]

The practice of the good people is ultimately crystallised into a body of customs and conventions, which then govern the workings of the ordinary people. Imitation is the way of the masses. गतानुगतिको लोक: न लोक: पारमार्थिक:। People blindly follow those who preceded them; they cannot find out truth for themselves. The Gitakar well says : "Whatsoever a great man deoth, that other men also do; the standard he setteth up, by that the people go."[41] Therefore, the customs of a people are naturally credited with certain value. "When a decision is passed in accordance with local custom, logic, or the opinion of the traders the issue of the case is overruled by it. The time-honoured institutions of each country, caste, and family would be preserved intact; otherwise the people would rise in rebellion; the subjects would become disaffected towards their rulers; and the army and treasure would be destroyed. The maternal uncle's daughter is taken in marriage among the twice-born inhabitants of the South. In the central country they become labourers or artisans and eat cows. The inhabitants of the East are fish-eaters, and their women are unchaste. In the North the women take intoxicating drinks, and in their courses can be touched. The people of the Khasa marry the widow of a brother who has died. These men are not subject to the performance of a penance or to punishment on account of any such offence. Cultivators, artisans, artists, money-lenders, companies of tradesmen, dancers, persons wearing the tokens of religious orders, and robbers should adjust their disputes according to the rules of their own profession."[42] "The usage of the counrty should first be attended to; that which is observed in the country should alone be observed. Wise men abstain from what is hated by the people. A wise man should go by the path of the people. The deities, the Brahmins, the (notious of) purity, the (kind of) earth, the water, and the religious observances of a country should not be ridiculed in that country, for that is the law of the country."[43] Even the wise and clever people who are capable of rising above the conventions of the people occasionally do well to follow the dictates of the social conscience. "An action which is religious but disapproved by the people does not lead to heaven."[44] "Ordinary people are the guides and instructors of the wise men for all ordinary activities. Hence the men versed in Shastras should follow these people for social functions. One should not abuse the king, the country, the race, the family, and the religion, and should not even mentally break the customs of the folk though that were possible."[45] Apastamba upholds the authority of the Shrutis against the local customs of a community. "The authority (for these duties) is the agreement of those who know the law and the Vedas.[46] For (explicit) revealed texts have greater force than custom from which (the existence of a permissive passage of the revelation) may be inferred.[47] Besides (in this particular case) a (worldly) motive for the practice is apparent.[48] For no (worldly) motive for the decision of those Aryas is perceptible; (and hence it must have a religious motive and be founded on a passage of the Veda).[49] By this (discussion) the law of custom which is observed in (particular) countries for families, has been disposed of.[50]

All doubtful points of morality may be referred to a council of experts, whose decision will be held as final. "Whatever a council of ten, or of three qualified Brahmins, faithful to their duties, shall lay down as the law, must be accepted as such. Such a council must consist of at least ten Brahmins, who have studied the Vedas, are acquainted with rules of reasoning and are well-versed in the Nirukta and law codes."[51] The *Rishis* did not believe in the infallibility of Majority and justly thought that wisdom ought to decide all cases and not number. "Even what-ever a single Veda-Knowing Brahmin shall determine as the law shall be accepted an such to the exclusion of what has been said by ten thousand ignorant Brahmins. A council consisting of thousands of assembled Brahmins, who are devoid of penan-ces and Vedic knowledge and live by the emblem of their caste, can never acquire the status of a true council."[52]

(2)

It will be interesting to know the Hindu view on the problem of the connection between virtue and happiness. The idea that virtue is inseparably connected with prosperity and happiness and vice with misery is a very deep-rooted one in the consciousness of man-kind. "To him who keeps the Law, both old and young, thou givest happiness, and energy that he may live."[53] "Riches with many heroes, thou has for the man who offers gifts."[54] " Yea Heaven and Earth, ye hold in your possession full many a treasure for the liberal giver."[55] "Indra and Soma, plunge the wicked in the depth, yea cast them into darkness that hath no support."[56] "When thou with thunder and with roar, *Parjanya*, smitest sinners down, this universe exults threat, yea, all that is upon the earth"[57] The Upanishads clearly say that God leads those whom He impels to goods acts to higher regions; while those whom He prompts to evil acts He leads them to lower regions.[58] "O daughter of Drupada, religion is the only raft for those desirous of a going to heaven, like a ship to merchants desirous of crossing the ocean. If the virtues that are practised by the righteous people had no fruits, the universe then would be enveloped in infamous darkness. No one then would pursue salvation, no one would seek to acquire knowledge, not even wealth, but men would live like beasts. If asceticism, the austerities of celibate life, sacrifices, study of the Vedas, charity, honesty,–all these were fruitless, men would not have practised virtues, generation after generation. If acts were all fruitless, a dire confusion would ensue. For why, then do Rishis and gods and Gandharvas and Rakshasas who are all independent of human conditions, cherish virtue with such affection? Knowing it for certain that God is the giver of fruits in respect of virtue, they practise virtue in this world. This is the eternal source of prosperity! When the fruits of both knowledge and asceticism are seen, virtue and vice cannot be fruitless."[59] "Through (observing) good conduct one acquires a long life, through good conduct one acquires a desired progeny; through good conduct one acquires decayless wealth, and good conduct kills all inauspicious traits of a person. A man of misconduct is condemned in the world, suffers perpetual misery, is afflicted with disease, and dies a premature death."[60]

A man's life should be guided by four ends : duty (धर्म), fulfilment of worldly purposes (अर्थ) , happiness (काम), and salvation (मोक्ष). Each of these ends has a definte value, and if possible, should not be neglected. Desire for happiness may not be the highest of impulses in us, but it need not be rooted out. All healthy, sane views of life make provision for the thirst for happiness in man. It is the raw material of a higher life and hence must not be entirely ignored. "Not commendable is the spirit of desire in man, nor the total absence of such a spirit (in him) is detected in this world. The study of the Vedas and the performance of the Vedic rites and sacrifices fall within the boundary of acts with a desire. Desire is based on volition or determination, and the religious sacrifies are based on solemn determination. All vows, Niyamas (Self-control), and religious duties are said to be born of desire. No action is found in this world, of a man without desire. Whatever act a person does is but the effect of his desire."[61] An exaggerated assertion of the rights of hedonistic impulses is made in the following passage; but is contains elements of truth in it. "One without Desire never wishes for wealth. One without Desire never wishes for Virtue. For these reasons, Desire is the foremost of all the three. It is under the influence of Desire that the very *Rishis* devote themselves to penances, subsisting upon fruits, or living upon roots or air only. Others possessed of Vedic lore are engaged upon the Vedas and their branches, or upon rites of faith and sacrificial acts, or upon making gifts or accepting them. Traders, agriculturists, keepers cattle, artists and artisans, and those who are employed in rise of propitiation, all act from Desire. Some there are that dive into the depths of the ocean, induced by Desire. Desire, indeed, takes various forms. Everything is pervaded by the principle of Desire. A man outside the pale of Desire never is, was, or will be seen in this world. This is the truth. Both virtue and profit (fulfilment of religious and secular purpose) presuppose the operation of Desire. As butter represents the essence of curds, even so is Desire the essence of all spiritual and temporal life."[62]

The secret of success in worldly concerns lies in wealth or the control over material means and resources. This constitutes अर्थ or wealth. Ascetic ideals of life may entirely rule out wealth as an object of ambition; but an all-round realisation of our nature requires a possession of material resources as an indispensable means to it. "Agriculture, trade, keeping of cattle, and diverse kinds of arts, constitute what is called अर्थ. Wealth, again, is the end of all such acts. Without wealth, both virtue and happiness cannot be won. This is the declaration of the

Shruti. Even persons of uncleansed souls, if possessed of diverse kinds of wealth, are able to perform the highest acts of virtue and gratify desires that are apparently difficult of attainment. Virtue and happiness are the limbs of wealth as the Shruti declares. With the acquisition of wealth, both virtue and happiness may be won."[63]

It is necessary therefore, to look to all the ingredients of a complete life. Not one of these elements should be sought at the expense of the other. "Morality is always afflicted by two things, viz; the desire for wealth entertained by those that covet it, and the desire for pleasure cherished by those that are wedded to it. Whoever without afflicting virtue and wealth, or virtue and pleasure or pleasure and wealth followeth all three, viz., virtue, wealth and happiness, always succeeds in obtaining great happiness."[64] Here it is made very clear that the Hindu view of life is not in the least one-sided. It fully recognizes the claims of worldly success and pleasure in a full, rounded life. The ideal laid down here is as rich and many-sided as the ideal laid down by Aristotle. It is neither hedonistic nor ascetic. No one aspect of life is to be exalted at the complete sacrifice of the other equally important aspects. "And that virtue which tortureth one's self and friends is really no virtue. It is rather vice, producing calamities. Virtue is sometimes also the weakness of men. And though such a man might be engaged in the practice of virtue, yet both virtue and wealth forsake him like pleasure and pan forsaking a person that is dead. He that practiseth virtue for virtue's sake always suffereth. He can scarcely be called a wise man, for he knoweth not the purpose of virtue, like a blind man incapable of perceiving the solar light." In the same way wealth is to be properly subordinated to the acquisition of virtue and happiness. "He that regardeth his wealth to exist for himself alone, scarcely understandeth the purposes of wealth. He is really like a servant that tendeth kine in a forest. He, again, that pureth wealth too much without looking to virtue and enjoyments, deserveth to be censured and slain by all men..... He that wisheth to obtain wealth, seeketh for a large share of virtue to crown his wish with success. He that wisheth for pleasure seeketh wealth." Thus, virtue is necessary for worldly success, which in its turn leads to happiness. An exclusive pursuit of happiness leads nowhere. "He also that ever pursueth enjoyments without pursuing virtue and wealth, loseth his friends and virtue and wealth also. Destitute of virtue and wealth, such a man indulging in pleasure at will, at the expiration of his period of indulgence, meeteth with certain death." Pleasure is essentially connected with both virtue and wealth; but it is a normal accompaniment of these and not as a means leading to any of these ends that it exists, Pleasure, therefore unlike the other two is incapable of being a fresh source of moral growth. "They that are wise are ever careful of both virtue and wealth, for a union of virtue and wealth is the essential requisite of pleasure. Pleasure hath always virtue for its root, and virtue also is united with pleasure. Know that both are dependent on each other, like the ocean and the clouds, the ocean causing clouds, and the clouds filling the ocean." "The joy that arises from the senses, the intellect, and the heart being directed to the objects proper to each is called pleasure. That pleasure is one of the best fruits of our action." Pleasure therefore should be welcomed as a result of all normal and healthy activities; but it should not be an end by itself. "Pleasure, however, yieldeth nothing in its turn. One pleasure cannot lead to another, being its own fruit; as ashes may be had from wood, but nothing from those ashes in their turn...He, therefore, who misled by pleasure, or covetousness beholdeth not the pleasure of virtue, deserveth to be slain by all, and becometh wretched both here and hereafter." A synthetic union of all there, each in due subordination to the other is the best things to be aimed at.[65]

Much scepticism is the result of the apparent sundering of the two moments of all activity, virtue and happiness. Life gets its complexity and depth through this divorce. If a life of persistent practice of duty were a life of perpetual pleasure, there would be little heroism in all life of virtue. Heroism lies in its connection with suffering. Then alone faith would be tried; and accordingly it gains in depth and richness which would not otherwise be there. An interesting passage–bursting out in a weak moment from Laxman–shows that the author was alive to the arduous nature of the task of pursuing duty even at the cost of happiness. Here cynicism as regards all high ideals breaks out; virtue is considered illusory, and wealth is lauded high. "Virtue is profitless. It is incapable of delivering from calamity thee, who hast ubdued thy senses, and who ever abidest in thy good path. The beings, whether mobile or immobile, cannot have that direct perception of virtue which they have of happiness. Therefore, I think, Virtue is a non-entity, in as much as the immobile world (although devoid of any regard for virtue) is nevertheless happy and as the mobile world also is so, this virtue cannot lead to happiness. (If it were so), one like thee would not have been placed in peril. If unrighteousness would bring happiness on creatures, Ravana should go to hell, and thou possessed of virtue should not come by misfortune. And seeing that he is free from danger and thou art in it, righteousness and its opposite have tendencies the very reverse of those assigned to them respectively."[66] Draupadi similarly despairs of the fruits of a virtuous life. "And the supreme Lord, according to his pleasure, sporteth with his creatures, creating and destroying them like a child with his toy..... Like a vicious person, he seemeth to bear himself towards his creatures in anger."[67]

When therefore, there is a conflict between virtue and happiness then the question as to the superiority of either arises. The authority of virtue is naturally more stable and more majestic than the authority of fluctuating inclinations; and virtue leading to suffering is preferred to the fulfilment of desires, contradicting the dictates of duty. "It is by virtue that the *Rishis* have crossed (the world all its difficulties). It is upon virtue that all the worlds depend (for their existence). It is by virtue that the gods attained to their position of superiority. It is upon virtue that wealth or worldly success rests. Virtue is foremost in point of merit. Wealth is said to be middling. Desire or pleasure is the lowest of the three."[68] The sense of duty must be paramount over all other considerations. If there is a conflict between duty and worldly good or duty and life, the former must be unhesitatingly preferred. "O sire, I would impart to thee another sacred lesson which is the highest of all teaching, viz., virtue should never be forsaken from desire, fear or temptation, nay, not for the sake of life itself ! Virtue is everlasting; pleasure and pain are transitory, life is indeed everlasting; but its particular phases are transitory."[69]

Such considerations gradually lead to the practice of a higher type of virtue, in which it disengages itself from all idea of reward. The idea of duty for duty's sake comes into prominence; and morality becomes more and more inward, more and more an independent attitude of the soul. In reply to Draupadi's sceptical reflexions, Yudhishthira says : "Thou speakest the language of atheism, I never act, solicitous of the fruits of my actions ! I give away, because it is my duty to give; I sacrifice, because it is my duty to sacrifice! O Krishna, I accomplish to the best of my power whatever a person living in the domestic life should do, regardless of the fact whether those acts have fruits or not. I act virtuously, not from the desire of reaping the fruits of virtue, but of not transgressing the ordinances of the Veda, beholding the conduct of the good and the wise. My dearth is naturally attracted towards virtue. The man who wisheth to reap the fruits of virtue is a trader in virtue. His nature is mean and should never be counted among the virtuous"[70]

The idea that the connection between virtue and happiness is a very intrinsic one, and that in spite of appearances to the contrary, virtue is more rooted in the nature of things than its opposite leads to the Hindu belief in the objective character of morality. Morality is not a caprice of individual will or wills; it is not an accidental phase of civilisation. It is not a fabrication of the weak and depressed, as Nietzebe thought. "One should not take what belongs to others. That is an eternal obligation.

Powerful men regard it as one that has been introduced by the weak. When, however, the destiny of these men becomes adverse, this injunction meets with their approval .... They that are possessed of wealth think that this duty has been laid down by those that are indigent. When, however, those wealthy men meet with poverty inconsequence of some turn of fortune, the practice of morality then recommends itself to them".[71] Moral law is as deep-laid, as organically connected with the foundations of the universe as the natural law. There is nothing arbitrary, nothing subjective about it. "Eating, sleeping, fearing, and enjoying are the pursuits which men share with beasts; but the consciousness of duty alone lifts up men from the animal level." "Those that are not righteous should not be counted among men even as rains without kernel are not counted among grain, and as cockroaches are not counted birds."[72] Morality is, therefore, the prerogative of human beings. It is the most precious possession of the virtuous. In them righteousness becomes dear for its own sake and all other things are sacrificed at its altar. It becomes the one mainspring of all activity. We realise Kant's famous sentence: Nothing in this world is good without qualification except good will. "Neighter in those days of prosperity nor in those days of thy adversity, thou, O Bharata, hath ever known anything so dear to thee as virtue, which thou hast even regarded as dearer to thee than life! That thy kingdom is for virtue alone, that thy life is for virtue alone, is known to Brahmins, and thy superiors, and even to the celestials. I think thou canst abandon Bhimasen and Arjuna and these twin sons of Madri along with myself, but thou canst not abondon virtue! I have heard that a king protected virtue; and virtue protected by him, protecteth him (in return)"[73] "Yudhishthira can abondon the whole world full of wealth, but he will never sacrifice morality."[74] Morality is distinguished from other things by its superior stability, its superior reality. "Let your hearts be fixed on virtue, for virtue is the one only friend of him that has gone to the other world. Even the most intelligent by cherishing wealth and wives can never make these their own; nor are these possessions lasting."[75] Righteousness is the best species of wealth. "Do thou earn that wealth which has no fear from either kings or thieves and which one has not to abandon even at death. Earned by one's own acts, that wealth has never to be divided among co-owners. Each enjoys that wealth which each has earned for himself."[76] Wordsworth says with regard to Duty that "the ancient heavens through thee are fresh and strong." The universe is sustained by the righteousness of the good, who are the salt of the earth. "They that are righteous always practise eternal morality.........And verily it is the righteous who by their truth make the sun move in the Heaven. And it is the righteous upon whom both the past and the future depend."[77]

All these three ideals of duty, of happiness and social success are not ultimate; they are all very important for the attainment of success in the universe; but none of them either singly or in combination constitutes the Highest Good. "Vedic acts may be divided into two classes, such as the *Pravrittam* and *Nivrittam*; by Pravrtittam acts one enjoys happiness and prosperity, by Nivrittam acts one enjoy emancipation. An act or rite, done or instituted for the fruition of a definite object either in this act or in the next, is called *Pravrittam;* an act voluntarily done without any prospect of gain or reward, is called *Nivrittam* one."[78] " All the three (धर्म, अर्थ and काम) again have their root in will. Will is concerned with objects. All objects, again, in their entirety exist for gratifying the desire of enjoyment. Upon these three does the aggregate of three depend. Entire abstraction from all objects is Emancipation. It is said that virtue is sought for the protection of the body, and wealth is for the acquisition of virtue. Pleasure leads only to the gratification of the senses. All these have, therefore, the quality of passion. Virtue, wealth and pleasure, when sought for the sake of heaven and such other rewards are said to be remote, because the rewards themselves are remote. When sought, however, for the sake of knowledge of Self, they are said to be proximate. One should seek them when they are of such a character ....The aim of the triple aggregate is Emancipation."[79] Disinterested pursuit of worldly objects and virtues leads gradually to the final salvation, which is the ultimate end highest end of human life.

(3)

To adjudge rightly the morality of an action, it is necessary to look both to the intention of the individual and to the consequences of the action. The former would yield to us what is subjectively right; the latter would enable us to arrive at an objective moral judgment. An action can never be moral if the agent is not conscious of righteous motives; the essence of moral actions of mental. To a great extent, our actions derive their moral worth from the intentions which inspire them. Thus Hanumana in his search after Sita has to pass through the harem of Ravana; and so he could not help seeing the faces of the ladies who were asleep. Now to look at the faces of other's wives is not held to be quite legitimate. But Hanumana maintains that it is a part of an act of duty that he has to see those faces; and further, he says that his mind is not affected by passion, hence it is not objectionable. It is mind that is at the root of all actions moral and immoral; and as there was no bad idea present in his mind, he was free from al blame.[80] The ultimate criterion of the morality of an action is clearly laid down to be the sanction of the conscience, the inward satisfaction which ensues at one's doing what is right. No action is moral which fails to satisfy this test. The intuition of the moral sense is necessary to ensure the moral character of the action, although it is not a sufficient condition of its morality. To whatever degree a man may be wedded to external standards, ultimately these must get the inward ratification of the individual. Morality is, therefore, obedience to one's sense of right, one's inner voice, even when this sense of right has behind it the weight of Shastras or the authority of tradition, or the example of great men. To this extent the right of moral autonomy must be conserved in all systems of ethics. The judgement of the individual is final. Manu says that "Virtue is that conduct, which pious men, wellread in the Vedas, and free from attachment and aversion have followed from time immemorial, and *as to the truth or falsity of which the dictates of the heart are the concluding proof.*[81] "The entire Vedas, the law codes framed by men well-versed in the Vedas, from their recollection as well as the rules of life observed by them, the costumes, etc. of the pious, and the *satisfaction of the heart* are the tests of virtue.[82] As Garga says whenever there are alternative courses of action, the inward test of the ratification of the heart is ultimate. (विकल्पके आत्मतुष्टिश्च) Intuitions of the moral faculty are indeed of final authority; but it is the intuitions of the very pious souls which are invoked on all occasions. *Morality is the practice of the best people in their best moments.* This is the real Hindu view (यद्यदाचरति श्रेष्ठ:) "All acts done by a good and pious person are good and laudable including even the touching of the hair of a cow's tail."[83] "One reposeth not even in one's self that confidence that one doeth in the righteous."[84] "That code of morality which is honoured in every respect by those that are good and which is approved by every honest heart should be followed."[85] Therefore, only the most refined souls are credited with a certain infallibility as regards the rightness or wrongness of actions. Note each and every one can claim for himself this right of seeing finally through the ethical character of every action. Kalidasa finely describes the state of mind of Dushyanta when he begins to feel overpowering love for Shakuntala. The instinctive longings of his heart, he says, guarantee that there is nothing wrong in the situation. (सतां हि संदेहपदेषु वस्तुषु प्रमाणमन्त:करण प्रवृत्तय:।) In cases of doubt the good always find in their own internal whisperings the final authority. The Smritikar also lays down that the authority of the conscience is final; मन:पूतं समाचरेत्। The Hindu ethics, therefore, preserves the claims of moral autonomy in two ways. The pious souls have a right of forming their own independent judgments which are not only valid for themselves but for all in similar situations. The ordinary persons are to follow the judgments of the wise, but they too are entitled to exercise their own judgments on the data before them. "The man of true knowledge should find out for himself the morality laid down for the good. If even a wise man speaks of morality under the influence of wrath or confusion of understanding or ignorance his deliverances go for nothing. Discourses on morality made with the aid of intelligence, derived from the true letter and spirit of the scriptures are worthy of praise, and not those which are made with the help of anything else. Even the words heard from an ignorant person, if in themselves they be fraught with sense, come to be regarded as pious and wise.[86] "These, O Jajali, are some of the wicked practices which are current in this world. Thou practisest them because they are practised by all men from ancient times, and not because they agree with the dictates of thy cleansed understanding. One should practise what one considers to be one's duty, guided by reasons instead of blindly following the practices of the world."[87]

The interests of systematic morality require us to look to the objective content of all actions carefully. It is not sufficient to be assured of the purity of the intention of the agent. Morality will then become quite subjective and will lose entirely the character of universality. A full insight, therefore, into all the circumstances connected with an action is necessary to arrive at a just moral judgment on it. "Righteousness becomes unrighteousness and unrighteousness becomes righteousness according to place and time."[88] However, some standard of uniform application to all cases is necessary for building up ethical judgments. In other words, we must know the exact content of the idea of righteousness. Here we have a two-fold answer. Morality has reference to the good both of the individual and of society; and these two ideas are connected with each other. Kanada defines morality as that which gives prosperity (अभ्युदय) in this life and the highest success hereafter. (नि:श्रेयस) This definition is laid down from the point of view of the individual but what is that which gives to an individual the success he tries for? Evidently the devotion to the good of society. The word Dharma (morality) is derived from धृ to uphold; it is so called because it upholds the order, the organisation of society, even of the three world.[89] "Righteousness was declared (by Brahmana) for the advancement and growth of all creatures. Therefore, that which leads to advancement and growth is righteousness. Righteousness was established for restraining creatures from injuring one another. Therefore, that is righteousness which prevents injuty to creatures. Righteousness (Dharma) is so called because it upholds all creatures."[90] "It is nothing else but that ancient morality which is known to all, and which consists of universal friendliness and is fraught with beneficence to all creatures. That mode of living which is founded upon total harmlessness towards all creatures or upon minimum of such harm is the highest morality.[91]

Morality of actions is, therefore, to be judged by a reference to this standard viz., the welfare of humanity. Objective utility of actions, the actual consequences of these must be taken into consideration in all our moral judgments. Actions in this sense may be wrong even if the agent is not conscious of any moral guilt. "One who is not possessed of clear vision does wrong even when one wishes to do right. Such a person, by even exercising his judgment, does such acts of virtue as partake the nature of inquity. Desiring to do what is right one does what is wrong, similarly desiring to do what is wrong one does what is right. Not knowing the two kinds of acts, one has to undergo repeated re-births and deaths.[92] Here the greatest amount of tact and caution is necessary. The welfare of humanity is a very vague phrase; and many crimes may be committed in its name. Morality will become quite vague and elastic; faith in the very primary judgments of our conscience will be lost. One has to look, therefore, as much to his own conscience or his own inner, fundamental, moral intuitions as to the outer consequences of an action, and should not tamper with the highest moral virtues in the name of the welfare of society. "The man of intelligence would never do an act that is sinful in character even if it lead to the greatest advantage."[93]

"That man who is endued with intellegence would never do an act which is dissociated from virtue, however high may be the advantages of that act. Indeed such an act is not regarded as truly beneficial. That lawless king, who, snatching thousands of kine from their lawful owners, gives them away, acquires no fruit beyond an empty sound. On the other hand he incurs the sin of theft."[94] "The man possessed of wisdom would not seek wealth for the performance of religious rites, by ways that are unrighteous, and that involve an abandonment of morality. Wealthy earned by such means can never prove beneficial."[95] Men are tempted to do evil that good may come when they are left free to make an unfettered application of this test. Another limitation of the morality, which leans too much upon consequences, is the very circumscribed range of our knowledge. Of the very remote issues of any course of action we cannot have any knowledge; we can have only faith. One must not, therefore, think too much of consequences. "The fact, however, is that they can never arrive at the truth who under the influence of doubt proceed to inquire about the consequences hereafter of virtue and vice, or about the strenght and weakness of men. For it is seen that which is the cause of the success of a person's object becometh also the cause of his ruin. Human acts, therefore, are doubtful in their consequences. Learned men capable of judging of the evils of actions pronounce a particular course of action as worthy of being followed. It produces, however, consequences the very opposite of what were for-seen very much like the course of the wind. Indeed even those acts of men that are the results of deliberation with conside-rations of propriety are baffled by the dispensations of Provi-dence.[96]

Whatever may be the limitations of reflection as an instrument of investigating moral truths, its use is indispensable in fixing the degrees of objective rightness of an action. Consequences are almost a part of acts and judgment about them must colour our judgments about acts. "From the worldly point of view, acts that are evil lead to good and those that are good to consequences that are bad. From the worldly point of view, therefore, virtue and sin are to be distinguished by the good and evil character of their consequences. Acts that are (apparently) evil, when undertaken from considerations connected with with gods, the scriptures, the life itself, and means by which life is sustained, produce consequences that are good. When an act is undertaken from the expectation, however doubtful, that it will produce mischeif (to some one) in the future or when an act is done whose consequence is visibly mischievous, expiation has been laid down.[97] In the same way when the respective importance of duties is to be adjudged, a reference to their effects is unavoidable. Yudhishthira inquired "which, of snake, is the higher of the two; truth or alms-giving." The snake replied "the relative merits of these virtues: truth, alms-giving, kind speech and abstention from injury to any creature are known by their objective utility. Even so it is, O king, depending on effects.[98]

Many criteria, external and internal, are laid down for distinguishing between right and wrong. But each of them has its own limitations. The ancient sages knew too well the nature and power of these and when they laid down dogmas they simultaneously pointed the exceptions and modifications in the case of each. "Thou sayest that righteousness or duty depends upon delicate considerations that, it is indicated by the conduct of those that are called good, that it is fraught with restraints and that its indications are also contained in the Vedas.... All these embodied creatures take birth exist and leave their bodies of their own nature. Duty and its reverse, therefore, cannot be ascertained by the study of the scriptures alone. The duties of a person who is well-off are of one kind. Those of a person who has fallen into distress are of another. How can duty respecting seasons of distress be ascertained by reading the scriptures alone? The acts of the good, thou hast said, constitute duty. The good, however, are to be ascertained by their acts. The definition involves, therefore, a begging of the question with the result that what is meant by conduct of the good remains unsettled. It is seen that some ordinary person commits unrighteousness, while apparently acheiving righteousness. Some extraordinary person again may be seen who achieves righteousness by committing acts that are apparently unrighteous. Again, it has been heard by us that the ordinances of the Vedas disappear gradually in every successive age. The duties in the Krita age are of one kind; those in the Treta are of another kind; and those in the Dwapara again are different. The duties in the Kali age again are of an entirely different kind. It seems therfore that duties have been laid down for the respective ages according to the powers of human beings in the respective ages. When, therefore, all the declarations in the Vedas do not apply equally to all the ages, the saying that the declarations of the Vedas are true is only a popular form of speech indulged in for popular satisfaction. From the Shrutis have originated the Smritis whose scope again is very wide. If the Vedas be authority for everything, then authority would attach to the Smritis also, for the latter are based on the former. When, however, the Shrutis and the Smritis contradict each other, how can either be authoritative? Whether we know it or not, whether we are able to ascertain it or not, the course of duties is finer than the edge of the razor, and grosser than even a mountain. That conduct by which one becomes meritorious impedes another in the acquisition of merit. One may thus see that all courses of conduct are seen to lose singleness of purpose and character."[99] This scepticism is natural to those who have thought deeply on moral questions. But it is only an occasional phase; and it is important inasmuch as it prevents us from becoming dogmatic. Morality is indeed a very subtle affair requiring the co-operation of various factors, a fine intelligence, a through-going knowledge of the Shastras, a familiarity with the practice of the great people, a knowledge of the customs, traditions and history of the society, and a firm and unerring character. To define it is hopeless as we have seen. The good is indefinable in the last resort. All attempts at definition inevitably involve us in a vicious circle. If morality is to be judged by consequences we must first know what consequences are good and what are bad; we must beg the question. If morality is the practice of good people how are we to know the good people without knowing what good is? All the same, people can know broadly what constitutes the virtuous acts and what the unrighteous ones. Subjectively, we have within us the sense of duty, the categorical imperative which is the ultimate court of appeal in all questions of right and wrong. Objectively, the content of virtue and vice, of the higher and lower life becomes increasingly clear to people who have very acute and trained intellects, very refined conscience, very exalted and delicate sense of humanity and very extensive acquaintance with the customs of various people, the lives of saints and the Bibles of all the great Faiths.

(4)

Hindu moral system was far from being a rigid, inelastic structure. Ample provision is made for all possible situations. An unbending compliance with the strictest ethical injunctions at all costs would aften land men in very awkward situations and force them to make uncalled for sacrifices which would take away a large part of their usefulness. Morality is a means by which individuals and societies secure their self-preservation by the trying to bring about as perfect an adaptation as possible between themselves and their environment, Catastrophic changes in the latter necessitate equally great important changes of front on the part of the former. A large amount of relativity, therefore, necessarily enters into every deed of morality. Time and place, capacity and opportunity, all help to mould man's actions and any defiance of these limiting factors brings down upon man gratuitous ruin. "Righteousness becomes unrighteousness, and unrighteousness becomes righteousness, according to place and time; such is the power of place and time. The friends of humanity, by doing even acts of cruelty, have attained to high heaven. Righteous Kshatriyas, by doing even sinful acts, have attained to blissful ends. The Brahmin, by taking up arms on the occasions, does not incur sin, viz. for protecting himself, for compelling the other orders to betake themselves to their duties, and for chastising robbers."[100]

In our humble opinion, this was one of the most remarkable characteristics of our system of morality. It requires very great stretch of human power to be able to establish main distinctions between right and wrong. These constitue main principles true for all time and space. Thus the Yoga-Sutras refer to Ahimsa, Satya, Asteya, Brahmacharya, and Aparigraha as principles of universal validity. "जातिदेशकालसमयानवच्छिन्ना: सार्वभौमा: महाव्रतम्"[101] But very soon these distinctions become stereotyped and take the shape of customary morality. A far greater exertion of human capacity is necessary to transcend these self-imposed bonds and to establish modifications, limitations, exceptions to copy-book, dogmatic, primary assertions of moral sense. The world, the mass-mind-cannot be taken safely into the confidence of the moral expert. However, morality is not always a routine thing, a matter of course thing, which he who runs may read. It is the most subtle of all subtle things, and requires very shrewd insight to find out one's duty in complicated situation of life. Here precisely the set rules of morality fail and guidance of experts becomes so necessary.

The Mahabharata is full of instances revealing the difficult nature of ethical problems. A hunter of animals called Valaka used to kill animals for the sake of the maintenance of himself and his family. Here the deed was cruel, but his intentions were honest. Once he happened to kill a beast of prey, which was a source of great destruction to animal lives. This deed enabled Valaka to go to heaven. An ascetic called Kaushika vowed to speak truth and nothing but truth. Once certain persons hid themselves in a forest owing to fear of robbers. When the robbers came, Kaushika revealed the truth and those persons were killed. He fell into hell "ignorant of the subtleties of morality."[102] Bhishma after laying down that there is nothing higher than truth says :–"There where falsehood would assume the aspect of truth should not be said. There, again, where truth would assume the aspect of falsehood, even falsehood should be said. That ignorant person incurs sin who says truth which is dissociated from righteousness.[103]

The following passage shows how subtle are the windings of the moral sense of ancient writers, how while they lay down every ethical proposition, are equally keen to point out its limitations when applied to actual situations, how finely they draw our attention to time, place, and circumstance on the one hand and the inner intention of the author on the other in fixing the ethical character of an action, how they see necessity of measureless thought in adjudging the character of an action. "One who slays a Brahmin that has fallen away from his own duties and that advances, weapon in hand, with intent to slaughter, does not truly become the slayer of a Brahmin. In such a case it is the wrath of the slayer that proceeds against the wrath of the slain. A person by drinking alchoholic stimulants in ignorance or upon the advice of a virtuous physician when his life is in peril, should have the regenerating ceremonies perfomred once more in his case. All that I have told thee, 6 son of Kunti, about all eating of interdicted food, may be cleansed by such expiatory rites. Connection with the preceptor's wife at the preceptor's command does not stain the pupil. The sage Uddalaka caused his son Shwetaketu to be begotten by a disciple. A person by committing theft for the sake of his preceptor in a season of distress is not stained by sin. One, however, that takes to thieving for procuring enjoyments for himself becomes stained. A falsehood may be spoken for saving one's life, or that of another, or for the sake of one's preceptor, or for gratifying a woman, or for bringing about a marriage. One's vow of Brahmacharya is not broken by having wet dreams.[104] The art of calculating less and more is necessory in weighing an action. A smaller good must yield to a greater good. "If by slaying a single individual a family may be saved, or if by slaying a single family the whole kingdom may be saved, such an act of slaughter is no transgression. Sin, O King, sometimes assumes the form of virtue, and virtue sometimes assumes the form of sin. They, however, that are learned, know which is which.[105]

A logical development of this principle of relativity is the ideal of what is known as आपद्धर्म–morality of exceptional situations. Abnormal circumstances justify resort to abnormal expedients. What is true of a man who is healthy is not true of a diseased man. What is true of a man in famine is not true of a man in a good season. Every situation carries its own peculiar moral. "For men that are able and competent the duties are of one kind. In season of distress, however, one's duties are of a different kind.[106] The main object must be self-preservation. Men have no right in their moral or altruistic enthusiasm to forget the most elementary duties towards themselves. It was in this sense that Shakespeare said :–"Self-love is not so vile a sin as self-neglecting." If a man sticks to the essence of virtue, he must be prepared to let go its accidental appearance sometimes; otherwise, the essence will be lost. That a man should not steal is ethics quite good enough for ordinary times. But if a man is dying for want of food, will pedantic adherence to the mere letter of the law be either sound wisdom or sound morality? The fact to be borne in mind is that the act of stealing is not the material thing; the disposition to steal is the real thing. Action is merely, as a poet said, the movement of a muscle this way or that. The real act is the character behind it. No man who has a deeply religious disposition can lightly do away with life for the sake of a mere formal adherence to a law of morality. The man who is at heart a thief is none the less a thief whether he steals or not. The man who is at heart not a thief is never a thief whether he steals or not. The man who fundamentally loves chaste life is not polluted by mere outward touch as Sita's words testify; the man who is at heart vicious is not chaste even if he studiously abstains from all contact with women. Even this formal breach of certain well-established moral conventions is justifiable, only if an extreme exigency almost jeopardising a man's life arises. It is in this sense that we are told not to be over-scrupulous as regards the means to preserve life, in times of crises. If a man's existence on the whole, stands unambiguously for higher ideal, an over-literal conformity to minute points of morality often becomes undesirable. समर्थो धर्ममाचरेत् "It hath been said that in a season of distress one should protect his life by any means.[107] "That by which life may be preserved should certainly be accomplished without scruple. Life is better than death. Living, one may acquire virtue.[108] "The hungry saga Ajagartah, for having attempted to kill his son in order to appease his hunger, was not associated with the sin. The famished Vamadevah, the knower of sin and virtue, for having wished to eat dog's flesh in order to avoid death from starvation, was not associated with the sin.......Oppressed by hunger, the holy Vishwamitra, the knower of merits and demerits, for having accepted the gift of the flesh of a dog's thigh from the hand of a Chandala, was not associated with sin".[109] The Mahabharata comments thus on the latter's action. "Burning all his sins afterwards by his penances, the sage after a long time acquired the most wonderful (ascetic) success. Even thus when the end in view is the preservation of life itself, should a high-souled person possessed of learning and acquainted with means rescue his own cheerless self when fallen into distress, by all means in his power.........A person, if alive, can win religious merit and enjoy happiness and prosperity."[110]

But the Hindu moralist goes a step further and challenges the very distinction between right and wrong. There is a redical distinction between the morality of the man of the world and morality of the superman. A super-moral state is the goal of life. Moral categories are not ultimate; they dominate only a particular stage of life. But man has higher and vaster possibilities. This stage is variously described by sages as गुणातीत or जीवनमुक्त निस्त्रैगुण्ये पथि बिचरतः को विधिः को निषेधः। No moral injunctions and no moral prohibitions bind a man who has gone beyond the qualities or worldly. The Gita also says तस्य कार्यं न विद्यते– He has left nothing to be done. The underlying idea is, that morality is merely a provicialism of our planet, an outcome of Maya, a product of our circumscribed ego. Once we transcend the empirical limits of time, space, and causality, we become free. We are neither moral, immoral, or unmoral, we are super-moral. There is a world 'beyond good and evil.' The whole struggle of right against wrong goes on as long as the power of worldly temptations and worldly terrors survives. But once we understand that all is illusion, that there is one Atman alone which is real, we pass automatically into a higher, and more unfettered region.

The transition from moral life to super-moral one is a transition from an ego-centric view to a cosmocentric view. A right view of soul transports man from his narrow sphere to a vast timeless, spaceless region where his egoism does not conflict with other rival egoism above him or beneath him but has an undisputed sovereignty. Morality presupposes the limitation of the I by the Not-I; it presupposes the reality of time and space and causality; it presupposes the separate and independent existence of man, God, and nature. But a higher view of spiritual reality emancipates man from these illusions, points out that time, space and causality have empirical validity but not transcendental reality, that man, God, and nature are unreal as abstractions, as autocratic entities, that the supreme Reality is essentially transcendental. "Passages such as 'He is to approach his life at the proper time' and 'He is not to approach the wife of his Guru' are examples of permissions and prohibitions.......Permissions and prohibitions of this kind are possible, because the Self although one is connected with various bodies. Of what kind then is the connection? It consists in the origination in the Self of the erroneous notion that the Self is the aggregate consisting of the body and so on......And thus, although the Self must be admitted to be One only, injunctions and prohibitions are possible owing to the difference effected by its connection with bodies, and other limiting adjuncts, the products of nescience."[111]

The Gita describes the super-moral soul in a few verses. "Balanced in pleasure and pain, self-reliant, to whom a lump of earth, a rock, and gold are alike, the same to loved and unloved, firm, the same in censure and praise; the same in honour and ignominy, the same to friend and foe, abandoning all undertakings, he is said to have overcome the power of the qualities."[112] Man in this way can travel beyond his family, guild, state and even caste and reach a transcendental plane where the tyranny of ritualism, of worldly convention, does not touch him, but where even the words good and evil, right and wrong. Moral and immoral become meaningless to him. "This indeed is his (true) form: free from desires, free from evil, free from fear. Now as a man when embraced by a beloved wife, knows nothing that is without, nothings that is within, so this person when embraced by the intelligent Self, knows nothing that is without, nothing that is within. This, indeed, is his (true) form, in which his wishes are fulfilled, in which the Self (only) is his wish, in which no wish is left, free from any sorrow. Then a father is not a father, a mother not a mother, the worlds not worlds, the gods not gods, the Vedas not Vedas. Then a thief is not a thief, a murderer is not a murderer, a Chandala not a Chandala, a Paulkasa (the son of a Shudra father and Kshatriya mother) not a Paulkasa, a Shraman not a Shraman, a Tapasa not a Tapasa, He is not followed by good, not followed by evil, for he has then overcome all the sorrow of the heart."[113] A similar position is found in Buddhistic writings. "A true Brahmin goes scatheless, though he has killed father and mother, and the two valiant kings, though he has destroyed a kingdom with all his subjects.[114]

References

1. Rg.I. 105. 4-6.
2. Rg.III. 56. 1.
3. Rg.IX.113.4.
4. Rg.IX. 110.4.
5. Rg.IX.94. 2.
6. Rg.VIII. 75.5.
7. Rg.VII.63. 3.
8. Rg.X. 48. 11.
9. Rg.X. 170.2.
10. Rg. X, 62. 3.

11. Rg.VIII. 89. 4.
12. Rg.1. 2. 8.
13. Rg.VII.66. 13.
14. Rg.X, 133. 6.
15. Rg.VIII. 23.8.
16. Rg.IX, 73. 6.
17. Vana. 31. 35-40.
18. Rg.III. 54. 5.
19. Shanti. 132. 19-22.
20. Shanti., 136.11.
21. Shanti. 179. 21.
22. M.II. 8.
23. M. II. 8- 10. 14., M. XIII. 94-95. 97. 99.
24. Naradiya Purana cited in the Hemadri.
25. S.B. III. 1. 25.
26. Bg. 16. 23-24.
27. Bhishma. 5. 11-12.
28. M. II. 11.
29. M. XII, 105-106.
30. Shanti. 142, 17-23.
31. Shanti, 142, 7-10.
32. Shanti. 252, 13.
33. Rg. X, 14, 7.
34. Rg.VIII, 30. 3.
35. Vana. 314, 88.
36. Vana. 314, 119.
37. M.IV, 178.
38. M.II. 17-18.
39. M. I. 108. 110. IV. 156.
40. S. N. VII.80.
41. Bg. III.21.
42. Brihapati. Ch. II.26. 28-31, I.26.
43. Devala cited in the Smriti Ratnakar.
44. S.N. III. 130.
45. S.N. III. 65.68.
46. P. I. P. I. K. I. S. 2,3.
47. P. I. P. I. K. 4. S.8.
48. *ibid.* 9.
49. P. I. P. 4. K. 12. S. 8.

50. P. 2. 6. K. 15. 5.
51. M. XIII. 108-111.
52. M.XIII, 113, 114.
53. Rg. I. 91. 7.
54. Rg. VIII. 60.6.
55. Rg.VII. 53. 3.
56. Rg. V. 104. 3.
57. Rg.V. 83. 9.
58. Kau. Br. 3. 8.
59. Vana. 31. 24-41.
60. M. IV. 156.157.
61. M.II, 2-4.
62. Shanti. 165, 29-30.
63. Shanti. 165. 11-14.
64. Shalya. 61. 23-24.
65. Vana. 33, 21-48.
66. R. VI, 83, 14-39.
67. Vana. 30, 37-43.
68. Shanti. 165, 7-9.
69. Udyoga. 40, 12-13.
70. Vana. 31, 2-6.
71. Shanti, 265, 12-13, 18-20.
72. Shanti. 330, 7.
73. Vana. 30. 5-8.
74. Sobha. 89. 60.
75. Adi. 2. 392.
76. Shanti. 329. 54-6.
77. Vana. 298, 48-51.
78. M. XII, 88. 89.
79. Shanti. 123, 3-10.
80. R. IV, 11, 37-45.
81. M.II. 1.
82. M. II, 6.
83. Shanti. 191, 18.
84. Vana. 298, 43-44.
85. Shanti. 132, 19.
86. Shanti. 142, 17-23.
87. Shanti. 269, 52-53.
88. Shanti. 78, 32.

89. R. VII.
90. Shanti. 109, 11-21.
91. Shanti., 268, 5-6.
92. Shanti. 241,31-32.
93. Shanti. 297, 7.
94. Shanti. 299. 8-10.
95. Shanti. 300. 25.
96. Udyoga. 76, 5-10.
97. Shanti. 35. 11-15.
98. Vana. 183. 3-7.
99. Shanti. 266.
100. Shanti. 78, 32-35.
101. II. 30-31.
102. Karna. 72, 40-50; 56-66.
103. Shanti. 109., 10-21.
104. Shanti. 33. 21-34.
105. Shanti. 32. 18-21.
106. Shanti. 130. 14.
107. Adi. 167. 23.
108. Shanti. 141. 63-65.
109. M.X, 105-108.
110. Shanti. 141, 101-104.
111. S.B. II. 3. 48.
112. Bg. XIV. 22-25.
113. Br. U. IV. 3. 22.
114. Dhammapada 21. 294-5.

Chapter - III

VALUE OF LIFE : POSITIVE AND PRUDENTIAL QUALITIES

It is often supposed that the Hindu view emphasizes negative elements of life to the exclusion of positive qualities. Nothing can be further from truth. "Tis more life and fuller that we want." A love of life and all the elements which go to make a life strong, and radiant, and beautiful, and happy was a predominant characteristic of Hindu thought in all its phases. This will be clear from a detailed consideration of this question.

The Vedas are full of prayers for long life. The longer the span of time one's life covers the more useful to the society and to oneself one becomes. "Adityas....grant to our children and their seed, extended terms of life that they may live long days."[1] "A hundred autumns may we live."[2] Among other objects of proper were victory prosperity and children. "Vouch-safe us food, prosperity, and progeny, and lengthen our days that we may see long life.[3] "Make thou my chariot to be first. And bring the fame of victory near."[4] Indra is "Lord of spoil and wealth."[5]

The Hindu, therefore, cannot look upon suicide with complacency. All attempts to escape life's burdens and responsibilities by voluntary resort to death argue cowardice and want of faith in God. There is expiation of three fasts for persons who attempt to commit suicide from grief.[6] "The death that one meets with by taking poison, by hanging, by burning, at the hands of robbers, and at the teeth of animals is said to be an inglorious one. Those men that are righteous never incur such or similar deaths even if they be afflicted with mental and physical diseases of the most agonising kind."[7] The Upanishads consign a man to sunless regions for the sin of self-destruction, However, wilful suicide are distinguished from willing acceptance of death when the psychological moment arrives. They only know how to live, it is said, who know how to die. There are two types of death,–we read in the Mahabharata,– voluntary and involuntary. An old man who has fulfilled all his obligations and whose health is quite shattered may die by either walking out his existence, or fasting or by entering water or fire. A Kshatriya may accept death for protecting the people; a student may die for his Guru's sake; a man may die for the defence of cows, and Brahmins and for the sake of his fatherland. A servant is free to die for his master. Life may be sacrificed for the poor. But a man who abandons life in anger, or lust, terror goes to hell.[8]

It was realised that to be weak is miserable. Virtue is, after all, virility. "Force thou art: force mayst thou give me: hail ! Power thou art: power mayst thou give me: hail,"[9] The Upanishads expressly say: नायमात्मा बलहीनेन लभ्य: Atman is not for the weak. True power is a combination of bodily and spiritual force. "Spiritual power is veritably greater than understanding. Here in this world, one powerful man of spirit makes a hundred men of understanding tremble.....By power the Earth stands firm, by power the intermediate world stands firm, by power the Deva Loka stands firm, by power the mountains and divine men, by power the cattle and birds and herbs and trees and beasts down to worms, insects, and ants stand firm, by power the world stands firm. Meditate on Brahman in power."[10] The Mahabharata also emphasizes this element. "If, however, the two be compared, Power will appear to be superior to Righteousness. It is from Power that Righteousness springs. Righteousness depends upon Power as all immobile things upon the Earth."

From consciousness of power springs courage. The Gita

calls it अभयं–Fearlessness and places it in the forefront of the catalogue of the spiritual goods. The Vedic age above all praised courage in war. "All manliness that is in heaven........Bestow, ye Ashwins upon us."[11] "Make me a bull among my peers, make me my rivals' conqueror."[12] A blind heroism is not appreciated; discertion is the better part of valour. कातर्यं केवला नीतिः शौर्यं श्वापदचेष्टितं. Kalidas says that mere policy (diplomacy divorced from strength) is cowardice; and mere courage (divorced from wisdom) is the courage of beasts. A happy combination of both is necessary for success. "One, However, that is destitue of valour, though possessed of every (other) merit, can scarcely accomplish anything......One, however, that is possessed of valour doth not yet deserve success if he acts with carelessness."[13]

The Gita well sums up the situation in the last verse :

यत्र योगेश्वरो कृष्णः यत्र पार्थो धनुर्धरः।
तत्रश्रीर्विजयो भूतिर्ध्रुवानीतिर्मतिर्मम।।

Wherever there is Krishna with his policy and wherever their is Arjuna with his heroism, there is victory and prosperity.

Body should be the last things to be neglected: because it is the vehicle of higher life. शरीरमाद्यं खलु धर्मसाधनं. Kalidas called it the one instrument of the realisation of Dharma. It is the temple of gods; its gratuitous contempt is downright folly "The human body is the residence of many intelligent creatures of great energy, of Shakra, of Vishnu, of Saraswati, and of other beings. A man of knowledge therefore, should never disregard the body."[14] The Veda cries: "Let thy body become a stone ![15] "Let thine heroic strength come from behind us, before us, from above us, or below us. From every side it may approach us."[16] "May my energy and my force, and my self, and my body, and my shelter and my shield, and my limbs, and my bones, and my joints, and my members, and my life, and my old age prosper by sacrifice. May my pre-eminence and overlordship, and my wrath and my angry passion, and my violence, and my impetuosity, and my victorious power, and my greatness, and my breadth and my width, and my height, and my length and my increase and my improvement prosper by sacrifice. May my religious rite and my immortality, and my freedom from consumption and my freedom from disease and my life and my longevity, and my fair dawn and my fair day prosper by sacrifice."[17] This passage is such a powerful testimony to the Vedic Hindus love of all the good things of life. The Yoga-Sutras specially praise celibacy for this purpose.

"ब्रह्मचर्यप्रतिष्ठायां वीर्यलाभः।"

The importance of property as an ingredient of a complete life was well perceived by Hindu writers : "Bring cattle, bring us ornament, bring us embellishment and steeds. Give us beside two rings of gold."[18] "Give us not up, Agni, to want of heroes, to wretched clothes, to need, to destitution. Yield us not, Holy one, to fiend or hunger."[19] "May we subdue all famine and evil want with store of grain and cattle."[20] "Wealth was considered the very basis of higher life in the Mahabharata. A close connection exists between material prosperity and morality.

"Poverty is a state of sinfulness. I do not see the difference between a fallen man and a poor man! From wealth spring all religious acts, all pleasures; and heaven itself. O king ! Without wealth, a man cannot find the very means of sustaining his life.......From wealth one acquires family honour. From wealth one's religious merit increases. He that is without wealth hath neither this world nor the next !" The great sages like Bhishma when approached by Yudhishthira confess that they are helpless: "A man is the slave of wealth, but wealth is no one's slave.[21]

It must be clearly understood, however, that wealth is to be a means to an end, not an end in itself. Bhartrihari says that there are three possible outlets for wealth: charity, enjoyment and destruction. The Hindu sage clearly said that उपार्जितानां वित्तानां

त्याग एव हि रक्षणं। We shall see that charity was highly praised and greediness condemned in the Rig-Veda. The Upanishads also lay it down: "Don't covet anybody's wealth ![22] The Gita calls लोभ or greed one of the three roads to destruction. Worship of mammon leads one to all sorts of vices. "From covetousness proceeds sin.....It is the spring of all the cunning and hypocrisy in the world. From covetousness proceeds wrath; form covetousness flows lust; and it is from covetouness that loss of judgment, deception, pride, arrogance and malice, as also vindictiveness, shamelessness, loss of prosperity, loss of virtue anxiety, and infamy spring."[23]

Many sociologists associate pleasure with virtue and call the former a life-furthering process. The Hindu theory also as we have seen considers काम (gratification of desire) one of the ends of life. Even Brahman is called joy (आनन्द). It is called रस (रसोऽवै ब्रह्म:)" When one knows Him as pleasure he knows Him as the Creator, he who does not know Him as pleasure, does not know His as Creator."[24] Shri Krishna calls himself Kama: (धर्माविरुद्धः भूतेषु कामोऽस्मि भरतर्षभ।) when it is not opposed to Duty. The Hindu theory is not a rigorism of the Kantian type' it is as comprehensive as the Aristotelian theory, with a finer and deeper spirituality about it than is to be found in the highest Greek speculation.

The very breath of human life is, after all, work. Action is of three types : the pure selfless, disinterested action is Satwik. That action which is egoistic is Rajas, and the action undertaken from delusion, without regard to capacity and consequences-loss and injury to others-that is Tamas (dark).[25] Under no circumstances cessation of work is possible. "Man winneth not freedom from action by abstaining from activity, nor by mere renunciation doth he rise to perfection. Nor can any one even for an instant, remain really actionless; for helplessly is every one driven to action by the qualities born of nature."[26]

Apart from this philosophical view of work, it is considered infinitely superior to idleness. Success is bound up with work. Passivity is not the teaching of the Hindu Shastras. A life of negation leads nowhere. "Only the active conquers, dwells in peace and thrives: not for the niggard are the gods."[27] 'May we allied as with princes obtain possessions by our own exertion.'[28] Agni gives all things unto him who strives.[29] Indra responds to the call of "the early rising one, the active one."[30] "Savitar, God hath sent us forth to labour, each quadruped, each biped to be active."[31] "Never may sleep or idle talk control us.[32] "They (the gods) desire not sleep; they punish sloth everlastingly.[33] The dignity of labour is so well established. Especially agricultural labour was highly regarded.[34] In the time of the Smritis, however, professional labour all artistic activity, al handicrafts were considered unworthy of higher castes. This were a clear falling-off ! Thus food from artisans, physicians, blacksmiths, goldsmiths, washerman, dyers of cloths, is unacceptable to a Brahmin.[35] A truer expression of the Hindu creed is found in the emphatic assertion that even God is an humble labourer. "That great ascetic Hari, though the Lord of the whole universe, still betaketh himself to work like a humble labourer that tilleth the fields."[36]

A brief description of various qualities leading to worldly success is necessary to round up this subject. We may call this part sententious morality. It is the morality of the man of the world. The books like Vidura-Niti are specially devoted to what may be called wisdom of the world. It is not quite possible to be exhaustive in our treatment here. Perseverance is the most noted characteristic of a man of the world. The first mark of wisdom is abstention; the second is persistence till the end. Heroism is well defined to be persistence. न निश्चितार्थाद्विरमन्ति धीराः। "By exertion the Amrita was obtained; by exertion India himself obtained sovereignty in heaven and on earth. The hero of exertion is superior to the hero of speech."[37] Abstinence from sleep during the day-time leadeth to success.[38]

The ancient Hindus were emphatic in their praise of travelling. Overseas commerce with other countries is frequently referred to. Persons desirous of wealth sent ships to the sea.[39] Bodies of merchants went on voyages in ships with a hundred oars to distant lands for sale and barter.[40] Merchants went to far-off countries for interchange of merchandise.[41] A writer has cleverly pointed out how the very words Avara-parina,[42] Paraga (one who has gone to the other side,) Anukula (favourable, when the wind blows towards the coast), Pratikula, (hostile-away from the coast), Sagara (the king was so called because he first crossed the ocean), Bhagiratha (who has traced the river Ganges from the source to its mouth), show the prevalence of sea-voyage among the ancient Aryans. Mercantile fleets are referred to in Vana Parva. (168). Indra says– "Fortune belongs to one who travels. Indra is a friend of those who more. A travelling man becomes prosperous; his sins are consumed by his pilgrimage: travel, The luck of a man sits when he is sitting, stands when he is standing, sleeps when he is sleeping, and moves when he moves. When a man sleeps, there sets in Kali Yuga; when he sits the Dwapara sets in; when he moves the Treta begins; and the Satya-Yuga commences when he works."[43] These are the finest verses exhibiting the majesty of action. It is especially essential for Brahmins to travel far and wide in pursuit of culture. "If remaining in the abode of his sire he masters all the Vedas.....people still condemn his as home-keeping. Like a snake swallowing mice, the Earth swallows up these two, viz. a king who is unwilling to fight and a Brahmin who is unwilling to leave home for acquiring knowledge."[44] "He who desireth to obtain a knowledge of the different customs of different countries, of also the languages of different nations, and of the usages of different orders of men, knoweth at once all that is high and low; and wherever he may go he is sure to acquire ascendency even over those that are good.[45]

Independence is an absolutely necessary condition for happiness as well as good life. Manu calls "service the vocation of a dog; hence it should be shunned.[46] Liberty is the very essence of happiness; it is the unhindered growth of one's inner self. "Works, which make one dependent on others, he must studiously avoid: works, which are entirely under his own control, he must diligently pursue. Liberty (in all respects) is happiness; and independence, (in all matters) is misery. These, know to be the general definitions of happiness and misery. A work, by doing which the inner man is satisfied, do by all means; avoid the contrary."[47] "Dependence upon another, even if that other happens to be possessed of splendour, is not desirable or praise-worthy.[48] "The fear that arises in the heart of a person who is summoned by the king is unknown to persons passing their days contendly in the woods, supporting life upon fruits and roots. Simple food and drink obtained without effort, and luxurious food procured with fear, widely differ from each other."[49] Here it is clearly pointed out that luxury and freedom cannot go together.

Men gather their characters from their association and environment very often. The company, therefore, one selects, should be well chosen. "He that waiteth upon one that is good or upon one that is wicked, upon one that is possessed of ascetic merit, or upon one that is a thief, soon taketh his colour from that companion of his, like a cloth from the dye in which it is soaked."[50] "A person becomes like those with whom he dwells, and like those whom he reverences, and like to what he wishes to be."[51] "Devoid of religious acts as we are, we shall yet reap religious merit by association with the righteous, as we should come by sin by waiting upon the sinful. The very sight and touch of the dishonest, and converse, and association with them cause diminution of merit, and men never attain purity of soul."[52] Brahmins should avoid contact with the degraded, with thieves, with sceptics and with the illiterate.[53] Contagion inevitably spreads by contact. "As oil drops poured on water soon spread over its surface, so the contagion of sin spreads from one person to another by the use of the same bed, seat, or cushion, or through contact and conversation."[54] The sight or *darshana* of the holy is a very purifying things and of the unholy is degrading.[55]

Shrewdness is very necessary in our commerce with the world. An excess of confidence in others may be chivalrous; but it is nothing but folly. "One should never trust a person who does not deserve to be trusted. Nor should one repose blind confidence upon a person deserving of trust. One should always endeavour to inspire others with confidence in himself. One should not, however, himself repose confidence in foes. In brief, the highest truth of all treatises on policy is mistrust."[56]

Procrastination should be avoided on the one hand and too much hastiness on the other hand, "That man, again, who, regarding himself clever, does not seek his own good in proper time, incurs great danger. Hence these two only, viz., he that has much forethought, and he that has presence of mind, succeed in obtaining happiness. He, however, that is procrastinating meets with destruction."[57] There is the story of Chirkarin who reflects and reflects and in this way avoids precipitate action. Inaction is often the best kind of action. The man was called Chirkarin "because he used to reflect upon all matters, to remain awake for a long time, to sleep for a long time, and to take a long time in setting himself to the accom-plishment of such acts as he accomplished." He was branded idle and foolish. Once his father asked him to do away with his mother in wrath. But this fellow in his characteristic way thought on and on till the father changed his mind and was highly pleased with his son. "That learned and best of Rishis then uttered these verses .....If the matter is the death of a friend, one should accomplish it after a long time. If it is the abandon-ment of a project already begun, one should accomplish it after a long while. A friendship that is formed after a long exami-nation lasts for a long time. In giving way to wrath, to pride, to haughtiness, to disputes, to sinful acts, and in accomplishing all disagreeable tasks he that delays long deserves applause."

The *rationale* of prosperity is briefly given "Exertion, self-control, skill, carefulness, steadiness, memory, and commencement of acts after mature deliberation-know that these roots of prosperity." "Prosperity never resides in one who suffers himself to be tortured by grief, who is addicted to evil ways, who denies godhead, who is idle, who hath not his sense under control. Also those who are excessively liberal, who are over-bold, who practise the most rigid vows, and who are proud of their wisdom."[58]

A few marks of folly are indicated. "He, who, forsaking his own concerneth himself with the objects of others, and who practiseth deceitful means for serving his friends is called a fool. He, who wishes for those things that should not be desired, and foresaketh those that may be desired, and who beareth malice to those that are powerful, is regarded to be a foolish soul. He who regarded his foe as a friend, and hateth his friends.....is a fool. He, who divulgeth his projects, doubteth all things, and spendeth a long time in doing what requireth a short time, is a fool. The person, who entereth a place, uninvited and talketh much without being asked......is a fool. That man, who being himself guilty casteth the blame on others, and who though impotent giveth way to anger, is the most foolish of man."[59]

References

1. Rg. VIII, 18.
2. Rg.VII, 66, 16.
3. Rg.Val. 11, 7.
4. Rg.VIII, 69, 5.
5. Rg.VIII, 81, 30.
6. Shanti. 35, 18.
7. Shanti. 303, 25-26.
8. Anu. 242.
9. Yj. II, 17, 1-2.
10. Ch. Up. VII, 8, 1.
11. Rg.VIII, 9, 2.
12. Rg. X. 166.
13. Sabha. 16, 7-14.
14. Shanti. 120, 46.
15. II, 13, 4.
16. Rg. I, 27, 9.
17. Yj. XVIII, 3-6.
18. Rg. VIII. 67. 2.
19. Rg. VII. 1.

20. Rg. X. 43. 10.
21. Bhishma. 43, 58.
22. Ish. Up.
23. Shanti. 156. 2-20.
24. Ch. U. VII. 22-1.
25. Gita XVIII. 23-25.
26. Gita III. 4-5.
27. Rg. VII. 32. 9.
28. Rg. X 42.10.
29. Rg. I. 128. 4.
30. Rg. I. 132. 2.
31. Rg. I. 124, 1.
32. Rg. VIII, 48. 14.
33. Rg. VIII. 2. 18.
34. Rg. VIII. 22.6. VIII. 31. 14.
35. M. IV. 212-219.
36. Udyoga. 67. 14.
37. Shanti. 57. 13-16.
38. Shanti 110.6.
39. Rg.I 48. 3.
40. Rg. I 56. 2, I. 116.5; Av. III 15.4.
41. Av. III. 15.4.
42. Panini V. 2.11.
43. Ai. Br. 33.
44. Anu. 71. 14-17.
45. Udyoga. 33. 121-122.
46. M. IV. 6.
47. M. IV. 159-161.
48. Shanti. III. 28.
49. Shanti. III. 30. 33.
50. Udyoga. 36. 10.
51. Shanti. 305, 32.
52. Vana. I, 23-31.
53. M. IV, 60-1; 79, 133.
54. M. IV, 71.
55. Kat. XIX, 9-10.
56. Shanti. 138, 194-197.
57. Shanti. 137, 19-20.
58. Udyoga. 39.
59. Udyoga 33, 39-45.

Chapter - IV

TRUTHFULNESS

The conception of Truth and Law were at first hardly distinguished from each other. Truthfulness is such a fundamental moral conception that it is often considered identical with morality itself. "The Law is what is called the true, and if a man declares what is true, they say he declares the Law; and if he declares the Law, they say he declares what is ture. Thus both are the same."[1] Truth is then conformity to Law; and falsehood is conscious breach of Law. "All falsehood, Mitra Varuna! Ye conquer and closely cleave unto the Law eternal."[2] "The Babe Unborn (Sun) supporteth the world's burthen, fulfillest Law and overcomest falsehood."[3] "Thrice, Agni, let thy noose surround the demon who with his falsehood injures Holy Order."[4] Law or Truth supports the very foundation of the universe. "Truth is the base that bears the earth; by Surya are the heavens sustained. By Law the Adityas stand secure and Soma holds his place in heaven."[5] "And by his (Indra) truth supporteth earth's foundation."[6] "He lays it down so as not to be separated from the truth; he thereby establishes the earth on the truth; hence this earth is established on the truth; and hence the truth is this earth, for this earth is the most certain of these world."[7] Truthfulness gives a man as much strength as the performance of a sacrifice.[8] A man becomes sacrificially impure on account of his speaking untruth.[9] Truth is the special virtue of gods, as lying is the vice of Asuras; and though truthfulness exposes its devotees to severe trials at first, it ultimately triumphs. "Two-fold, verily, is this, there is not third, viz., truth and untruth. And verily the gods are the truth and man is the untruth. Therefore, in saying 'I now pass from untruth into truth'. he passes from the man to the gods. Let him then speak only what is true; for this vow indeed the gods do keep, that they speak the truth; and for this reason they are glorious; the truth."[10] " The god speak nothing but truth, and the Asuras nothing but untruth. And the gods, speaking the truth diligently were very contemptible and very poor: whence he who speaks the truth diligently is very contemptible and very poor: but in the end he assuredly prospers, for the gods indeed prospered. And the Asuras speaking untruth diligently throve even as a salt-soil, and were very prosperous: whence he who speaks untruth diligently, thrives indeed, even as a salt-soil and becomes very prosperous; but in the end he assuredly comes to naught, for the Asuras indeed came to naught."[11]

All deceit and falsehood are strongly condemned in the Rigveda. "The gods Aryaman, Varuna, Mitra are the chastisers of all guilt and falsehood."[12] "Oh Indu, overcome and drive the false afar."[13] "Burn up the fool who ruins truth with falsehood."[14] "Let arrows pierce the liar in his vitals."[15] "Whatever sin is found in me, whatever evil I have wrought, if I have lied or falsely sworn, waters, remove it from me."[16] Gods protect and strengthen the true people and punish the liars. "The prudent find it easy to distinguished the true and the false; their words oppose each other. Of these two that which is the true and honest, Soma protects and brings the false to nothings"[17] "Never doth Soma aid and guide the wicked or him who falsely claims the warrior's title. Who slays the friend and him who speaks untruly, both lie entangled in the noose of Indra."[18] "Agni, to us with speech that hath no falsehood, grant riches."[19] Hell is the creation of the untrue and the faithless. "They who are full of sin, untrue, unfaithful, they have engendered this abysmal, station."[20] All double-dealing, slander, breach of contracts are considered different forms of falsehood. "Guile follows close the men who are untruthful."[21] "The sinful man who worships not, oh Agni, who offering naught, harms us with double-dealing, be this in turn to him a double sentence: May he distress himself by his revilings."[22] "Who so accuses me with words of falsehood when I perceive my way with guileless spirit, may he the speaker of untruth be, Indra, like water which the hollowed hand compresses."[23] "Men who lead evil lives, who break agreements, and injure Varuna, Aryaman and Mitra, against these foes, Of, mighty Indra, sharpen as furious death thy bull of fiery colour."[24]

Truthfulness was one of the fundamental essentials of moral life as pictured in the Ramayana. It was held in almost divine regard by the Hindus." Kingdom is essentially based upon truth; and this world itself is established in truth. Saints and celestials regard truth alone as all-important. In this world a truthful person attains the regions of Brahma. Untruthful persons harass people as much as serpents. In this world virtue, which is said to be the root of everything, is itself established in truth. In this world truth is the Lord; in truth is established righteousness. Everything has truth for its basis. No condition is superior to truth. The Veda, which inculcates gift, sacrifice, Homa and asceticism, is based on truth.....We have heard that the gods and the Pitris (ancestors) do not accepts offerings from one inclined to untruth, or who is unsteady and of volatile faculties. This duty of maintaining truth, whose influence radiates all over one's soul, I certainly find to be the prime one; and this burthen has (ere this) been borne by worthy people....The earth, and fame, and renown, and auspiciousness pay court unto the truthful person. The good follow truth, therefore, truth is to be sought by all."[25] Rama says to the councillors :–"That assembly is not an assembly where there are no old men, nor are they old men who do not dwell upon religious topics. That religion is not a religion where there is no truth, and that is not the truth where there is hypocrisy. Those councillors are liars who do not give proper replies in time on the subjects on which they are well-informed. He who does not give reply to a question under the influence of passion, anger, or fear, binds himself with a thousand nooses of Varuna and at the expiration of full one year he is released from a single sin."[26] Here the conception of falsehood is extended; all *supressio veri* and *suggestio falsi* (suppression of truth and suggestion of falsehood) is mere lying. To Dasharatha Rama says: "I desire neither dominion, nor happiness, not the earth, not any object of enjoyment, nor heaven nor life. All I wish for is that you may not come by falsehood and abide by truth."[27] The regard for truth expressed itself in the regard for one's promises. Vasishtha thus advises Dasharatha: "Do thou maintain thy habit of adhering to promise; for it does not behove thee to act unrighteously. If having promised 'I will do so' thou dost not act up to thy word, the merit thou hast achieved by digging tanks etc. shall come to naught, therefore do thou renounce Rama."[28] Kaikeyi asks of Dasharatha the fulfilment of his word: "Do thou by proving true to thy word become the king of kings; and preserve thy race, character, and birth. Truthful speech, say the ascetics, is of supreme welfare unto men in the next world."[29] "If, Oh, monarch, having conferred the boon, thou repentest afterwards, how O hero, wilt thou speak of thy righteousness in the world? When the Rajarshis assembled around thee shall ask thee ragarding this matter, what wilt thou answer?.....Surely, Oh Lord of men, thou wilt bring disgrace unto all the monarchs (of thy line), since having conferred the boons this very day thou speakest otherwise. Shaibya granted his own flesh unto the bird in the matter of the hawk and the pigeon. And Alarka having granted his eyes (unto a blind Brahmin) attained excellent state. And the ocean, having bound himself by pro-mise, never passes beyond his shores."[30]

The supremacy of truth over other virtues is spoken of in very eloquent terms in the Mahabharata : "Those cognisant with virtue and morals have said that truth and honesty are the highest virtues. Virtue that is eternal is difficult of being understood. But whatever it is, it is based on truth."[31] "Holding all the Vedas in memory, or ablutions performed in all the sacred waters, may or may not be equal to telling the truth everyday in one's life. A thousand horse-sacrifices and truth were once weighed in the balance. It was seen that truth weighed heavier than a thousand horse-sacrifices. It is by truth that the sun is imparting heat; it is by the truth that fire blazes up; it is by truth that the winds blow; verily everything rests upon truth. It is truth that gratifies the Deities, the Pitris and the Brahmins. Truth has been said to be the highest duty. The Munis are all devoted to truth. Their prowess depends upon truth. They also swear by truth. Hence truth is pre-eminent."[32] "He who is addicted to falsehood hath neither this world nor the next. Such a person fails to rescue his (deceased) ancestors. How again, shall he succeed in doing good to his (unborn) progeny? The reward of sacrifices and gifts, as also of fasts and religious observances, are not so efficacious in rescuing (a person from evil and hell) as truth in both this and the next world.–Truth is the one undeteriorating Brahma. Truth is the one undeteriorating Penance. Truth is the one underteriorating sacrifice. Truth is the one underteriorating Veda. Truth is awake in the Vedas. The fruits attached to truth have been said to be the highest. From truth arise righteousness and self-restraint. Everything rests on truth."[33] Truth is the foundation of all morality; because it leads to knowledge of what is right; and practice of what is right depends upon this mental illumination. "Untruth is only another form of darkness. It is darkness that leads downwards. Those who afflicted by darkness fail to behold the lighted region of heaven. It has been said that heaven is light and hell darkness. The creatures that dwell in the universe may obtain both heaven and hell. In this world also, truth and untruth lead to opposite courses of conduct such as righteousness and unrighteousness, light and darkness, pleasure and pain. Amongst these that which is truth is righteousness: that which is righteousness is light; and that which is light is happiness. Similarly that which is unrighteousness is darkness; and that which is darkness is sorrow or misery."[34] Even the Vedas cannot purify a liar. "The Vedas never rescue from sin a deceitful person living by falsehood. On the other hand, they forsake him while he is on his death-bed, like newly fledged birds foresaking their nests."[35] No association of men is possible if man cannot trust man, and society will be dissolved. Even an association of robbers or thieves or rebels must be pledged to maintain truth among themselves; otherwise confidence, the only bond of union, will be lost and they will collapse. "Even the sinful and ferocious swearing to keep the truth amongst themselves, dismiss all grounds of quarrel and uniting with one another set themselves to their tasks, depending upon truth. If they behave falsely towards one another, they would then be destroyed without doubt."[36]

A spirit of uncompromising adherence to truth is commended. "But know, O Bhima, my promise can never be untrue ! I regard virtue as superior to life itself and a blessed state of celestial existence. Kingdom, sons, fame, wealth, all these do not come up to even a sixteenth part of truth.[37] "There is this, moreover, that both the Kurus and the Brahmins assembling together, speak of thy firm adherence to truth, in that thou hast never from ignorance, from meanness, from covetousness, or from fear, uttered an untruth."[38] "They that always speak truth in this world even when life is at stake and that are exemplars for all creatures to imitate, succeed in overcoming all difficulties."[39] "Oh Satyavati, I repeat the pledge I once gave, viz. I would renounce the three worlds, the empire of heaven, or anything that be greater than that, but truth I would never renounce. Earth may renounce its scent, water may renounce its moisture, light may renounce its attribute of exihibiting forms, the atmosphere may renounce its attribute of being unperceivable by the touch, the sun may renounce its glory, fire its heat, the moon her cold waves, space its capacity of generating sound, the slayer of Vritra his prowess, the god of justice his impartiality, but I cannot renounce truth !"[40] There is something inexpressively grand in this attitude. It is the spirit running riot, intoxicated with its own superiority over circumstance. Truth also raises its devotees almost to the height of divinities, when it is perceived in this lofty fashion. "Both the earth and the fermament exist owing to my truth and virtue; fire yet burneth in the world of men, owing to my turth and virtue. Never hath a word spoken by me been untrue. It is for this that the wise adore the truth."[41] "I do not remember having told a single falsehood even in jest. Let my father-in-law and mother-in-law hold their lives by virtue of that truth."[42]

Lying is of various degrees of guilt, according as the circumstances under which it is practised vary. "He that speaketh a lie on account of an animal casteth from heaven five of his sires in the ascending order. He that speaketh a lie on account of a cow casteth from ten of his ancestors. A lie on account of a horse couseth the downfall of a hundred, and a lie on account of a human being, the downfall of a thousand of one's sires in the ascending order. An untruth on account of gold ruineth the members of one's race, both born and unborn, while an untruth for the sake of land ruineth everything. Therefore, never speak an untruth for the sake of land."[43]

The attitude of perfect honesty is especially necessary in the presence of very important or learned or intimate persons. "One should never appear deceitfully before a King; nor before a Brahmin; nor before one's wife when that wife is possessed of every wifely virtue. Those who appear in deceitful guise before these three every soon meet with destruction. The power of kings consists in their sovereignty. The power of Brahmins, conversant with the Vedas, is in the Vedas, Women wield a high power in consequence of their beauty, and youth, and blessedness. There three are powerful in the possession of these powers. He, therefore, that is desirous of accomplishing his own object should always approach these three with sincerity and candour. Insincerity and deciet fail to produce success."[44] A king, Lomapada by name, was guilty of a falsehood towards a Brahmin. The result was that all Brahmins deserted him and even there were no rains in his territory owing to his sin.[45]

There are certain occasions on which lying is allowable. "It has been said, Oh king, that it is not sinful to lie on the occasion of a joke, in respect of women sought to be enjoyed, on occasions of marriage, in prospect of immediate death and the loss of one's whole fortune. Lying is excusable on these five occasions."[46] A literal adherence to truth would make us all perhaps pure matter-of-fact fellows Humour requires that there should be a certain elasticity in our talk, that the materials of our conversation must be a little malleable in the interests of social pleasure. The most truthful person can indulge, therefore, in untruthful statements by way of joke. Rama says to Surpankha that Laxman was unmarried and was desirous of having a wife.[47] In such pleasantries it was quite allowable to make statements which may not be strictly true. "A falsehood spoken for saving the life of a good man (falsely accused of an offence) constitutes no sin; but such a lie for the sake of saving the life of a wicked person should never be told."[48] The magnitude of the guilt of falsehood varies with the motives of the agents or with his state of mind. "For giving false evidence out of lust one shall be punished with a fine of two thousand and five hundred Panas; for giving false evidence out of anger or spite, the penalty shall be a fine of three thousand Panas; for giving false evidence out of ignorance one shall be punished with a fine of two hundred Panas; while the penalty for giving false evidence through inadvertence shall be a fine of a hundred Panas."[49] "An untruth spoken by an angry, elated, frightened, agonised or a greedy person, as well as by an infant, old man or an idiot, or by an intoxicated or an insane person, constitutes no sin."[50]

The anecdote of Yudhishthira shows that the ideal is this: Truth under all circumstances is preferable to falsehood; but that it is better to indulge in some falsehood for the sake of other important ends, to incur all the necessary sin on that account and to get the necessary punishment for it. Life is not a smooth, clear-cut thing; simple formulae would not suit it. Its complexity would require a corresponding complexity in morality which is to guide it. "If Drona fighteth for even half a day, I tell thee truly, thy army will then be annihilated. Save us then from Drona ! Under such circumstances falsehood is better than truth! By telling an untruth for saving a life one is not touched by sin. There is no sin in untruth spoken unto women, or in marriages, or for saving kine, or for rescuing a Brahmin."[51] Drona was to be paralysed by the circulation of the report of the death of his son Ashwathaman. At that time one elephant called Ashwathaman was killed. Yudhishthira was asked to say that 'Ashwathaman was killed', because in him Drona had complete confidence. Fearing to utter an untruth, but earnestly desirous of victory, Yushishthira distinctly said that Ashwathaman was dead, adding indistinctly the word '*elephant*' (after the name.)[52] For this act of deception he had to see hell. The following passage shows that it is not meant that lying even on exceptional occasions is quite an allowable things. "Unto children, an women, in jest, danger, or calamity, in distress or at dice, I have never spoken a falsehood! By that truth ascend thou to heaven! I can, O king, give up all objects of desire and enjoyment, my kingdom, yea, life itself, but truth I cannot give up! By that truth ascend thou to heaven!"[53]

There are three moments in truthfulness: the heart must sincerely feel one thing, or the head must clearly conceive one idea; then the tongue is to express it; and lastly it is to be embodied in a concrete activity. It is when these three factors are closely interconnected that a man is said to be truthful. There must be first, fidelity to fact or intuition of the hear; secondly, fidelity to the inner idea in utterance; and lastly, fidelity to both the idea and the utterance in the actual achievement. The Hindu view always insisted upon this unity of thought, word, and deed. "Having first settled a thing mentally, it is expressed in words, and then it is carried out in practice" says Savitri. The definition of a good man (साधु) is: "The speech reflects the soul and the action corresponds to the speech. In the case of good persons there is uniformity of thought word, and deed."

Truthfulness, however, is a delicate duty; and when other more important interests suffer, a bare adherence to truth cannot be recommended. The concept of truthfulness, therefore, is widened; and this extended notion takes sin all other important virtues. "It is the dictum of the ages that the ways of righteousness are subtle, diverse, and infinite. When life is at stake and in the matter of marriage, it is proper to tell an untruth. Untruth sometimes leads to the triumph of truth, and the latter dwindles into unturth. *Whichever conduces most to the good of all creatures is considered to be truth.*"[54] "Leniency is the best of virtues, and forbearance is the best of powers, the knowledge of our spiritual nature is the best of all knowledge, and truthfulness is the best of all religious obligations. The telling of truth is good, and the knowledge of it may also be good, but what conduces to the greatest good of all creatures is known as the highest truth."[55] It is by the application of this test that all apparent exception to the duty of veracity can be explained. "Righteousness was declared for the advancement and growth of all creatures......Sometimes men (robbers) desirous of obtaining wealth of some one, make inquiries. One should never answer such inquiries. That is a settled duty. If by maintaining silence, one succeeds in escaping, one should remain silent, If, on the other hand, one's silence at a time when one must speak rouses suspicion, it would be better on such an occasion to say what is untrue than what is true. This is a settled conclusion. If one can escape from sinful man by even a (false) oath. One may take it without incurring sin.... When life is at risk, or on occasions of marriage, one may say an untruth. One who seeks virtue, does not commit a sin by saying an untruth, if that untruth be said to save the wealth of others or for religious purposes.[56] Truthfulness is not an isolated virtue; it must be rendered duly consistent with or subordinate to the whole scheme of righteousness, "Silence, it is said, is better than speech; if speak you must, then it is better to say the truth; if truth is to be said, it is better to say what is agreeable; and if what is agreeable is to be said, then it is better to say what is consistent with morality."[57] Truth is, in fact, fidelity to the highest order of Reality. It is, therefore, defined as "immutable, eternal, and unchangeable." "Truth as it exists in all the world, is of thirteen kinds. The forms that truth assumes are;

impar-tiality, self-control, forgiveness, modesty, endurance, goodness, renunciation, contemplation, dignity, fortitude, compassion, and abstention from injuty. These are the thirteen forms of truth : *Truth is immutable, eternal, and unchangeable....* Those thirteen attributes, though apparently distinct from one another, have but one and the same form, viz. truth. All these support truth and strengthen it."[58]

Truthfulness has a two-fold aspect; one has reference to society, and the other has reference to self. The former is frequently emphasised because it is the outer aspect of the question and the one which concerns society more directly. The social bond consists in mutual confidence which depends upon the amount of veracity in a people. But falsehood is not only a violation of what we owe to others, it is also a violation of what we owe to ourselves. In this sense, veracity may be defined as fidelity to self; and this is sufficiently comprehensive :–

"To thine own self be true,
Thou canst not then be false to any man."

The social aspect of veracity is clear. Language is the one bond which makes society possible; and if this very language is perverted in the interests of a man's designs, it is evident that society loses its cohesion. "All things are inherent in the meanings of (spoken) words, all things are founded on speech; all things emanate from speech; *he, who speaks falsehood is said to be a universal thief.*'[59] But one injures his own self as much as he injures society by misrepresentation. "His self is the witness of his own self (*i. e.* to all his acts); self is the refuge of self; hence by bearing false witness *one must not insult his own self.* Miscreants think that there is none to witness their secret vices; the gods and their inner selves are the witnesses to their misdeeds."[60] "Knowing everything, O monarch, how canst thou, like an ordinary person, thus say that thou knowest not? This heart is the witness to the truth or the falsehood of this matter. Therefore, speak truly without degrading thyself. He who being one thing representeth himself as another thing to others, is *like a thief and a robber of his own self.* Of what sin is he not capable? Thou thinkest that thou alone hast knowledge of thy deed. But knowest not thou that the Ancient, Omniscient One (Narayana) liveth in thy heart? He knoweth all thy sins, and thou sinnest in His presence! He that sins thinks that none observe him. But he is observed by the gods and by Him also who occupies every heart. The sun, the moon, air, fire, earth, sky, water, the heart, Yama, the day, the night, both twilights, and Dharma, all witness the acts of man! Yama, the son of Surya, takes no account of his sins with whom Narayana the witness of all acts is gratified! But he with whom Narayana is not gratified is tortured for his sins by Yama! Him who degradeth himself by representing his self falsely the gods never bless! Even his own soul blesses him not."[61]

Perjury is a specially condemnable form of lying because through it, justice is liable to be perverted. "Giving false evidence and killing a friend, these two crimes are equal to the drinking of spirituous liquor."[62] " A witness, who has spoken in the assembly of venerables (in court) anythings other than what he has actually seen or heard shall be ousted out of heaven, and fall headlong into hell after death. A witness, who alleges truth in his deposition, attains the exalted regions after death and acquires excellent fame in this life; this is a statement which Brahma has approved of. Truth purifies a witness; and it is truth that augments virtue; hence witnesses of all castes must speak truth."[63] "He (i. e. the judge) shall say unto a Brahmin (witness) 'speak'; 'speak truth' unto a Kshatriya; by the sin of stealing the cow, gold, or seeds he shall charge a Vaishya witness to speak truth; and a Shudra (witness) by all sins."[64] Terrible punishment is the lot of the perjurers. "To regions which are said to be reserved for killers of Brahmins and women, for infanticides, for the violators of friendship and for the ungrateful, go (the souls of) those who speak falsehood."[65] False evidence given in respect of a land is more sinful than that given in respect of gold, human beings, horses, kine, and other animals.[66] Motives are also taken into account in adjudging the crime. "False evidence is said (to proceed) from greed, ignorance, fright, friendship, anger, desire, foolishness, and juvenile fickleness. For giving false evidence, out of greed, out of mental agitation, out of terror, or out of affection, one shall be respectively punished with a fine of a thousand, two hundred and fifty, one thousand, and a thousand Panas."[67] Here, too, in certain cases it is excusable to bear false witness. "A witness, who, out of compassion, has knowingly stated a fact otherwise than it is in reality, shall not be ousted out of heaven, since such a speech is called divine allegation. In cases where the allegation of truth would lead to the lawful execution of a Shudra, Vaishya, Kshatriya, or a Brahmin, a witness is warranted to speak falsehood. In such a case lie is greater than truth. Such (false) witnesses shall worship the deity of speech with offerings of sacrificial porridge, that being a good expiation for the sin of speaking such lies.[68] Wilful maintenance of silence is equivalent to perjury. "Those who, though acquainted with the facts, and appointed to give evidence, stand mute, are equally criminal with, and deserve the same punishment as, false witnesses."[69]

If any sin is committed in the presence of an assembly, the whole assembly becomes responsible for it. Men are not merely to do right and abstain from evil; they are to stop the actual evil if they are in a position to do so. A passive attitude in such circumstances is very iniquitous. An aggressive crusade against evil is what duty requires us to do. "If the members of an assembly are conversant with morality, nothing improper should be permitted by them to happen. Where, in the presence of the virtuous members of an assembly, righteousness is sought to be overpowered by unrighteousness, and truth by untruth, it is these members that are vanquished and slain. When righteousness, pierced by unrighteousness, seeketh the protection of an assembly, if the arrow is not extracted, it is the members themselves that are pierced by that arrow. Indeed, in that case, righteousness slayeth the members of that assembly like a river eating away the roots of the trees on its banks."[70] "All the members of the tribunal, in which truth is conquered by falsehood and falsehood is not pierced by the needle of justice, should be regarded as smitten with impiety. Rather one should not attend a tribunal, but once there, he must speak nothing but truth; by keeping silent or speaking falsehood in a tribunal, a man becomes guilty of vice. The members of a tribunal, where in truth is killed by untruth, and virtue by vice, are killed by the sight. A quarter part of the (sin of) injustice goes to the person making the false complaint; a quarter part is attached to his false witnesses; a quarter part is attached to the members of the tribunal; and another quarter part is attached to the king."[71]

Swearing is an allowable and even a necessary practice under certain circumstances, "In a suit without witnesses, the truth should be ascertained by causing the contending parties to swear or affirm on oath. The gods and great sages have sworn for determining the truth (in suspicious cases); Vasishtha swore in the court of king Paivana."[72] "A swear (falsely made by a husband of many wives as to his preference to one of them, present at the time), as well as that made in respect of a matrimonial (negotiation), in respect of forage for cattle, in respect of fuel, or the one made for the advancement of a Brahmin, does not entail any sin."[73] Oaths should not be taken on any and every occasion. "A wise man should never wantonly swear for a small thing; by unnecessarily swearing a man is destroyed both in this world and the next."[74] One should swear by that which is dearest to him. "A Brahmin shall be caused to swear by truth; a Kshatriya by his weapons and riding animals; a Vaishya by his cattle and seed-grains; and a Shudra by the sin of all the crimes."[75]

Hypocricy is mere misrepresentation of one's self. "Who sitteth, controlling the organs of action, but dwelling in his mind on the objects of the senses, that bewildered man is called a hypocrite."[76] Hypocricy is one of the demoniacal properties.[77] Sacrifices offered out of hypocrisy are condemned as Rajas.[78] "One should achieve righteousness alone or single-handed. Verily, one should not proclaim oneself righteous and walk with the standard of righteousness borne aloft for purposes of exhibition."[79] Religious hypocrisy is shrewdly exposed in unmeasured terms by Manu. The ignorant world has suffered much through this form of deceit. "He, who, though extremely covetous of wealth, carries a cloak of religion, is deceitful, arrogant, and envious, and cannot bear the praise of others, and hence tries to snub down all men, is called cat-natured, (*i.e.* he is like a cat which assumes meekness only to decoy his prey out of his safe hold and then pounce upon it.) With eyes cast down to conceal his ferocious purpose, he, who, to gain his own ends, roams about in deceit and falsehood, like a crane, is called *Baka-vrati.* Those Brahmins, who are cat-natured or crane-natured, fall into the hell of extreme darkness through the effects of their (treacherous deeds.) After committing a crime let him not practise the expiatory penance under the pretext of practising a virtue, for the purpose of duping females and Shudras. A vow or a penance practised out of hypocrisy goes to the monsters; the Brahmins who do it are condemned by the *Brahm-Vadins.* A person, who tries to earn a livelihood by falsely wearing the badges or marks of an order he does not belong to, robs the sin of all that order, and is reborn in the womb of beasts. He, who gives himself out to honest persons as something different from what he really is, is called the worst of miscreants; truly he is a thief, inasmuch as he dissimulates his real self."[80]

Honesty is the application of the principle of truthfulness to all the details of business, "All kinds of crookedness mean death, and all kinds of sincerity are called Brahma. This constitutes the subject of knowledge. The rhapsodies of system-builders cannot affect this."[81] Acquisition of wealth is not a bad thing; but the means employed for it must be honest. "One should not seek for advancement by performing any wicked or censurable act. That wealth which is earned by righteous ways is true wealth. Fie on that wealth, however, which is earned by unrighteous means. Righteousness is eternal. It should never, in this world, be abandoned from desire of wealth."[82] "The man possessed of wisdom would not seek wealth for the performance of religious rites by ways that are unrighteous, and that involve an abandonment of morality. Wealth earned by such means can never prove beneficial."[83]

Gambling is a dishonest way of gaining wealth; and the practice of it leads to many disastrous consequences. People were fond of it in the time of the Rig-Veda and realised the bitter result of it. It is the outcome of greed; it interferes with one's normal work. It brings into contempt healthy professions in society. It brings poverty and want into the house and all the consequent wretchedness. "Play not with dice: no cultivate thy corn-land."[84] "For the die's sake, whose single point is final, mine own devoted wife I alienated. My wife holds me aloof." "Her mother hates him; the wretched man finds none to give him comfort. Others caress the wife of him whose riches the die hath coveted, that rapid course; of his speak father, mother, brothers, saying we know him not, bind him, and take him with you. The gambler's wife is left forlorn and wretched; the mother mourns the son who wanders homeless. In contant fear, in debt, and seeking riches, he goes by night into the home of others."[85] Cheating at play is common. "If we, as gamesters cheat at play, have cheated etc."[86] The numerous evils of gambling are exposed in the Mahabharata. "I would have shown the many evils (of dice) through which thou hast fallen into such distress and the son of Virasena was formerly deprived of his kingdom. O king, unthought of evils befall a man from dice....Women, dice, hunting, and drinking to which people become addicted in consequence of temptation, have been regarded as the four evils that deprive a man of prosperity"[87] It plants enmity between man and man and provokes dissensions. "From very olden times it hath been seen that gambling provoketh quarrels. Therefore, he that is wise, should not resort to it even in jest."[88]

"It is evident that dice soweth dissensions. And dissensions are the ruin of the kingdom."[89] Its dishonesty renders it specially immoral. "Deceitful gambling is sinful. There is no

Kshatriya prowess in it. There is certainly no morality in it. The wise applaud not the pride that gamesters feel in deceitful play."[90] "To obtain victory in battle without cunning or stratagem is the best sport. Gambling, however, is not so, as a sport. Those that are respectable never use the language of the Mlechhas, nor do they adopt deceitfulness in their bahaviour....I do not desire either happiness or wealth by means of cunning. The conduct of one that is a gamester even if it be without deceitfulness, should not be applauded."[91] Gambling-houses are, however, tolerated by the Smritikaras and the king is to derive revenue from these. Special keepers are appointed for these, to superintend them. "The king should make those, who play fraudulently or with a motive to cheat, first under go the operation of the brand-iron, and then banish them."[92]

Honest industry and peaceful life cannot thrive as long as there is fear of theft, robbery or other misappropriation of one's well-earned property. The fiend, O Agni, who designs to injure the essence of our food, kine, steeds, or bodies, may he, the adversary, thief, and robber, sin to destruction himself and offspring."[93] "Who lurks about the path we take, the robber with a guileful heart: Far from the road chase away."[94] "May mighty Indra....bestow on us good road and perfect safety.[95] Robbers are enemies of all orderly society; they are not healthy parts of the social organism. "The robber has no connection with men, with the deities, with the Gandharvas, and with the Pirtris. What is he to them? He is not anybody to any one. This is the declaration of the Shrutis. The robber takes away the ornaments of corpses from cemeteries, and wearing apparel from men afflicted by spirits. That man is a fool who would make any covenant with those miserable wretches or exact any oath from them."[96]

Property is of three kinds : white, mottled, and black. "What has been inherited, through friendly gifts, and the dowry of a wife, that is called white property. What has been acquired as a fee, or by the sale of forbidden articles, or as a return for a benefit conferred, is denoted mottled wealth. What has been acquired by servile attendance, by gambling, by thieving, by begging, by deceit, by robbery, or by fraud, is called black property."[97] All forms of acquisition of 'mottled' and 'black' property are crimes and punishable as such. "A deposit-holder is not liable to make good the deposited article in the event of its being stolen by a thieves in the event of its being stolen by a thief or in the event of its destruction by water or fire. He who refuses to give back a deposited article, and he who demands an article without having kept it as a deposit, both of them should be punished as thieves."[98] All deceit as regards the bride is punished.[99] Servants must do their work regularly, they are liable to punishment otherwise. But they are entitled to their wages if they are ill.[100] Merchants should be scrupulously honest with regard to the quantity and prices of their goods. "An article (of one species) mixed with another of a different (species), a pithless substance, an article weighing less than its surface or manifest weight and an article that is under a cover, or lies at a distance, must not be sold."[101] " (In cases relating to) the destruction of landmarks, transgression of the boundary lines, and misappropriation of field, one should be punished with the lowest , middling, and highest penalty."[102] All property of others in land should be scrupulously respected; especially the property of Brahmins must not be touched. "The stealer of lands is not purified by (the gift of) a thousand wells and tanks, by (the celebration of) a hundred horse-sacrifices, and by the gift of a crore of kine." (Brihaspati 39). "To speak false for land destroys all. Therefore, one should never cherish an inclination for a Brahmin's property, even if his vital breath comes up to the throat. That dreadful poison has no medicine and no physician......Poison kills only one man; but a Brahmin's property destroys even his son and grandson. One can digest iron, powdered stone, and even poison. What man in three regions, can digest a Brahmin's property?"[103]

All forms of theft and robbery are to be put down; punishment varies with the circumstances "The king shall assiduously endeavour to repress the thieves in his kingdom; by repressing theft the fame and kingdom of a king are augemen-ted."[104] A fine double the value of the stolen articles is inflicted on a thief in case of such things as cotton threads etc.[105] Theft of gold calls for the heaviest punishment. Capital punishment should be inflicted on a thief for having stolen a tula weight of gold or silver, or precious clothes, weighing more than a hundred Palas. Mutilation should be the punishment for stealing the above-said articles, numbering more than fifty and less than one hundred Palas: Death should be the punishment for stealing jewels and precious gems belonging to high-born ladies and men.[106] The forcible taking away of a things constitutes what is called Sahasa (robbery).[107] It is a more serious crime than that of theft. "A robber should be regarded as a worse miscreant than a thief, assaulter, or foul-mouthed person. The king who tolerates (the depredations of a robber) soon incurs the wrath (of his subjects) and meets his doom."[108]

Some other forms of misappropriation are mentioned. A washerman is to be punished, if he wears a cloth, belonging to another. All quacks are liable to punishment of humbuging the patients. All who make imitations of various articles and pass them as originals are fined eight times the value of the article. All tampering with scales or weights and measures brings down heavy fine upon the merchant. Forgery is dealt with seriously. "He who counterfeits or forges scales, or plates inscribing grants of land, or standards of measures and coins and makes use of them, should be punished with the highest form of pecuniary punishment."[109] It is interesting to note some rules touching commerce. The government was to stand between merchants and the public. It used to fix prices, the amount of legitimate profits and such other things. All monopolistic exploitation is to be prevented. "Sale and purchase shall be conducted daily according to the value fixed by the king. The surplus, on the fixed value, is to be recognized as the profit of the trade. On indigenous articles, the trader, who sells them immediately after purchase, shall make a profit of five per cent; and ten percent on those coming from other countries. Calculating the intrinsic value of commodities and the charges for bringing them, the king shall so fix their price that the seller or buyer may not suffer any loss.[110] The evils of trusts and huge combines are foreseen. "The highest form of pecuniary punishment is laid down for them, who, knowing the standard value (of a thing) settled by the king, in a body so increase or decrease its value as is painful to the artist or artisan. The highest form of pecuniary punishment is laid down for these merchants, who in a body obstruct the sale of foreign articles, and those who sell them (at a higher price)[111]

References

1. Br. U. 1.4 .14.
2. Rg. I. 52.2.
3. Rg.I. 152. 3.
4. Rg. X. 87, 11.
5. Rg. X. 85, 1.
6. Av. XIV. 1.1; Rg. X.111.4.
7. Sh. Br. VII, 4.1.8.
8. Sh. Br. II.2.2.19.
9. Sh. Br. I. 1.1.1.
10. Sh. Br. I. 1.1.4-5.
11. Sh. Br. IX. 5. 1. 16-17.
12. Rg. VII. 60. 5.
13. Rg. IX. 105. 6.
14. Rg. X. 87. 12.
15. Rg. X. 87. 15.
16. Rg. I. 23. 22.
17. Rg. VII, 104.12.
18. Rg. VII, 104. 13.
19. Rg. III. 14. 6.
20. Rg. IV. 5.5.
21. Rg. II. 61. 5.
22. Rg. I. 147. 4.
23. Rg. I. 147. 5,
24. Rg. X. 89.9.

25. R. II. 109; 10. 22.
26. R. VII प्रक्षिप्तसर्ग: 3.
27. R. II 34. 47. 48.
28. R. I. 21. 7. 8.
29. R. II 11.29.
30. R.II. 72. 39-44.
31. Vana. 209. 42. 43.
32. Anu. 110. 29-32.
33. Shanti. 197. 67-76.
34. Shanti. 188. 1-5.
35. Udyoga. 35.53.
36. Shanti. 265. 10-11.
37. Vana. 34. 22.
38. Vana. 33. 77.
39. Shanti. 110-11.
40. Adi. 112. 15-19.
41. Adi. 87. 47.
42. Vana. 298. 101.
43. Udyoga. 35. 44-45. M. VIII. 98-99.
44. Shanti. 325. 72-74.
45. Vana. 111.20.
46. Adi. 76, 24-26.
47. R. III 18. 3-5 etc.
48. Gautama XIII.
49. M. VIII, 121.
50. Gautama. V.
51. Drona. 191, 45-46.
52. Drona, 19. 54.
53. Udyoga. 122, 9-10.
54. Vana. 213, 3-4.
55. Vana. 215, 46-47.
56. Shanti. 109. 11-21.
57. Udyoga. 36. 12.
58. Shanti. 160. 3-10. 22-26.
59. M. IV, 256.
60. M. VIII, 84-85.
61. Adi. 98. 5-14.
62. Vishnu. XXXVI., 2

63. M. VIII, 81-83.
64. M. VIII. 88.
65. M. VIII. 89-90. 93.
66. M. VIII. 98-100.
67. M. VIII. 118-120.
68. M. VIII, 103-105.
69. Vishnu. VIII, 37.
70. Udyoga. 95, 47-57.
71. M. VIII, 12-14, 18.
72. M. VIII, 109-110.
73. M. VIII, 112.
74. M. VIII, 111.
75. M. VIII, 113.
76. Bg. III, 6.
77. Bg. XVI. 4.
78. Bg. XVII, 12.
79. Anu. 268, 41.
80. M. IV, 195-200, 256.
81. Shanti. 79, 21.
82. Shanti. 298, 18-19.
83. Shanti. 300. 25.
84. Rg. X. 34. 13.
85. Rg. X. 34, 2-4; 10.
86. Rg. V. 85. 8.
87. Vana. 13. 5-7.
88. Udyoga. 37. 19.
89. Sabha. 77. 11-12.
90. Sabha. 84. 5-6.
91. Sabha. 84. 9-13
92. Yaj. II. 202-205.
93. Rg. VII. 104. 10.
94. Rg. I. 42. 3.
95. Rg. 1. 42. 3.
96. Shanti. 273. 21.22.
97. Vishnu. LVIII, 9-11.
98. M. VIII. 189-191.
99. M. VIII. 204-205.
100. M. 215-216.

101. M. VIII. 203.
102. Yaj. II. 158.
103. Brihaspti. 45-48.
104. M. VIII. 302.
105. M. VIII. 326.
106. M. VIII. 323.
107. M. VIII. 332.
108. M. VIII. 345-346.
109. Yaj. II. 243.
110. Yaj. 254-256.
111. Yaj. II. 252-253.

Chapter - V

PURITY AND IMPURITY

A comprehensive conception of purity is met with in the secred writings of the Hindus. It takes in its range both outward cleanliness required by society and inward cleanliness guaranteed only by a high character. Purity of heart is the highest of all purities; it is the one fundamental thing in all moral and spiritual life. The heart must be a seat of holy thoughts and holy feelings. It must be a temple of humane intentions, lofty enthusiasm, pious ideas, and chaste feelings. Morality is not punctilio or outward behaviour, it is other than formal correctness of conduct. Its essence, in Hindu thought, lies in pure ideas, pure feelings, and pure volutions. Kant realised the truth when he said that good will is the one thing in the world which is good without qualification; and even if it is impotent and does not issue in deeds owing to an adverse environment or unfit medium its value is there; it shines by its own light. The capital fact of moral life, therefore, is to ensure the possession of this good will. All the rest well follow. The realm of fact is but a projection or a reflexion of the realm of ideas. It has no independent existence.

The Vedic seers very clearly expressed this truth. The highest prayer with them was for pure thoughts. "May our thoughts be holy." "Further (Indra) the holy thoughts of Vamadeva."[1] " Assist our holy thoughts, wake up our spirit."[2] "For over every thought thou (Agni) art the ruler; thou furtherest even the wisdom of the pious."[3] Hindus' great faith in the potency of thoughts is revealed in the most popular prayer of theirs. The Gayatri Mantra is recited by Hindus every day. It is nothing but an appeal to God to send one pure thoughts. "Let us adore the supremacy of that divine sun, the godhead, who illuminates all, from whom all proceed, to whom all must return, whom we invoke to direct our understandings aright in our progress towards the holy seat."[4] Holiness is constituted by holy thoughts; sinfulness means similarly wicked ideas. "Slay ye the wicked man whose thought is of the demon kind."5 I'll thoughts, that visit us awake or asleep, seize the man who hate, the man who hateth us.[6] Purification requires purification from malice, from sin. "Burn up all malice with those flames, O Agni, wherewith of old thou burnest up Jarutha."[7] " May the gods company make one clean, and Vasus make me pure by song. Purify me, O general gods; O Jatavedas, make me pure."[8] "Cleanse us with thine own cleansing power, O Agni, that is bright with flame. And by libations poured to thee.[9] It was supposed that because agencies like fire, the sun, water, can cleanse us outwardly they can also wash away our sins and make us inwardly pure. "The reason why he touches water is, that man is sacrificially impure, on account of his speaking untruth, and because, by that act an internal purification (is effected)"[10]

Formal behaviour is very insistent on the claims of cleanliness and decency in all matters Elaborate rules are laid down for the detailed observance of these. "Let him not eat in the company of his wife, nor see her eating, nor while she is yawning or sneezing, or sitting at case. He must not vauntingly strike the muscle of his upper arms, nor gnash his teeth, nor bray like, an ass, out of an exuberance of emotional feeling. A holy thread, an ewer, a cloth, a garland of flowers, an ornament, and shoes previously used by another, he must not wear. He, who (wantonly) grinds earth (with his finger) or cuts his finger nails (with his teeth) as well as a malicious calumniator, and one who neglects his personal cleanliness, soon meets with destruction. Let him not lie down entirely naked in the bed, nor go anywhere without washing, his mouth after eating.

Voiding stool, bathing, cleaning the teeth, applying collyrium along the eyelids, and worshipping the deities must be performed before sun-rise at the close of the night."[11] " One should not eat, sit down, lie down, welcome or bow down (to a superior) with one's shoes on."[12] The value of a good bath is rendered quite explicit. "The Rishis highly speak of early bathing in the morning; for it yields fruits seen and unseen. If a Vipra, getting up from the bed at dawn, takes his daily bath early in the morning for three years, he has the sins of his entire birth dissipated."[13] "A man should bathe after having dreamt a bad dream, or vomited, or shaved himself, or after having known a woman, or after an exposure to the smoke of a cremation ground."[14] The advantages of bathing are well summed up. "He that performeth ablutions winneth these ten, viz., strength, beauty, a clear voice, capacity to utter all the alphabetical sounds, delicacy of touch, fineness of scent, cleanliness, gracefulness, delicacy of limbs, and beautiful women."[15]

Personal uncleanliness results from various causes such as contact with a Shudra or Mlechha, birth or death among the relatives, the menses of women. "He should not hold any conversation with a Mlechha, or with a pariah, and must not forget to mentally recite the names of saintly persons, or to talk to a Brahmin immediately after, in the event of being forced to enter into such a conversation."[16] The Bandhus (near relations) of a male child become unclean on his death; likewise his Bandhus become unclean on the birth of a male child, Death-uncleanliness continues for ten days among Sapindas or until the bones are collected, or for three days, or for an entire day and night."[17] The same is the period of birth-uncleanliness. This period of mourning is to be systematically observed. "During the term of a (death-uncleanliness) they shall eat their meals without any (artificial) salt, must bathe on each of the three days, forswear meat-diet, and must sleep separately on the ground."[18] The death of a fellow-student, or a disciple or a priest, or a king entails on one a similar period of mourning.[19] A woman in her menses is regarded as specially unclean.

"A woman becomes as object as a Chandali on the first, a Brahmaghatini on the second, and a Rajaki (laundress) on the third day of her menstrual flow."[20] Contact with all unclean beings is degrading. "Happening to touch a Chandala, a woman in her flow, a degraded person, a (newly) parturient woman, a dead body, or a person who has touched a corpse, one shall regain his purity by bathing."[21] Any personal uncleanliness on one's part exposes one to an attack at the hands of superior beings.

The rigour of the regulations affecting these matters is modified in various ways. Persons who have exacting duties to perform connot afford to be handicapped by these ceremonial restrictions; and there are occasions on which all persons require exemption from them. "There is not impurity for a king, for a persons killed by lightning; (for those killed) for kine and in the battlefield, (as well as for those) whom the king wishes (to have for state business). (Purification is immediate) for sacrificial priests,....for religious students, for those who make gifts and for these who know Brahma. Immediate purification is laid down in a gift, marriage, sacrifice, war, devastation of the country, calamity and distress."[22] In the same way things are also considered fit for acceptance if they are very useful.

There are various agencies for purification, "Time, fire, action (bathing etc.), earth, air, mind, spiritual knowledge, austerity, water, repentance, and fasting,–all these are the instruments of purification"[23] Baths, purificatory rites, and pilgrimages are agencies mainly of bodily purification. (Purification is effected) by bathing, (of a person) touched by a woman in her menses, or by one who is impure. If touched by such a person, (one) should rince the mouth, recite the Mantras, and the Gayatri once mentally."[24] "Care should always be bestowed on the purificatory rites. The purificatory rite has been described as the root of the twiceborn."[25] Holy places are objects of special reverence to the Hindus. It is the religious atmosphere there which is thought to inspire a person with pious thoughts. To visit all the sacred places with all heir romantic and hallowed associations, is one of the objects dearest to the imagination of a very orthodox Hindu. Persons used to travel thousands of miles even in those days when the Railways were unknown, in order to drink deep at the fountains of spirituality which are supposed to be rempant in the holy places. "O thou best of the Bharata race, sojourns in Tirthas (holy places) which are meritorious are even superior to sacrifices! He is a poor man who having gone to a Tirtha hath not fasted for three nights, who hath not given away gold, and who hath not distributed kine."[26]

The Brahmins were not pharisees insisted on mere outward cleanliness. The spirit of don't touchism was not all important. Purity of body and neatness of environment were aspects indeed of a moral life; but they were subordinate aspects. "Purity is being spoken of as being two-fold, external an internal. It is said in the Smriti that external purity (is effected) by earth, water etc. Purity of thought is internal (purity). External purity is superior to impurity; and internal purity is superior to that (external purity). He who is pure in both is (said to be) in a state of purity and no one else."[27] Both the elements are here held to be essential in a perfect life. The performance of both the earthly vows and spiritual vows is aimed at. "Purify your hearts and then set out for the Tirthas! The Brahmins have said that regulations in respect of the body are called earthly vows, while efforts to purify the heart, so that it may be free from evil thoughts are called spiritual vows. O king, the mind that is free from all evil thoughts is highly pure! Purifying yourselves, therefore, harbouring only friendly feelings for all, behold ye the Tirthas! Observing (earthly) vows in respect of your bodies, and purifying your minds by spiritual vows, observe ye the fruits, as recited, of sojourns in Tirthas."[28] A perfect purity, inward and outward, of soul as well as body is the ideal. " Calamities befall not those who constantly be of auspicious conduct; let him nourish a clean spirit in a clean body."[29]

The ceremonial purity can, however, never be a substitute for inward purity. People have a tendency of mistake the shell for the kernel; and outward marks are often supposed to be quite sufficient. But true morality is inward and concerns the spirit and not the body. "The carrying of three staves, the vow of silence, matted hair on the head, the shaving of the crown, covering one's body with barks and skins, the practice of vows, ablutions, the worship of fire, abode in the woods, emaciating the body, all these are useless if the heart be not pure....Those high-souled persons that do not commit sins in word, deed, heart, and soul, are said to undergo austerities, and not they that suffer their bodies to be wasted by fasts and penances. He that hath no feeling of kindness for relatives cannot be free from sin, even if his body be pure. That hard-heartedness of his is the enemy of his asceticism......It is in consequence of holiness and virtue alone that men attain to regions of blessedness, and fasts and vows become efficacious."[30] " Of all purities, the purity of the mind is the greatest purity. He who is pure in intent is truly pure; purification with the help of clay and water is no (real) purification."[31] "All the rites of a person, who is divorced from the purity of conduct become futile."[32]

Spiritual purity is attained by the practice of various virtues. "Charity purifies the perpetrators of forbidden acts; current, the river; earth and water, those articles that are worthy of being purified; and renunciation, the twice-born. Austerity (purifies) those that are well-versed in the Vedas; forgiveness, the learned; water, the body; recitation (of the sacred verses) those who have their sins concealed; and truth, it is said, the mind. Practice of the duties of one's own caste, and worship of the Brahmins are the (instruments of) purification of a soul that considers the body as (one's) own; knowledge is the purifier of intellect; and the knowledge of Ishawara. (God) is the purifier of individual souls."[33] Persons who have any moral or intellectual or physical taint clinging to them are all impure. "Personal impurity attaches to one who is always sickly, one who does not perform religious rites, one who is ignorant, one who is notoriously henpecked, one who is grossly inclined to vile practices, one who abstains from Vedic study and the vow of celibacy."[34]

A pure soul is not a simple entity; he is the most complicaied being. Nothings but inward perfection, perfect holiness, is sufficient to constitute a pure soul. He is the home of all virtues, of all graces, and of all finer humanity. The Gita says: The Yogins practise acts without being attached to them for the sake of attaining inward purity. (आत्मशुद्धये) This inward purity is almost the climax of moral life, although it is but the first step in the Pathway to Reality. The following passage gives us some idea of the contents of a purified being: "That man, whose limbs only are washed; is not regarded as one that is washed. He, on the other hand, is regarded as washed who has washed himself by self-denial. Even such a person is said to be pure both inwardly and outwardly. They who never concern themselves with what is past, they who feel no attachment to acquisitions that are present, indeed, they who are free from desire, are said to be possessed of the highest purity....Purity of conduct constitutes the purity of the mind. The purity that one attains by ablutions in sacred waters is regarded as inferior. Verily, that purity which arises from knowledge, is regarded as the best"[35]

References

1. Rg. IV. 16. 18.
2. Rg. IV. 50. 1.
3. Rg.IV. 6. 1.
4. Sir. W. Jones. Rg.III 62. 10.
5. Rg. VII. 94. 12.
6. Rg. X, 164. 5.
7. Rg. VII. 1.7.
8. Rg. IX, 67. 27.
9. Rg. IX. 67. 24.
10. S. Br. I. 1.1.1.
11. M.V. 43-45; 56; 64; 66; 71; 75; 152.

12. Gautama. IX.
13. Daksha. 12. 10.
14. Parashara. XII.
15. Udyoga. 37. 33.
16. Gautam. IX.
17. M.V. 58-59.
18. M.V. 73.
19. M.V. 80-82.
20. Parashara. VII. 19.
21. M.V. 85.
22. Yaj. 27-29.
23. Yaj. III. 31. M.V. 105.
24. Yaj. III. 30.
25. Daksha. V.2.
26. Vana. 80. 17-19.
27. Daksha. V. 3-4.
28. Vana. 91. 22-24.
29. M. IV. 146.
30. Vana. 203. 96-109.
31. M.V. 106.
32. Dsksha. V.2.
33. Yaj. III, 32-34.
34. Atri. I. 102-3.
35. Anu. 170, 9-14.

Chapter - VI

CULTURE AND CHARACTER

(1)

A high appreciation for the value of culture is met with even in the Rig-Veda. Wisdom is well regarded as better than riches. " Send to us all, intelligence and wisdom."[1] " O Indra give us wisdom as a sire gives wisdom to his sons."[2] "Let them (Ribhus) speed us to wealth wisdom and victory."[3] "Give, Pavamana, high renown, give kine, and steeds and hero sons: Win for us wisdom, win the light."[4] "These Mitra Varuna, whom none decieveth, with great power quicken even the fool to wisdom, and wakening, moreover, thoughtful insight, lead it by easy paths o'er grief and trouble."[5] "Speed us to mental power and skill."[6] " Wisdom leads us to long life and riches; folly betrays us into ruin. "Wisdom, most Sapient. One, brings force that lengthens life."[7] "Not our own will betrayed us, but seduction, thoughtlessness, Varuna! wine, dice, or anger."[8] " Down sink the unintelligent."[9]

The superiority of intellect over material goods is clearly seen. The Upanishads at times consider intellect the highest part of our nature. "Different from this, which consists of mind, is other, the inner-self, which consists of understanding. The former is filled by this...Faith is its head. What is right, is its right arm. What is true is its left arm....All Devas worship understanding as Brahman, as the oldest....." Intellect is here considered the same as the supreme essence–the Absolute Knowledge is considered to be not only power, but the highest power. "Men are said to have five different kinds of strength. Of these the strength of arms is regarded to be the most inferior kind. Blessed be thou, the acquisition of good councillors, is regarded as the socond kind of strength. The wise have said that acquisition of wealth is the third kind of strength. The strength of birth, O king, which one naturally acquireth from one's sires and grand-sires, is regarded as the fourth kind of strength. That, however, O Bharata, by which all these are won, and which is the foremost of all kinds of strength, is called the strength of the intellect."[11]

An exalted homage was paid to learning in India. The study of the Vedas was considered as fraught with the highest blessings. "The study and teaching (of the Veda) are a source of pleasure to him; he becomes ready-minded, and independent of others, and day by day, he acquires wealth. He sleeps peacefully; he is the best physician for himself; and (peculiar) to him are restraint of the senses, delight in the one things, growth of intelligence fame, and the (task of) perfecting the people."[12] Learning is a capital ground for reverence. "Wealth, friends, age, work, and erudition, these are the sources of honour; each succeeding one being more honourable than the one preceding it (in the order of enumeration)."[13] "The kingdom, where the ignorant partake of the food, which should be taken by the learned, courts draughts; or a great calamity appears there. There the god of rain pours down showers where the king adores these the Brahmins learned in the Vedas, and well-versed in all the scriptures."[14] Manu considers one who is master of the Vedas, perfectly competent for all great tasks. "A Veda-Knowing man is fit to be entrusted with generalship, sovereignty, or the highest judgeship of the land, nay, with the overlordship of all the regions."[15]

The persons who are advanced in learning and wisdom are considered really senior, and not those who are merely old in years. Age is generally held in the Hindu society to be a special ground of reverence; but the seniority in age yields to the seniority in culture. "The son who knows rightly is his father's father."[16] "An ignoramus is veritably a boy, the imparter of the Mantras is like unto a father, for since the ancient time, it has been a practice to call an ignoramus a boy, and the imparter of the Mantras, a father."[17] Ashtavakra was but a boy, but as he was very learned, he claimed reverence on that ground. "True growth cannot be inferred from the mere development of body, as the growth of the knots of the Shalmali tree cannot signify its age. That tree is called full-grown, which although slender and short, beareth fruits. But that which does not bear fruits, is not considered as grown."[18]

Reverence for the Guru or teacher was the key-stone of the ancient Aryan culture. In those days, the Gurus were the real universities; and all knowledge was to be had only from them. Hearing was the one main source of knowledge, and not reading. The three main stages of acquiring knowledge were called Shravana (hearing), Manana, (meditation) and Nididhyasa (final assmilation). The words as Upanishad, or Antewasin, clearly show that sitting near a Guru was the one essential of receiving education. The pupils were sent at an early age, just after their thread ceremony, to these forest universities. The hermitages of these Rishis became the centres of all culture, and hundreds of students used to flock to these. A very close personal service of the Gurus was, therefore, a necessary condition of getting any culture. "Let thy teacher be to thee like a god![19] The Guru says to the pupil: "To me alone thou shalt adhere. In me thy thoughts shall dwell. Upon me thy veneration shall be bent. When I speak, thou shalt be silent."[20] The Gurus should not be insulted or lightly treated on any account. "Let him not say 'thou' to his Gurus. If he has offended any one of them, he must keep a fast and not eat again till the end of the day, after having obtained his forgive-ness. He must not quarrel with his spiritual teacher and argue with him from emulation."[21] The debt, one owes to his Guru, is almost incalculable. "Of one's own progenitor and imparter of the Veda, he, who teaches him the Vedas, is superior to his progenitor, since the birth of a Brahmin through the Vedas is his enternal existence both in this world and the next."[22]

The period of studentship was a very important period in a man's life. A life of severe discipline is laid down for a student. The end of culture is investigation of Truth. All the other ends are either secondary or irrelevant. "Those Shrotriyas constantly pursue their studies for the investigation of Truth."[23] ते श्रोत्रियास्तत्त्वविनिश्चयाय भूरिश्रुतं शाश्वतमाद्रियन्ते। A Brahmacharin has to put on garments made of the skin of goats or deer or antelope and carry a staff in his hands. He has to maintain himself by begging. A life strictly of poverty and renunciation is to be led by him."[24] A Vedic student, until he returns to his father's house, shall kindle the fire at morning and evening, beg alms, lie on the bare ground, and do what I conducive to the good of his preceptor, each day....Let him forswear the use of unguents, collyrium shoes, and umbrella; let him renounce lust, anger, greed, dancing, singing, and music; gambling with dice, idle gossips, scandal, falsehood, embracing and casting lustful eyes on females, and doing injury to others....He shall fetch pitchers-ful of water, flowers, cowdung, clay, and Kusha grass."[25] The life of study is a very hard, arduous life; it is not a bed of roses. A student should carefully avoid all temptations lying in his way. "Carelessness in waiting upon the preceptor, haste, and boastfulness, are the three enemies of knowledge. Idleness, inattention, confusion of the intellect, restlessness, gathering for killing time, haughtiness, pride, and covetousness,–these seven constitute, it is said, faults of students in the pursuit of learning. How can they, that desire pleasure, have knowledge? Students, again, engaged in the pursuit of learning cannot have pleasure. Votaries of pleasure must give up knowledge, and votaries of knowledge must give up pleasure."[26]

The word *Brahmacharin* specially connotes two things; celibacy and devotion to one's Guru. These are the two most essential features of a student's life. The practise of *Brahmacharya* or celibacy is always highly regarded by the Hindus. The Brahmacharin is a member of God's own body.[27] Wonderful capacities flow from a life of rigid self-control. "The Brahmacharin goes on setting in motion both firmaments; in him the gods become like-minded; he maintains earth and heaven; he fills his teachers with fervour.....By Brahmacharya, by fervour a king defends his kingdom; a teacher, by it seeks a Vedic student. By Brahmacharya, a girl wins a young husband; by Brahmacharya, a draft-ox, a horse strives to gain food."[28] "He (a religious student) must sleep always alone, and let him not cast his seed. A lustful casting of seed kills one's vow. A Brahmin religious student, who has unintentionally spent himself in sleep, shall bathe and worship the sun."[29]

The period of studentship lasts for forty-eight (years), or twenty-four (years), or twelve (years), or until one has learnt (the Veda.)[30] The period of Brahmacharya may be prolonged upto death; and although ordinarily the duty of begetting sons and other duties devolve upon a man, a Brahmacharin for life can secure the highest goal by his penance. "They that departed (unmarried) but are assiduous, abandoning hatred, having no progeny,–going up to heaven, have found place, (they) shining upon the back of the firmament."[31] A student is expected to pay at the end of his career some honorarium called *Guru Dakshina* to his teacher.[32]

Guru must maintain a very lofty standard of life, in order to deserve fully the homage of his pupils. "That high conduct which the preceptor should always adopt towards his disciples should be adopted by thee towards thy younger brothers. If the preceptor happens to be unendued with wisdom, the disciple cannot possibly behave towards him, in a respectful or proper way. If the preceptor happens to be possessed of purity and highness of conduct, the disciple also succeeds in attaining to conduct of the same kind."[33] The highest ideal here is mutual reverence, the Guru for his pupils, and the pupils for their Guru. "May it (the Brahman) protect us both (teacher and pupil)! May it enjoy us both! May we acquire strength together! May our knowledge become bright! May we never quarrel! Peace! Peace! Peace!"[34] There are checks to Guru's power of chastising his pupils. "A preceptor should admonish his disciple without beating him, or inflicting any kind of corporal punishment on him. In cases of emergency he may be chastised with a cut piece of rope, or a bamboo twig without leaves. A king should punish a preceptor for chastising his pupil in any other way."[35] "A wife, sons and pupils who are contaminated by sinful deeds must first be admonished, and then forsaken. He, who forsakes them in any other way, becomes (himself) an outcaste."[36] A pupil also can desert or even punish his Guru under certain extraordinary circumstances, "An officiating priest or preceptor, who neglects to perform sacrifices or to teach (the Veda) shall be forsaken."[37] A preceptor, old man, infant, Brahmin, or vastly erudite person, coming as an *Atatayin* (assassinator, etc.) must be killed without the least hesitation.[38] "Even a spiritual teacher deserves chastisement, if he is puffed up with pride, and is devoid of the power of judging good actions and bad, and when he is gone astray."[39]

The communication as well as reception of knowledge were considered equally important. "Do not neglect the learning and teaching of the Veda![40] Knowledge was to be gathered from all sources, however humble and upretentious they may be. "One should extract truths from the ravings and the prattlings of the children, like gold from stone. A wise man should learn good behaviour, good words, and good acts from every side, like the leader of the Shila mode of life, picking grains of corn from the field that have been abandoned by the reapers."[41] Pride of birth should not prevent a Brahmin from learning from all-other castes. "Respectful, let him acquire auspicious knowledge even from a Shudra, the highest virtue even from a man of vile caste; and a good wife even from a bad family. Ambrosia may be taken even out of poison, a good word even from an infant; good conduct even from an enemy; and gold, even from an unhallowed person. Women (wives), gems, knowledge, virtue, purity, good words, and the various kinds of arts may be acquired from anywhere."[42]

Knowledge, however, was considered a very sacrosanct

thing; it can be communicated only to the worthy few. The ancients thought knowledge to be a mystery which could not be safely scattered broadcast among the unthinking multitude. A great reserve was maintained as regards all culture; a very heavy load of responsibility lay on the teacher, with regard to the selection of proper recipients of his lore. "The son of the preceptor, one who is devoted to service, a virtuous person, one who is pure, a relation, one who is capable of comprehending the meaning of the Vedas, an honest youth, a son, and a paying student, these ten are fit to be taught."[43] Knowledge would be wasted, if the recipient were not capable of making a proper use of it, or if the recipient had not the requisite appetite for it or capacity to assimilate it. Adhikara or qualification of a pupil was always first looked to. The Shudra was debarred from the Vedic study.[44] It is deemed desirable that knowledge should perish, rather than it be either imporperly received or communicated. "He, who, disregarding all righteous rules, solicits knowledge, and he who, disregarding the rules of righteousness communicates knowledge, either of them falls off, and instead of that affection which should prevail between preceptor and disciple, such questioning and communication are sure to produce distrust and suspicion."[45] "The presiding deity of knowledge came to a Brahmin, and said, preserve me, I am thy highest treasure. Do not impart me to a malicious person, thereby my potency will be kept unimpugned. To him, whom thou shalt know to be pure, perfectly continent, and free from the follies of the world. To that Brahmin, to that custodian of the treasure of knowledge, shalt thou impart me".[46] "Even in the absence of a means of livelihood, rather let a Vedic preceptor die with his knowledge than impart it to an unworthy recipient."[47] Knowledge should not be stolen. "He, who acquires the knowledge of the Vedas from a studying pupil, or from a teaching preceptor, without his permission, stands guilty of the theft of Brahma and goes to hell for his crime."

It is necessary for the candidate for knowledge to seek some Guru. "Learn thou this by discipleship, by investigation, and by service. The wise, the seers of the essence of things, will instruct thee in wisdom."[49] "That cleansed understanding again, it is said, is unattainable without one's connection with a preceptor The preceptor is the helmsman, and knowledge is the boat. After having acquired that boat, one becomes crowned with success. Indeed, having crossed the ocean, one may abondon both."[50]

The questioning spirit was allowed its legitimate scope. "Without being asked, one must not speak anything to any person, nor should he speak if any question is put to him without decorum. In such cases, the intelligent one shall behave like a dumb person. He who puts an improper question, or he who answers an improper one, either of them meets his doom or incurs the enmity of the other."[51] The Hercules pillars of human knowledge must be duly recognised; and the spirit of asking the why of things must not to be pushed beyond its proper limits. Yajnavalkya says to Sakalya; "Thou hast gone on questioning me beyond the Deity, beyond which there must be no questioning: thou shalt die ere such and such a day and not even thy bones shall reach thy home."[52]

It is forbidden to a teacher to sell his learning or to pervert it to private uses. "He, who, having collected sacred knowledge gains his substance by it in this world, will derive no benefit from it in the world to come. Neither will he (derive much benefit from it), who uses his knowledge, in order to destroy the reputation of others, by defeating them in argument."[53] "Those who sell the Shrutis are outcasts. Those, who teach unknown persons, those who give instructions on receiving fees, those who study the Vedas by paying fees are described as Vritakas."[54]

An intelligent mastery of the contents of books is to be sought rather than mere learning these by rote. "A reader of books is greater than an illiterate one; one who has got those books by heart is better than a mere reader; one who has got a true knowledge of their contents is greater than one who remembers them."[55] The Niruktakara says : "He, who crams the Vedas, without understanding their meaning, is a mere bearer of burden like as ass." "That person who bears in his understanding merely the texts of the Vedas and the other scriptures, without being conversant with the true sense or meaning of those texts, bears them fruitlessly. Indeed, one who holds the contents of a work in memory without comprehending their meaning, is said to bear a useless burden."[56]

We shall briefly summarise some aspects of technical and higher education. "Arts, consisting of work in gold, husbandary, and the like, and the art of dancing and the rest are called *human* sciences; let him who studies these perform work in his teacher's house."[57] In fact, all secular knowledge was styled *human* knowledge. A period or apprenticeship is laid down for a pupil, during which he stays at his master's house and works at the art or craft. It is for the teacher "to instruct him, give him a maintenance in his own house, and not to employ him in any other work, but to treat him as a son." (Narada) It is for the pupil to fulfil the contract, to stick to him to the end of the period and to pay the teacher handsomely in the end. All money that accrues to the pupil from the practice of his art during the period goes to the teacher. The teacher had a prior right to the service of his pupil. During the period, the relations between them should not be commercial but spiritual, the teacher studiously abstaining from exploiting the pupil, and the pupil giving his Guru his full due to reverence. "For science is like a river, ever advancing to a humbler lever, therefore as one's knowledge grows broader and deeper one should become even more humble towards the source of one's knowledge."[58]

(1)

Hindu seers put a broad interpretation upon the Socratic dictum, virtue is knowledge, and vice is ignorance. All morality was dependent upon a certain enlightened state of soul, a certain inner attitude, and not upon the mere fact of knowledge of virtues and vices and their consequences. However, the belief in the power of intellectual illumination to create moral regeneration ,in man was very powerful. The ends of culture were severely practical. The indulgence in one's literary tastes, or revelry in the formal aspects of literature was not very useful. The thing that mattered above everything else was the ,attainment of clear vision which unmistakably let to its corresponding action. The knowledge of the soul was , therefore, the one absolutely essential things. Metaphysics was not meant to be one among many branches of knowledge, but the discipline of disciplines, the science of sciences, upon a proper training in which depended both man's here and his hereafter. All the other culture was a mere lumber if it did not lead directly or indirectly to this goal. Hence we find even in such treatises as Tarka-shastra or books on logic, that the end aimed at is Moksha. Knowledge was not to be prized for any material ends such as the acquisition of mastery over nature, not was its pursuit to be an end in itself. It was to be strictly subordinated to practical ends, but not so-called practical which govern the scientific mind of the West. Its end was to be salvation. "You, indeed, are our father, who carry us from our ignorance to the other shore." The study of the Vedas was, therefore, to be preferred to all other learning. "Let the foremost of the twice-born ones constantly commit the Vedas to memory inasmuch as the study of the Vedas is said to be the highest Tapasya for a Brahmin. Even he, who indulges in such articles of luxury as the garland of flowers, etc. by studying the Vedas, each day, according to his might, acquires such an efficiency in Tapas that it (energy) surcharges his whole body from the tips of his fingernails to the crown of his head. A Brahmin, who, not having studied the Vedas, tries to acquire other forms of learning, is degraded to the status of a Shudra with all his progeny, even in his life-time."[60]

A clear vision, a right view of the higher entities, intellectual, is a factor of very great importance in moral life. "Untruth is only another form of darkness. It is darkness that leads downwards........It has been said that heaven is light, and hell is darkness...In this world also, truth and untruth lead to opposite courses of conduct such as righteousness and unrighteousness, light and darkness, pleasure and pain. Amongst these, that which is righteousness is light; and that which is light is happiness. Similarly that which is unrighteousness is darkness, and that which is darkness is sorrow and misery."[61] Intellectual insight is often more valuable than the will to do right. "One, who is not possessed of clear vision does wrong even when one wishes to do right. Such a person, by even exercising his judgment, does such acts of virtue as partake the nature of iniquity.[62] "For thoughts alone cause the round of births; let a man strive to purify his thoughts. *What a man thinks, that he is;* this is the old secret. By the serenity of his thoughts a man blots out all actions, whether good or bad.[63] The absence of proper insight or ignorance becomes from this point of view, a cardinal sin. Napoleon said: "It is not a crime; it is a blunder." Intellectual confusion, he believed, to be worse than moral perversity. "In consequence of ignorance one sinks into hell. Ignorance is the spring of misery. Through ignorance one suffers afflictions and incurs great dangers."[64] Not only does thought act on life, but life in its turn acts on thought. Intellectual errors are the cause of sins, but sins in their turn become fruitful source of intellectual confusion. "How miserable is the fruit I see of sinful acts! Through sin the very vision of the sinner becomes perverse, and he confounds his body and its unstable accompaniments with the soul!"[65]

Intellectual culture was rightly regarded as a mere waste if it did not lead up to a corresponding development of a man's moral character. Character is the central fact with regard to a man's life and not his intellectual polish. Man's academic acquisitions are comparatively a superficial part of him; these touch the mere fringe of his nature. The real man in him speaks through his Swabhava, his own innate nature and disposition. Continued practice alone can enable a man to weave his principles into the texture of his life. "One who has got a true knowledge of the contents of books is greater than one who remembers them, and one who acts according to that knowledge is greater than one who has merely gained a knowledge of their contents."[66] "Knowledge of the Shastras is said to bear fruit, when it resulteth in humility and good behaviour."[67] "Neither friends nor wealth, nor high birth, nor scriptural learning, nor Mantras, nor energy, can succeed in rescuing one from sorrow in the next world. It is only by conduct that one can attain to felicity there.[68]

The sentiment expressed in the following lines by Karna in the Venisamhara was as dear to the ancient Hindus as it is to the modern democracy.

सूतो वा सूतपुत्रो वा यो वा को वा भवाम्यहं।
दैवायत्तं कुले जन्म मदायत्तं तु पौरुषम्।।

If birth in a noble family is not a guarantee of good manners and excellent morals, what is the use of it.? "Mere lineage, I think, in the case of one whose behaviour is not good, should command no respect. Even persons that are of low birth should be regarded as respectable, if their conduct be so."[69] " Whether of low or high birth, he who doth not transgress the rules of polite intercourse, who hath an eye on virtue, who is endued with humility and modesty is superior to a hundred persons of high birth."[70] " Vidura was a Shudra, but none commanded greater reverence that he, "But of all present in that assembly it is Vidura whom I worship! Neither by learning nor by wealth doth one beome worthy of homage! It is by disposition alone that one becomes respectable. O Krishna, endued with great intelligence and profound wisdom, the character of the illustrious Vidura like unto an ornament, adorns the whole world."[71] Families are to be judged as high or low according as they are characterised by fine traits of morality or not. "Those families that are possessed of members, wealth, and kine, are not regarded as respectable, if they be wanting in good manners and conduct, while families wanting in wealth, but distinguished by manners and good conduct are regarded as such and win great reputation."[72]

Character is the fundamental things in man, rather, character is the man. Bhartrihari very well says : The very root of all that is good and great in a man is character: सर्वेषामपि सर्वकारणमिदं शीलं परं भूषणं। It is character which rules society. "One attired in excellent robes prevaileth over an assembly; an owner of kine possess power as regards the desire of eating sweets; a possesses or of vehicles is a master of the situation on roads, but he that is righteous in behaviour is triumphant over everything. Righteous character is essential to a man; he that loseth it gaineth nothing by life, wealth, and friends."[73] Rama refuses to return to Ayodhya, on the ground that persistence in a right course of action is the very essence of character. A man sinful and unstable character does not command any prestige, in the circles of the respectable people. A steady practice of the highest virtues alone can enable us to distinguish between a hero or a coward, a high-born or a low-born, a pure or an impure man.[74] Character becomes a veritable power, a weapon of no mean potency to guard those who possess it. This power is alluded to in Sanskrit literature as तेजस् or वर्चस्; it is the lustre which goes in the train on the practice of good deeds. We, thus, hear that Sita's chastity once protects her from fire when she submits to the ordeal; it protects her as well as Hanuman from the conflagration set up by the latter. The Rishis were great also owing to this force of will शमप्रधानेषु तपोधनेषु गूढ हि दाहात्मकमस्ति तेज:। There is a talent power lodged in tne saints who are full of शम or tranquillity of soul. "A virtuous Brahmin must not complain of any wrong done to him, to the king; he shall punish the wrong doer by means of his own (psychic) power. The Brahmanic (psychic force) is stronger than the royal prowess; hence let a Brahmin punish his enemies by means of his own (psychic) powers."[75] The Brahmins are to use their soul-force, not brute-force; their power lies in their *Satyagraha.* Miraculous powers are attributed to this soul-force. "Without doubt, one may, by character alone, conquer the three worlds.

There is nothing impossible of attainment by persons of character. Mandhatri conquered the whole world in course of only one night, Janmejaya, in course of three; and Nabhaga, in course of seven. All these kings were possessed of compassion and virtuous character. For this reason, the Earth came to them of its own accord, won over by their virtues."[76]

We will close this chapter with the following anecdote which vividly illustrates how every virtue, every excellence in man is bound up inseparably with his character. In days of yore, the Daitya Prahlad, by the merit of his behaviour, snatched from the high-souled Indra his sovereignty, and reduced the three worlds to subjection. Shakra (Indra) then, with joined hands, approached Brihaspati. Possessed of great wisdom, the chief of the celestials addressed the great preceptor, saying,–I desire thee to tell me, what is the source of felicity? Thus addressed, Brihaspati said unto him that knowledge is the source of the highest felicity. Indeed, Brihaspati indicated knowledge to be the source of supreme felicity. Indra, however, once more asked him as to whether there was anythings higher than that. Brihaspati said,–There is something that is still higher. The high-souled Bhargava will instruct thee better. Indra is sent away ultimately to Prahlad, whom he satisfies by serving him as a Brahmin. He then asked Prahlad as to what means enabled him to acquire the sovereignty of the three worlds. Prahlad said,–I do not feel any pride in consequence of my being king, nor do I cherish any hostile feelings towards the Brahmins!....I am ever obedient to the teaching of Shukra. I wait upon and serve the Brahmins and my seniors. I bear no malice. I am of righteousness soul. I have conquered wrath. I am self-restrained, and all my senses are under my control. Those regenerate ones that are my instructors pour beneficial instructions upon me like bees dropping honey into the cells of their comb. I taste the nectar dropped by these learned men, and like the Moon among the constellations, I live among the members of my race. The Brahmin then asks for a boon from Prahlad and requests him to grant him his (Prahlad's) character.

While the Daitya chief sat boarding over the matter, a flame of light issued out of his body... Prahlad asked the form, saying,– who art thou? The form answered, saying,–who art thou? The form answered, saying–I am the embodi-ment of thy character.

Cast off by thee I am going away...The form, then entered Indra's body. After the disappearance of that form another of similar shape issued out of Prahlad's body. The Daitya chief addressed it, saying: who art thou? The form answered, saying– know me, O Prahlad, for the embodiment of Righteousness....I reside there where character dwells! Upon the disappearance of righteousness, a third form, blazing with splendour, issued out of Prahlad's body. Asked by Prahlada as to who he was, that form answered saying–know, that I am Truth! I shall leave thee following the way of Righteousness. After Truth had left Prahlad, following in the wake of Truth, another great person issued out of Prahlad's body. Asked by the Daitya king, the mightly being unswered,–I am the embodiment of Good deeds! Know that I dwell there where Truth dwells! After this one had left Prahlad, another being came out, uttering loud and deep cries. Addressed by Prahlad, he answered–know that I am Might. I dwell there where good deeds are!....After that a goddess of great effulgence issued out of Prahlad's body. The Daitya chief asked her and she answered him saying that she was the embodiment of prosperity. On being asked other, particulars, she said: O righteous one, it was by thy character that thou hadst reduced the three worlds to subjection. Knowing this, the chief of celestials robbed thee of thy character. Righteousness, and Truth, and good deeds, and might, and myself, all have our root in character![77]

References

1. Rg.IV. 22. 10.
2. Rg. VII, 32. 26.
3. Rg. I. 111. 4.
4. Rg. IX. 9.9.

5. Rg. VII. 60. 61.
6. Rg. IX. 36. 3.
7. Rg. X. 144. 5.7.
8. Rg. VII. 86. 6.
9. Rg. IX. 64. 21.
10. Tai. Up. II. 4-5.
11. Udyoga. 37. 52-58.
12. Sh. Br. XI. 5.7. 1.
13. M.II. 136.
14. Atri. I. 23-24.
15. M. XII. 100.
16. Rg. I. 164. 16.
17. M.II. 150. 154-156.
18. Vana. 135. 8-13.
19. Tai. Up. I. 11. 2.
20. Gr. H. I. 2. 5.
21. Vishnu. XXXII. 8-10.
22. M. II. 144. 146-148.
23. Malati Madhav.
24. M. II. 48. 50-51.
25. M.II, 108, 175-179, 182-183, 186.
26. Udyoga. 40, 4-6.
27. Rg. X. 109, 5.
28. Av. XI, 5. 1, 17-18.
29. M. II, 180-181.
30. Gr. H. 1, 3, 9, 14.
31. Av. XVIII, 2, 47; M. II, 243-244.
32. M.II, 245-246.
33. Anu. 162, 2-4.
34. Tai. Up. II.
35. Gautama. II.
36. Vasishtha. XI.
37. Vasishtha . XI.
38. M. VIII. 350.
39. R. II, 21, 13.
40. Tai. Up. I. 11.1.
41. Udyoga. 34. 33-34.
42. M.II, 238-242.
43. M. II. 109.
44. M. IV. 80-81.

45. Adi. 91. 52. Shanti. 335.
46. M. II, 114-115.
47. M. II. 113.
48. M. II. 116.
49. Bg. IV. 34.
50. Shanti. 334, 22-23.
51. M. II. 110-111.
52. Sh. Br. XI. 6. 3. 11.
53. Vishnu. XXX, 39-40.
54. Ushanas, IV. 23-26.
55. M. XII. 103.
56. Shanti. 310. 24-28.
57. Brishaspati, See Colebrook's Digest of Hindu Law: also Dr. Mookerjee's Local Self-Government in Ancient India.
58. Narada. V. 12.
59. Pr. VI. 8.
60. M. II. 166-168.
61. Shanti. 188. 1-5.
62. Shanti. 241. 31-32.
63. Mu. Up. VI. 3-4.
64. Shanti. 157. 2-3.
65. Shanti. 297. 7-8.
66. M. XII. 103.
67. Sobha. 5. 116.
68. Shanti. 292. 15.
69. Udyoga. 34, 42.
70. Udyoga. 34, 49.
71. Udyoga. 90, 53-54.
72. Udyoga. 36, 23-32.
73. Udyoga. 34, 48-49.
74. R. II, 109, 3-8.
75. M. XI, 31-34.
76. Shanti. 124, 15-17.
77. Shanti. 124.

Chapter - VII

WOMAN : HER STATUS AND FUNCTIONS

A problem of very great importance both in the ethics and sociology of a people is the position assigned to women in social life. It is one of the criteria of considerable value in estimating with precision the proper rank attaind by a particular people in the comity of civilised nations. In this respect, the Hindu ideas have gone through various vicissitudes. The general trend, however, is towards degradation of woman. In the time of the Vedas, all writers are agreed that she enjoyed much freedom and was clearly in most cases an equal of man. Nevertheless, from the very first we must recognise the fact that two conflicting views are set forth regarding woman's character. "With women there can be no lasting friendship; hearts of hyenas are the hearts of women."[1] "Indra himself hath said, the mind of woman brooks not discipline. Her intellect hath little weight."[2] A few passages both in the Ramayana and the Mahabharata picture woman as very degraded; full of all sorts of faults and blemishes. Dasharatha says to Rama: "Neither lineage, nor benefit, nor learning, nor gift, nor forbearance of faults, can secure the hearts of females,–surely their hearts are unstable."3 In the Mahabharata, even a more humiliating pictur is drawn. As an advisor she is quite worthless. "Those object that depend upon women....are all doubtful of success. The sink helplessly, O king, like a raft made of stone, who have a woman, a deceitful person, or a child, for their guide."[4] "There is nothing that is more sinful than woman. Verily, women are the root of all faults... . Women, even when possessed of husbands having fame and wealth, of handsome features and completely obedient to them, are prepared to disregard them, if they get the opportunity....Even those women that are loved by their husbands and treated with great respect, are seen to bestow their favours upon men that are dwarfs...The destroyer, the deity of wind, death, the nether regions, the equine mouth that roves through the ocean vomiting ceaseless flames of fire, the sharpness of the razor, virulent poison, the snake and fire,–all these exist in a state of union in women."[5]

Side by side with this picture, exist many fine delineations of the highest traits of feminine character. Her status in the Vedic period was sufficiently high. She was the presiding deity of the house. "Over thy husband's father and thy husband's mother bear full sway."[6] " Over the sister of thy lord, over his brothers rule supreme."[7] "Go to the house to be the household's mistress and speak as lady to thy gathered people."[8] She has more character than impious men. "Yea, many a women is more firm and better than the man who turns away from gods, and offers not."[9] "As the (mighty) river won the supremacy of the streams, so be thou supreme, having gone away to thy husband's home."[10] "Be thou supreme among father-in-law, supreme also among brothers-in-law, be thou supreme over sisters-in-law, supreme also over mother-in-law."[11] Another proof of the former greatness of her position is to be found in equality of her position is to be found in the equality in religious rites which she shared with her husband. The term Patni in the Brahmanas is used to indicate a woman's role as a partner with her husband in sacrifices; while the term Jaya points out her conjugal capacity. It is clear also from many references in the Vedic literature as well as the epics that there was a stage in the history of the Hindu civilization when all the very highest religious privileges were freely shared by her. She seems once capable of going through the Brahmacharya stage of life and entering even the last stage. "By Vedic studentship a girl wins a young hunsband."[12] There is a verse in the Smritis which definitely says that in former times women were admitted to the privilege of sacred thread ceremony and so on. The evidence of the epics also is important. Sita is mentioned as one capable of performing the Samdhya ceremony. Hanuman says: "Surely the beautiful and the graceful daughter of Janaka fond of performing morning Samdhya shall come to this river of pure water to perform it."[13] Kaushalya unhesitatingly kills a horse in a sacrifice–a sign surely of great manliness.[14] She is described as performing her Puja (worship) every day. "Worshipful Kaushalya, seeking her son's welfare, kept up the whole night being absorbed in meditation, and was worshipping the God Vishnu. Wearing silk cloth, pleased, and accustomed to the performance of religious rites every day, she performing benedictory ceremonies, was offering oblation unto the fire."[15] Instances of woman performing penances and Yoga practices were not rare. "Hare a Brahmin maiden, leading from youth the life of Brahmacharya, became crowned with ascetic success. Ultimately, in the possession of Yoga powers, that lady proceeded to heaven. The high-souled Shandilya, O king, got a beautiful daughter who was chaste, wedded to severe vows, self-restrained, and observant of Brahmacharya. Having performed the severest penances such as are incapable of being performed by women the blessed lady at last went to heaven, worshipped by the gods and Brahmins."[16] In the same Satya Yuga, a woman of the name of Sulabha, belonging to the mendicant order, practised the duties of Yoga and wandered over the whole Earth.[17] Anasuya is thus introduced to Rama by her husband Atri "The people were ceaselessly burning in consequence of a famine extending over ten years. Anasuya who had practised rigid asceticism and voluntary penances, created fruits and roots, and the Jahanvi (the Ganges) was made by her to flow through the asylum. She performed mightly austerities for ten thousand years, which were instrumental in stopping the disturbance to the asceticism of the sages; and she brought ten nights within the compass of one. Let Vaidehi always resort to this aged ascetic devoid of anger, *who is worthy of being bowed down to by all creatures.*"[18]

Gradually, however, woman loses her privilege in this respect. Manu is quite explicit on this point. "For the purification of their persons, these rites excepting that of the initiation with the thread shall be done unto woman, in due time and in due order, without any Vedic Mantras. The sacrament of marriage is to a female, what initiation with the thread is to a male. The service of the husband is to the wife, what his residence in the preceptor's house, as a religious student is to the husband; the household duty is to a woman, what the making of burnt offerings is to a man."[19] Vyasa says: "The recitation of any Mantra by a woman is prohibited in the ten ceremonies commencing with the *Jatakarma*, and ending with the *Karna-Vedha*; but she is privileged to recite Mantras in connection with the celebration of her marriage ceremony."[20] Woman was, however, allowed Fire-worship and in some cases, even the performance of Shraddha ceremony.[21] Woman's position slowly becomes degraded; all the higher types of spiritual life became too high and sacred for her; in fact, the inner circle of religious thought and action was closed to her. Her one religion was the worship of her husband. "Recitation (of the Gayatri), austerity and journeys to sacred places, adoption of a Sannyasa–life, practice of Mantras and adoration of deities,–these six bring about the fall of women and Shudras."[22] "The woman, who, during the lifetime of her husband, fasts while performing a religious rite, robs the longevity of her husband. Such a woman goes to hell."[23]

It seems that woman used to bear some share in public administration in the Vedic period.

They come to him as dames to an assembly.[24] "Let Bhaga lead thee hence, grasping thy hand;.....thou, having control, shalt speak unto the council."[25] Women had access the highest culture of the day and they contributed their own share to the creative work of the age. Thus we find that many hymns of the Rigveda were written by women. Yajnavalkya discoursed on the highest philosophical problems with his wife. Maitreyi received in this way from her husband the highest metaphysical truths and prized them above all worldly treasures. Again, when Yajnavalkya silenced the Brahmins who challenged his supremacy in the court of Janaka, a lady got up and said: "O Yajnavalkya, as the son of a warrior from the Kasis or Videhas might string his loosened bow, and take two pointed foe-piercing arrows in his hand and rise to battle, I have risen to fight three with two questions. Answer me these questions." Then Yajnavalkya answered these questions of Gargi. Women used to be teachers also in those times.[26] Savitri is represented in the Mahabharata as well versed in all the Shastras.

There is nothing to show that women in the Vedic period did not move freely in society. Then presence in assemblies and participation in the discussions taking place there, are adequate proofs of their free position. The custom of having veils had begun early; but it was capable of considerable modification. But we have ample evidence that woman enjoyed free atmosphere of life as much as men. "From olden times the matron goes to feast and general sacrifice."[27] "They trooped to festal meetings, decked, shining forth with sunbeams."[28] The presence of charming ladies added much to the lustre of social life. They were agreeable at festivals.[29] They embellished their bodies with garlands, and scents, and unguents and walked out glancing to the right and left.[30] The harem, however, is referred to.[31] "And that Sita whom formerly the very rangers of the sky could not see, is to-day beheld by the passers by."[32] Rama clearly exposes the futility of this custom and rises superior to it. When Vibhishana begins to drive out people in order that Sita may present herself before Rama, Rama says :- "Why dost thou insult me by disturbing all these? Do you remove their anxiety; they are all my own men. It is not houses, clothes or walls which constitute the veil of women; character is the real veil of women. There is no sin consequent upon seeing women in danger, difficulty, war, Swayamvara (self-choice), sacrifice, and marriage."[33] Sita herself gives reception to Ravana, who came disguised as a Brahmin, in the absence of her husband. Here is a description of Draupadi when she is alone in the presence of a guest. She asks the king who visits her hermitage: "Is everything right with thy kingdom, thy government, thy exchequer, and thy army? Art thou, as sole ruler, governing the rich countries of Shaivya? Do thou, O prince, accept this water for washing thy feet.[34]

In general, in the time of the epics and the law-books, woman's position became markedly inferior to her partner in many respects, although respectful treatment to her is enjoined upon men in her various capacities. A woman was not to have independence in any state of life. "One of the refuges of a woman is her husband, a second is her son; and a third is her relatives and a fourth she has none.[35] "A girl, or a maid, or an old woman must not do anything independently in the house. In childhood let her remain under the control of her father; under the control of her husband in youth; and under the control of her son after the demise of her Lord in old age. A woman must not assume independence in any circumstances whatever."[36] The following verse marks the extreme degradation of woman's position; she became almost a chattel, a thing, not a person. "A wife, a son, and a slave can never acquire any property for themselves; what ever they earn go to him to whom they belong."[37] 'A single non-avaricious, male witness should be regarded as enough and competent for testifying to a fact, while a host of virtuous women should not be regarded as competent witness owing to the fickleness of the female temperament."[38]

Although shorn in this way of some of her fundamental rights, woman did not lose everything in the way of happiness. "Women should (always) be adored by the husband, brother, father, kinsmen, mother-in-law, father-in-law, husband's younger brother and the other relatives with ornaments, clothes, and food,"[39] "(The deities smile on the family) where the females are honoured; fruitless are the acts (in the family) where they are dishonoured."[40] "The moon has conferred on them (women) purity; the Gandharvas, sweet speech; (and)

Fire, the most exalted state of holiness; (therefore) women are most holy."[41] The sight of a lady with a husband is quite auspicious.[42]

Here we have given details regarding woman's position in general. It is a mixed impression which we receive from this picture. The Hindu theory was quite sound in the Vedic period; but it showed considerable decline in its purity in the later period. However, it is clear that in its purest form it contains all the essential of truth in this matter. The inner sanctity, the fundamental holiness of woman's soul was recognised. Her sphere of activity was gradually narrowed down; but in that sphere she always maintained her supremacy. The influence which she was allowed to exercise was moral and spiritual influence; and hence while on the one side she lost much as regards the goods of this world and position in it, she became purer, holier and more spiritual than ever. Her authority became less extensive, but more intensive, less material but more moral and religious. We do not mean to say that this was the consummation most devoutly to be wished; but there is an element of truth in this position. It is so gratifying to find that even Manu considers it absolutely essential for males, for moral and economic prosperity, to worship (पूज्) women; to hear Bhavabhuti proclaiming that it is character that we worship in the virtuous not their sex nor age."[43] and to read in the Gita Lord Krishna's description to the highest feminine qualities as "Glory, Magnificence, Refinement of speech, Memory, Intellect, Fortitude, and Forbearance," surely a collection of some of the finest moral and intellectual excellencies."[44] Some earthly privileges were cruelly denied to women; but the very highest goal which a human being can attain was within her reach. The doors of paradise indeed were open to her; even Moksha or final salvation was possible for her. In the Shanti Parva, persons belonging to the inferior orders and women were considered capable of attaining the highest end.[45] The same fact is confirmed by a verse in the Gita.[46]

References

1. Rg. X. 95. 15.
2. Rg. VIII. 33. 17.
3. R. II. 39. 20-23.
4. Udyoga. 38. 42-43.
5. Anu. 73. 11-30.
6. Rg. X. 85.
7. Rg. X. 46.
8. Rg. X. 26-27.
9. Rg. V. 61. 6.
10. Av. XIV. 1. 43.
11. Av. XIV. 1. 44.
12. Av. XI. 5. 18. (See स्मृतिचंद्रिका)
    पुरा कल्पे कुमारीणां मोञ्जीबन्धनमिष्यते।
    अध्यापनं च वेदनां सावित्रीवचनं तथा।। –यम:
    Harita-Smriti also divides women into सद्योवधू and ब्रह्मवादिनी—those who are married and those who take to Brahma.
13. R. V. 15. 49.
14. R. I. 14.33
15. R. II. 20. 14-19
16. Shalya. 55. 6-9.
17. Shanti. 325, 7.
18. R. II, 117, 8-12.
19. M.II, 66-7.
20. I. 16.
21. Kat. XIX, 3.
22. Atri 135.
23. Atri. 136-7.
24. Rg. X. 168. 2.
25. Av. XIV. I,20.
26. Br. Up. III, 3. 1.; 7. 1.
27. Rg.. X. 86. 10.
28. Rg. I 124,8.
29. Av. II 36, 1.
30. Rg. V. II, 39, 2. VII, 55, 8, X, 85 7, 1, 75, 1.
31. Kaus. Sutras. 17, 6.
32. R. II. 3, 8.
33. R. VI, 114, 26-28.

34. Vana. 268, 11-13.
35. R. II. 61. 24.
36. M.V. 147-9.
37. M. VIII. 416.
38. M. VIII. 77.
39. Yaj. 1. 82.
40. M. III. 56-59.
41. Y. I. 71. Atri. 139.
42. Kat. XIX. 9.
43. शिशुत्वं स्त्रैणं वा भवतु ननु वन्द्यासि जगतः।
    गुणाः पूजास्थानं गुणिषु न च लिंग न च वयः॥
    Kalidas also emphasizes the importance of woman in social life
    'प्रभुता रमणेषु योषितां etc.
    'गृहिणी सचिवः सखी मिथः प्रियशिष्या ललिते कलाविद्यौ।'
44. Rg. X.34.
45. Shanti. 246. 34.
46. Bg. IX. 32.

Chapter - VIII

MARRIAGE CONSIDERATIONS

The Hindu looks upon marriage as not only a very important social institution, but an equally important religious institution also. It is held to be the pivotal fact of a man's life, transforming him from a self-centred into a social being, from an isolated unit into a unit essentially connected with the past as well as the future of the race. Marriage is not a contract in the eyes of a Hindu, temporarily entered into under the influence of his wandering fancy or dissolved at his pleasure. It was essentially a sacrament, necessary for every individual to realize the capabilities of his social nature fully and to fulfil the responsibilities which he owed to himself, his ancestors and to the society at large. It is a fundamental social fact in man's life, constituting an important stage in the development of his individuality, a stage in which he essentially belongs to society and not to himself. Marriage, therefore, is to every Hindu not an act of mere pleasure, not primarily a source of gratification to his sentimental longings or romantic loves, but an act of duty, a matter of moral and religious obligation, absolutely incumbent on him in all normal circumstances. The following verses show that marriage is considered an act of positive merit. "He, who out of stupefaction, puts impediments in an impending marriage, sacrifice, or gift, O Vasava, is born as a vermin after death."[1] "For one dying without purificatory rites being performed unto one, the nuptials for a bachelor should be performed."[2] Of all gifts, the gift of a maiden is the best.[3]

Marriage was, therefore, regarded as in indispensable duty

for men and women alike, but especially for the latter. The phenomenon, of old spinsters was not altogether unknown.[4] They lived in their parents' home 'till the hair was white with age.'[5] An old maid restlessly tried for a husband and at last secured him.[6] Manu also entitles a girl to remain unmarried if a suitable husband is not found.[7] But this state of things was quite exceptional. "May she long sit with her relatives until her hair drops from her head."[8] Such was the curse given to a lady. Manu says that marriage is the only sacrament for women; it is to them what the ceremony of putting on sacred thread is to the males.[9] The following story from the Mahabharata illustrates the Hindu sentiment on this point. "Though her sire had been giving her away to a husband, she yet did not wish for marriage, for she did not see a husband that could be worthy of her. Continuing to emaciate her body with austere penances she devoted herself to the worship of the Pitris, (manes), and the gods in that solitary forest. At last when she (became very old so that) could no longer move even a single step without being aided by any one, she set her heart upon departing for the other world. Beholding her about to cast off her body, Narada said unto her : O sinless one, thou hast no regions of blessedness to obtain in consequence of thy not having cleansed thyself by the rite of marriage."[10] She had to go through married life and then she became qualified for heaven. The moral of Rishyashringa's story is plain. There was a severe famine in a kingdom. The king consulted various sages and ultimately he found out that famine could be removed only by one means. It was this. There was in a forest one son of a saint called Rishyashringa, who was kept so much out of contact with human society that he could not distinguish males from females. Now if the king could persuade him to marry his daughter, the famine would cease. Even nature felt an uncomfortable void as long as such an isolated being existed who had potentially the keenest capacity of participation in conjugal happiness, but whom circumstances had absolutely debarred from even a rudimentary understanding of married life. Had Rishyashringa been a voluntary Sannyasin, there was no wrong to be redressed; but as it was, when that isolation of the absolute celibate was so harmoniously removed, nature herself felt joy and burst out in rains.

There were four objects in the Hindu marriage: creation of progeny (प्रजाति) ; conjugal fecility (रति): spiritual happiness (आनन्द); and comradeship in the performance of Dharma.[11] Here we will bring out only one aspect of the problem, viz., the importance of marriage as a guarantee of race continuance. The command 'Increase and multiply' was very sacred to a Hindu whose present bliss and prosperity depended, indeed, upon male children; but above all, his future and the future of his ancestors hinged upon the male descendants of the line. The Rigveda is full of cries for children; sons were a source of strength and power to people in those days. They were called "cancellers of the father's debt."[12] To have children was to become immortal.[13] 'O bounteous Indra, make this bride blest in her sons and fortunate. Vouchsafe to her ten sons and make her husband the eleventh man."[14] "Great riches with a multitude of hero sons."[15] Barrenness was deprecated. "The lot of childlessness remove ye from us."[16] Daughters were not at first out of favour. "With sons and daughters by their side they reach the full extent of life."[17] The Aitareya Brahmana has a very eloquent passage in praise of son. "When the father sees the face of the born living son, he places his debts (wordly and the three Vedic) on him. There is more enjoyment (of pleasures) of the father by the son, than there are in the earth, in the fire, and in the water, of living beings. Fathers are delivered from great darkness by the son. Self is born from self. He (the son) is a ferry in a great river. What is the good of the four Ashramas? Desire the son, O Brahmins. He is the happy unblameable regions. Food is the life, clothes are refuge, gold is beauty, cattle are marriage, friend is wife, grief is daughter, light is the son in the great heavens. The husband enters the wife having become the embryo in the womb of the wife who becomes the mother. He is born again in the tenth month after being a new (being). Therefore the wife is called Jaya, because he (husband) is born again.....There are no heavenly region for the sonless man." "To a childless being there is no world; of this all creatures, however low are aware. Hence it is that the son approaches even the mother and the sister." (the same). The Hindu view is that the son is the reproduction of one's self, and hence he is entitled to take up one's burden of responsibilities. "From the several limbs (of my body) art thou produced, from my heart art thou born; thou art 'self' called a son; mayst thou live a hundred autumns." The Hindu idea is that there are three big debts on all persons; for one of these a son is quite essential.[18] Here is a description of संप्रदान ceremony, when the father gives over his charge to his son. "There are three worlds : the world of men, the world of fathers, the world of the gods. The world of men is conquered only by a son and not by other work. By work, the world of the fathers, and by learning the world of the gods is conquered. The world of the gods is the best of the worlds, therefore they praise learning above all. Now about the giving of charge. When he thinks he is dying, he says to the son :–'You are Brahma, you are the Yajna, you are the Loka.' The son answers :–'I am Brahma (i.e.I shall study the Vedas); I am the Yajna (i.e. I shall perform the Yajnas); I am the Lokas' (i.e. I shall by getting a son conquer the world of men, by performing meritorious works conquer the world of ancestors, and by learning, conquer the world of gods."[19] "And because the son rescueth ancestors from hell called Put, therefore, hath he been called by the self-create himself Puttra (the rescuer from Put.)"[20] It is not only necessary to have sons but grandsons and great-grandsons. In fact, the mandate is "Don't sever the thread of the human species." (प्रजातन्तुं मा व्यवच्छेत्सी:) " By a son one conquereth the three worlds. By a son's son, one enjoyeth eternity, and by a grandson's son, great-grandfathers enjoy everlasting happiness."[21] It is needless to point to the natural agreeableness of a child. But the question arises whether children should be desired as objects of pure religious interest or secular interest or both. In the Vedic period, we hear of an undoubted sanction for many children. "Vouchsafe to her ten sons and make her husband the eleventh man."[22] In the Mahabharata we read that: "The wise say that he that hath one son hath no son."[23] Manu draws the distinction between the first son whose birth is necessitated by religious considerations and the other sons who are there owing to the lust of the parents. "He (i.e. the eldest son) on whose birth the debt (to the manes) is discharged and the father obtains immortality is called the son according to virtue (धर्मज:) the rest are sons of lust (कामज:)"[24] If the line threatens to fail, sons could be adopted; but in the Rigveda we find that adoption was not popular "Agni, no son is he who springs from others... Unwelcome for adoption is the stranger, one to be thought of as another's offspring. Though grown familiar by continual presence."[25]

The choice of the partner often lay in the hands of the bride or the bridegroom in the Vedic period. "Embrace, another, Yama; let another, even as the wood-bine rings the tree enfold thee. Win thou his heart and let him win thy fancy and he shall form with thee the best alliance."[26] The selection of girls was not always happy; "Many a woman is attracted by the wealth of him who seeks her. But the woman who is of gentle nature and of graceful form, selects among many, her own loved one as her husband."[27] It was often clearly recognised that the maiden's wishes should but be a matter of indifference in the marriage transaction. "Manu does not applaud the practice of a girl living with a person whom she does not like. Living as wife with a person whom she does not like, leads to disgrace and sin."[28] The Brahmin is to marry a girl who is not unwilling to marry him.[29] "One is certainly one's own friend, and one certainly may depend upon one's own self. Therefore, according to the ordinance, thou canst certainly bestow thyself."[30] Devayani says to her father : "This, O father, is the son of Nahusha. He took hold of my hand when I was in distress. I bow to thee. Bestow me unto him. I shall not wed any other person in the world."[31] An instance, which we have already quoted, refers to a lady who asserts herself so far as to remain unmarried. "Though her sire had been for giving her away to a husband, she yet did not wish for marriage, for she did not see a husband that could be worthy of her."[32] Savitri's father says to her: "Daughter, the time for bestowing thee is come! yet none asketh me. Do thou (therefore) thyself seek for a husband equal to thee in qualities. That person, who may be desired by thee, should be notified to me by thee. Do thou choose thy husband as thou likest. I shall bestow thee with deliberation."[33] Manu also points out circumstances in which a girl is justified in making her own selection of a husband. "A girl, who has attained puberty, shall wait (unmarried in her father's house) for three years (after the appearance of her first flow); after that she shall take a husband of her own caste and status. For taking a husband herself, a girl, not given away in marriage at the proper time by her father, acquires no demerit, nor does the man who takes her as his wife."[34]

The following passages from the Kamasutras of Vatsayana throw some light on the prevalence of courtship in Ancient India. "III. According to Ghotakmukha, a man should marry the woman whom he deems likely to make him happy, if he can do so without incurring the censure of his friends. IV. The proper persons to present the suit are the father and mother of the young man, and their connections : friends, too, on both sides who are likely to be trusted V. Such friends should din into the ears of the girl's mother and father, the faults observed and by them foretold, of other suitors for her hand; when they see an inclination to consent, they should cultivate that by dwelling on the good qualities, personal and hereditary of their man. Let them dwell very specially on such of his advantages as are likely to commend themselves to the girl's mother....X. Let him give up, who, when the wooers come to woo, is found asleep, in tears, or out....XI. He will be a happy husband who marries the woman on whom his heart and his eyes are set. Let a man not think of any other : So some say. XII. Accordingly, when a girl is of an age to be given in marriage, her parents should dress her well. Every afternoon she should play with the girls of her acquaintance, always faultlessly got up. At a sacrifice or a marriage, or wherever people come together, care should be taken to show her off. So also at festivals. For she is of the nature of merchandise. XIII. When men fair to look on, conscious in speech and accompanied by their connections come to propose marriage, the parents of the girl should receive them hospitably, and on some pretext or another show them the girl in her ornaments. They should come to no decision as to giving the girl before they have consulted the oracles.... Here ends the chapter on wooing."[35]

The question of guardianship as regards marriage arises only in connection with girls. Men are generally free to contract marriages for themselves; but if they are minors, the consent of parents or guardians is necessary. Even if a man is not a minor, it is a matter of duty for him, though one of legal obligation, to marry with the permission of the parents or elders. "With their permission (of parents) he should take a wife....[36] In the case of females, persons who are fit to be guardians are mentioned. "The father, parental grandfather, brother, kinsmen, and mother, being of sound mind, are the persons to give away a damsel–the latter respectively on failure of the preceding."[37]

Hindus have a custom of betrothment, according to which a verbal promise is exchanged between the two parties as regards their future marriage. It does not create a positive obligation to marry.[38] Yajnavalkya thinks that if a better husband is found betrothal is void.[39] It is important, therefore, to note that mere verbal gift cannot be the basis of legal marriage. "The nuptial Mantras import the status of a wife, and the rite of Saptapadi (walking seven steps), gone through by the bride completes the creation of wifehood."[40] Devala says that marriage ceremony is necessary in the case of all the three castes even when the marriage has been consummated previously by the Gandharva form.[41] Narada also takes the same view.[42] The Mahabharata also endorses this position. "The engagement made by the kinsmen of a girl is, no doubt, binding and sacred. But the engagement that is made by the wedder and the wedded with the aid of Mantras is very much more so."[43]

Eight types of marriage are distinguished. These are: The Brahma, Daiva, Arsha, Prajapatya, Asura, Gandharva, Rakshasa and Paishacha.[44] The first four are proper for the Brahmins; the Rakshasa and Gandharva forms are specially appropriate for the Kshatriyas; and the Asura for the Vaishyas and Shudras, "The form (of marriage) in which a well-attired bride, decorated with ornaments, is given in marrige to an erudite and worthy bridegroom, especially invited by the bride's father himself to receive her is called Brahma. The form of marriage in which the bride is given in marriage to the person duly officiating as a priest at a Vedic sacrifice, which is being celebrated, is called Daiva by the holy sages. The lawful form (of marrige) in which a bride on the receipt of an ox and a cow, or of two oxen and two kine for the performance of religious sacrifices, is duly given in marriage to the bridegroom according to the ordinance, is called Arsha. The form, in which after having worshipped the bridegroom, the bride is given to him in marriage, with the injunction, 'Let both of you jointly discharge the duties of a householder', is called Prajapatya. The form is which the bridegroom, on paying money to her father and to herself, out of the promptings of his own desire, receives the bride in marriage is called Asura. The form, in which, for the reason of a reciprocal marriage of hearts, the bridegroom is mated with the bride, is called Gandharva. It originates from a couple's passionate desire of being united with each other. The form of marriage, in which the bridegroom by killing or hurting the guardians or relations of the bride, and by forcing open the doors of her house, forcibly carries her away weeping and screaming, is called Rakshasa. The form, in which the bride when alone, asleep, senseless, intoxicated or delirious with wine, is ravished by the bridegroom, is called Pishacha, the eighth and the most sinful form of marriage."[45]

The significance of the marriage ceremony lies in the Mantras. The bridegroom with his party goes to the house of the bride where the ceremony takes place.[46] A cow used to be slain for the entertainment of guests.[47] The bridegroom accepts the hand of the bride and hence the ceremony is called the acceptance of the hand. They go round the fire and walk seven steps, at each step reciting verses. The husband says : "I seize thy hand and we may be blessed with offspring, that thou mayset live to old age with me thy husband Bhaga, Aryamana, Savitri, Purandhi, the gods have given thee to me that we may rule our house. This am I; that art thou, the heaven I, the earth thou, the Saman I, the Rik thou. Come! Let us join together. Let us unite our sperm that we may generate a male child, for the sake of the increase of wealth, of blessed offspring, of strength. Bountiful Indra, bless this woman with sons and with a happy lot. Give her ten sons. Let her husband be the eleventh person in the house."[48] The wife says looking at the polar star: "Firm art thou: May I.N.N. become firm in the house of N.N. my husband.[49] After the circumambulation of fire, the husband says to his wife: "With seven steps we have become friends. May I attain to friendship with thee. May I not be separated from thy friendship. Mayest thou be not separated from my friendship."[50] Brahmin women should sit by the bride's side pronouncing auspicious words (such as) "A mother of valiant sons! A mother of living sons! A living husband's wife!"[51] For three nights "they (husband and wife) should both avoid saline or pungent food and should sleep together on the ground, without having conjugal intercourse."[52] After three nights have passed, they should cohabit according to some teacher. According to others, the time of cohabiting is after her monthly illness.[53]

Marriage by capture, marriage by purchase and marriage by choice are subjects of frequent discussions; and conflicting judgments are often given on these subjects. "Other forms of marriage are seen, practised by men, such as marrying girls after abducting them by force, from amidst their kinsmen.

Those persons who have sexual intercourse with a maiden, after reducing her to subjection by force, are regarded as perpetrators of sin. They have to sink in darkest hell.[54] Nevertheless, instances of marriage by capture are often highly approved of.[55] The very words Vivaha, Udvaha testify to the prevalence of this type of marriage. "She is the best of women whose garments are pure. Therefore, let him approach a woman whose garments are pure or whose fame is pure and address her. If she does not give in, let him, as he likes, beat her with sticks or with his hand, and overcome her saying, 'With manly strength and glory I take away thy glory'."[56] Bhishma says: "But the sages have said that the wife is clearly to be prized who is taken away by force, from amidst the concourse of princes and kings invited to a self-choice. Therefore, Ye Monarchs, I bear away these maidens hence by force!"[57] "In the case of Kshatriyas that are brave, a forcible abduction for purposes of marriage is applauded as the learned have said. Therefore, O Arjuna, carry away this my beautiful sister by force, for who knows what she may do in a self-choice!"[58] Perhaps it is necessary to make a distinction between violent abduction and the establishment of superior strength.

Marriage by mutual choice, the Gandharva form, is specially recommended for Kshatriyas. Dushyanta's union with Shakuntala, even before marriage had this foundation; and it afterwards secured the approval of Kashyapa. "Amiable one' what hath done by thee to-day in secret without having waited for me, viz. intercourse with a man, hath not been destructive of thy virtue. Indeed, union according to Gandharva form of a wishful woman with a man full of desire without Mantras of any kind is the best for Kshatriyas."[59] Here it may be remarked that the subsequent repudiation of Shakuntala at the hands of Dushyanta must have discredited this form of marriage; and the need of publicity became sufficiently apparent. A special type of Gandharva form was called Swayamvara (self-choice). Sita and Draupadi secured their husbands through Swayamvara. In this type of marriage, a large assemblage of princes was called together and the girl accepted the husband suitable to her. Savitri was asked to select her husband, and was required to go in search for him. But this institution was pronounced doubtful in its results.[60]

Marriage by purchase, though sometimes approved, is mostly condemned. Society was gradually passing from the former stage to the latter. The worthless son-in-law had to pay a heavy price for a wife.[61] Bhishma says to the king of Madra: "O king, this, no doubt, is virtue. God himself has said it. Thy ancestors have observed the custom. There is no fault to find in it. It is also well-known that this custom with regard to family dignity has the approval of the wise and the good." Bhishma then 'gave unto Shalya much gold, both coined and uncoined, and precious stones of various colours by thousands and elephants and horses and cars, and much cloth and many ornaments, and gems and pearls, and corals. And Shalya accepting with a cheerful heart those precious gifts then gave away his sister decked in ornaments unto that bull of the race."[62] The practice, however, is unequivocally condemned in other passages. "The erudite father of a girl shall not take anything by way of Shulka (price) from her bridegroom. By taking a dowry out of greed, he becomes the seller of his offspring"[63] Dowries constitute a sale and the sale of a girl is not allowed even to the lowest castes.[64]

We find : "wedding a girl after purchasing her at a high cost and after gratifying the cupidity of her kinsmen," is the practice of the Asuras. Maidens married in the commercial way of sale and purchase cannot attain to the status of wives. "A wife should never be purchased. Nor should a father sell his daughter. Only those persons of sinful soul, who are possessed of cupidity, and who sell and purchase female slaves for making serving women, regard the status of wife as capable of arising from the gift and acceptance of dower."[65]

Parents generally managed the marriage affairs of thier children. But they were not allowed to be arbitrary in this matter. Responsibility as regards the disposal of a daughter was recognised as very great. "Wherever a daughter is conferred, a daugher stays placing in uncertainty the three races (of father, mother, and husband) to which she is related."[66] That, is upon a proper wedlock depended not only the happiness of the parties concerned, but the future of the three lines or races. Hence certain considerations of propriety are not to be neglected. The quesiton of age of the parties entering in to marriage is not a little important. It is clear that early marriages were unknown in the Vedic period. "Hither hath this woman come, desiring a husband, desiring a wife I have come."[67] There are numerous reference to the practice of courtship, to the wife keenly desiring a suitable husband, and to the husband seeking a suitable wife. All this presupposes full development. "Enjoyable is she to suitors, agreeable at festivals; be there quickly good fortune to thee in a husband."[68] " May this woman, O Agni, find a husband......giving birth to sons; she shall become chief consort, having gone to her husband, let her, having good fortune, bear rule."[69] Only mature ladies long for husbands; only mature ladies are courted by lovers; only mature girls can discriminate between suitable partners or unsuitable partners; only mature girls can be expected to exercise rule over the household. Again, an examination of the marriage ceremonies and Mantras shows that both the bridegroom and the bride were really active partners in the affair, understanding fully the nature of the sacrament and the responsibilities involved in it. The three nights Brahmacharya had no meaning unless the parties were mature; and the act of cohabitation which used to follow clearly indicates the full growth of the parties. It appears that marriages were encouraged at a comparatively tender periods in the time of the Ramayana. Rama was nearly sixteen at the time of marriage.[70] Sita says to Ravana that she stayed for twelve years in the house of the Ikshwakus, and at that time she was eighteen; this means that she was married at six.[71] But other statements confirm the impression that she was fit for marriage at that time. Sita says to Anusuya; "Seeing me fit for the company of a husband, (पतिसंयोगसुलभंवय:) my father in distress was plunged in thought."[72] In the case of Rama, too, although he was sixteen, he was capable of wielding a weapon which no other kings or princes could wield. Other evidence also shows that girls were mostly full-grown before they were wedded. From the accounts of Savitri and Damayanti seeking husbands for themselves it may be reasonably assumed that they were mature. Nagnika girls are considered specially suitable in the Sutras.[73] Now the term is translated into 'naked' by many writers. But as Dr. Ghosh says: "नग्निकां मैथुनार्हाम् is the commentary of Matridatta. Nagnika, therefore, in ancient times meant a young but mature girl. It is difficult to believe that Nagnika meant a naked girl, having regard to the fact that the Mahabharata advocates the marriage of a girl, Nagnika of sixteen."[74] Manu recommends early marriages, but has no serious objection to marriage after puberty. "A girl, even before having attained the proper age of marriage, should be duly married to a handsome, qualified husband of her own caste, (if such an opportunity occurs.)"[75] "A girl, who has attained puberty, shall wait (unmarried in her father's house) for three years (after the appearance of her first flow); after that, she shall take a husband of her own caste and status."[76] "A man aged thirty years, shall marry a maiden of twelve who pleases him, or a man of twenty-four a girl eight years of age; if (the performance of) his duties would (otherwise) be impeded, (he must marry) sooner."[77] The texts of some of the later Smritis show that the standards of age in the case of girls had quite fallen.

It is true that ancient Hindu thought at certain epochs deliberately considered love as a very subordinate element in the formation of marriage unions. But in very early period, as well as in the classical period, mutual love was regarded as the most essential condition of all healthy marriages. "Let that (man) love me; being dear let him love me; ye gods send forth love; let yon (man) burn for me."[78] "Let thy heart dry upon me, then let (thy) mouth dry up; then dry thou up by loving me; then go thou about dry-mouthed."[79] "The eyes of us two (be) of honey-aspect; our face (be) ointment; put thou me within thy heart; may our mind verily be together."[80] "Let the Creator assign to this spinster a husband that is according to her wish."[81] The bridegroom recites the following text when he accepts the bride : "Who gave her? To whom did he give her? Love gave her. To love he gave her. Love was the giver. Love was the taker. Love has pervaded the ocean. With Love I accept her. Love! May this be thine." In the Jatakas we read instances of unions of various types justified on the ground of mutual love. "Whomsoever the lover loves, be it a low Chandali, all are alike : in love there is no unlikeness." The king Vasudeva married Jambavati–a Chandali, because he had fallen in love with her.[82] Apastamba has laid down love as the most necessary presupposition of happy wedded life. "He will be a happy husband who marries the woman on whom his heart and eye are set. Let not a man think of any other; so some say." (quoted in Vatsayana, Malati-Madhava and others.) The following remarks from Vatsayana are interesting. "A poor man, however excellent, a man who has all other virtues but is of mean birth, a rich man if he be a neighbour, a man who is not his own master, and one or two others, need not hope for any favourable answer to any deputation they may send. They are accordingly enjoined to woo the girls for theselves. They get minute directions as to how to do this, and are in the end warned that, however great their success may be, they must not expect their lady to confess their love. 'For all the world knows that a girl, however much she may be in love, will not herself, make any overtures to the man.' Accordingly he must be quick to read the signs by which she will betray her passion....It ought to interest the sufferer of the present day to know that Vatsayana held that the girl might be taken to be yielding if it was found that she could not look her lover in the face, and was put out when he looked at her, if she liked to be in his company, and made his friends her friends, if she gave him the flower from her hair and made a point of wearing the flowers he sent her."[84] An ancient verse refers to various stages of love between man and woman. The first stage is complete absorption in each other's personality. There is one person–an integral unit. (अविभिन्ना तनु:) The next stage marks the growth of dualism. The husband is called a 'lover' (प्रेयान्), and the wife a 'beloved' (प्रियतमा). But when they grow married, they begin to be less and less idolatrous with regard to each other. Then the former is called a 'husband' (नाथ); and the latter a 'wife' (कलत्र). Readers of Sanskrit classical literature must be familiar with the romantic pictures of the love-marriages of Shakuntala and Dushyanta, Malati and Madhav, Urvashi and Pururava, Kadambari and Chandraketu, Mahasweta and Pundarika. It is not meant that in the other periods love as an element of married life was ignored, but in most cases it followed rather than preceded the union. This love between husband and wife may be distinguished from that between the lover and his beloved; the former belongs to this chapter; the latter will fittingly come later on.

The selection of husband or wife being a solemn duty, we find various considerations urged which ought to enter into all reasonable choice. Equality of rank and status is always desirable. "Social games,....marriages, and intercourse generally, should be with a man's equals, not with those either above him or below him." "Where the love between husband and wife adds lustre to both, and is a source of joy to both families, that is the only marriage which is approved."[84a] Here only in the case of mutual love an exception is allowed. Love transcends all distinctions of rank and condition. Purity and nobility of race were often looked to. Both Vasishtha and Janaka entertain each other with long accounts of the pedigrees of their respective families. The ancient Rishis fully realised the value of the problem of heredity and hence they emphasized this question. It does not, however, follow that this racial question proved a veritable bar to healthy interfusion of blood. Manu says that the jewel of a female may be taken even from a low family. (स्त्रीरत्नं दुकुलादपै) There must be equality not only of status and race; there must be quality of charaters also. Kalidas says with regard to the hero and heroine: "Thou (Dushyanta) art the foremost of the great; Shakuntala is the very embodiment of the spirit of good-will. The Creator does not deserve any blame as the union of the bride and bridegroom of equal excellence is brought about."[84b] Indeed, if a girl cannot find out a husband of her own mould, she is free to lead a single life. "The Rishis have find the command upon all men that maidens should never be bestowed upon persons unless the latter happen to be most fit or eligible."[84c] "But the maiden though she had attained puberty should rather stop in her father's house death than that he should give her to a men destitute of good qualities."[85]

Now we will refer to certain special consideration which determine the choice husbands and wives. "Marry a daughter to an intelligent person."[86] "A bridegroom should be endued with all the accomplishments, be of the same caste and social standing, well-read in the Vedas, carefully examined about his manly power, youthful, intelligent, and agreeable to all the people."[87] Narada mentions the following defects disqualifying a person for being a suitable husband : "Madness, loss of caste, impotence, misery, being forsaken by his relatives and the two first faults of a maiden (in the above text, i.e. affliction with a chronic or hateful disease and deformities.)"[88] "In order that the girl may be happy all her life, and purity of the race may be preserved, she should be bestowed on a well-qualified husband. High caste, learning, young age, powers, health, many-sidedness, character, and wealth, these are the eight qualifications of a husband. A girl should not be married to one who stays at a great distance or who is illiterate or who is hungering after salvation, or who is very great, or very brave, or very poor. She should not be given to one who stays very far or very near, to one extremely rich or poor, to one devoid of character or intelligence."[89]

Equal attention is to be paid to the selection of a girl.[90] "Therefore, let a man select a girl who is such an one as follows.

She should be of good family. Her father and mother should both be alive. She should be younger, and younger by at least three years than himself. She should be the daughter of a house that reverences the sacred ordinances, that is rich, the members of which are kindly disposed one to the other and that is rich in adherents. Her connections both on the mother's and the father's side should be influential. She should have beauty, virtue, and auspicious marks. Her teeth, nails, ears, hair, eyes, and breasts must be neither too large nor too small, and she must not have lost any of these parts. She must be of sound constitution.[91] The young man should be of the same kind; but in addition he must have completed the prescribed course of study."[92] The girl must be decidedly younger in age than her husband.[93] Seniority in age on her part conflicts with the Hindu ideas of obedience to a husband. While manliness and learning are emphasized as the best qualities of a husband, beauty and grace are deemed the best qualities of a girl. The Hindus hold that there is some subtle but real connection between outward form and inward soul, that the two generally correspond with each other. (आकृतिर्गुणान्कथयति।) "Face is the index of the qualities." "A female having the upper lip very high, and the hair coarse at the ends, is fond of quarrelling. Generally speaking, vices will be found with the ugly, whereas the virtues reside where beauty dwells."[94] Above all, the girl must be a virgin. It was, therefore, emphasized that a girl who has no brothers should not be married, because her character could not be relied upon.[95] "The nuptial texts are applied solely to virgins, (and) nowhere among men, to females who have lost their virginity, for such (females) are excluded from religious ceremonies."[96]

All the above texts are directory and not imperative. Marriages contracted on the above basis were approved of; but those which violated the conditions were not invalid. We shall now mention the actual limitations on marriage. There is no age disqualification in the case of Hindus; all minors are eligible for marriage. It is, indeed, considered advisable that a twice-born man should marry after his period of studentship.[97] But as this ideal has disappeared the age limit, too, has changed accordingly. Even insane persons and eunuchs were considered fit to contract marriages. "A eunuch, a degraded person, a person born blind or deaf, an idiot, or those devoid of any organ, shall not take any share in the paternal property...But if these eunuchs, etc. should be inclined to marry, and if the wife of the eunuch should raise up a son to him by a man legally appointed, that son and the issue of such as have children shall be capable of inheriting."[98] However, as this method of raising offspring is not warranted now, it may be questioned how far such marriages may be allowed. It is an offence to marry when one's elder brother is unmarried; but if the elder brother is not in a position to marry owing to some infirmity, there is no harm.[99] Similarly, all girls are qualified to marry; but a girl must not be married before her elder sister's marriage is accomplished.

Almost all persons are held competent to contract marriage, but not with any and every person. Absolute disqualification there is little or none; relative disqualification there is. Here then are two main questions; how far it is permissible to marry outside one's caste; and within what limits one cannot marry within one's family. It is not necessary to confine oneself to one's own caste for marriage; a man may marry any women of the lower caste but it was not good for live to marry a woman of the higher caste. "A Shudra woman is the wife of a Shudra, a Vaishya can marry a Shudra or Vaishya wife; a Kshatriya can take a Shudra, Vaishya, or a Kshatriya wife, and a Brahmin can marry a Shudra, Vaishya, Kshatriya or a Brahmin wife."[100] Marriage with a Shudra wife gradually fell into utter contempt.[101] Marriage with persons of the same caste, however was the ideal. "A girl belonging to his own caste is recommended to a Brahmin for holy wedlock; for desire, he may take from any of the three remaining castes, her precedence being according to her caste."[102] Marriages of the loose, miscellaneous type are condemned; and the progeny of all hybrid unions is said to degenerate. "In the destruction of a family the immemorial family traditions perish in the perishing of tradition, lawlessness over comes the whole family. Owing to predominance of lawlessness, the women of the family become corrupt; women corrupted, there ariseth caste-confusion."[103] Even the marriages of the males of the twice-born castes, although allowed, involve some degradation to the offsprings of such unions. The children do not belong to the castes of their fathers but of their mothers.[104] The children born out of the unions of females of the higher stock with the males of the lower stock (प्रतिलोमजः) are the low-born ones.[105] It is possible for the children of the mixed unions to rise to the status of the higher castes by carefully marrying in the higher castes. "If the daughter of a Brahmin by his Shudra wife is married to a Brahmin, and the daughter of that union is again married to a Brahmin, and so on uninterruptedly up to the seventh generation in the female line, then at the seventh generation the issue of such union is divested of its Parashava caste and becomes a Brahmin."[106] The children begotten by Aryan men on non-Aryan women become Aryans; but those begotten by non-Aryan men on Aryan women remain non-Aryans.[107]

The limits of the circle of relationship within which marriage was forbidden became gradually more and more marked. The dialogue of Yama and Yami in the Rig-Veda is very interesting; it is a very early expression of the growing consciousness to avoid near blood-relations. Yama says to Yami :–

I will not fold mine arms about thy body; they call it sin when one comes near his sister.[108]

Rules about the prohibition to marry within one's Gotra (family) were not crystallised in the time of the Brahmanas. "In the third or fourth generation we unite."[109] But the Sutras clearly establish the position that marriage within the same Gotra or primitive stock was not allowed to the twice-born ones.[110] "A girl with whom there is no relationship unseemly for marriage should be married. The relationship such as make the pair like parent and child to each other is relationship unseemly for marriage, e.g. the daughter of the wife's sister, the sister of the wife of the paternal uncle. Some exclude the mother's Gotra."[101] The point of importance is that owing to the existence of the joint-family system, persons of some six generations often stay together under the same roof as a group; and if marriage is allowed within these degrees, there is likelihood of the sanctity of family ties being weakened.

The question of competence to marry, raises the problem whether a husband, who has one living wife, is capable of entering on a new marriage and whether a wife, who has one husband, is capable of having two or more? In other words, are polygamy and polyandry allowed to the Hindus and if so under what limitations? The Hindus are monogamous rather than polygamous people; but they are not rigid adherents to the institution of monogamy. In the Vedic period, many wives were allowed; Manu had ten wives.[112] A reference to rival wives brings out the same fact. "Like rival wives on every side enclosing ribs oppress me more."[113] Chyavana was made "Lord of youthful maidens."[114] "I have subdued as conqueror these rivals, these my fellow-wives, that I may hold imperial away over this Hero and the folk."[115] The king has four wives attributed to him, the Mahishi[116] the Parivrikti[117] the Vavata[118] and the Palaguli.[119] The first is the chief wife, the second means one having no son, the third is the favourite, and the fourth is the daughter of the last of the court officials. "Three wives are allowed to a Brahmin in accordance with the order of castes. Two to a Kshatriya and one to a Vaishya. One Shudra wife bedsides, to all, according to some teachers without using the Mantras."[120] Clearly the sanction for polygamy exists; but is it the ideal? The ideal is of one man and wife, known in the Hindu books as एकपत्नीव्रत. Manu says that marriage with the first wife is for Dharma; only pure inclination is responsible for other wives.[121] Association for the performance of religious rites is allowed only to the wives of one's own caste. All this evidence shows that the permission to marry many wives was a mere concession to human nature. It is not to be taken seriously. However, polygamy was quite rampant in the royal families. Dasharatha had four principal wives, but he had three hundred and fifty other wives.[122] Rama's single-minded devotion to one wife has become proverbial, perhaps because the contrast it afforded to the practice of other people. The marriage of only one wife is expressly applauded in the Ramayana; it is equal to the merit acquired by penance or study of the Vedas or gift of land or Agnihotra-ceremony.[123]

Polyandry is entirely opposed to all the Hindu scriptures and traditions. It is unvedic. There is no mention of it in the Vedas; it is clearly repudiated therein. "As in one piece of wood there may be two strings, therefore, a man may have two wives. As there cannot be one string for pieces of wood for Yagna, so a woman cannot have two husbands."[124] "A man may have several wives but a woman cannot have many husbands."[125] "Polygamy in men is an act of great merit. In women it is very sinful to betake to a second husband after the first."[126] The fact of Draupadi's marriage to five Pandavas raises the question of existence of polyandry. Vyasa says that the practice had become obsolete. Drupada says "it is sinful in my opinion, being opposed to both usage and the Vedas. Nowhere have I seen many men having one wife between them. The illustrious ones also of the former ages never had such a usage." Yudhishthira replies :"My tongue never uttereth an untruth, and my heart never inclineth to what is sinful. What my heart approves can never be sinful. I have heard in the Purana that a lady by name Jatila, the foremost of all virtuous women, belonging to the race of Gotama, had married seven Rishis. So also an ascetic's daughter born of a tree had in former times united herself in marriage with ten brothers, bearing the same name of Prachota and who were all of souls exalted by asceticism." Yudhishthira takes his stand upon obedience to the command of his mother. (who had unknowingly asked the brothers to divide their alms) The story is mythologically explained by Vyasa. The case of Draupadi remains, therefore, an isolated one, having no rootage in the Vedic past, nor any future after it. The inference, however, is possible that the practice was not entirely unknown in those times.[127]

Under certain circumstances, a sort of divorce is possible in the Hindu system. Generally speaking, in life and in death, the husband and wife are one; separation in their case is inconceivable. Once married, always married. The wife is declared to be one with the husband. "Neither by sale nor by repudiation is a wife released from her husband. Only once can a partition of an estate be made, only once a girl can be given away in marriage, and only once can a thing be gifted. Each of these three things can be made only once."[128] "Let mutual fidelity continue till death, this in a few words may be considered as the supreme law between husband and wife."[129] But this rigidity of extreme theory is modified in various ways. The Hindu theory allows Tyaga or separation, which however, does not amount to dissolution of marriage. "In the event of one's wife becoming a drunkard or faithless, hostile, invalid, extremely hot-tempered, or spend thrift, one shall marry a second wife. The husband of a sterile woman shall remarry on the eighth, the husband of a wife whose children die in infancy on the tenth, and the husband of a wife who has given birth to daughters only on the eleventh year of their respective marriages, while the husband of a harsh-tongued wife may remarry without the least delay. If a wife of good conduct, who is attached to the good of her lord, happens to be afflicted with (an incurable) disease, let her husband marry again with her consent; but he must not insult her under any circumstances whatever."[130] But a wife failing to nurse an insane, degraded, sexless or seedless husband, or one affiliated with a sinful disease, is not fit to be abandoned by that husband for that hostile conduct, nor the things which he might have presented to her can be taken from her.[131] All the authorities are agreed that a dutiful and son-bearing women, should not be abandoned. "(He who) abandons an obedient, attentive, son-bearing and sweet-speaking wife, should be compelled (by the king) to give her a third of his property. If poor, he should (be ordered to) maintain her."[132] Apastamba maintains that co-operation in religious duties absolutely consolidates woman's rights; she becomes a धर्मपत्नी. If the wife belongs to the same Gotra and comes within the prohibited degrees, she must be abandoned at once.

But it is not the husband alone who has the right to desert a wife; the wife is not entirely without her privileges. Here, too, pure theory requires that under all circumstances the wife must follow her husband. "Like a deity, a chaste wife shall always serve her husband, even if he be found devoid of learning, character, and conjugal fidelity."[134] But, as we have seen, a wife who neglects her husband who is mad or sinner or eunuch or diseased, is to be severely punished.[135] Parashara says: "If the husband be missing, or dead, or retired from the world, or impotent, or degraded, in these five calamities a women may take another husband."[136] Narada and Devala take the same view. Narada goes furthest in allowing separation and even marriage to a woman during the life of a husband. No wanton cause, however, justifies a divorce. "Husband and wife must not lodge a plaint against one another with their relations, or the king, when a quarrel has arisen through passion which has its root in jealousy or scorn. When husband and wife leave one another, from mutual dislike, it is a sin, except when a woman, who is kept under supervision, commits adultery."[137] Manu entitles a husband to repudiate a wife if a blemish, previously unsuspected, is afterwards detected in her.[138] Narada entitles a woman to seek another man if the former husband is found to be defective in a way not known before. "When a faultless lady has been married to a man who has a blemish unknown (before his marriage) and does not repair to another man (after discovering it), she shall be enjoined to do so by her relations. If she has no relations living, she shall go (to live with another man) of her own accord."[139] The usual cases of the disappearance or degradation or renunciation or death or impotence of her husband justify a woman to take to a second husband.[140] Here are his bold utterances. "For the wife of one who spills his semen, or whose semen is devoid of strength, though he may have discharged his marital duties, another husband must be procured after she has waited for half a year. Women are created for the sake of propagation, the wife being the field and the husband the giver of the seed. The field must be given to him who has seed. He who has no seed is unworthy to possess the field."[141]

Widow remarriage is perhaps a strictly Vedic institution. Niyoga or marriage of a widow with a husbands' brother when she had no child was recognised.[142] "Go up, O woman, to the world of the living; thou liest by this one who is deceased. Come! to him who grasps thy hand, thy second spouse, thou hast now entered into the relation of a wife to a husband."[143] The following verse refers to the union of the second husband with the woman even in the next life. "Whoever having gained a former husband, then gains another later on, if they shall give a goat with five rice-dishes, they shall not be separated."[144] In the time of Mahabharata the custom was very much prevalent. Vyasa himself creates sons on the basis of this institution. Manu represents both the old and the new view. "The wife of an elder is said to be like a preceptor's or superior's wife unto his younger brother, and the wife of a younger brother is said to be like unto a daughter-in-law to his elder brother. Except in the case of a failure of issues, an elder, by going unto the wife of his younger brother, or a younger brother by going unto the wife of his elder brother, even under an appointment, becomes degraded. In the absence of a son, a woman wishing to obtain progeny, shall lie down under an appointment, with a younger brother, or with a Sapinda relation of her husband, for the procreation of a son. A man appointed to procreate a son on a widow, shall anoint his person with clarified butter and silently procreate a son on her in the night; but he must not procreate a second son under any circumstances whatever."[145] In the verses which follow Manu condemns the custom absolutely. "Brahmins shall never allow a widow of their own to get a son procreated on her by any one under an appointment; by so engaging her one kills the eternal virtue."[146]

There is much difference of opinion as regards the proper place of widow-remarriage in the orthodox system. Remarriage of widows was a regular custom in the Vedic age. "Let these women without suffering the pain of widowhood, after obtaining husbands of their choice enter the house with collyrium and clarified butter. Let these married women without shedding tears, without being distressed with sickness, after wearing excellent ornaments first enter the house."[147] But the institution gradually underwent a change. Manu is evidently against the custom.[148] But he refers to such a thing : "the son, whom one's widow or deserted wife voluntarily gets procreated on her person by her second husband, is said to be the Paunarbhava (the son of a remarried woman) son of the latter. If that wife, with unruptured hymen, takes another husband, then the second husband lawfully marries her again."[149] Apastamba considers the marriage of a woman sinful. "If a man approaches a woman who had been married before they both commit sin. The son born is also sinful." Vasistha, Parashara, Narada, Devala have no objection to the remarriage of widows.[150] Vasishta recommends marriage to a near relative of the husband. "Of those who are connected (with her husband) by libations of water, funeral cake, birth and by family, each preceding person is more preferable. But if a member of her family survives, she shall certainly not go to a stranger."[151] Widows possess according to the Hindu theory the right to remarry but the strict orthodox view still looks upon all such marriages with horror and contempt. Manu's view remains current. "A son begotten by a man on another wife can never be called a son and nowhere a virtuous woman has been advised to take a second husband. A woman, who discarding a former though inferior husband, marries a better and a greater husband, for the second time, is condemned in society and is called a fore-enjoyed wife."[152] The general view clearly recommends to a widow strict spiritual adherence in death as well as in life to her former husband. "After the demise of her lord, let her control her passion by living on auspicious flowers, bulbs, and fruits, and never dream of taking the name of another man. Forbearing, self-controlled, and emulating the excellent virtues of chaste wives, let her pass the whole life in constant practice of asceticism. After the demise of her lord a virtuous wife, by taking to the life of asceticism may go to heaven even though not blessed with child, like the Brahmacharins."[153]

Manu makes no reference to the institution of Sati. In the Vedic literature, only once the custom is merely referred to. "This woman, choosing her husband's world lies down by thee that art departed, O mortal, continuing to keep (her) ancient duty; to her assign thou progeny and property."[154] The implication of progeny and property makes the verse quite ambiguous. The later Dharmashastras sometimes recommend the immolation of the widow on her husband's funeral pyre. "A widow, who immolates herself on the same funeral pile with her deceased husband resides in heaven for ten million years, which is the number of hairs on the human body."[155] "After the death of her husband, to preserve her chastity or to ascend the pile after him" are the alternatives before a widow.[156] The Brahmin widows are forbidden to die after their husbands. "The woman of Brahmin caste who follows her husband in death does not take either herself or her husband to heaven owing to her act of suicide."[157] Madhavacharya brands the practice as opposed plainly to the Vedas प्रत्यक्षश्रुतिविरुद्ध. It was a practice among the Kshatriyas mainly, and that, too, was never a universal one. Dasharatha's wives did not follow him; and this was quite common. When Madri and Kunti insist upon following their husband the sages said to them: "Following the husband in death is indeed good; but in your case it is difficult. A good lady on the death of her husband abides by celibacy, controls herself by penances and vows, thinks of her lord and saves herself, her husband, and her son. Hence in your case, continuance of life may be recommended."[158] There is a remarkable passage in the Kadambari which clearly anticipates the spirit of Akbar and Bentinck and exposes the futility and unscriptural character of the institution. Chandrapida says :

"This practice of self-immolation on the death of a relative is exceedingly fruitless. It is the path of the illiterate; it is the outcome of infatuation. It is due to rashness. It is the standpoint of the mean; it is a great mistake; it is downright folly–to abandon one's life when one's father or brother, or friend, or husband dies. If life does not go away of itself in such cases, it should not be artificially given up. Here if we think, we find the real motive is selfish, since one wants to remove by suicide the extreme grief. The act does not do any good to the dead. It does not raise him to life. It is not a means to either virtue or heaven. It does not avoid hell. It cannot secure re-union with the dead. The dead are led to altogether different world owing to the diversity of the deeds. While this person who commits suicide merely incurs sin. By living, one can do much good to the dead as well as oneself; by dying to neither."

References

1. Brishaspati. 70.
2. Shatatapa.VI. 36.
3. R. IV. 24. 38., Samvarta, 61-62. 64. 75.
4. Rg. II. 17. 7.
5. Av. I. 14. 3.
6. Rg. I. 117. 7.
7. M. IX. 89.
8. Av. I. 14. 3.
9. M. II. 67.
10. Shalya. 53. 5-14.
11. Kau. Br. U. II, 15, Sabha. 5. 116; M.IX, 96; Br. U.I, 4. 17.
12. Rg. VI. 61. 1.
13. Rg. V, 4. 10.
14. Rg. X, 45,
15. Rg. X. 15, 11.
16. Rg. III, 54. 18.
17. Rg. VIII, 8.
18. Tai. S. VI. 3. 10. 5, Sh. Br. I. 7, 2, 1, 2, 3.
19. Sh. Br. 14, 4. 3, 24-25.
20. Adi. 98. 18-21.
21. Adi. 98, 18-21.

22. Rg. X. 45.
23. Adi. 107, 69.
24. M. IX. 107.
25. Rg. VII. 4, 7, 8.
26. Rg. X. 10.14.
27. Rg. X. 27. 12 tr. R. Dutt.
28. Anu. 79. 25.
29. Anu. 79. 57.
30. Adi. 94. 13.
31. Adi. 75. 39-40
32. Shalya. 53. 7.
33. Vana. 294, 33-37.
34. M. IX. 90-92.
35. Quoted in Dr. Peterson's Article. J.B.B.R.A. Vol. XVIII.
36. Gr. H.I. 6. 19.1
37. Yaj. I. 63.
38. M. IX. 69.
39. Yaj. I. 65.
40. M. VIII. 227.
41. As quoted by Kulluka M. VIII. 226.
42. Narada. XII. 2-3.
43. Anu. 79. 27-29.
44. M. III. 21.
45. M. III. 27-34.
46. Rg. IV. 58. 59, Av. VI. 60.
47. Rg. X. 85. 13.
48. Gr. H. I. 6, 20-1-2.
49. Gr. G. II. 3.9.
50. Gr. H. I. 6. 21-2.
51. Gr. II. 7. 12.
52. Gr. G. II. 3. 12-15.
53. Gr. G.II. 5, 7-8.
54. Anu. 80, 18-23.
55. Rg. I. 112, 19, 116, 1, 117, 20.
56. Br. U. VI 4, 6-8.
57. Adi. 109. 17-18.
58. Adi. 239, 22-4.
59. Adi. 94, 59-60.
60. Adi. 239, 22-24, 245, 4-6.
61. Rg. I. 109, 20.

62. Adi. 122, 12, 16.
63. M. III. 51.
64. M. IX. 98.
65. Anu. 79, 46-48.
66. R. VII. 9, 8-10; Udyoga. 97.15-16.
67. Av. II. 30. 4-5.
68. Av. II. 36. 1.
69. Av. II, 36. 3.
70. R. I. 20.2.
71. R. III. 47. 4.11.
72. R. II. 118. 34
73. H. Gr. S.I.I. 19.3 M. Gr. S.I. 7-8.
74. Hindu Law p. 707.
75. M. IX. 88.
76. M. IX. 90.
77. M. IX. 94.
78. Av. VI. 130.2.
79. Av. VI. 139.2.
80. Av. VII. 36.
81. Av. VI. 60. 3.
82. No. 546; Cowell and and Rouse V.VI.
83. यस्यां मनश्चक्षुषोर्निबन्धस्तस्यामृद्धिः। नेतरामाद्रियेत।
84. Dr. Peterson, J.B. B.R.A. XVIII.

84a. Verses quoted in Vatsayana.

84b. Sh. IV.

84c. Anu. 79. 37.

85. M. IX. 89.
86. A. Gr. S. 1-3.
87. Yaj. I. 55.
88. Narada 12. Ch. 2-4.
89. Brihat Parashariya 4. 17. 26-27.
90. M. III. 6-10.
91. Mutatis Mutandis.
92. Vatsayana.
93. Yaj. I. 52.
94. Varaha Mihira. Brihat Sanhita. Quoted by Dr. Peterson.
95. M. Gr. S. I. 7-8.
96. M. V. 151.
97. Manu. III. 4.
98. M. IX. 201. 203.

99. M. III. 171; Atri. 103-4-5-6; Kat. 6. 2-8.
100. M. III. 13.
101. M. III. 14-16.
102. M. III. 12.
103. Bg. I. 40-44.
104. M. X. 6.
105. M. X. 41.
106. M. X. 64, Y. I. 96.
107. M. X. 67.
108. Rg. X. 10.
109. S. Br. I. 8. 3. 2.
110. H. Gr. S. I.I. 19. 2; Gobhila Gr. S. 3, 4, 1, 2, 5, 7.
111. A. Gr. Parishista.
112. M. Sam. I. 5, 8.
113. Rg. I. 105, 8, X. 33, 2.
114. Rg. I. 116, 10.
115. Rg. X. 159. 4-6.
116. S. Br. V. 3, 1, 4.
117. S. Br. V. 3, 1, 13.
118. S. Br. XIII. 2, 6, 5.
119. S. Br. XIII. 4, 1, 8.
120. M. Gr. S. I. 5-10, I. 5; Vishnu. 24, 4.
121. M. III. 12.
122. R. II. 34, 13.
123. R. II. 64, 43.
124. Ta. S. 6. 6. 4. 3.
125. Ai. Br. 3. 2. 12.
126. Adi. 172. 46.
127. See Brahaspati. XXVII. 20; Apastamba. II. XXVII. 2.
128. M. IX. 45-47.
129. M. IX. 101.
130. M. IX. 80-82.
131. M. IX. 77-79.
132. Yaj. I. 76; Narada. 12. 95.
133. Kulluka. Manu. III. 5. 11.
134. M. V. 154.
135. M. IX. 79.
136. Parashara. IV. 26.
137. Narada. XII. 89, 90.
138. M. IX. 72-73.

139. Narada. XII. 96.
140. Narada. XII. 97-101.
141. Narada. XII. 16, 20.
142. Rg. X. 18. 8; X. 40-2; A. Gr. S. IV. 2. 18.
143. Av. XVIII. 3. 2.
144. Av. IX. S. 27.
145. M. IX. 57. 60.
146. M. IX. 64-66.
147. Rg. X. 18, 7.
148. M. IX. 65, quoted above.
149. M. IX. 175, 176.
150. Vasistha. XV; Narada XII. 46; Manu. IX. 176; Vishnu. XV. 8.
151. Vasistha. XV.
152. M. V. 162, 165.
153. M. V. 157, 158, 161.
154. Av. XVIII. 3, 1.
155. Parashara. IV. 28.
156. Vishnu. XXV. 14.
157. Angiras. Dr. Ghosh, 671.
158. Adi. 134, 83-86.

Chapter - IX

HUSBAND AND WIFE

The Hindu view regards husband and wife as one person not two and hence requires on their part complete identity of feelings, interests, and duties. Even the Vedas recognise that the essence of wedded life lies in the profound reciprocal love between the parties to marriage. "So may the universal gods, so may the waters join our hearts; may the Mataraishwan, Dhatar, and Deshtri together bind us close."[1] "Perfect the well-knit bond of husband and wife."[2] Fond and affectionate wives dressed themselves gaily to please their husbands, displayed their beauty to them, clung to them as round the tree the woodbine clings.[3] A devoted husband and a loving wife are compared to the Chakravak and its mate.[4] The word Dampati shows the joint rulership of the house. In the Brihadaranyaka we read how the man, who was originally one, divided himself into two parts. "But he felt no delight. Therefore a man who is lonely feels no delight. He wished for a second. He was so large as man and wife together. He then made this hismelf to fall in two; and thence arose husband and wife. Therefore Yajnavalkya said; We two are thus (each of us) like half a shell. Therefore the void which was there, is filled by the wife. He embraced her, and men were born."[5] "It is only with his wife and progeny that a man becomes complete. Hence, the wise call the husband and wife as identical."[6] "The god Brahma cleft his body into two of yore. Out of one part sprang the husbands, and out of the other the wives. This is what the Shrutis declare. A man so long as he does not take a wife, is but (a) half (incomplete) being. A half (thing) cannot beget. A whole (thing) only can beget. This is the dictum of the Shruti."[7] Kulluka places the essence of marriage in the union of the souls : "Marriage according to the Rishis is a holy sacrament, a kind of psychic transformation, the two parties to it being blended together in spirit and for all eternity. Both the parties are transformed into that 'human centaur' which is called man and wife."[8] The fact that each one is meant for the other is brought out by Bhavabhuti when he says that it is not in youth but in old age that real affection develops. जरसा यस्मिन्नहार्यो रस:।। It is only in advanced age that one enjoys the climax of conjugal felicity.

The supreme duty of a wife is absolute and unconditional devotion to her husband. Anasuya says to Sita : "They that love their husband whether living in the city or in the forest, whether well or ill-disposed towards them attain great status. Wicked, or libidinous, or indigent, a husband is a supreme deity unto a wife of noble character."[9] Sita says to Rama at the time of the latter's departure to forest : "O dear husband, father, mother, son, brother, daughter-in-law, all of them abide by the consequences of their own actions; it is the wife alone that shares the fate of husband...Neither father, mother, son, friends, nor her own self is the stay of a woman in this or in after-life, it is the husband alone that is her only support....Unto woman is preferable under all circumstances the shade of her husband's feet to the tops of a palace, the celestial car, or the excursion in the airy Path..."[10] In reply to Dasharatha Sita says : "The Vina (lute) without strings does not sound; and the car without wheels does not move, so although having an hundred sons, a woman without husband cannot attain happiness. The father gives in measure, the brother and the son give in measure, but who does not worship that bestower of limitless treasure–the husband?....A husband is a deity unto the wife."[11] A woman should unhesitatingly prefer the wishes of a husband to those of a son. Kaikeyi is thus rebuked by Sumantra : "You ought not to bring down your boon-bestowing lord and husband

Dasharatha; for surely the wish of a husband to a wife outweighs a crore of sons."[12] Similarly Tara says : "I would rather die with this hero than have hundred sons like Angada."[13]

The Mahabharata is full of pages, giving vivid details of the duties of a wife. Draupadi gives an account of her own attitude: "Keeping aside vanity and controlling desire and wrath, I always serve with devotion the sons of Pandu with their wives. Restraining jealousy, with deep devotion of heart, without a sense of degradation at the services I perform, I wait upon my husbands. Ever fearing to utter what is evil or false or to look or sit or wait with impropriety, or cast glances indicative of the feelings of the heart, do I serve the sons of Prithu..."[14] "Devotion to her lord is woman's merit; it is her penance; it is her eternal heaven...The husband is a god which women have. The husband is their friend. The husband is their high refuge...If the husband that is poor, or distressed, or fallen among foes, or afflicted by a Brahmin's curse, were to command the wife to accomplish anything that is improper or unrighteous or that may lead to the destruction of life itself, the wife should, without any hesitation, accomplish it, guided by the code, whose propriety is sanctioned by the Law of Distress."[15]

The woman's devotion in its highest form becomes transcendental; it is given irrespective of the husband's response to it. It is, therefore, directed towards the husband both in life and in death. Sita's devotion rises to its height, when although chaste, she is repudiated by her husband. Kalidas puts the very finest verses into her mouth. She only prays that Rama may be her husband even in the next life and she may not have separation from him. त्वमेव भर्ता न च विप्रयोग: Kashyapa says to Shakuntala : भर्तुर्विप्रकृतापि रोषणतया मा स्म प्रतीपं गम:। "Don't oppose your husband even if he insults you." Nala deserts Damayanti and yet her fidelity is unshakable. "Chaste women, although fallen into distress yet protect themselves, and thus certainly secure heaven. They may be deserted by their lords, they do not yet become angry on that account, for women that are chaste lead their lives encased in the armour of virtuous behaviour.....Whether treated well or ill, such a wife should never indulge in anger."[16] Death does not dissolve the marriage tie of those spiritually united. Anasuya says : "I find no other friend greater than the husband, who is worthy of being served both in this world and the next."[17] "She, who has been given away as wife by her father to one, with due rites of gift peculiar to each class, touching holy water, shall be his, even in her after life."[18]

A reference is made to other duties of women. Women took a substantial share in the work of the household by fetching water from the wells, and doing other duties.[19] They were early risers and used to awaken the other members of the family.[20] Husking rice, churning butter out of curds, weaving embroidery, dyeing were some of her activities.[21] The bride used to weave the garment to be put on by the bridegroom on the marriage day with beautiful borders.[22] Old ladies often used to grind corn even, as a profession.[23] 'Wool and thread' is said to be woman's work.[24] Draupadi shows herself as not only a devoted wife, but an able mistress of the house. "I always keep the house and all household articles and the food that is to be taken well-ordered and clean. Carefully do I keep the rice and serve the food at the proper time. I never indulge in angry and fretful speech, and never imitate women that are wicked. Keeping idleness at a distance I always do what is agreeable. I never laugh except at a jest, and never stay for any length of time at the house-gate...Those duties that my mother-in-law had told me of in respect of relatives, as also the duties of alms-giving, of offering worship to the gods, of oblations to the deceased, of boiling food in pots on auspicious days for offering to ancestors and guests, of reverence and service to those that deserve our regard, and all else that is known to me, I do...Indeed, I knew everything about what the maid-servants of the palace and other classes of attendants, even what the cow-herds and shepherds of the royal establishment, did or did not. It was I alone amongst the Pandavas who knew the income and expenditure of the king, and what their whole wealth was."[25]

Vyasa very minutely describes the daily duties of a Hindu woman. "A wife should quit her bed before her lord, clean her person, fold up the beds and make her house clean and tidy. Then having entered the chamber of Homa (sacrificial fire), she should (first) wash and plaster its floor, and then the yard of her house; and after that, wash with warm water the vessels of oil, clarified butter etc. which are used in connection with Agnikaryas (fire) and keep them in proper places. The oven should be repaired and re-plastered with earth and clay, and the fire should be lighted therein. Then having performed the morning duties and pondered over the dishes of different flavours (to be prepared that day) and allotment of work to different workers, and the daily expenditure of the household, she should make obeisance to her elders and superiors. Then she should decorate her person with the ornaments given to her by her father-in-law, husband, father, mother maternal uncle, or relations...Then having finished cooking, she should report about it to her husband saying, 'The rice is cooked'. The husband having made offerings to the Vishvedevas, she should first feed the children, and then should serve out the morning meal to her lord. Then, with the permission of her lord, she would partake of the residue of the boiled rice and cooked dishes, and spend the closing portion of the day in contemplation of the family earnings and expenditure."[26] The following verse so aptly describes the woman's manifold functions.

कार्येषु मन्त्री करणेषु दासी
भोज्येषु माता शयनेषु रम्भा।
मनोनुकूला क्षमया धरित्री
गुणैश्च भार्या: कुलमुद्धरन्ति।।

Husband and wife were called co-partners in moral and religious life. सहधर्मचारिणी is the title of a wife. She used to take part in religious ceremonies of the household.[27] "Pairs waxing old in their devotion seek thee."[28] They jointly offer oblations; they are joint 'deities' of one hymn.[29] The wife had an appointed place in a sacrifice from which she would speak as a house-mistress to the gathered people.[30] Her sovereignty over the other elderly members of the house was equal with her husband.[31] The following seven assertions of a bride at the time of marriage throw considerable light over their mutual relations. "The bride says when taking the first step, to her husband; 'I share with you all happiness and misery : I am always with you.' On taking the second step : 'I will look to all the members of our family from a young baby to an old man or woman. I see all that is and all that is not.' On taking the third step she says : 'I shall be always devoted to my husband and shall speak sweet words.' On taking the fourth and fifth steps : 'I shall share your unhappiness, and shall obey your commands. I shall share your bed at the end of the menstrual period and shall not approach another person.' On the sixth step, she says : 'You have not deceived me : God is our witness; our love is a fact.' And on taking the last step, she says : *I shall help you* in your religious rites and *in all your pursuits relating to worldly or spiritual ends*."[32]

Husband has reciprocal duties and obligations towards his wife. In his case also devotion to his wife was a praise-worthy thing. "A wife, O Maghavan, is home and dwelling."[33] Wives aspire to supremacy in their own sphere. "I am the banner and the head, a mighty arbitress am I; I am victorious and my lord shall be submissive to my will. My sons are slayers of the foe. My daughter is a ruling queen. I am victorious o'er my Lord, my song of triumph is supreme."[34] "Be vigilant to rule thy household in his home."[35] Kaushalya was to Dasharatha not merely a servant, but "a friend, wife, sister, and mother."[36] Rama says to Sita that : "I do not long for even the abode of celestials gained through they affliction...When thou art determined to repair unto the forest with me, I cannot leave thee behind, as one possessing self-knowledge cannot renounce munificence."[37] Vasishtha argues that Sita had the same rights and privileges as Rama, being his wife :–"Sita shall not go to the forest. She shall occupy Rama's seat. Of those that marry, wife is the (other) soul. Sita will govern the earth as she is Rama's self."[38] Women often used to take a very intelligent interest in their husbands' affairs. A wife is as needful to the life of a husband as a husband is to a wife. "A householder's home, even if filled with sons and grandsons, and daughters-in-law, and servants, is regarded empty if destitute of the housewife. One's house is not one's own home; one's wife only is one's home. A house without a wife is as desolate as the wilderness."[39] "The wife is a man's half. The wife is the first of friends. The wife is the root of religion, profit, and desire. The wife is the root of salvation. They that have wives can perform religious acts. They that have wives can lead domestic lives. They that have wives have the means to be cheerful. They that have wives can achieve good fortune. Sweet-speeched wives are as friends on occasions of joy. They are as fathers on occasion of religious acts. They are as mothers in hours of sickness and woe. Even in the deep woods, a wife to a traveller is his refreshment and solace. A wife, therefore, is the most valuable possession. Even when the husband leaving this world goeth into the region of Yama, it is the devoted wife that accompanies him thither...For these reasons marriage exists...It hath been said by learned persons that oneself is born as one's son. Therefore, a man whose wife hath borne a son should look upon her as his mother...No man, even in anger, should ever do anything that is disagreeable to his wife seeing that happiness and joy and virtue depend upon the wife. A wife is the sacred field in which the husband hismelf is born."[40] A husband is not to consider his wife as his property, but "as an acquisition due to his own acts of previous life, or to what has been ordained by God."[41] "The wife is a friend bestowed on man by the gods."[42] The husband is called Bhartri, because he supports the wife; he is called Pati because he protects her.[43] "This eternal course of morality is ever followed by the virtuous viz. that the husband, however weak, protecteth his wedded wife."[44] A wife is not to be controlled by harsh means, but by things which please her. "Her life is indeed, crowned with success who has controlled his friends by gifts, his foes in battle, and wife by food and drink."[45] "Respect, kind treatment, and everything else that is agreeable should be given unto the maiden whose hand is taken in marriage. Her sire and brothers and father-in-law, and husband's brother should show her every respect and adorn her with ornaments, if they be desirous of reaping benefits, for such conduct on their part always leads to considerable happiness and advantage. If the wife does not like her husband or fails to gladden him, from such dislike and absence of joy the husband can never have issue for increasing his race. Women should always be treated and worshipped with affection. The begetting of offspring, the nursing of children already born, and the accomplishment of all acts necessary for the needs of society, behold, all these have women for their casue....Deities of prosperity are women. ...By cherishing women, one cherishes the goddess of prosperity, and by afflicting her, one is said to afflict the goddess of prosperity."[46] Women is not to be roughly handled, and she is generally incapable of being slain. Sugriva says to Tara : Beholding thee, Laxman will not be angry : great men never behave roughly towards the females."[47] Kind treatment of expectant mothers was a very attractive feature of the social life of ancient India. The future of the race depends upon such factors. "A pregnant woman forms a mental image of her child and in this attempt she is unfolding her own character; there is psychic continuity of the race through the medium of the mother, and she is, therefore, to be respected."[48] Anything that tends to injure the pregnant lady causes injury to the child.[49]

Complete protection is the woman's due at the hands of her husband. "Men should never give any license to their wives in day and night; by keeping them engaged in commendable pursuits, they should be kept under their own control...Women should be especially protected from the slightest of corrupting influence, since an unprotected woman aggrieves the two families. This (protection of wives) forms the highest duty of the members of all the four social orders. Even weak (i.e. diseased) husbands should endeavour to protect their wives.

By assiduously protecting his wife, a man protects (the purity of his) progeny and family as well as his character, self, and virtue...Wives cannot be kept by force : it is by the application of the following expedients that they can be kept under control. They should be employed in storing and spending money; in maintaining the cleanliness of their persons and of the house, and in looking after the beddings, wearing apparels, and household furniture. Imprisoned in the house and closely guarded by their male relations, (bad) women are not sufficiently protected. *Woman who guard themselves are said to be truly guarded.*'[50] Nothing would justify the desertion of a wife except some great sin on her part or her suffering from diseases and childlessness, or her being extravagant and hostile.[51] Shankha is of opinion that "A wife should be caressed and admonished, both fondled and checked."[52]

It is an imperative duty of a husband never to neglect his wife at the end of the menstrual period. "And the husband that knoweth not his wife in season meeteth with disgrace."[53] But on no account a man is to visit a woman during the four days of her menses. "Even extremely heated, he must not visit his wife during the three forbidden days of her period, nor share the same bed with her. Intellect, vigour, strength, eye-sight, and vitality of a man, who goes unto a woman in her menses, are impaired."[54] He must not have his connection with his wife "in the day-time, and in the twilight. And with unclean. And with one sick. And while he is sick himself. He must not have connection, if he wishes to enjoy a long life with a woman who has a limb too little, nor with one who has a limb too much, nor with one older than himself, nor with a pregnant woman."[55] But the Smritikaras, knowing the demands of human nature, have sufficiently relaxed these restrictions. "Remembering the vow of women, being faithfully devoted to one's own wife, and being influenced by desire proportionate to (hers), one can know (his wife) (even at any other time except the menstrual period); for it is laid down in the Smritis that woman should be protected (by every means)."[56]

References

1. Rg. X. 47.
2. Rg. V. 28. 3.
3. Rg. I. 124. 7, X. 71. 4, X. 10. 13.
4. Av. XIV. 2. 64.
5. Br. U. I. IV. 3.
6. M. IX. 45.
7. Vyasa. II. 13. 14.
8. Kulluka's Commentary on Manu.
9. R. II. 117. 22-28.
10. R. II. 27. 4-23.
11. R. II. 39. 29-31.
12. R. II. 35. 8.
13. R. IV. 21. 13.
14. Vana. 234. 13-61.
15. Anu. 249. 5-29. 250. 1-62.
16. Vana. 68. 8-121.
17. R. II. 117. 22-28.
18. R. II. 29. 17-18.
19. Rg. I. 191. 14; Av. X. 8. 14.
20. Rg. I. 79. 1; Av. VII. 13.2; Rg. I. 113. 5, I. 124. 4.
21. Av. XII. 3. 13; Rg. I. 28. 4; Rg. II. 3. 6, X. 26. 6., V. S. XXX.
22. Av. XIV. 2. 51.
23. Rg. IX. 112. 3.
24. S. Sr. XII. 7. 2. II.
25. Vana. 234. 13-61.
26. Vyasa. II. 20-35.
27. Rg. I. 72. 5.
28. Rg. V. 43. 15.
29. Rg. I. 131. 3.
30. Rg. V. X. 85. 24, X. 85. 26.
31. Rg. X. 85. 46.
32. Samskara-Bhaskara.
33. Rg. III. 53.4.
34. Rg. X. 159. 2-3; Av. VI. 78. 1-2.
35. Rg. X. 27.
36. R. II. 12. 68-69.
37. R. II. 30. 27-29.
38. R. II. 37. 23-24.

39. Shanti. 144. 5-17.
40. Adi. 98. 22-43.
41. Anu. 79, 29.
42. Vana. 314, 74.
43. Adi. 113, 30-31.
44. Vana. 12, 71-73.
45. Udyoga. 39, 83.
46. Anu. 8, 1-15.
47. R. IV. 33, 36.
48. Ai. Up. II. 5, 3.
49. Yaj.
50. M. IX. 2-12.
51. Yaj. I. 72-74.
52. Shankha. IV. 16.
53. Vana. 294. 36.
54. M. IV. 40-41.
55. Vishnu. LXIX. 9-17.
56. Yaj. I. 81.

Chapter - X

CHASTITY

The enormous importance of the purity of sexual life was recognized from the Vedic period and all deviations from it was regarded with disfavour. A certain amount of freedom and gallantry was shown towards young women. Life was not yet cast in a rigid mould. "Bees take honey in their mouth as a woman goes to an assignation."[1] "Wake up intelligence as when a lover wakes his sleeping love."[2] A lover prayed for immunity frem harm for going to a beloved at night time, when he lulls to sleep all the people of the house and the dogs.[3] Children born of irregular connections, brotherless girls going astray, prostitutes going about displaying their beauty, are referred to.[4] Agru, a child born out of an illicit union was thrown into an ant-hill but was saved by Indra, and became a Rishi.[5] However, the high appreciation shown for normal wedded life, with its attendant conjugal felicity brings out the fact of wide prevalence of healthy relations among persons of both the sexes. The sin of women who conceive without their husbands is noticed. "Upholders of the Law, ye strong Adityas, remove my sin like her who bears in secret."[6] Hell is the creation of female adultery. "Like youthful women without brother, straying like dames who hate their lords, of evil conduct. They who are full of sin, untrue, unfaithful, they have engendered this abysmal station. (hell)."[7] Adultery with a Brahmin's wife is very dangerous. "Dire is a Brahmin's wife led home by others; in the supremest heaven she plants confusion."[8] The grave character of incestuous union also is well brought out.

"Prajapati conceived a passion for his own daughter : either the sky or the dawn. May I pair with her? Thus (thinking) he united with her. This assuredly, was a sin in the eyes of the gods. 'He who acts thus towards his own daughter, or sister, (commits a sin)' they thought."[9]

Chastity was recognised as the central and most indispensable aspect of a woman's character. Rama complains that nothing was more painful to him than the touch of Sita by another person.[10] Jatayu says : "It becomes every man to save another's wife, just as he saves his own wife, from the touch of a second man."[11] Sita's character is called in question by Rama. She, thereupon, wants to enter fire. "As my heart has never gone away from Raghava, may thou protect me, O fire, the witness of the people. As Raghava considers me vile who have got a pure character may fire, the witness of the people, protect me on all sides."[12] The god of fire appears and vouches for her chastity. "O Rama, here is thy Vaidehi–no sin has visited her. Neither by words, mind, understanding, nor eyes, she hath deviated from thee." Rama replies : "The vicious Ravana could not even by his mind get Maithili, who was beyond his reach like unto the burning flame of fire. Her mind could not have been moved although she lived in the inner apartment of Ravana. She belongs to none else : Sita is mine as the rays of the sun."[13] Forcible touch, however, cannot detract from the merit of a lady. Sita refuses to go with Hanuman, saying : O monkey, being guided by my love for my husband, I do not like willingly to touch anybody's body but Rama's. When Ravana by force touched my person I had no other help."[14] And she says to Rama : "Though my person was touched by another, but it was not in my power; nor was it any wilful act (of mine); accident is to blame in this. My heart is under my control and that is in thee; and what could I do of my body which was subject to another, and if which I was not the mistress."[15] The following passages from the Mahabharata are important : "Virtue I shall never sacrifice, seeing that in this world the keeping of their persons inviolate is deemed as the highest duty of women, and is held in high regard."[16] "Amongst them both kinds are to be seen, that is those that are virtuous and those that are not so. Those women that are virtuous are highly blessed. They are the mothers of the universe. They, it is, that uphold the Earth will all her waters and forests."[17]

Male chastity is not, indeed, a matter of complete indifference; it is an object of much praise in the sacred books. Sita praises Rama's virtue in this respect. "Nor yet canst thou ever even in fancy be (guilty of) going after other people's wives."[18] Even Kaikeyi testifies to this : "Rama does not look with his eyes upon another's wife."[19] Hanuman is filled with some regret at his seeing the harem of Ravana. "Beholding a female who is the righteously wedded wife of another, while she is asleep, verily causes loss of righteousness."[20] Laxman confesses his ignorance of the ornaments of Sita because he had never looked full in her face. "I do not know her bracelets : I do not know her ear-rings but I know full well her bangles on account of my always bowing down unto her feet."[21]

This high ideal of chastity is often modified. The practice of Niyoga or Levirate was departure from this ideal. Pandu even asks his wife to have connection with some person to secure sons for him during his life-time. He traces the evolution of marriage from a state of promiscuous relationships. 'Women were not formerly immured within houses and dependent on husbands and other relations. They used to go freely enjoying as much as they liked. They did not then adhere to their husbands faithfully, and yet they were not regarded sinful, for that was the sanctioned usage of the times. That very usage is followed to this day by birds and beasts without any exhibition of jealousy. That practice, sanctioned by precedent, is applauded by great Rishis. The practice is yet regarded with respect amongst the northern Kurus. Indeed, that usage so lenient to women, has the sanction of antiquity. The present practice, however, (of women being confined to one husband for life) has been established but lately." Pandu then gives this story of Uddalaka. His wife was once being taken away by a

Brahmin, in the presence of her son, who became very angry at this. Upon this Uddalaka says : "This is the practice sanctioned by antiquity. The women of all orders in the world are free. O son, men in this matter, as regards their respective orders act like kine." The Rishi's son Shwetaketu, however, disapproved of usage and established in the world the present practice as regards men and women. Accordingly, since the establishment of the present usage, it is sinful for women not to adhere to their husbands...The woman, also, who being commanded by her husband to raise offspring refuses to do his bidding becomes equally sinful[22] Many other passages also indicate possible modifications in the rigorous practice of chastity. Virgins were once said to possess special freedom. "It is because a virgin desireth the company of every one, that she has received the appellation of Kanya, from the root Kama meaning to desire. Therefore, a virgin is by nature free in this world...That all men and women should be bound by no restraints is the law of nature. The opposite condition is the perversion of the natural state."[23] Another curious idea is that women's wishes must be gratified by males especially in season. It is a duty. "That male person, who being solicited by a woman in season doth not grant her wishes, is called, by those cognisant of the Vedas as a slayer of the embryo. He who solicited in secret by a woman full of desire and in season, goeth not unto her loseth virtue and is called by the learned a killer of the embryo. O son of Bhrigu, for these reasons, and anxious to avoid sin, I went unto Sharmishtha."24 The prime function of maternity was so important for females, that chastity was often subordinated to the utilitarian consideration of raising offsprings. "And when the Earth was thus deprived of Kshatriyas by that great Rishi, the Kshatriya ladies all over the land raised offsprings by means of Brahmins skilled in the Vedas. It has been said that the son so raised belongeth to him that had married the mother. And the Kshatriya ladies went unit the Brahmins not lustfully, but from motives of virtue. Indeed, it was thus that the Kshatriya race was revived."[25]

Narada has bold views on the subject. "A man is not punishable as an adulterer for having intercourse with the wife of one who has left his wife without her fault, or of one impotent, or consumptive, if the woman herself consents to it."[26] Connection with a virgin girl is allowed, but the man must be ready to marry her. "When, however, he has connection with a willing maiden, it is no offence, but he shall bestow ornaments on her, honour her (with other presents) and (lawfully) espouse her."[27] "Intercourse is permitted with a wanton woman, who belongs to another than the Brahmin's caste, or a prostitute or a female slave, or a female not restrained by her master, if these women belong to a lower caste than oneself : but with a woman of superior caste, intercourse is prohibited. When, however, such a woman is the kept mistress (of another man, intercourse with her) is as criminal as (intercourse) with another's wife."[28] Manu recognises the illegitimate unions but considers the offsprings as possessing varying degrees of rights.[29] A man may lawfully remarry a wife who has deserted him and known another man.[30] The idea, that women are intrinsically pure and hence free from all guilt, is frequently expressed. "Practices of women are not to be discussed; (they are always) pure; rain-drops are always unsullied; and so the dust driven by the wind."[31] "A woman is not sullied by being known by another; nor a Brahmin, by (harmful) Vedic rites, nor (a river) water, by urine and excreta; not fire by burning impure articles. Women were first enjoyed by the celestials; then by the moon, the Gandharvas, and the Fires. Afterwards men came to enjoy them. They are never affected by any sin. When a woman conceives by being known by an Asawarna (one belonging to a higher caste than her), she remains impure as long as she does not give birth to a child...If despite her complete unwillingness, a woman is known deceitfully, forcibly, or stealthily, that woman, unaffected by any sin, should not be renounced; for she has not done so willingly. The woman, who has once been known by the Mlechhas, or by the perpetrators of crimes become purified with the Prajapatya and the menstrual flow."[32]

The Hindu ideal of purity is undoubtedly high; but it often makes enormous concessions to various circumstances. Adultery, however, stands condemned and its varieties are distinguished. "Sexual intercourse is of eight kinds :–viz., thinking of woman, talking (about her), dalliance with a woman, looking (at a woman with an impure desire), speaking to her secretly, determination (for holding a sexual congress), persistent endeavour (for doing it), and the actual deed. This should never be thought or spoken of, nor should it ever be done."[33] No greater sin exists on earth than carrying away another's wife.[34] "Nothing so shortens the life of a man in this world as the act of (clandestinely) visiting another's wife."[35] All adulterers are to be expelled from the country. "The king, having clumsily mutilated their persons, shall cause the defilers of other men's wives to be banished from the country, since it is through such men that hybridisation of castes is effected; and intermixture of castes is the primal cause of vice which leads to universal destruction."[36] All activities which are connected with adultery are punished. Suspected persons must not talk with other men's wives; or they are punished with a fine of hundred Panas.[37] A person is to be fined one gold coin if he talks with another's wife although forbidden to do so.[38] "If one accosts, and converses with another's wife in a lonely wood or forest, or at a holy pool or confluence of rivers, he shall be guilty of the offence of adultery punishable with a fine of one thousand Panas. Sending presents of scents and flower-garlands to another's wife, cutting jokes with or embracing her, touching her ornaments and catching hold of her wearing apparel, and eating or sharing the same bed-stead with her are acts which are said to constitute the Stri-sangraha (adultery with another's wife). A woman, who tolerates being touched at her private parts by a man, and a man, who tolerates similarly being touched by her, are said to be guilty of adultery by mutual consent.[39] Adultery with an unwilling woman is more heinous and amounts to a rape. He, who defiles a maid not amatively disposed, should be punished (with the mutilation of his reproductive organ).[40] "The fingers of him, who forcibly ruptures the hymen of a virgin therewith, shall be clipped off and he shall be further liable to pay a fine of six hundred Panas."[41]

Women are held equally responsible for all participation in forbidden intercourse. "A wife who out of pride of personal beauty and opulent relationship, has made transgression against her husband, the king shall cause to be devoured by ferocious dogs in a well-crowded locality."[42] Adultery is the main ground upon which the desertion of a wife can be justified. "(One should make) an unchaste wife–deprived of (all her) rights, living poorly, taking only a morsel of food, always lying on earth, living in his own house."[43] "The woman having intercourse with four different men is called a Swairini, while she having intercourse with five becometh a harlot."[44] The rape of woman on a woman is referred to. "A girl committing the same offence (forcibly rupturing the hymen of a virgin) upon another girl be punished with stripes and a fine of two hundred Panas."[45] A woman, who is the victim of a rape, is allowed to expiate her condition by an ordinary penance. A woman forcibly ravished by a man in captivity, as well as she, who accommodates a man on account of being physically overpowered or out of a sense of danger to her life, should regain her purity by practising a Santapana penance.[46]

The illicit connections possess varying digress of guilt according as the objects of these are of different castes. The highest form of pecuniary punishment is the penalty, if adultery is committed by a man with a woman of the same caste; the second form is (the penalty) when a similar offence is committed with a woman of a lower caste. Death (is the penalty when it is committed with) a woman of a higher caste. The cutting of the nose etc. is the penalty for women."[47] Adultery with a woman of an inferior caste is not an offence : but rape is not permitted. "No offence is committed, if a maiden of an inferior caste is lustfully disposed of; otherwise there is a penalty (for the offence). (If a woman of an inferior caste) is ravished (against her will with scratches of her person, made) by nails, the cutting off of fingers (is the penalty). Death (is the penalty, if a similar offence is committed with) a woman of a higher caste."[48] A Shudra is punished with the mutilation of his organ or loss of his life and forfeiture of his estate for connection with a woman of a higher caste.[49]

Now we will deal with varieties of defects of blood on the part of males. Wanton assertions concerning another woman are forbidden. "When a man actuated by vanity, folly, or braggartism, declares himself that he has enjoyed the love of a certain woman, that is also termed an adulterous proceeding."[50] "For making known the real defects of a maiden (one should be made to) pay (a fine of) a hundred Panas; for making a false accusation two hundred."[51] Women in their menses and pregnant women are to be specially avoided. "A highly distressing penance is laid down for the expiation of his sin, who co-habits with a woman in her menses or with one who is in the family way, or with a degraded woman."[52] The connection with low-born and degraded females is to be deprecated. "If one knows them (the women of the Chandalas etc.) willingly and procreates children, he is degraded to the same caste; there is no doubt in it for that man is born as her son."[53] A wife also is not fit to be enjoyed in all ways. "By knowing a dead wife one is born as one whose wife dies ...By knowing one's own wife who is initiated, one is born suffering from the vitiation of blood."[54] All unnatural intercourse is severely condemned. "By co-habiting with a beast, one is born, suffering from urinary diseases."[55] "Having gone to a she-animal, prostitute, she-buffalo, she-camel, female monkey, she-ass, one should practice penance."[56]

"By discharging semen into inhuman females except a cow, into a woman in her menses, into others that have no female organs (i.e. a male or a eunuch) or into water should perform the penance of Santapana.[57] "A person holding an intercourse (with his wife) at any other place but the sexual organ; or knowing a religious mendicant should be punished with twenty-four Panas."[58] "The ancestors of a man who commits intercourse through the mouth of his wedded wife, feed that month on his semen; for unnatural intercourse is against the sacred law."[59] "An emission of one's semen during sleep, or out of fright, or on account of a disease should be atoned by begging for seven days.....An act of masturbation should be atoned for in the following ways. Observing perfect continence, a masturbator should stand up from sunrise to sunset and take a single meal each day."[60] Waste of semen in connection with eunuchs, barren women, sexless beings is equal to Brahmanicide.[61]

The enormity of all acts of incest is exposed. "Sexual connection with one's mother, or daughter or daughter-in-law are crimes in the highest degree.... Such criminals should proceed to flames; for there is not any other way to atone for their crime."[62] "Killing a Brahmin, drinking spirituous liquor, stealing the gold of a Brahmin, and sexual connection with a Guru's wife are high crimes...Sexual connection with the wife of a paternal uncle, of a maternal grandfather, of a maternal uncle, of a father-in-law, or of the king, are crimes equal to sexual connection with a Guru's wife. And so is sexual intercourse with the father's or mother's sister and with one's own sister. And the sexual connection with the wife of a learned Brahmin, or a priest, or an Upadhyaya or a friend. And with a sister's female friend, with a woman of his own race, with a woman belonging to the Brahmin caste, with a (Brahmin) maiden, with a low caste women, with a woman in her courses, with a woman come for protection, with a female ascetic, and with a woman entrusted to one's own care."[63] Narada lays down excision of the organ as the only punishment for incest.[64]

The following passage from the Skanda Purana as regards harlots is interesting : "The Veshyas are known as Kalavati, Rambha, Nayika, Ulukhali. Among Veshyas, the Nayika is known by her beauty, and is celebrated for the splendour of her dress. Kalavati is versed in amorous intercourse and is one who has worked for the art of singing, and Rambha is known to be adept in matters of beauty, art and dress. That woman who always has intercourse with two, three, or six men, and who is absolutely wanting in art of beauty, is known as Ulukhali. That woman who abandons her own husband and goes to another man of her own Varna out of love (for him) is called a Swairini. Restrained in speech, and restricting herself to intercourse with a man of higher tribe she is regarded as a Dharma-patni, and is considered as a Pativrata even among harlots. She, who having once accepted a fee from one man does not desire another who offers one or many rupees, or one who offers the (sovereignty) over the three worlds, or even Indra, even though a Veshya, is to be regarded a virtuous and chaste woman, and is respected as a lawfully married wife."

References

1. Rg. X. 40. 6.
2. Rg. I. 134. 3.
3. Av. IV. 5.
4. Rg. II. 29. 1, IV. 5. 5, I. 87.1.
5. Rg. IV. 19. 9, IV. 30. 6.
6. Rg. II. 29.
7. Rg. IV. 5. 5.
8. Rg. X. 109. 4; Br. Up. VI. 4. 12.
9. S. Br. I. 7. 4. 1-2.
10. R. III. 2. 21.
11. R. III. 50. 7.
12. R. VI. 116. 25-26.
13. R. VI. 118. 15-18.
14. R. V. 37. 62-63.
15. R. VI. 116. 8-9.
16. Vana. 307. 23.
17. Anu. 78. 23-4.
18. R. III. 9. 5-6.
19. R. II. 72. 48.
20. R. V. 11. 38.
21. R. IV. 6. 22-23.

    नाहं जानामि केयूरे नाहं जानामि कुण्डले।
    नूपुरे त्वभिजानामि नित्यं पादाभिवन्दनात्॥

22. Adi. 128. 3-48.
23. Vana. 308. 12-16.
24. Adi. 77, 54-56.
25. Adi. 113, 5-7.
26. Narada. XII. 61.
27. Narada. XII. 72.
28. Narada. XII. 78. 79; Manu VIII. 362.
29. M. IX. 167-173.
30. M. IX. 176.
31. Atri. 258.
32. Atri. 189-197.
33. Daksha. VII. 31-33.
34. R. III. 38. 30.
35. M. III. 134.
36. M. VIII. 352-353.
37. M. VIII. 354-355.
38. M. VIII. 361.
39. M. VIII. 356-358.
40. M. VIII. 364.
41. M. VIII. 367.
42. M. VIII. 371.
43. Yaj. I. 70; Narada. XII. 91.
44. Adi. 132. 64.
45. M. VIII. 369.
46. Parashara. X. 20.
47. Yaj. II. 289.
48. Yaj. II. 291.
49. M. VIII. 374-375-379.
50. Narada. XII. 69.
51. Yaj. II. 292.
52. Samvarta. 163.
53. Atri. 184.
54. Shatatapa. 31-34.
55. Shatatapa. 36.
56. Parashara. X. 15.
57. Atri. 268.

58. Yaj. II. 296.
59. Vasishtha. X.
60. Gautama XXIV.
61. Anu. 213. 2-4.
62. Vishnu. XXXIV. 1-2.
63. Vishnu. XXXVI. 4-7.
64. Narada. XII. 73-75.

Chapter - XI

OBEDIENCE TO ELDERS

A coherent type of family organization was already established very early–the main features of which survive in the Hindu Society to this day. Its essential basis was the authority of elders. A measureless devotion towards the parents and Gurus is demanded by the Hindu ideas. There is scarcely any limit to the amount of obedience and love and gratitude which children are expected to cherish for their parents. "Eagerly they who hear his word fulfil his wish as sons obey their father's behest."[1] "Like a son folowing his father's wishes, grant to this family success and safety."[2] Sons are said to express their affection in various ways. "One seeks another as he talks and greets him with cries of pleasure as a son his father."[3] "We come with gifts of pleasant food, invoking thee (Indra), as sons invite a sire."[4] "I bend to thee as thou approachest, Rudra, even as a boy before the sire who greets him."[5] The mere word of a father is a law to a son; accordingly, Rama consents to renounce kingdom and go to the forest with the utmost readiness. This is no external obedience; the position is accepted with all willingness.(प्रीत्या च नियमेन च।)[6] The ethical value of the worship of parents is very high. "Truth, almgiving, honour and sacrifices with profuse gifts are not so strengthening (in the life to come) as the services rendered unto the parents. Heaven, wealth, grains, learning, son and happiness–nothing remains inaccessible unto us."[7] Sons are expected to save their parents from a certain hell called Put, by offering oblations to their manes at sacred places; this is the derivation of the word

Putra (son).[8] The dependence of the son on a father's wishes is often extreme. King Ambarisha wanted to perform a sacrifice. The horse was stolen by Indra. He, therefore, requested one sage called Richik, to sell him one of his sons, who might serve as a substitute for the horse. The parents could not part with either the youngest or the eldest son; so the middle one Shunashepa offered himself for sale to be sacrificed in the Yajna of Ambarisha.[9] This was indeed an extreme assertion of the parental authority.

The situation sometimes arises when the wishes of the two parents are contradictory. There is a clear answer given to all doubts in such cases. The authority of a father has a prior right to respect, to the authority of the mother. Kaushalya thus appeals to Rama at the time of his departure to the forest. "As the monarch is worthy of reverence unto thee so am I. I do not permit thee to repair hence into the forest. Separated from thee I do not need life or happiness."[10] Rama replies : "There is no power in me to transgress my father's behests; bend my head low unto thee. I want to proceed to the forest. The learned Rishi Kandu, who lived in the forest, keeping the word of his father, killed a cow, knowing it to be unrighteousness. In our line the descendants of Sagara, at the command of their father, met with signal destruction, while digging the earth. Rama, the son of Jamdagni, at his father's word decapitated his mother in the forest. These and other godlike personages obeyed heroically the orders of their fathers; and I shall do my father's welfare, therefore...I am not introducing some such unrighteousness, unfavourable unto thee, that has never been practised before."[11]

The Mahabharata enjoins the same worship of parents. "He conquereth both the worlds that payeth homage unto his father and mother, and preceptor, and Agni, and fifthly the soul."[12] Among sons, he is entitled to the greatest regard who serves his parents most and not he who is eldest or most learned. "The wise say that he is no son who disobeys his father. That son, however, who doth the bidding of his parents, who seeketh good, who is agreeable to them, is indeed the best of sons.[13] The following passage is full of the feeling of reverence which the father naturally inspires in a Hindu son. "The father places his own self within the mother's womb, and takes birth as the son, for continuing his practices, conduct, name, and race...The words uttered by the sire while performing the initial rite after birth, and those that were uttered by him on the occasion of the subsidiary rite (after the return from the preceptor's abode are sufficient (evidence) for the reverence due to him. In consequence of his bringing up the son and instructing him, the sire is the son's foremost of superiors and the highest religion. The very Vedas lay it down as certain that the son should regard what his sire says as his highest duty. Unto the sire the son is only a source of joy. Unto the son, however, the father is all. The body and all else that the son owns have the sire alone for their giver. Hence, the behests of the sire should be obeyed without ever questioning them in the least. The very sins of one that obeys one's sire are cleansed (by such obedience). The sire is the giver of all articles of enjoyment, of all articles of food, of instructions in the Vedas, and of all other knowledge regarding this world."[14] A full measure of respect and protection should be extended to the parents. "The father, the mother, and the preceptor should never be insulted...They that injure in thought and deed their preceptors or fathers, or mothers incur the sin of killing a foetus. There is no sinner in the world equal to them. That son of the sire's loins and mother's womb being brought up by them does not support them when he comes to age, incurs the sin of killing a foetus. There is no sinner in the world like unto him."[15] "He, who, without adequate cause casts off his sire, mother, or preceptor, surely becomes fallen."[16] Manu's ideas about filial piety are the same.[17]

Ancestor-worship prevalent among the Hindus indicates their great regard for their parents even after their death. It insures reverence for the past, and consequent organic continuity of future development. The ceremony was called Shraddha. "Come hither Fathers, who deserve the Soma, by the deep-pathways which the Fathers travel. Bestow upon us life and store of children, and favour us with increase of riches."[18]

Worship of mother is a specially pleasing feature of Hindu morality. It is useless, we believe, to trace in early records any proofs of matriarchy. However, it is clear that woman attains greatest sanctity in her capacity of a mother. All the devotion which is to be directed to the father is to be shared by the mother as well. "A mother should be as much regarded by a son as a father."[19] Yaksha asks Yudhishthira : "What is weightier than the earth itself? What is higher than the heavens?" He replies : "The mother is weightier than the earth; the father is higher than the heavens."[20] Mother's services to the child are simply incalculable; all these deserve reciprocal regard on the part of the child. "I shall now think upon (what is due to) the mother. Of this union of five elements in me due to my birth as a human being, the mother is the (chief) cause as the fire-sticks of fire...She is the panacea for all kinds of calamities. The existence of mother invests one with protection; the reverse deprives one of protection. The man, who , though divested of prosperity, enters his house, uttering the words :–O, mother! hath not to indulge in grief. Nor doth decrepitude assail him. A person, whose mother exists, even if he happens to be possessed of sons and grandsons, and if he is hundred years old, looks like a child but two years age. Able or disabled, lean or robust, the son is always protected by the mother. None else, according to ordinances is the son's protector. Then doth the son become old, then doth he become stricken with grief, then doth the world look empty in his eyes, when he becomes deprived of his mother. There is o shelter like the mother. There is no refuge like the mother. There is no defence like the mother, there is none so dear as the mother."[21] Very often the authority of the mother becomes almost paramount. Kunti asks her sons to enjoy the alms they had obtained, not knowing that the alms that they had brought was a lady. This creates a delicates situation for the five brothers; but considering that unquestionable obedience is due to the wishes of the mother, they took Draupadi as a common wife. Hindu writers with a rare insight often place mother in the very forefront of Elders as a person worthy of respect. "मातृदेवो भव" 'Let mother to you be a deity.' "O foremost of all that are acquainted with the rules of morality, it is said that obedience to superiors is every meritorious. Amongst all superiors, it is well known that the mother is the foremost. Even she hath commanded us to enjoy Draupadi as we do anything obtained as lams. It is for this that I regard the act as virtuous."[22] "An Acharya excels ten Upadhyayas, a father excels a hundred Acharyas, and a mother excels a thousand fathers in veneration."[23] There is no duty higher than truth. There is no superior more worthy of reverence than the mother."[24] Displeasure of mother is, therefore, at all costs, to be avoided. "And the son that doth not protect his mother when her husband is dead also suffereth disgrace."[25] "Remedies certainly exist for all curses, but no remedy can avail those cursed by their mother."[26]

The parental authority, as is apparent, is pushed beyond its legitimate limits. An unquestioning obedience to their wishes good or bad is considered to be the due of the parents. The case of Shunashepa shows that a child must be sold at the will of his parents. The story of Parashurama reveals the length to which a son is required to go in fulfilment of a father's wishes. He killed his mother at the command of his father. Jajali says : "I consider it to be my highest duty to do what is agreeable to them though it be not strictly justifiable."[27] There are, however, definite limits to parental obedience. An unjust wish of parents does occasion protests. Laxman says : "The king is uxorious, old, and therefore of perverted judgment, and is addicted to worldly affairs; being under the influence of his wife and passion, what could he not speak?"[28] Bharata is full of indignation and hatred towards his mother : "O Kaikeyi, thou hast been guilty of homicide in consequence of destruction of this race. Do thou go to hell...O thou enemy of mine in the guise of my mother...O slayer of thy husband...thou art a Rakshashi. (demoness)"[29] Parents may be renounced if they are hopelessly estranged from morality. "A man should renounce a father who is a regicide, or an insultor of the Vedas, or attends on Shudras as a priest, or procures abortion."[30]

The whole family organization, in fact, is based here upon the reverence of the younger people for their elders. The parental and priestly authority is based upon this principle. It is the same with other elders : they have a general right to respect and obedience at the hands of their juniors. "The elder brother, father, and the instructor–these three should always be regarded in the light of a father if they tread the paths of virtue and morality."[31] Bharata calls Rama his father, brother, and friend. "The eldest brother of one that is noble and cognisant of morality becomes his father. I shall take hold of his feet; he is now my refuge."[32]

The authority of the elder brother is next to that of the parents. He was largely responsible for the morals of his unmarried sisters.[33] "After the father has ceased to breathe, the eldest brother should be regarded as the father. It is the eldest brother who should assign to them their means of support and protect and cherish them. All the younger brothers should bow to him and obey his authority. Indeed, they should live indepen-dence upon him; even as they did upon their father while he was alive."[34] "The preceptor is the living image of Brahma, the father is that of Prajapati; the mother is the living image of the earth and the uterine brother is one's own image. Hence a man and especially a Brahmin, even when much oppressed by them shall not insult a father, mother, or an elder brother."[35]

All the other senior relations are entitled to a similar respectful treatment. "One shall stand up in the presence of one's uncles, father-in-law, maternal uncles, and preceptors, although younger than him in years, and welcome them as, I am that so and so etc. (that accost you). A mother's sister, the wife of a maternal uncle, or a father's sister shall be revered as the wife of a Guru. All these are equally venerable as the preceptor's wife. One shall accost a wife of his elder brother, belonging to his own caste, by clasping her feet, on returning from distant country; one shall accost his aunt and mother-in-law by clasping their feet. One shall behave unto his elder sister, mother's sister, or father's sister, as his own mother; but his brother is the most venerable of all."[36] Ushanas adds to this list the maternal and paternal grandfathers and grandmothers and says : "all of them are spoken of as the female and male elders : one should follow them with mind, words and deeds."[37]

Respect and honour are not to be confined within the family circle; all persons entitled to respect on one ground or the other should be objects of special attention and courtesy. The sin of withholding respect from the worthy people is very great. (पूज्यपूजाव्यतिक्रम:) It was on such a ground that a king suffered from childlessness. Good manners were not deemed idle; they were the very core of morality, of course when they were the fruits of noble natures and loyal hearts. The Hindus hate indeed too much of formality; objects of courtesy must be specially deserving and courtesy must be a matter as much of heart as of outward etiquette. For very near relations such as wife and husband no code of manners is laid down. "No kind of formal courtesy or obeisance need be observed or made in an assembly of fools or among husband and wives."[38] Various grounds of respect are mentioned. "Wealth, friends, age, work and erudition are the sources of honour; each succeeding one being more honourable than the preceding one. Among members of the three castes, he, who, has the best of the five above–said qualifications is entitled to the highest honour. Even a Shudra of ninety years shall be respected by the twice-born ones. (Elderliness) among the Brahmins is according to knowledge, that among the Kshatriyas is proportionate to prowess; that among the Vaishyas is proportionate to wealth, that among the Shudras is proportionate to age."[39] Nothing entitles a person to greater reverence as possession of high moral and saintly qualities. It is character which ultimately governs all. "If the Ritwij, the Purohita, the preceptor, the Acharya, the disciple, the relative (by marriage) and kinsman, happen to be possessed of learning and free from malice, then they should be deemed worthy of respect and worship. Those persons that do not possess such qualifications cannot be regarded as worthy of gifts or hospitality. Hence, one should with deliberation examine persons with whom one comes into contact."[40] These views reveal a very exalted conception of reverence,–its high value as a part of character, and its useful function in society. The sentiment of hero-worship is very strong in the Hindu mind; but it is directed not merely to persons who display all the pride and pomp of circumstance of heroes, but to persons who have any intrinsic moral or intellectual worth whatsoever. Profound reverence is to be felt and duly expressed for all who are our seniors,–be they seniors in age, or wealth, learning, or character. At the same time, the unworthy persons are to be carefully avoided. 'मान्यान्मानय'–says Bhartrihari : "Honour those to whom honour is due." "By worshipping one who should not be worshipped, and by refusing to worship him who should be worshipped, a man incurs the sin of homicide for ever."[41] "Only they that are firmly devoted to such seniors, that speak what is agreeable to them that seek their welfare, and that are submissive to them in behaviour, can obtain the merit of devotion."[42] "The duration of life, fame, and bodily strength of him who sits in the assembly of the old and serves them faithfully are found to increase each day."[43] In those days when learning was not diffused through books, it was specially necessary to wait upon the old people for these were the depositaries of all traditional culture. "It is by the (study of the) Shrutis that a person becometh learned : it is by ascetic practices that one acquireth some great object; it is by serving the old that one becometh wise."[44]

Man feels constraint in the presence of man; good manners remove all this constraint and thus lubricate the wheels of society. "At the advent of an old man, the vital airs of a youth heave up and attempt to leap over to him; they are restored to their normal condition by his rising up from his seat and duly welcoming him in. Having accosted an elderly person, a Brahmin after the accosting, shall enumerate his own name as, I am that so and so who accost you. A Brahmin accoster shall be re-accosted as 'be long-lived, O you handsome-looking one.' In meeting a Brahmin his spiritual good will be the first thing that shall be enquired; similarly the worldly peace of a Kshatriya, the opulence of a Vaishya, and the good health of a Shudra are the things that shall be asked after the first meeting. One shall address another man's wife, not related to him by marriage, as Bhavati (revered lady etc.); he shall address the younger sister as, O thou fortunate one (सुभगे)."[45]

It is not to be supposed that all rights exist on one side and all obligations on the other. The younger members of a family are entitled to protection and kindness at the hands of the elders. Parents are all kindness and sweetness to their children. "Whose gracious favour like a father's is most sweet."[46] "Be sweet as a kind father to a son, O Soma"[47]. "When will you take us by both hands as a dear sire his sons."[48] "Like a dear son who must be decked."[49] The father is bound to protect his son; and often he becomes the teacher of a son, too. If the boy goes wrong, he punishes him. "Agni claims protection like a son."[50] "I from my father have received deep knowledge of the Holy Law."[51] "I singly have sinned many a sin against you, and ye chastised me as a sire."[52] A father was condemned for depriving his son of his eyesight when the latter was guilty of extravagance.[53] Parents also leave their property to their sons. "Thou (Indra) and my mother appear alike, to give me wealth abundantly.[54] "Men have served thee in many and sundry ways, parting as it were, an aged father's wealth."[55] The kindness of parents was at first extended almost equally to both boys and girls. But the Aitareya Brahmana (33.I) shows that girls were falling into contempt.[56] The father kisses the son as well as the daughter when he returns from a journey.[57]

Parents are responsible for the protection as well as education of their children. "In consequence of his bringing up the son and instructing him, the sire is the son's foremost of superiors and the highest religion....The sire is the giver of all articles of enjoyment, of all articles of food, of instruction in the Vedas, and of all other knowledge regarding the world."[58] Kalidas mentions the functions of a father :–education (विनया-धान), protection (रक्षण), and maintenance (भरण). Bhavabhuti's masterly definition runs as follows :–"A child is the knot of joy binding the very essence of the souls of the parents owing to their common affection for it." A child is the objective manifestation of their mutual love, and a perpetual witness to the affections of their souls. A son should, therefore, on no account be abandoned. "Sons support the religion and achievements of men, enhance their joys, and rescue deceased ancestors from hell. It behoveth thee not, therefore, to abandon a son who is such. Therefore, cherish thy own self, truth and virtue, by cherishing thy son...The dedication of a tank is more meritorious than that of a hundred wells. A sacrifice, again, is more meritorious than the dedication of a tank. A son is more meritorious than a sacrifice."[59] "The mother is but a sheathe of flesh; the son sprung from the father is the father himself... Therefore, Dushyanta, cherish thy son born of Shakuntala. To live forsaking one's living son is a great misfortune."[60]

Next to sons, daughters are the objects of all attention. "The son is as one's own self and the daughter is like unto the son. How, therefore, can another take the wealth when one lives in one's own self in the form of one's daughter?"[61] The birth of a daughter, however, is not always looked upon with joy, and the Hindu sentiment is not quite unfaithfully reflected in the verse quoted by Sayana. "At the time of her birth a daughter is a source of annoyance to all relatives ; at the time of her bestowal she is a source of pecuniary loss; in her youth she is often the seat of much mischief; indeed a daughter burns the very heart of a father."[62] The affection of the Hindus, however, for their daughter is sufficiently keen, as is evinced by the fine verses put in the mouth of Kashyapa at the time of Shakuntala's departure.

The authority of the elders over the younger ones is very clearly asserted. But it is bounded by definite limits. The junior people pay obedience to their elders and in return are bound to get kindness and protection. "One should not chastise by harsh words the son after the sixteenth year, the girls after the twelfth year nor should punish the daughter-in-law."[63] Chanakya's verse also is very important. "One should fondle a child for five years, should chastise him up to ten, and when he reaches sixteenth year, he should behave towards him as a friend." The absolute authority of the parents, therefore, ends at the sixteenth year. "That eldest brother who injures his younger brothers ceases to be regarded as the eldest, and forfeits his share in the family property and deserves to be checked by the king."[64]

The householder's important duty is to see that all the relations are duly protected and maintained. "The chaste wife, step-mother, mother, daughter, father, wife, widowed daughter, or sister who has no offspring, aunt, brother's wife, sister of father or mother, grandfather, preceptor who has no son, father-in-law, uncle, grandson who is young and orphan–these must be maintained carefully to be best of one's ability even under adverse circumstances. One should maintain the families of both parents, friends, wife's family and the tendants, servants and maid-servants. One should also maintain the poor, the deformed, the stranger, and the helpless. Woe to the person who does not maintain his kith and kin. All his virtues go for nothing. In fact, though living, he is dead."[65] "The whole circle of relatives must be delicately looked to; all of them have power over man's future destiny. "The old, the young, the afflicted, the wasted, have power over the sky. The eldest brother is like unto the sire himself. The wife and the son are one's own body. One's menial servants are one's own shadow. The daughter is an object of great affection. For these reasons, a householder, endued with learning, observant of duties, and possessed of endurance, should bear without warmth or anxiety, every kind of annoyance and even censure from the last-named relatives."[66]

The relations between masters and servants are to be characterised by a spirit of mutual love and service.[67] "The worst servants desire wealth, the medium want both wealth and fame, the best want fame. Reputation is the wealth of the great."[68] Rama says to Hanuman : "As long as the worlds will last, so long will your fame and life persist. I may give one life to you for every one act of service of yours; and for the residual services, we shall remain indebted to you."[69] Loyalty to masters is a servant's duty. "One should never desert a good master who has fallen into distress. One should daily wish for the good of him whose food he has taken even once in life. Should not that of the protector be wished for always."?[70] A man attains heaven if he dies for the sake of his master.[71] The best servant would not flatter his master, but be bold enough to tell him the truth. He speaks out : "even when unasked if there be some danger, or if there be something wrong in the affairs, or if the time appointed for some action is seen to be expiring. He should say what is pleasant, true, useful, and virtuous, and always explain to him what is his good on terms of equality."[72]

But the master's task with regard to his servants is none too easy. Of course, the spirit of devotion on the part of loyal followers carries these often to very difficult heights. "The duties incidental to service are indeed very mysterious; even the yogis cannot efficiently perform these." The master have to reciprocate the devotion of their followers. In the Uttarram the old servant forgets for the time that Rama is a king and addresses him in the old style "Ramabhadra." When he corrects himself, Rama checks him and says he must address him in his old wonted way. Kalidas beautifully says that when servants attain success in the great achievements, it is due to the exalted opinion entertained by their masters about them. "That master who doth not give vent to his displeasure with devoted servants zealously pursuing his good, enlisteth the confidence of his servants. In fact, the latter adhere to him even in distress. By confiscating the grants to one's servants or stopping their pay, one should not seek to amass wealth, for even affectionate counsellors deprived of their means of life and enjoyment, turn against him and leave him. (in distress)... That officer who fully understanding the intention of his royal master, dischargeth all duties with alacrity, and who devoted to his master, always telleth what is for his master's good.... should be regarded by the king as his own second self."[73] Masters must possess certain qualities if they are to command the devotion of their servants. "A person should never wait upon these six types of men, viz. one that is a foe, one that always errs, one that is wedded to falsehood, one that is wanting in devotion to the good, one that is without affection, and one that always regards himself competent to do anything."[74] A master is to share his food with his servants. "One should not make distinctions between one's guests and attendants and knismen in matters of food. Equality (in this respect) with servants is applauded."[75] Desertion of servants without any fault on their part is a very sinful act.[76] "They who abandon and cast off preceptors and loyal followers without any offence have to sink in hell."[77] Yudhishthira refused to go to heaven leaving the faithful dog who accompanied him. "Hence, O Indra, I should not abandon this dog to-day from desire of my happiness. Even this is my vow steadily pursued, viz, that I never give up a person that is terrified, nor one that is devoted to me nor one that seeks my protection saying that he is destitute, nor one that is afflicted, nor one that has come to me, nor one that is weak in protecting one self nor one that is solicitous of life. I shall never give up such a one till my life is at end."[78]

The love for one's settled home had sunk deep even in the minds of our Vedic forefathers. It meant the triumph of pastoral and agricultural life over purely nomadic life of the previous people. Progress of civilisation very early required man to settle down peacefully in one abode, which gradually became the centre of his family and home of all virtue and prosperity. "May he, (Surya) grant us a sheltering home, a house that wards the fierce heat off on every side."[79] Grant us

(Rudra) protection, shelter, and a home secure."[80] Fixity and security are specially valued. Specious dwellings are objects of frequent prayers. Home derives its peculiar charm from the fact that its prosperity represents the prosperity of the family which it shelters. "Adityas, Gods, vouchsafe that this our home may be praiseworthy, prosperous, our heroes' sure defence. For cattle, for our sons, for our progeny, for life."[81] The following lines chanted by the traveller as he traces back his footsteps homewards are very expressive of deep passion for home in man's heart and the exact significance of it. "House do not fear, do not tremble; bringing strength we come back. Bringing strength, gaining wealth I come back to the house, rejoicing in my mind. Of which the traveller thinks, in which much joy dwells, the house I call. May it know us as we know it. Hither are called the cows; hither are called goats and sheep; and the sweet essence of food is called hither to our house. Hither are called many friends; the sweet companionship of friends. May our dwellings be always unharmed with all our men. Rich in sap, rich in milk, refreshing, full of joy and mirth, free from hunger and thirst, O house, do not fear us. To thee I turn for the sake of safety, of peace."[82]

The community possesses important claims upon everybody, which must not be ingnored.[83] Both the advantages and the disadvantages of one's relatives are set forth in the following passage :–"Thou shouldst fear they kinsmen, as thou shouldst fear death itself. A kinsman can never bear a kinsman's prosperity even as a feudatory chief cannot bear to see the prosperity of his overlord. None but a kinsman can feel joy at the destruction of a kinsman, adorned with sincerity, mildness, liberality, modesty, and truthfulness of speech. They, again, that have not kinsmen, cannot be happy. No men can be more contemptible than they that are destitute of kinsmen. A person that has no kinsmen is easily overridden by foes. Kinsmen constitute a refuge of one that is afflicted by other men, for kinsmen can never bear to see a kinsman afflicted by other people. When a kinsman is persecuted by even his friends, every kinsman of the persecuted regard the injury as one inflicted upon himself. In kinsmen, therefore, both merit and demerit may be marked. One should, for this reason, always know and worship his kinsmen in words and acts; and do them agreeable offices without injuring them at any time."[84]

References

1. Rg. I. 68. 5.
2. Rg. IX. 97. 30.
3. Rg. VII. 130. 3.
4. Rg. I. 103. 1.
5. Rg. II. 33. 12.
6. R. II. 25. 3.
7. R. II. 30, 35-38.
8. R. II. 107, 12.
9. R. I. 61, 19-21.
10. R. II. 21, 22-28.
11. R. II. 21, 30-36.
12. Vana. 160. 14.
13. Adi. 79. 25. 26.
14. Shanti. 272. 11-23.
15. Shanti. 108. 29-31.
16. Shanti. 163. 63.
17. M. II. 227-235.
18. Av. XVIII. 4. 62.
19. R. II. 101-21.
20. Vana. 314. 62.
21. Shanti. 272. 24-43.
22. Adi. 211. 16-17.
23. M. II. 145.
24. Shanti. 351. 18.
25. Vana. 294. 36.
26. Adi. 37. 4.
27. Vana. 217. 19-29.
28. R. II. 21. 3-12.
29. R. II. 74. 4-9.
30. Gautama. XXI.
31. R. IV. 18. 13.

32. R. II. 72. 32-33.
33. Rg. I. 124. 7; Av. I. 14. 2, iv. 55.
34. Anu. 162. 13-15.
35. M. II. 225-226.
36. M. II. 130-133.
37. U. I. 26-27.
38. Gautama. VI.
39. M. II. 136-137, 155.
40. Anu. 72, 6-10.
41. Shanti. 290, 17.
42. Shanti. 303, 1-2.
43. M. II. 121.
44. Vana. 314, 50.
45. M. II. 120, 122, 125, 127, 129.
46. Rg. VIII. 75. 4.
47. Rg. VIII. 48. 4.
48. Rg. I. 38. 1.
49. Rg. XI. 107. 13.
50. Rg. VI. 2. 7.
51. Rg. VIII. 6. 10.
52. Rg. II. 29. 5.
53. Rg. I. 117. 17-18.
54. Rg. VIII. 1. 6.
55. Rg. I. 70. 5.
56. Also Av. VI. 2. 4.
57. Gr. G. II. 8. 21. 22. 25.
58. Shanti. 272. 11-23.
59. Adi. 99. 24-30.
60. Adi. 100. 2-4.
61. Anu. 80. 11-15.
62. Sayana's Com. Ai. Br. 33. 1.
63. S. N. 334-335.
64. Anu. 162. 2-7.
65. S.N. III. 243-253.
66. Shanti. 249. 18-21.
67. R. VI. 16, 2-9.
68. S. N. II. 836-841.
69. R. VII. 40, 21-23.
70. S.N. 495-497.
71. R. VI. 92. 9.

72. S. N. II. 441-448.
73. Udyoga. 37. 22-27.
74. Udyoga. 37. 37.
75. Shanti. 191. 9.
76. R. II. 75. 37.
77. Anu. 62. 34.
78. Mahaprasthanik. 3. 11-12.
79. Rg. V. 44. 7.
80. Rg. I. 114.5.
81. Rg. X. 35. 12.
82. Gr. H. I. 8. 29. 2.
83. R. VI. 16. 2-9.
84. Shanti. 80. 33-40.

Chapter - XII

RIGHTS OF PROPERTY

The idea which bound together ancient society was the idea of kinship. Consanguinity was the one powerful cement holding families and tribes together. The same self persisted in the family for nearly four or seven generations. There was identity of body so far (सपिंडता) ; body being the same, property, worship, food must remain joint. "Of members of the same family divided or undivided, living together, there should be partition of the heritage among the descendants of the fourth degree. Up to that degree the members of the family are the same body. After that, there is difference of body. Sages desire that there should be separation in body and in wealth at the same time."[1]

The main features characterising a joint family are common religious worship, common food, common income and expenditure, and a common legal personality. The eldest or the ablest member becomes the representative of this Gens. All the other members of the family, however old they may be, have no financial autonomy. Children have no economic freedom as long as their parents survive. "Wives, sons, slaves and attendants are dependent. The head of the family who has got property descended from ancestors, is independent in regard to it."[2]

It must not be forgotten that the unit in such cases in the family, not the individual. The rights of the head therefore remain severely limited. Certain forms of property such as deposits, borrowed things, joint property are inalienable even in the worst plight. Ancestral property can be enjoyed only; there can be no gift or sale of the same.[3] Sacrificial gains, land, written documents, food, water, and women remain indivisible even to the thousandeth degree.[4] All actions with regard to immovable property, must be duly authorised by the consent of every co-heir. Land alienation cannot be done without the consent of co-villagers, of kinsmen, of neighbours, and of heirs.[5] Only extreme crises can justify such alienations. Rights of family must be fully conserved before any sacrifice of property for charitable purposes can be allowed.[6]

Primogeniture seems to be at first the prevailing custom. Unity and indivisibility of executive in a family required such concentration of power.[7] First father, then mother, then the eldest son was the head of the family, in early times.[8] The eldest member was bound to support the junior people, who in turn were bound to give him honour. Minors must be carefully protected. A joint-family assured to all those who were old, who were disabled, who were defective complete protection. The work of poor-relief, of insurance for old age and accidents, which is being organised in Europe now, was a normal function of a family here, which was held together not by naked economic ties, but by moral and spiritual affinities as well. The spirit underlying certain modern schemes suggesting artificial restriction of families, segregation of the effete, and the doing away with the undesirables was wholly alien to the ancient law-givers who took into account not only the biological and economic factors but also moral and spiritual ones. "Let them carefully protect the shares of those who are minors, as well as the increments. Granting food, clothing, they shall support those who are incapable of transacting legal business, the blind, idiots, those immersed in vice, the incurably diseased and so forth. Those who neglect their duties and occupations; but not the outcast, nor his offspring."[9] Perpetrators of very grave sins become outcasts. These must never be supported.[10]

Equal division of property soon took the place of primogeniture. "Manu divided his wealth equally among his sons."[11] Manu's reference to primogeniture, therefore, relates to some pre-Vedic period. "O fire, men obtain wealth from you as sons obtain from their old father."[12] For a long time, it was maintained share.[13] Apastamba was a great reformer; he put up a fight against this custom and pleaded for equality in partition. "Therefore all (sons) who are virtuous inherit. But him who expends money unrighteously, he shall disinherit, though he be the eldest son. He should, during his lifetime, divide his wealth equally among his sons, excepting the eunuch, the mad man, and the outcasts."[14]

Family was not a mere economic organization, but a cultural organization as well. It was one of the most powerful instruments to train up the younger people in higher ideals and to keep in check the idler and the vagabond. The younger brothers should be given a share in the self-acquired property of the eldest brother, *provided they have made a due progress in learning.* (यदि विद्यानुपालिन:)[15] All brothers who habitually commit forbidden acts are unworthy of (a share of) the property.[16] A distinction is made between those who are in capable, and those who are morally perverse. The former are not entitled to a share, but entitled to maintenance; the latter are not entitled to either. But while the undesirables may be outcasted, their wives and children are entitled to support as well as inheritance.[17] All persons who contract illegitimate marriages, those who are apostates from a religious order are excluded from inheritance; so also hermits, ascetics, long-long students, and heretics.[18] The principle upon which these rules are based is here enunciated. "Wealth is made for sacrifices. Those that are incompetent to perform them are not entitled to inherit property. They are only entitled to maintenance. Wealth is for sacrifice. (यज्ञार्थं विहितं वित्तं.) Therefore it should go to a proper person and the virtuous, and not to a woman, an ignorant person, or an apostate."[19]

Members of a joint family form a company with an unlimited liability, However, there are certain limitations to the power of each member to involve others in ruin, and also certain safeguards by which the special interests of a zealous, studious, intelligent man are conserved. Sons are liable for their father's debts; but if these debts are incurred for spirituous liquor, for gratification of lust, for gambling, and for idle gifts, sons have no responsibility for their payment.[20] Certain types of property belong only to the person who acquires them even if he stays in a joint family. "Property (acquired) by learning belongs solely to him to whom (it was given), likewise the gift of a friend, a present received on marriage or with the honey mixture. What one (brother) may acquire by his labour, without using the patrimony, that acquisition made by his own effort, he shall not share unless by his own will."[21] Narada lays it down that all property gained by valour, or the gains of science, or Stridhana : these three types of property are not subject to partition. An unlearned brother, if he finances the education of a younger brother, shall be entitled to a share of the wealth gained by the : latter. [22] Katyayana defines the position further and adds the gains from arts and crafts to the list of articles over which the rights of co-heirs do not extend. "What has been obtained from a pupil, or by officiating as a priest, or for answering a question, or for determining a doubtful point, or through display of knowledge, or by success in disputation, or for superior skill in reading, the sages have declared the gains of learning, and not subject to distribution."[23]

The Hindu sages thought so seriously of the necessity of the continuation of the line that they laid it down that in the absence of legitimate sons, others could be improvised for the fulfilment of, religious duties. Manu, accordingly, mentions twelve types of sons : the legitimate son of the body, the son begotten on a wife, the son adopted, the son secretly born, and the son cast off are the six heirs and kinsmen. The son of an unmarried damsel, the son received with the wife, the son bought, the son begotten on a remarried woman, the son self-given, and the son of a Shudra are neither heirs nor kinsmen.[24] Aupjanghani asserts that only the Aurasa (legitimate) sons are entitled to inheritance.[25] Apastamba calls all such connec-tion sin and says that a man of later times should not blindly imitate the great men of preceding times.[26] Brihaspati says that eleven types of sons (excluding the Aurasa type) cannot be adopted by men of the present age; they can only be substitutes as oil may be a substitute for ghee. They are entitled to maintenance only.[27]

From very early times the custom of adoption prevailed. The Aryan man and wife could not without a son, either for worldly of spiritual purposes. At first this custom was not popular. It seems to be an unpleasant innovation in the Rig-Vedic time. "The son of another of a different family should never be acknowledged as a son even in mind."[28] "Atri gave his son to the son of Urva who desired a son; childless he thought he was without power, weak, and without substance."[29] 'नापुत्रस्य लोकोस्ति।'[30] "There is no place for a sonless man." Atri is supposed to be the first person to initiate the system of adoption.[31] Vishwamitra adopted Shunahshepa as his son and gave him the right of the eldest. We hear in the Mahabharata that Kunti was the adopted daughter, and in the Ramayana that Shanta, the daughter of Dasharatha, was adopted by Lomapada. The adopted son takes the family name of the person adopting him.

Opinion is divided as regards the power of the parents over the children as regards their gift of sale. Apastamba here as elsewhere, stands for a purer position. "The gift (or accepta-nce of a child) and the right to sell (or buy) a child are not recognized."[32] But actual necessities gradually prevailed. Extreme distress justifies such a step. "A wife or a son or the whole of a man's estate shall not be given away or sold without the assent of the persons interested; he must keep them himself but in extreme distress he may give or sell them; otherwise he must attempt no such thing."[33] Other sages assert the power of the father over the boy to the extent of his gift or sale for adoption. "Man formed of uterine blood and virile seed proceeds from his mother and his father (as an effect) from its cause. (Therefore) the father and the mother have power to give, to sell, to abandon their (sons). But let him not give or receive (in adoption) an only son. For he (must remain) to continue the line of the ancestors."[34]

An interesting light is thrown on the position of females in a society by the examination of their economic position. A girl in a family had three possibilities. She gets married; and if she has brothers it seems that she had no property rights. "Some hold that daughters do not inherit. Therefore the Vedas says that a male is the taker of wealth, and that a female is not a taker of ."[35] "The legitimate son of the body does not give the inheritance to the sister."[36] Daughters have a right to the ornaments of their mother, which custom assigns to her.[37] Property sufficient for their marriage should be given to them.[38] The rights of unmarried girls are fully recognised even when these have brothers. "(O Indra) as the daughter being with her parents asks for share of wealth from the father's family."[39] Vishnu allots to daughters shares equal to those of their brothers.[40] Narada also takes this view. "To the eldest son a larger share shall be allotted and a less share is assigned to the youngest son, the rest shall take equal shares and so shall an unmarried sister."[41] Manu assigns a share equal to that of her brother to a daughter, who is first appointed Putrika but afterwards a son being born to her father who becomes an ordinary girl.[42] Subsequently, it was ruled that unmarried sisters should receive one share for every three shares of a brother.[43] The third possible position for a daughter is be the only child of the parents. She is then made Putrika i. e. her son is entitled to perform the funeral rites of her father, and she is entitled to her father's property. "The sonless man who has a daughter fit to be a Putrika having observed the Putrika rite gets the son of that daughter as his son's son knowing that this daughter's son will perform his Shraddha."[44] The brotherless female remains a part of her father's house.[45] Manu says : "A son is even as one's self, a daughter is equal to a son; how can another heir take the estate while one's self lives. The daughter's son shall take the whole estate of his maternal grandfather who leaves no male issue."[46] Apastamba, Vishnu, Narada entitle a brotherless damsel to be the sole inheritor of her father's estate.[47]

A widow who has no sons succeeds to the entire property of her lord.[48] But she is not entitled to bestow gifts or to sell property. Under all circumstances she is entitled to food and raiment. She is also entitled to her share of the joint property as long as she stays in the joint family, but she is not competent to dispose it of. But if the widow is in charge of the house (कुलपालिका) her proprietorship is for the life-time, in gift, mortgage, and sale. But widows who have sons receive shares proportionate to their son's share.[49]

Women have a general right to maintenance and protection. "A mother and a father in their old age, a virtuous wife, and an infant son must be maintained even though doing a hundred times that which ought not to be done."[50] Women are under the protection of either their father, or sons, or other relations. The position of an unchaste wife is rendered harsh by poor accommodations. She is deprived of her rights, poorly dressed, fed with a view to sustain life only.[51] But it must be remembered that males also lose their rights of inheritance if they lead immoral lives.

The ancient law first assigned no separate property to females. The growth, therefore, of Stridhana–woman's property was a slow growth. The Hindus were the first to give females rights which they had not elsewhere. "What (was given) before the (nuptial) fire, what (was given) on the bridal procession, what was given in token of love, and what was received from her brother, mother, or father, that is called the six-fold property of a woman. (Such property) as well as a gift subsequent and what was given (to her) by her affectionate husband, shall go to her offspring, (even) if she dies in the life-time of her husband."[52] Her power over the property called Saudayika i.e. What is received from her brothers, parents, or her husband's father's family, is complete, both in respect to sale and gift. She can even dispose of the immovables according to her pleasure. She is to preserve what she has received from her husband with care while he is alive; afterwards her right is supreme. Neither the husband, nor the son, nor the father, nor the brothers can assume power over a woman's property to take or bestow it.[53] Only exceptional circumstances such as famine, performance of religious duties, illness, or imprisonment can justify a husband to touch his wife's property.[54] Of course, each partner has complete right over the property of another when mutual affection subsists; in fact the idea of separate property of either husband or wife does not arise in normal wedded life. "दम्पत्योर्मध्यगं धनं." "Wealth is common to the married pair."[55]

References

1. Devala cited in Madhava.
2. Narada. I.
3. Vriddha Yaj.
4. Ushanas quoted in Smritichandrika.
5. Mitakshara.
6. Narada. IV.
7. M. IX, 105-108.
8. Narada. I.
9. Baudhayana. II.3, 36-40.
10. Gautama. 21.1, 28. 43, 44.
11. Ta. S. III. 1, 9, 4.
12. Rg. I. 70, 5; Rg. X. 61,1; M. IX. 104.
13. Ta. S. II. 5, 2-7; M. IX.112, etc.
14. Apastamba. II.6, 14, 15, 1.
15. M. IX. 204.
16. M. IX. 124.
17. Narada. XIII. 21, 22.

18. Katyayana cited in the Kalpataru, Vriddha-Harita IV. 152.
19. A text cited by Madhava.
20. M. IX. 107; VIII. 159.
21. M. IX. 206, 208.
22. Narada. XIII. 6. 7. 10.
23. Quoted in Ratnakar.
24. M. IX. 158-160.
25. Baudhayana. 2. 2. 3. 31-33.
26. Apastamba. 2. 6. 13. 1-6; 8-11.
27. Vishnu. XXIV. 14; XXV. 33. 35.
28. Rg. VII. 4. 8.
29. Ta. S. 7. 1. 8.
30. Ai. Br. VII. 3. 1.
31. See Harivamsha II. 7.
32. Apastamba. 2. 6. 13. 10.
33. Katyayana cited in the Mayukha.
34. Vasishtha. XVII. XV.
35. Nirukta.
36. Rg. III. 31. 1. 2.
37. Baudhayana. 2. 2. 3. 43.
38. Devala quoted in the Ratnakar.
39. Rg. II. 17. 7.
40. Vishnu. XVIII. 35.
41. Vishnu. XIII. 2. 13.
42. M. IX. 134.
43. M. IX. 118. Yaj. II. 126. 127.
44. Rg. III. 31.1.
45. Rg. I. 18. 124.
46. M. IX. 130-133.
47. Apastamba. 2. 6. 14. 2-4.; Vishnu XV; Narada XIII. 50.
48. Narada. I.
49. Vishnu. XVIII. 35.
50. Manu as quoted in Mitakshara.
51. Yaj. I. 70.
52. M. IX. 194-195.
53. Katyayana quoted by the commentators.
54. Yaj. II. 147.
55. Datta.

Chapter - XIII

ETHICS OF THE STATE

(1)

The incapacity of men for self-government gives rise everywhere to the institution of government. If men were left to themselves, all order and peace would vanish. Civilization, therefore, rests ultimately on the basis of force. Anarchy is the prolific parent of all lawlessness and disorder. The evils of anarchy are frequently referred to. "In a kingless kingdom no one sows corn. In such a state, the son does not obey his sire, nor the wife her husband. The country possesses no wealth and wives are hard to keep. All morality, in fact ceases to exist. Men do not form themselves into associations nor do they inspired with cheerfulness, make elegant gardens or sacred edifices. In big sacrifices the wealthy Brahmins do not confer (on the officiating priests) the Dakshinas. Neither social gatherings, nor festivities characterised by the presence of Merry the atrical managers and performers increase. Disputants cannot decide their points. Bevies of virgins decked in gold do not repair to gardens for purposes of sport. The wealthy are not well protected; nor do shepherds and cultivators sleep with their doors open."[1]

It is very interesting to find very early anticipations of the contract theory in the Mahabharata. Like Hobbes the ancient thinkers believed in an original state of war and anarchy, the violence and unpleasantness of which led men to surrender their freedom to an external agency, and entrust all the power of the state to it. "It hath been heard by us that men in days of old, in consequence of anarchy, met with destruction, devouring one another, like stronger fish devouring the weaker ones in water. If hath been heard by us that a few amongst them then assembling together made certain compacts saying. He who becomes harsh in speech or violent in temper, he who seduces or abducts other people's wives or robs the wealth that belongs to others should be cast off by us. Assembling after some time, they protested in affliction to the Grandsire, saying,-Without a king, O Divine Lord, we are going to destruction. Appoint some one as our king! All of us shall worship him and he shall protect us."[2]

The position of the king in a Hindu state is always very high. He represents the government; he is the one upholder of the whole social and political organization. "Firm is the sky and firm the earth, and steadfast also are these hills, steadfast all this living world and steadfast is the king of men."[3] There is a divinity that hedges a king in the eye of the orientals. "The king, if he be an infant must not be belittled in the knowledge of his human birth. He is the great divinity manifest in the shape of man."[4]

The Hindu view, therefore, does not look with favour upon the institution of a phantom monarchy. The king represents the majesty and power of the people; in him is concentrated the whole might of the demos. He is, therefore, to be a virtual ruler of men, a true leader of society; he is to play the role of a true heroking as Carlyle pictured it. The whole governmental structure hinged upon the royal personality; hence it is very important to inquire into the main elements which went to constitute it. "In Rama are united beauty and magnificence; and even as a father inquireth after the welfare of his sons, he returning from the field on horse or elephant, exhaustively inquireth after the weal of the citizens, concerning their sons or their (sacrificial) fire, or their disciples. And that tiger-like Rama always asketh the Brahmins,–Do your disciples tend you? and the Kshatriyas–Do your disciples always remain mailed? When calamity befalleth the people, he experiences excess of sorrow; and on festal occasions he rejoiceth ever like their own father. He ministers unto the aged and has controlled his senses. He preludes his speech with a smile, and will equal thee in good fortune, or in talent, or in subtle apprehension, or in the capacity of answering a controversialist."[5] Humility, tact, and power of conciliation are required in a leader of men. "Many kings, with their progenies have been destroyed through arrogance; and kings who had been exiles in forest, have regained their kingdoms, through humility."[6]

Qualifications, therefore, of a very high order are required in a king. A highly trained intellect, and an acquaintance with various arts and sciences are the very necessary prerequisites of kingship. "From Brahmins, well-versed in the Vedas, he must learn the three Vedas, the eternal principles of punishment, the science of reasoning, the science of Self-knowledge, the principles of trade, agriculture, cattle-rearing, and the science of wealth."[7] Perfect self-control is an essential trait of a good king. "Day and night, he must be engaged in conquering his senses, a king, who has conquered his senses, is enabled to keep his subjects under control. Let him assiduously avoid the ten evil habits, which originate from desire, as well as those eight, which result from anger, and which are sure to end in grief. A hunting excursion, a game with dice, day-sleep, calumny, promiscuous intercourse, intoxication, singing, dancing, music, and idle rambling, these are the ten vices which originate from desire."[8] An ideal king must combine the stern and humane virtues in equal proportions; he must err neither on the side of leniency nor on the side of severity. He should simultaneously inspire both love and awe and should be accessible without compromising his dignity. "In a king are united lustre and heroism along with gentleness, and a capacity of inflicting punishments along with a capacity of showering favours."[9] A complete balance of character is good for a king, who should not be excessively obsessed by pure righteousness, pure interests, or pure desires.[10]

The king's prime function is the administration of the kingdom for the happiness and well-being of his subjects. All personal and private ends are to be sternly set aside for the sake of the public. In the Vedic period he was called the protector of the tribe. (गोपा जनस्य) "The king is the Lord and father of the whole universe. He is time, he is Yuga, and he is the creation, mobile and immobile. He is called Dharma because he holdeth all." (R. प्रक्षिप्तसर्ग:) "The king by behaving with compassion towards his people is called their father. The subject that behaves falsely towards him takes birth in the next life as an animal or a bird. By doing good to the people and by cherishing the poor, king becomes a mother unto his people. By scorching the wicked, he comes to be regarded as fire, and by restraining the sinful he comes to be called Yama..... By giving instruction in morality and virtue, he becomes a preceptor, and by exercising the duty of protection, he becomes the protector."[11] In fact, the good of the people is the very first and the foremost aim of government; government exists for people and not people for government. The very titles of king such as नृप, राजन्, and others bring out the significance of his social role. "And because he gratified all people, therefore, was he called Rajan (king.). And because he also healed the wounds of Brahmins, therefore, he earned the name of Kshatriya."[12]

The proof of the pudding is said to be in the eating of it. The proof of the excellence of a government, its ultimate standard and criterion is in the happiness and elevation of the people. Rama was an ideally perfect king, because no man was a better leader of man; no man inspired such boundless attachment and love as he did in the masses. He was held up as a veritable God on earth, the adored centre of people's affections and joys, and hero of the popular imagination. His influence over the mind of the people was quite wonderful; it was the influence of his magnetic personality. The secret of his popularity was sympathy; he entered not merely into the skin but the soul of the people. And secondly, the greatness and elevation of his character,–the touching simplicity, the saintly self-control, the perfect disinterestedness, and the capacity for boundless self-sacrifice,–this was the root of his popularity and his empire over the mind of man. "Rama loves us even as he loves his own brothren" said a man from the ranks of ordinary people.[13] "That righteous one showed mercy unto all, old and young of the four castes and hence they were all obedient to him."[14] "And leaving aside our gardens and fields and abodes, will we, making the righteous Rama's misery and happiness our own, follow him.... Let the forest to which Raghava repairs resemble a city and this city renounced by us be converted into a wilderness."[15] "And they forgot to rejoice and the traders did not spread (their stores) and stalls did not grace the place, and the house-holders did not cook, and people did not rejoice on recovering lost property or gaining a profuse accession of wealth, and mothers did not feel any delight on beholding their first-born."[16]

The part which government is expected to play in social life is far from an unimportant one. Hindu thinkers made governments responsible not only for material prosperity or economic happiness of the people but also for such ideal values as the liberty of the soul, the character of the individual, and so on. "At the instance of the king, mind subjects perform many an action conducing to virtue, wealth, and desire though not mentioned in the Shastras. The king is the virtue, the king is the desire, and the king is the prime jewel of all subjects. Virtue, desire, or sin,-everything arises from the king."[17] Powerful personalities are at the botton of progress in civilization. These masterful men are almost the creators of their age; they initiate and pioneer new lines of thought, new institutions of civilization, They are, therefore, called epoch-making personalities. "The different cycles of time, such as the Kritam, Treta, Dwapara, and Kali are but the creations of kings. Hence, the king is called (the embodiment of) a Yuga, (a cycle of time). When the king sleeps (remains idle), he is the Kali Yuga; when he is awake, he is the Dwapara; when he energetically undertakes an exploit, he is the Treta; and when he is fully employed, he is the Kritam."[18] "Let not this doubt be thine, viz., whether the era is the cause of the king or the king is the cause of the era, for (know this to be certain that) the king is the cause of the era."[19]

(2)

It is pertinent to inquire what were the exact ways in which government was expected to be of substantial service to the people. The raison d'etre of government is made clear; it is the one most needful and beneficent organ of public good. But the detailed operations of this institution give rise to various problems of internal administration and foreign policy; and under these two aspects we will sum up the main influences of which the governing agency became the centre and the source, both directly and indirectly.

The important part of administration next to the royal personality is the body of ministers, who shape and mould the policy of kings. Much depended on the competence of these ministers; and hence their qualifications became an important subject. "A king desirous of prosperity and of shining in the midst of his contemporaries, should have for ministers men connected with his trusted friends, possessed of high birth, born in his own kingdom, incapable of being corrupted, unstained by adultery and similar vices, belonging to good families, possessed of learning, sprung from sires and grand-sires that held similar offices, and adorned with humility. The king should employ five such persons to look after his affairs, as are possessed of intelligence, unstained by pride, have a disposition that is good, energy, patience, forgiveness, purity, loyalty, firmness and courage, whose merits and faults have been well tested, who are of mature years, who are capable of bearing burden and who are free from deceit. Men that are wise in speech, that are possessed of heroism, that are full of resources under difficulties....that can read signs,...that are conversant with requirements of place and time, and that desire the good of their masters, should be employed by the king as his ministers in all affairs of the kingdom."[20]

Neither the king nor his ministers are to be puppet officers. Very heavy load of responsibility lies on the councillors; the king cannot act in his isolated capacity; at every step he is to be guided by his ministers. The king should hold conference with his ministers on all important questions of policy. "He that controlling his own self, consulteth with his counsellors, reasonably touching important matters of foreign policy, as well as matters of righteousness, and interest and personal happiness, does not come by calamity."[21] There are pseudo-counsellors as well as right ones, and these must be properly distinguished.[22] Mere orators, wits, flatterers, self-seekers, sophisters, bunglers, and traitors, are ruled out of court. "Learned men have declared that a king although powerful should never consult with these four, viz. men of small sense, men that are procrastinating, men that are indolent, and men that are flatterers."[23] A profound veil of secrecy is to be thrown over the deliberations of the inner council. "That king, whose counsels cannot be known by either outsiders or those about him, but who knoweth the counsels of others through his spies, enjoyeth his prosperity long."[24]

The organization of the civil and military service, and the selection of appropriate persons, are the most important part of the duties of the heads of government. The highest offices should be accessible to persons of solid merit and efficiency; no racial or colour bar should come in the way of the promotion of talent and scholarship. "Just as gold is tested by experts by reference to lightness or heaviness of weight, colour, sound etc. so also one should examine servants (or office-bearers) by reference to their work, companionship, merits, habits, family-relationships etc. and place confidence in one who is found to be trustworthy. Work, character, and merit-these are to be respected, neither casts nor family. Neither by caste nor by family can superiority be ascertained. In marriages and dinner parties, considerations of family and caste are compulsory."[25] Appreciation of all forms of merit and their due employment are very essential. "Appointments on unfit persons are not at all approved. That king, who confers on his servants offices for which each is fit, succeeds in consequence to enjoy the happiness attaching to sovereignty. A Sharabha should occupy the position of a Sharabha, a lion should swell the might of a lion, a tiger should be placed in the position of a tiger; and a leopard should be placed as a leopard... If thou wishest to achieve success, thou shouldst never appoint servants in situations higher than what they deserve."[26] "My child, dost thou employ the best servants upon the best offices, the middling upon middling and the worst upon the worst? And dost thou employ upon the most worthy offices, counsellors who are above bribery, who have served thy father and grandfather, and who are pure?"[27] No faith in the infallibility of majority guided the kings. It is wisdom not number which should rule the destinies of a country. "And passing by a thousand dunces does thou set thy heart on having a single wise man? In times of pecuniary stress, a wise man stands in excellent stead. And although a king might be surrounded by a thousand or ten thousand fools yet he cannot count upon any assistance (at their hands). And a single able counsellor, intelligent, heroic, and sagacious, bringeth great prosperity upon a king."[28]

The king should be very discriminating in his attitude towards his officers. Undue indulgence must never be extended to them.[29] "There should be no difference between him and them as regards objects of enjoyment. The only distinction should consist in his umbrella and his power of passing orders. His conduct towards them, before or behind, should be the same. The king, who behaves in this way, never comes to grief. That crooked king, who taxes his subjects heavily, is soon deprived of life by his own servants and relatives."[30] The ministers should be duly respected by the king. The prosperity of the kingdom requires that there should be perfect cooperation between them. "If masters and ministers follow each other for deriving support from each other, subduing pride and wrath and vanity and envy, they may then both become happy."[31]

When power, however, is liable to be abused in the hands of the officers, it is for the king to stand for the people against his men. He should be a substantial check to the powers of bureaucracy. Government is solely responsible for the mischievous work of its own agents. "When a weak person fails to find a rescuer, the great rod of divine chastisement falls upon the king. When all the subjects of a king (are obliged by distress to) live like Brahmins by mendicancy, such mendicancy brings destruction upon the king. When all the officers of the king posted in the provinces unite together and act with injustice, the king is then said to bring about a state of unmixed evil upon his kingdom. When the officers of the king extort wealth by unjust means, or acting from lust or avarice, from persons piteously soliciting for mercy, a great destruction is then sure to overtake the king."[32] "The king must personally inspect every year the Gramas (or villages), Puras (or cities) and Deshas (or districts) and must know which subjects have been pleased and which oppressed by the staff of officers, and deliberate upon matters brought forward by the people. He should take the side not of his officers, but of his subjects. He should accuse the officer, who is accused by one hundred men."[33] Corrupt officials must be excommunicated from the realm, and their goods confiscated.[34]

An active intelligence department was an essential part of every administration. Learned, upright spies, endowed with presence of mind, representing the truth, and possessed of wisdom are to be spread over all the provinces. The king is called चारचक्षु. (whose eyesight is represented by his spies.) Three spies must be appointed in connection with each of the following officers:–Minister, priest, heir-apparent, general, warder, gate-keeper of the harem, jailor, treasurer, conveyor of the royal orders, pleaders, judges, members of the council, distributer of pay and provision to the army, journeymen, justice of the peace, protector of the frontiers, magistrates, guards of rivers, hills, forests, and fortresses. These spies must be ignorant of each other's counsels.[35] Ravana addresses his spies : "Go hence, and acquaint yourselves with the exertions of Rama; as well as with those who, being the custodians of Rama's closest counsels, have gladly joined him. How he sleepeth and how he waketh, and what he engageth himself in,-having cleverly acquainted yourselves with all this do ye come back. The wise king, that gathers (a knowledge of) his enemy through spies, can, putting forth a little effort in conflict, neutralise (his exertions.)"[36] Rama asks his spy Bhadra to acquaint him with the currents of popular opinion. "Without hiding anything, do thou relate everything from the beginning as it is; what good and bad things have been given vent to by the citizens. Hearing the good and bad opinion of the citizens, I shall desist from bad actions and engage in good ones."[37] Such was the role of the C.I.D. in ancient organization of our society. It was employed to gauge the strength and weakness of surrounding peoples, to sound the level and direction of public opinion, and to be forewarned with regard to all contingencies.

The view of the functions of government adopted here leans towards the modern socialistic attitude. Government was the true Mabapa–the father and mother to the people. It was a paternal rule of which the ancients were so fond, based upon the mutual love and service of the governors and the governed. Not for a moment "the right divine of kings to govern wrong" was admitted. The people occupied the first and foremost place in the minds of the rulers. Power was essentially a trust and not an arbitrary privilege. The king was exalted above all earthly dignities because he was not a mouth-pieces of a section or a sect, of a particular race or caste, but he was the one supreme organ for the general good. All the varied interests of the kingdom were to find their supporter in him. The finer and rarer forms of spiritual and intellectual growth had the greatest claim upon the attention of government. Government was not a purely secular institution completely indifferent to all the spiritual interests of the community. "Spiritual preceptors , aged persons, ascetics, gods, guests, Chaityas (big trees situated on high ways which are supposed to be the abodes of gods), the emancipated ones, and Brahmins should be duly saluted."[38] "A king even at the point of death, must not receive any revenue from a Shrotriya Brahmin; nor must be suffer a Shrotriya, living in his territory, to be oppressed with hunger. The kingdom of a king, wherein a Shrotriya is overwhelmed with hunger, is soon consumed by that hunger."[39] Arts and sciences must be properly encouraged.[40]

The commercial and agricultural interests require special protection. All growth of capital depends upon the security and encouragement extended to the mercantile classes; and hence the efficiency and prosperity of the state depend ultimately upon the development of its trade and industries. "The king should always conciliate and protect the Vaishyas, adopt measures for in spring them with a sense of security, and for ensuring them in the enjoyment of what they possess, and always do what is agreeable to them. The king should always act in such a way towards the Vaishyas that their productive powers may be enhanced. The Vaishyas increase the strength of a kingdom, improve its agriculture, and develop its trade. A wise king, therefore, should always gratify them."[41]

Texation presents one of the knottiest points in the government of a country. "To tax and to please" said Burke "is no more given to man than to love and to be wise." Heavy and oppressive taxation ultimately defeats its own purpose. Excessive cupidity on the part of government is sure to overreach itself. Much tact is necessary in reconciling the people to necessary taxation; in fact, in this part of the administration of finance lies the main skill of government. "A king should milk his kingdom like a bee gathering honey from plants. He should act like the keeper of a cow, who draws milk from her without boring her udders and without starving the calf. The king should (in the matter of taxes) act like leach drawing blood mildly. He should conduct himself towards his subjects like a tigress in the matter of carrying her cubs, touching them with her teeth but never piercing them therewith. He should behave like a mouse which though posessed of sharp and pointed teeth, still cuts the feet of sleeping animals in such a manner that they do not at all become conscious of it."[42]

Certain general regulations are laid down regarding the methods of taxation and commercial transactions. "Taking into consideration the cost price as well as the selling price of his goods, the cost of conveyance, the cost of his daily living, and other contingent expenses, as well as the cost of ensuring safety to his goods, the cost of policing the forest etc., he shall levy taxes on merchants."[43] Non-interference in trade was not in fitting with ancient ideas; the commercial policy was more or less protectionist.[44]

No persons have greater claims upon society and government which is its organ that the weak, the poor, the distressed, and the helpless. Government is bound to provide for those who are rendered destitute of any provisions and it is a belief often expressed in the sacred writings that people never suffer nor starve unless there is somthing wrong with the government. A child cannot die prematurely under Rama's rule, if everything is well in his kingdom. Dushyanta in the Shakuntala says that evil spirits cannot affect people in his kingdom as his administration was faultless. A king insults a Brahmin and there is a famine for years together in the kingdom. All such instances clearly bring out the rooted belief of the Hindus in the omnipotent capacity both of good and evil of government. Government can become, if it chooses, averitable fountains of happiness to the unhappy and of strength to the weak.

The king is, above all, bound to uphold the rights of the minorities. It is his special mission to be a friend of the weak and the downtrodden. The poor, the old, and the pregnant women are all exempt from taxation. "The king shall levy a nominal tax on poor men living by plying small traders in his kingdom."[45] "A blind of lame man, an idiot, on above seventy years of age and one who does benefit to a Veda-knowing Brahmin must be exempted from paying any tax. Let the king always do honour to a Shrotriya, a sick man, an invalid, or an infant, as well as to the indigent, high-born, an the revered."[46] "He should always maintain and protect the helpless, the masterless, and the old, and the women that are widows."[47] In fact, government is not to be a soulless machine. Its office is clearly one of the highest humanity. Its duty is not to accelerate but to rectify the economic law which ordains that the rich shall be richer, and the poor the poorer. When Dushyanta comes to hear of the death of a sonless man he bursts out that he was ready to support all those who felt bereavement through the death of near relatives. "The eyes of the weak, of the Muni, and of the snake of virulent poison, Should be regarded as unbearable. Do not, therefore, come into (hostile) contact with the weak. Take care that the eyes of the weak do not burn thee with thy kinsmen."[48]

Government is credited with the capacity of substantially influencing the morality of a people by promulgating laws, regulating the private life of the citizen and by putting a ban on certain vices and evil practices. The following order issued by a king is very significant as illustrating the influence of law on morality. "At the command of Ahuka, of Janardana, of Rama and of Babhra, it was again proclaimed throughout the city, that from that day, among all the Vrishnis and the Andhakas no one should manufacture wines and intoxicating spirits of any kind, and that whoever would secretly manufacture wines and spirits should be impaled alive with all his kinsmen. Through fear of the king and knowing that it was the command of Rama also of unimpeachable deeds, all the citizens bound themselves by rule and abstained from manufacturing wines and spirits."[49] Asoka's edicts show the ways of propagation resorted to by the ancient kings. The Shukra-Niti also mentions such proclamations.[50]

The subjects owe to their sovereign the sacred duty of loyalty and obedience. The king is almost a God to the people over whom the rules. The sentiments of reverence should be the common property of all. All injury of the royal dignity or interest is highly condemnable. It is treason; and as such, it exposes those who practise it to fearful consequences. "Ever he (Agni) claims obedience as a king."[51] "Who is there that will not worship him in whose existence the people exist and in whose destruction the people are destroyed. That person who does what is agreeable and beneficial to the king and who bears (a share of) the burthen of kingly duties, conquers both this and the other world. That man, who even thinks of doing an injury to the king, without doubt, meets with grief here and goes to hell hereafter."[52] "To utter falsehood in a court of justice, to behave deceitfully towards the king, to act falsely towards preceptors and seniors, are regarded as equivalent to Brahmanicide. One should never do an act of violence to the king's person. Nor should one ever strike a cow. Both these offences are equal to the sin of foeticide."[53]

The duties of the subjects were not exhausted in a passive acquiescence in the royal wishes. The people were not ciphers in the administration. True, representative government on modern lines was unknown. But in various ways the influence of the people was felt. The king was expected to consult not only himself but his cabinet also. The task of administration was acknowledge to be a very complex one, making demands upon diverse talents, temperaments, and interests. "Even if the work be a trifling one, it can be done with difficulty by only one individual. What can be performed by an unfriended person for a kingdom that is considerable? The wise ruler should ever abide by the well-thought-out decisions of counsellors, office-bearers, subjects, and members attending a meeting-never by his own opinions. The monarch, who follows his own will, is the cause of miseries; he soon gets estranged from his kingdom and alienated from his subjects. The wealth of intelligence is seen to be different with different men,–according to (the various sources of knowledge) revealed wisdom, intuition, knowledge of Shastras, inferential reasoning, direct observation analogies, adventurous instinct, craft, and force. There are diversities of human conduct as well as grades of excellence according to the degree in which they are high or low. It is not possible for a single individual to represent all these, i.e. the differences in बुद्धिवैभव as well as varieties of व्यवहार."[54]

Assemblies were, therefore, deemed to be an essential part of the machinery of government as early as the Vedic period. Unanimity was highly prized in these gatherings. Eloquence in these assemblies was a very precious gift; and men tried to outshine one another in their boldness and fluency. Even ladies occasionally took part in these. We invoke gods, " that in the synod all the folk may be benevolent to us."[55] "But evermore may we, as friends of Soma, speak to the synod with brave sons around us."[56] "They come to him as dames to an assembly."[57] It was too evident that these gatherings were not mere debating societies; their part and lot in the government of the realm was quite substantial. Each individual was expected to speak out boldly and have his own say. "Assemble, speak together, let your minds be all of one accord, as ancient gods unanimous sit down to their appointed shore. The place is common, common the assembly, common the mind, so be their thought united. A common purpose do I lay before you, and worship with your general oblation. One and the same be your resolve, and be your minds be of one accord. United be the thoughts of all that may happily agree."[58]

These gatherings had various functions, administrative, deliberative, and judicial. In the time of the epics, and the Smritis, too, they were not quite ineffective. Matters of the greatest moment were often placed before vast, representative assemblies. The king Dasharatha, when he wanted to renouce his royal position and install the heir-apparent on the throne, called a big assembly, representative of various small principalities and cities. (नानानगरवास्तव्यान् पृथग्जानपदानपि) It was not merely an assembly of kings, it was an assembly of people as well. The king, after declaring his intention and the grounds for it, concluded; "If what have devised be meet, and also if it recommends itself to you, do ye accord your approval to it,- proposing what I am to do besides this, together with the ways and means of effecting it. If I have thought thus solely because it is personally agreeable to me, do ye suggest some other suitable course. The thought of the neutral persons is different from those that are concerned; and truth comes out from a friction of opposite forces."[59] Even the proud Ravana calls a conference of Rakshasas, and asks their advice.[60] A conference is summoned by Rama to decide the case of the Brahmin, who appealed to him for the restoration of his son's life. He sent for "Vasishtha, Vamadeva, his brothers, citizens and councillors" and asked their opinions.[61] Here is a picture of a normal assembly : "In the early morning, Rama sat on his royal throne in the company of Brahmins and citizens engaged in looking into state affairs. The assembly consisted of priest Vasishtha, the saintly Kashyapa; ministers well-versed in politics, and other religious preceptors, moralists, members, and kings."[62] The power of modifying laws was entrusted to a council of Brahmins. "Laws, not specifically laid down in this code, should be unhesitatingly accepted as virtuous Brahmins would lay down and interpret. Those, who have thoroughly studied the Dharma-shastras, are well-versed in the Vedas and Vedangas, and have led the life of Brahmacharins, and are the living monuments of the texts of the Shrutis, should be judged as duly qualified law-givers. Whatever a council of ten, or of three eqalified Brahmins, faithfully to their duties shall lay down as the law, must be accepted as such."[63] The decisions must be the result of collective wisdom, and not of mere passing of votes of counting of heads. "Even whatever a single Veda-knowing Brahmin shall determine as the law shall be accepted as such to the exclusion of what has been said by ten thousand ignorant Brahmins."[64] "When the question is which of the two sides should be adopted, thou shouldst not abandon the many for adopting the side of one. When, however, that one person transcends that many in consequence of the possession of many accomplishments, then thou shouldst for that one, abandon the many."[65]

Citizens must enjoy not only civil freedom which grants them immunity from undue restraints, but constitutional freedom which grants them active participation in the affairs of the kingdom. "He is the best of kings in whose dominions men live fearlessly like sons in the house of their sires."[66] This freedom is the privilege of citizens, in all rightly constituted governments. But this is not enough. It is always recognised that the advisers of the monarch are not to pander to his whims, but to do what is really good both for himself and his kingdom. The Hindus always maintain the superiority of the राज्यनीति (true statesmanship which looks to the interests of the kingdom) over the राजनीति (diplomacy or statecraft which thiks of the good of the government only); further, they are quite sure that, in the last analysis these do not conflict, but absolutely coincide. A true counsellor is he who speaks out boldly what he considers to be right; and a true king is he who has got the capacity of listening with patience to all criticisms and appreciating them at their true worth. "The man who even in the presence of a king can fearlessly speak out his demerits and never praises them like merits is the real speaker."[67] "One should advise the king for his benefit in some secret place when he is found to be an oppressor and punisher without rhyme and reason. One should not do anything that is good to the king but harmful to the people."[68] Maricha says to Ravana: "O king, the speaker of soft words is common, but the speaker and listener of unwelcome though beneficial words are rarities."[69] "He is obeyed in the world who, having listened to counsels of wisdom, accepts them, abandoning his own opinions."[70] Manu also thinks this quality of tolerance of even adverse and unfounded criticisms to be quite an essential one is government. "A king, seeking his own welfare, shall always tolerate the calumny of remarks made by suitors, defendants, infants, old men, and sick folk regarding himself. He, who bears well ill-report (adverse criticisms) made by the aggrieved, is glorified in heaven; he, who out of pride of wealth cannot tolerate such criticisms, goes to hell for that."[71]

Public interests must weigh more highly with the king than all his private interests put together. His private sentiments are not be allowed to stand in the way of public good. The king, therefore, has no right to waste any money in his charities any more than on his vices, if the public interest demands economy in that direction. "My wealth exists only for my subjects residing in the city and the country and not for my own comforts and enjoyments! That king, who giveth away for his own pleasure the wealth that belongeth to others can never earn virtue or fame!"[72] The leaders of public opinion are entitled to special consideration at the hands of the king. "All should follow the words of persons who speak in the interest of a public body. He, who acts otherwise, should be punished with the first form of penalty. The king should finish the business of persons, who approach him in the interests of a public body, and send them away after having honoured them with gifts and (other) marks of royal favour."[73]

People had often considerable share both in the election as well as the dismissal of a king. That the eldest son should succeed, became a very general rule very early. But the people and the ministers had a right to rule him out if he was unfit. There is ample evidence for it.[74] Yayati placed on the throne his youngest son, on the ground that the older ones were disobedient; and the public approved of his action. There are passages in the Rig-Veda which tend to show that monarchy was more elective in the Vedic period than it was subsequently. "Be with us; I have chosen thee; stand steadfast and immovable. Let all the people wish for thee; let not thy kingship fall away."[75] "And they like people, who elect their rulers, have in abhorrence turned away from Vritra."[76] Nor was there anything sacrosanct about government both in the vedic and post-vedic society. No doubt the passion for revolution was not ardent in the Hindu writers at any period. They did appreciate fully the blessings of order and stability. "Firm is the sky, and firm the earth, and steadfast also are those hills. Steadfast all this living world and steadfast is the king of them."[77] But, in the last resort, change was always considered possible, whenever strong public interest demanded it.[78] Loyalty of the masses is always conditional. "Even as elephants shun the muddy rivers, do people shun from a distance, the ruler that doth not send out spies, who showeth not himself and who hath lost his independence."[79] "People do not in times of peril assist a sovereign that is wrathful, stingy, intoxicated, haughty, and deceitful Even his own kindred slay a sovereign that sets immense store by himself, is of light worth, regards himself highly, and is irascible."[80] Deposition of kings was always advised to bring about a healthy change in society. "If the king be an enemy of virtue, morality, and strength, people should desert him as the ruiner of the state. In his place, for the maintenance of the state, the priest with the consent of the ministers, should install one who belongs to his family and is qualified."[81] "A king who has indiscriminately ploughed (the field of) his kingdom, shall be ousted thereof; he shall meet destruction with his relations. As the vitality of a man ebbs away through fasting, so the life of a king, ebbs away through the enragement of his subjects."[82] The ultimate outcome of tyranny is the outbreak of popul will and the overthrow of the monarch. "The fire engendered by the grief (consequent on) the oppression of the subjects does not return without consuming the family, prosperity, and vital airs of the king."[83] "The subjects should arm themselves for slaying that king who does not protect them, who simply plunders their wealth, who confounds all distinctions, who is incapable of taking their lead, who is without compassion, and who is regarded as the most sinful of kings. That king who tells his people that he is their protector, but who does not or is unable to protect them, should be slain by the combined subjects, like a dog that is affected by the rabies and has become mad."[84]

(3)

A very important part of the duties of the state lay in the proper administration of justice. A great step forward is taken when the sphere of private revenge is effectively supplanted by the authority of the state. We find that system of 'wergeld' (वैरदेय) was prevalent in the Vedic period.[85] The payment for killing a man varied very much; it often took the form of a number of cows which were handed over to the relatives of the person injured.[86] The power of receiving compensation was gradually shifted to Brahmins and kings. Among some other forms of punishment prevalent then, was the ordeal of the red-hot axe.[87] In some cases the punishment was binding to posts[88] or death. There is a reference to a prison,[89] to fetters of iron,[90] to the ordeals of fire, water, and a combat.[91] Thieves were to be severely beaten and crushed to bits.[92] The Atharva-Veda calls for a very horrible punishment on a man for injuring a Brahmin's cow. "Snatch thou the hair from off his head, and from his body strip the skin; tear out his sinews, causes his flesh to fall in pieces from his frame."[93]

The Ramayana clearly points to the existence of an elaborate organization of justice. Rama says to Laxman : "O gentle son of Sumitra, for not looking to state business for these four days, I have been pained very much. Do thou, therefore, call here men or women, priests or councillors who have come for business. For a king falls into the dreadful hell, who does not daily look into his state affairs."[94] Perfect accessibility to instantaneous justice to all was one of the marked features of the ancient Hindu regime. Once upon a time a king by name Nriga gave away in charity a crore of cows : by mistake he gave away among these a cow belonging to a Brahmin. This Brahmin and the new owner of the cow approached the king; but as the king did not open the gates for a long time they cursed him. "Since thou hast not granted us an interview though we have been waiting here for a long time, thou shalt, by our curse remain invisible, being a lizard."[95] A dog once presents itself for justice against a Brahmin. The Brahmin is punished by Rama for doing injustice to the dog.[96]

Impartiality was rigidly insisted on. Perfect justice is the due of all, the rich and the poor alike. No inequality ought to exist in a court of law. All persons irrespective of their rank and condition should have perfect access to the personality of the king and should be properly heard. The rich people who can offer bribes should never escape punishment when guilty. "O son of the Raghu race, the tears of those who have been falsely charged with any offence, destroy the sons as well as the beasts of the ruler who minds his own comforts only."[97] All personal considerations must be sternly set aside. "Hence the king shall conquer his anger and senses; and forswearing personal love and derision, he shall be, like unto death, impartial to all. The badsouled king, who fails to administers even-handed justice out of greed or folly, his enemies soon subjugate."[98] "Neither mother, nor father, nor brother, nor wife, nor priest is unpunishable with that king who rules agreeably to his duty."[99]

Hindu theories fully realised the importance of punishment as an instrument to preserve peace and order. The whole science of government was called the science of punishment (दंडनीति). Might is the greatest means to preserve Right. "That rod of sovereignty is in fact the sovereign; he is said to be the leader and regulator (of society) the surety for the due discharge of their duties by (the members of) the four social orders..... Punishment justly inflicted after due deliberation endears all subjects; unjustly inflicted it destroys them all.....Men are dominated by the fear of punishment, rare is the man who is moral for the sake of morality; it is the terror of punishment that enables all men to enjoy their earnings or possessions."[100] "If sin findeth not a punisher, the number of sinners becomes large. The man, who having power to prevent or punish sin doth not do so, knowing that a sin hath been committed is himself defiled by that sin."[101]

The end of punishment was recognised to be prevention of crime, not retribution against the wrong-doer. Two things were aimed at: Striking terror into the hearts of others, and purification of the guilty. "If thou dost not succeed in making honest men of those rogues and in saving them by means unconnected with slaughter, do thou exterminate them by performing some sacrifice...Good kings never slay the wicked from motives of retribution."[102] Hence mild punishments are comparatively better. Everything depends upon their efficaciousness. Punishment should never be severe out of vindictiveness. It is only when a particular crime becomes rampant that rougher punishments come into play. "In those days the mere crying of fie on offenders was sufficient punishment. After this came the punishment represented by harsh speeches and censures. Then followed the punishment of fines and forfeitures. In this age, however, the punishment of death has become current. The measures of wickedness has increased to such an extent that by slaying only others cannot be restrained."[103] The following passage is an eloquent testimony to the righteous motives which inspired punishment. "Without destroying the body of the offender the king should do that unto him which is directed by the scriptures....By slaying the wicked the king (practically) slays a large number of individuals that are innocent. Behold, by slaying a single robber, his wife, mother, father and children are all slain..Sometimes a wicked man is seen to imbibe good behaviour from a righteous person. The again from persons that are wicked good children may be seen to spring. The wicked, therefore, should not be torn up by roots. The extermination of the wicked is not consistent with eternal practice. By smiting them gently they may be made to expiate their offences. By depriving them of all their wealth, by chains and immurements in dungeons, by disfiguring them (they may be made to expiate their guilt). Their relatives should not be persecuted by the infliction of capital sentences on them. If in the presence of the Purohita and others, they give themselves up to him from desire or protection, and swear, saying,- O Brahmin, we shall never again commit any sinful act,–they would then deserve to be let off without any punishment."[104]

Various circumstances should be taken into consideration in administering justice. The fact of context is all-important. Innocent victims of some vicious tendency must be severely distinguished from hard and confirmed sinners. "Considering the wilful repetition of a crime, as well as the time, place, and circumstances of its perpetration, the light or serious nature of the offence committed, and the bodily strength, (and pecuniary circumstances of the offender), punishment should be inflicted on an offender.....A first offender should be let off (with a warning); an offender who is guilty twice should be let off with; a strong censure; one who has committed the offence for the third time, should be punished with a fine; while death (corporal punishment, or mutilation of a limb) should be the penalty for one who has committed the same crime for the fourth time."[105]

Minors were naturally exempt from responsibility. "An old man of eighty years and a minor below the age of sixteen, women and diseased persons have to perform only half of expiation."[105a] "A child is comparable to an embryo up to his eighth year. A youth who has reached the age of sixteen is called a minor. Afterwards he is no longer a minor."[106]

A characteristic feature of the ancient system of administration of justice was the discrimination of punishments according to the castes of the offenders. Here it must be remembered that all offences by members of the lower castes against members of the higher castes are considered far more iniquitous than those committed by members of the higher castes against those of the lower castes. Thus, it is said that the wergeld for the life of a Kshatriya is 1000 cows; for a Vaishya, 100 cows; and 10 for a Shudra.[107] But the crime of killing a Brahmin is too heinous for a wergeld.[108] A Brahmin using abusive language to a Kshatriya is liable to a fine of 50 Panas, and to a Shudra or Vaishya, is liable to a fine of 25 Panas. But a Kshatriya, a Vaishya or a Shudra guilty of the same offence against a Brahmin is liable to a fine of hundred Panas, a fine of hundred and fifty Panas, and a corporal punishment respectively.[109] This is one of those peculiarities of the ancient judicature of India which condemns it in the eye of a modern jurist. But it should never be forgotten that the Hindu law-makers at the same time lay down that in proportion to the greater knowledge of the delinquent, guilt is greater. Thus we read in Shantiparva, that "if great men transgress, their chastisement should be proportionate to their greatness."[110] The following two verses of Manu set the whole matter in right perspective : "For the offence for which an ordinary persons would be punished with a fine of one Karshapanam, a penalty of one thousand Karshapanam should be inflicted on the king, if he is found guilty thereof. For having committed theft, a Shudra cognisant of the law, shall be punished with a fine eight times the usual one in value; a Vaishya, with a fine sixteen times; a Kshatriya, with a fine thirty-two times; and a Brahmin, with a fine sixty-four, hundred, or hundred and twenty-eight times the usual one in value."[111]

A factor tending to humanize the system was the consideration of motives of delinquents. "A witness, who, out of compassion, has knowingly stated a fact otherwise that it is in reality, shall not be ousted of heaven thereofore, since such a speech is called is a divine allegation. In cases where the allegation of truth would lead to the lawful execution of a Shudra, Vaishya, Kashatriya, or a Brahmin, a witness is warranted to speak falsehood. In such a case a lie is greater than truth."[112] A Brahmin who merely wants to satisfy his hunger is allowed to take some fruits or edibles. "That Brahmin who has been forced by want to abstain from six meals, may take away without permission, according to the rule of a person that cares only for to-day without any thought of the morrow, only what is necessary for a single meal, from the husking tub or the field or the garden or any other place of even a man of low pursuits. He should, however, whether asked or unasked, inform the king of his act."[113]

Among the punishments prescribed for various offences, fining is the most conspicuous. It is the penalty for giving false evidence,[114] for non-payment of debt,[115] for misappropriation of property.[116] Corporal punishments are prescribed for cases of assault;[117] and for cases of theft.[118] Mutilation of limbs and even capital punishment are often the lot thieves of valuable property.[119] A robber deserves worse punishment.[120] A man incurs fine by privately talking with ladies; but the fine is small if the ladies concerned are maid servants and such other. A man incurs the penalty of having his fingers cut off, if he is guilty of rape.[121] An adulterous woman is liable to be devoured by dogs.[122] Very cruel punishment involving mutilation of limbs are inflicted on adulterers.[123] A Brahmin may be banished but not killed.[124]

(4)

Force is absolutely essential to keep up the order and organization of society. Society is held together by force. The existence of all fine and noble life, of higher morality, of all happiness, of all order, depends entirely upon the basis of force. "If force were abolished from the world, creatures would soon be destroyed. Like fish in the water, stronger animals prey upon the weaker. This truth was formerly spoken by Brahma himself viz., that force properly applied, upholds creatures. Behold! the very fires, when extinguished, blaze up again, in fright, when blown! This is due to the fear of force. If there were no force in the world distinguishing the good and the bad, then the whole world would have been enveloped in utter darkness, and all things would have been confounded. Even they that are breakers of rules, that are atheists, and scoffers of the Vedas, impressed by force, soon become disposed to observe rules and restrictions. Every one is kept straight by force. A person naturally pure and righteous is scarce. Yielding to the fear of force, man becomes disposed to observe rules and restraints. Force was ordained by the creator himself, for the happiness of all the four orders, and for making them righteous and modest."[125]

War is the one great mean to bring about the triumph of the righteous and the destruction of the wicked. Its foundations are laid in justice and equity. Non-destruction of the wicked is as great a sin as the destruction of the righteous. Possession of power is, therefore, a very necessary condition for the protection of all higher values of life. "It is from power that righteousness springs. Righteousness rests upon power, as all immobile things upon the earth. As smoke depends upon the wind, so righteousness depends upon the wind, so righteousness dependent upon power...Righteousness is dependent upon them that are powerful, even as pleasure is dependent upon those that are given to enjoyment. There is nothing which powerful men cannot do. Everything is pure with them that are powerful."[126]

The general principle to be observed in all warfare is that war must be righteous both in its aims and methods. The one essential condition of righteous fighting is that both the parties must have the same advantages. No unfair advantage is to be taken of the opponent's weakness. This is the principle of honour among all true Kshatriyas. "Persons equality circumstanced must encounter each other fighting fairly...Those engaged in contests of words, should be fought against with words. Those that left the rank should never be slain. A car-warrior should have a car-warrior for his antagonist; one seated on an elephant should have a similar combatant for his foe; a horse should be met by a horse; and a foot-soldier by a foot-soldier. Guided by considerations of fitness, willingness, daring, and might, one should strike another, giving notice. No one should strike another that is unprepared or panic-struck. One engaged with another, one seeking quarter, one retreating, one whose weapon is rendered unfit, one unceased in mail, should never be struck. Car-drivers, animals, (yoked to carter carrying weapons), men engaged in the transport of weapons players on drums and blowers of conches should never be struck. Having made these covenants, the Kurus and the Pandavas and the Somakas wondered much, gazing at each other."[127] All helpless persons, all persons in sleep, all members of the other sex are unslayable. "One that hath thrown away his weapons, one that hath fallen down, one whose armour hath slipped off, one whose standard is down, one who is flying away, one who is frightened, one who says,–'I am thine,' one who is a female, one who beareth the name of a female, one no longer capable of taking care of one's self, one who hath only a single son, or one who is a vulgar fellow, with these, I don't like to battle."[128] " One should not cast weapons upon kine, Brahmins, kings, women, friends, one's own mother, one's own preceptor, a weak woman, an idiot, a blind man, a sleeping man, a terrified man, one just risen from sleep, an intoxicated person, a lunatic, and one that is heedless."[129] Non-combatants should not be slain. "Thou hast with the Brahma weapon, burnt men, on earth that are unacquainted with weapons. This act that thou hast perpetrated is not righteous."[130] Certain other rules are mentioned. "No limb below the navel should be struck."[131] "Neither poisoned nor barbed arrows should be used."[132] "One should fight righteously, without yielding to wrath, or desiring to slay.... A wounded opponent should either be sent to his own home or if brought to the victor's quarters should have his wounds attended to by skilful surgeons."[133] There are exceptions. No party is expected to be more honest that its opponents. Deceit must be matched by deceit, and crookedness by crookedness. As regards ordinary combatants one should fight with them artlessly. As regards those that are possessed of powers of deception, one should fight with them, aided by the ways of deception.[134] It is said that when the war breaks out all laws are silent. In extreme crises, all means are justified for the ultimate end. "When the number of one's foes becomes great, then destruction should be effected by contrivances and means."[135]

Military strength, both for defensive and offensive purposes is the one most necessary thing for a government, situated in the midst of indifferent and hostile communities. Indeed, the capital thing for a government is to enlist popularity and enthusiasm on its own side by securing for the people both moral and material prosperity. The true strength of the government is the confidence and support it commands in its own people. The piling up of armaments does not serve any useful purpose if there is no peace and security at home. The foundations of efficiency are to be laid in the hearts of the subjects. "There is no treasure more valuable to kings than that which consists in the selection and assemblage of servants. Among the six kinds of citadels indicated in the scriptures, indeed, among every kind of citadel, that which consists of (the ready service and the love of the) subjects is the most impregnable."[136] Aggressive militarisms which starve out all the aspects of a national life except those which subserve their own ends are never popular with the moralists of Ancient India. "That energy, which is spent in grinding the hostile kingdom, should be utilised in looking to one's own kingdom."[137]

It was, however, very clearly recognised that countries which are too much obsessed by pacifist tendencies cannot hold their own in the existing state of international insecurity, and political brigandage. The best way, to prevent war, however, is often said to lie in the preparedness for war. "Even as serpent devoureth animals living in the holes, the earth devoureth these too, viz, a king who is incompetent to fight and a Brahmin who does not sojourn in holy places."[138] Efficiency, power, greatness, prosperity; these are the goals for which kings must day and night strive. "Discontent is the root of prosperity. Therefore, O king, I desire to be discontented. He that striveth after the acquisition of prosperity is a truly politic person,"[139] A state of meekness and poverty is not meant for states. "When one falls into distress, one should raise one's self by all means in one's power, mild or stern; and after such rise, when competent, one should practise righteousness."[140] Imperial dignity is a natural object of ambition to aspiring kings. There is nothing wrong about the idea of augmenting one's strength and enlarging the sphere of influence and overlordship. The Rig-Veda also speaks of paramount kings (सम्राट).[141] "It hath been heard by us that in the Krita age, having brought every one under their subjection Yauvanashuin, by the remission of all taxes, Bhagiratha, by the kind treatment of his subjects, Kartavirya, the energy of his asceticism, the Lord Bharata, by his strength and valour, and Maruta, by his prosperity,–these five became emperors. But O Yudhishthira, thou who covetest the imperial dignity, derervest it (not by one but) by all these qualities, viz, victory, protection afforded to thy people, virtue, prosperity, and policy."[142] There is the finest spiritual basis for many of these word-conquests; it is the conquest of the world not by sword but by soul.

Ways of the world are proverbially crooked. The path to prosperity and power is often a very thorny one. Hindu writers on political ethics or morality of nations frankly recommend unscrupulous courses of action on the plea that the end justifies the means. Protean are the shapes which morality assumes in the hands of statesmen वारांगनेव नृपनीतिरनेकरूपा. "I wonder at the ways of the statesmen that are myriad-shaped like the ways of fate. According as it suits their purpose, these ways at times are such as can be comprehended and at times they are too intricate to follow; at times they are set forth in all their magnitude, and at times they shrink to a vanishing point; at times their very trace is lost and at times they show ample results."[143] It is necessary, therefore, for the rulers to be deeply versed in all the mysteries of statecraft; but a naked acceptance of tortuous and heart-rending courses for merely selfish purposes is never recommended. "Both kinds of wisdom, straight and crooked, should be within the call of the king. Though acquainted with it, he should not, however, apply that wisdom which is crooked (for injuring others). He may use it for resisting the dangers that may overtake him."[144]

Unscrupulous measures should be fully resorted to achieve political purposes and these are hallowed in the light of the ultimate end. Prosperity never comes to those who are too honest. The higher morality of unambiguous sincerity is not meant for government. By means fair and foul, the politicians must aim at the regeneration of their country, at the development of ruthless efficiency and power which alone can cover a multitude of sins. "The king, therefore, in seasons of distress incurs no fault by oppressing his subjects for filling the treasury. For performing sacrifices many improper acts are done....If (at such times) such improper practices be not adopted, evil is certain to result. All those institutions that are kept up for working destruction and misery exist for the sake of collecting wealth........As animals and other things are necessary for sacrifices, as sacrifices are for purifying the heart, and as animals, sacrifices, and purity of the heart are all for final emancipation, even so policy and chastisement exist for the treasury which exists for the army; and policy, treasury, and army, all the three exist for vanquishing foes and protecting or enlarging the kingdom. I shall here cite an example illustrating the true ways of moralists. A large tree is cut down for making of it a sacrificial stake. In cutting it, other trees that stand in its way have also to be cut down. These also, in falling down, kill others standing on the spot. Even so they that stand in the way of making a well-filled treasury have to be slain."[145]

The general principle of foreign policy is here enunciated : "By means of all political expedients, a king, well-versed in the laws of state-craft, shall so exert that, his allies, foes, and indifferent sovereigns, may not acquire a higher supremacy than his own self."[146] Four expedients were recommended with regard to enemies; conciliation (साम), concession of territories (दाम), sowing of dissensions in the enemy's camp (भेद), and war (दण्ड). A military demonstration was to resorted to if the other methods failed. "The expedients,–conciliation, gifts, dissension and punishment, when duly applied, yield success. Punishment, (should always be applied) when there is no other means to follow."[148] "Brihaspati has said that a king possessed of intelligence should always avoid war for the acquisition of territory. The acquisition of dominions should be made by the three well-known means (of conciliation, gift, and disunion)."[149] In fact, circumstances alone can warrant the acceptance of the one method to the exclusion of others. Small kingdoms should not be exterminated on the mere ground of their weakness. With regard to more powerful enemies, discretion is always to be held the better part of valour. "A powerful king should never seek to exterminate weak kings, for these do good to the world, by cherishing the good and punishing the wicked."[150]

The most essential thing is to be able to measure the forces of one's own and one's opponents very accurately. "The king conversant with the scriptures that marches against a foe, should think of the three kinds of strength, and indeed, reflect on his own strength and the strength of his foe. Only that king, O Bharata, who is endued with alacrity, discipline, and strength of counsels, should march against a foe. When his position is otherwise, he should avoid offensive operations. The king should provide himself with power of wealth, power of allies, power of paid soldiery, and power of the mechanical and trading classes. Among all these, power of allies and power of wealth are superior to the rest. The power of classes and that of the standing army are equal. The power of spies is regarded by the king as equal in efficacy to either of the above, on many occasions, when the time comes for applying each."[151] Government must change its policy like a chameleon to suit different powers and different circumstances. Moderation, if it is interpreted as weakness, should be avoided. If diplomacy fails to convince the opponents of the soundness of one's policy, military demonstration must follow. Diplomacy is really effective when it is backed by force. Rama grows angry at the ocean and says : "Behold the hauteur of the Ocean in not presenting himself before me. Calmness, forbearance, candour, and soft speech-these virtues of the good are by the insolent taken for the effects of incompetency. The person that is self-laudatory, wicked, and impudent, publishes his own praise, and meteth out chastisement everywhere, is honoured in the world. By moderation, one cannot attain celebrity; by moderation, one cannot attain fame-and, in this world by moderatoin, one cannot attain victory in the battle-field."[152]

Self-preservation is the highest law for the community. It is the one foremost duty of the state to maintain its own existence and power as unimpaired as possible. All means that would lead to success are to be unhesitatingly adopted. "If thy son, friend, brother, father, or even spiritual preceptor becometh thy foe, thou shouldst if desirous of prosperity, slay him without scruples. By curses and incantations, by gifts of wealth, by poison, or by deception, the foe should be slain...And O Bharata, speak soft words before thou smiteth and even while thou art smiting. After the smiting is over, pity the victim, and grieve for him, and even shed tears."[153] Hypocrisy is a very essential part of statecraft. Policy requires statesmen to throw a veil of ambiguity over their real intentions. "In speech thou shouldst ever be humble, but at thy heart be ever sharp as a razor. And when thou art engaged in doing even a very cruel and terrible act thou shouldst talk with smile on thy lips."[154] "The hope thou givest into thy foe should be long deferred in the fulfilling; and when the time cometh for its fulfilment, invent some pretext for deferring it still. Let that pretext be shown as founded upon some reason and let that reason itself be made to appear as founded on some other reason. Kings should, in a matter of destroying their foes, even resemble razors in every particular : unpitying as these are sharp, hiding their intents as these are concealed in their leathern cases, striking when the opportunity cometh as these are used on proper occasions, sweeping off their foes with all their allies and dependents as these shave the head or the chin without leaving a single hair."[155]

(5)

We have so far dealt with the activities of the state in Ancient India. It might be supposed that the influence of the state was all-pervasive, that institutions owed their rise and extinction to a mere fiat of this Omnipotent Central Executive. Yet this is altogether an illusion. In the Greek Society, in the ancient Roman Republic, man had no existence apart from the state, that every part existed for the Whole and had no independent existence. In India, the state was a majestic institution, no doubt; but around it and behind it and within it lay large and extensive spheres of authority, which were to a great extent autonomous. Man as man did not come in contact with the state. The Greeks divided men into citizens and slaves. The Hindus transcended these limits and marked out for man large jurisdictions in which he could work independently of his position in the state. There was first the institution of family. Man was largely merged in this group : the state often dealt direct with families than with individuals. Patriarchs or heads of families represented the whole group: the state would not recognise the independent existence of individuals. A family was a vast group consisting sometimes of as many as a hundred persons knit together by blood-ties, owing allegiance to one adult head, generally the eldest male member living. Family was indeed a small state-an *imperium in imperio*. The family was the center where all property would concentrate, where all people would be properly looked after, where the children will be trained in the traditions and arts and learning of their elders, where the old will guide and direct the young and the young will respect and obey and support the old, where gods would be worshipped, sacrifices would be performed, and a corporate spirit fostered and nourished. It was a political, economic, religious, cultural institution, protecting and enhancing the traditional lore, safeguarding religion, morality, and means of existence of the group from generation to generation. Family here was a compact group-in which as many as seven generations used to pass a communal life.

Another institution which stood as a rampart between man and the state, between man and the outside world was Caste. Every Hindu is born into a caste, which is a larger group, standing for certain ideals and traditions. Caste determines to some extent a man's profession; caste determines a man's marriage; caste determines a man's social status; caste determines a man's cultural possibilities; caste determines a man's duties. In India the first question generally asked to a Hindu is–'What caste do you belong to?' Man ceased to have an independent existence as a man to some extent; he always used to think in terms of the group he was born into. Caste was a social not a religious institution, though not even the sacred relations between man and God escaped its influence. Man's status and functions, his rights and his duties, were determined by his caste irrespectively of the state. The state was an humbler institution bound to respect the limits of caste ethics. The secular agency of the state was powerless to raise the Shudras and run down the Brahmins. In this way, the fundamentals of peace, order, good administration, justice, and sound economic organization were secured. Our Swadeshi Samaj as Dr. Tagore calls it was thus able to preserve its existence intact in the midst of stormy changes and ceaseless political vicissitudes.

A third agency guaranteeing the stability of our social order was the indigenous system of local self-government so excellently developed by our ancestors. There were various types of institutions designed to meet common wants by concerted action. There were Shrenis–guilds of merchants and craftsmen. There were Kulas, which were assemblages of relatives and friends. There were Ganas, meaning assemblages of families or fraternities. Many Ganas were self-governing bodies. A Puga meant a federation of different bodies of workers–a vaster and more complex body than a Shreni. One of the functions of these guilds was to train the younger people in arts and crafts. Caste did not affect a man's entry into guilds. The Jatakas refer to king-craftsmen, to Brahmins acting as physicians, goat herds and merchants. Manu also allowed the use of handicrafts and the practice of other professions even to a Brahmin in time of distress. But these local bodies were not purely economic groups; they had administrative and judicial powers also. Brihaspati mentions the functions of Samuhas or municipal bodies: preservation and maintenance of public halls, temples, tanks, rest-houses, wells for supply of drinking water to travellers, construction of water-courses and places of worship, protection against incursions of wicked people and relief of the distressed.[156]

There is, therefore, plenty of evidence of corporate life among ancient Hindus. All these associations tended to delimit the sphere of the state. In India, therefore, it should never be forgotten that society and state were not identical, that each ran an independent course of life, their spheres now and then overlapping each other, now checking and balancing each other but maintaining always distinct, independent existence. All these institutions again, were not the gifts of the state to people; their roots were equally deep with those of the state in the ancient life and traditions of the people. The centre of gravity of man did not lie in the state; it lay in the body of Dharma or Laws to which the state, the caste, the family, the guild alike traced its existence.

Yet it would be a mistake to say that man's life was summed up in these associations. True, man as man had no civic rights; that was because Hindus did not believe man to be fundamentally a political being pure and simple. The idea of the nation, of the caste, of any group did not obtain that worship which it obtains at present in the West; because man as a spiritual being was a greater reality than man as a secular being. Man's soul was fundamental. Any man can leave the organization of the state, of the guild, and even of the caste, and the family, and become as free, as independent as he chooses. But not in the social, nor in the economic or political sphere was he allowed to have this unfettered existence. It was as a human being, as an Atman that he was allowed to wear the robe of a Sannyasin and transcend the local and sectional tyrannies of customs and conventions. The overwhelming emphasis that was placed on man's soul-life tended to weaken the harshness, the rigidity, the absoluteness of all secular organizations. Humanity, therefore, was not lost sight of; but the collective entities which so largely hem in the outlook of a Westerner ceased to have an unchecked control over men's minds. The tyranny of the nation-idea or the empire–idea was not so much felt. Hence that majestic development of economic and political structure, looking not to the past but to the future for its inspiration, building not for a generation or two but for ages together was not possible among the ancient Aryans, whose contributions towards the growth of free political spirit and building up vast industrial structures remained therefore handicapped.

References

1. R. II. 67. 8-36.
2. Shanti. 66. 17-27.
3. Rg. X. 173. 1-4. 6.
4. M. VII. 4-9. 11.
5. R. I. 22.
6. M. VII. 40-42.
7. M. VII. 43.

8. M. VII. 44-47.
9. R. III. 41. 12-13.
10. R. II. 100. 62-63.
11. Shanti. 139. 103-111.
12. Shanti. 58. 133-134.
13. R. II. 6. 23.
14. R. II. 17. 15.
15. R. II. 33. 12-17. 22.
16. R. II. 48. 4-5. 19.
17. R. III. 50. 9-10.
18. M. IX. 301-302.
19. Udyoga. 132. 15-16.
20. Shanti. 83.
21. R. VI. 63. 11-12.
22. R. II. 63. 14-17.
23. Udyoga. 33. 76.
24. Udyoga. 38. 15-20.
25. S.N. II. 106-113.
26. Shanti. 119.
27. R. II. 100. 25-26.
28. R. II. 100. 22-24.
29. Shanti. 55.
30. Shanti. 56.
31. Shanti. 83.
32. Shanti. 91; M. VII. 123-124.
33. S.N. I. 751-755.
34. M. VII. 124.
35. R. II. 100, 35-36.
36. R. VI. 29, 18-21.
37. R. VII. 43, 6.
38. R. II. 100, 60-61.
39. M. VII. 133-136.
40. S. N. I. 740-741.
41. Shanti. 87.
42. Shanti. 88.
43. M.VII. 127. 130-131.
44. M. VIII. 398-399. 401.
45. M. VII. 137.
46. M. VIII. 394-395.
47. Shanti. 86. 24.

48. Shanti. 91.
49. Mausala. 2.
50. S. N. 587-624.
51. Rg. I. 67. 1.
52. Shanti. 67.
53. Anu. 60.
54. S. N. II. 1-13.
55. Rg. X. 141. 4.
56. Rg. VIII. 48. 4.
57. Rg. X. 168. 2.
58. Rg. X. 191.2. 3. 4.
59. R. II. 2. 15-16.
60. R. VI. 6. 15.
61. R. VII. 74. 2.
62. R. VII. प्रक्षिप्त सर्ग.
63. M. XII. 108-110.
64. M. XII. 113-114.
65. Shanti. 83.
66. Shanti. 56.
67. S. N. 646-647.
68. S. N. II. 545-547.
69. R. III. 37. 2.
70. Shanti. 93.
71. M. VIII. 312-313.
72. Udyoga. 118.
73. Yaj. II. 191-192.
74. See Yaska. Nirukta. II. 10.
75. Rg. X. 173. 1.
76. Rg. X. 124. 8.
77. Rg. X. 173. 4.
78. Rg. X. 124. 4; Av. III. 3. 4; S. Br. XII. 9. 3. 3.
79. R. III. 33. 2-9.
80. R. III. 33. 15-16.
81. S. N. II. 550-552.
82. M. VII. 111-112.
83. Yaj. I. 341.
84. Anu. 96.
85. Rg. II. 32. 4.
86. Apastamba. I. 9. 24. 1-4.
87. Ch. U. VI. 16.

88. Av. XIX. 47. 9.
89. Rg. IV. 12. 5.
90. Av. VI. 63. 2.
91. Rg. I. 158. 4-5.
92. Av. IV. 3. 5.
93. Av. XII. 5. 65-71.
94. R.VII. 53. 4-6.
95. R.VII. 53. 7-18.
96. R. VII.
97. R. II. 100. 58-59. IV. 18.61.
98. M. VIII. 173-174.
99. Shanti. 121. 60.
100. M. VII. 17-22.
101. Adi. 196. 9-11.
102. Shanti. 273, 23-31.
103. Shanti. 273, 19-20.
104. Shanti. 273, 9-16.
105. M. VIII. 126-129.
105A. Angira Smriti. V. 33.
106. Narada. IV. 35-36.
107. Apastamba.
108. Av. I. 9, 24, 7.
109. M. VIII. 267-269.
110. Shanti. 273.
111. M. VIII. 336-338.
112. M. VIII. 103-104.
113. Shanti. 163. 11-12.
114. M. VIII. 120-1.
115. M. VIII. 139.
116. M. VIII. 264.
117. M. VIII. 280-283.
118. M. VIII. 322-325.
119. M. VIII. 334, 322-323.
120. M. VIII. 345.
121. M. VIII. 367.
122. M. VIII. 371.
123. M. VIII. 370-380.
124. M. VIII. 380.
125. Shanti. 15.
126. Shanti. 134. 3-9.

127. Bhishma. I.
128. Bhishma. 107. 77-78.
129. Sauptika. 6. 21-22.
130. Drona. 191, 38.
131. Shalya. 61: 6.
132. Shanti. 95.
133. Shanti. 95.
134. Udyoga. 193. 10.
135. Shalya. 62.
136. Shanti. 55.
137. Udyoga. 34. 31.
138. Udyoga. 33. 60.
139. Sabha. 81.
140. Shanti. 140. 38.
141. Rg. IV. 19. 2.
142. Sabha. 15. 16-18.
143. Mudrarakshasa. V. 3.
144. Shanti. 100. 5.
145. Shanti. 130. 35-51.
146. M. VII. 177.
147. R. V. 2. 27.
148. Yaj. I. 346.
149. Shanti. 68. 25-26.
150. Ashrama. 7. 17-20.
151. Ashrama. 8.
152. R.VI. 21. 14-17.
153. Adi. 153, 62-66.
154. Adi. 153, 62-66.
155. Adi. 153, 106-107.
156. See Dr. Mookerjee's Local Self-Government in Ancient India.

Chapter - XIV

CASTE MORALITY

A very characteristic institution of the Hindus is caste. From the time almost of the Rig-veda, the Hindus have accepted this typical institution. It stands for the natural inequality of men and tries to utilise this fact in the interests of society, by making it one of the main principles of division of social labour. It is, therefore, fundamental in the view accepted of social organization by the Hindus. The ordering of society on the lines of justice and utility requires that each man should take to that work for which he is most fitted by nature, by temperament, and by education. Every man is not fit for every thing. There are certain typical tendencies of human nature which each person embodies in himself; and according as men represent the one or the other of these, they fall into the one or the other division of society based on these. The perception of this fact is not peculiar to the Eastern mind; the earliest establishment of this principle in the Western thought, we find in Plato. Plato, however, tempered his view of caste by advocating systematic changes in it, corresponding of similar changes happening in the merits of individuals. His view is so excellent that we will put it in brief here. "These have different natures, and some of them God framed to rule, whom he fashioned of gold; others, he made of silver to be auxiliaries; others, again to be husbandmen and craftsmen, and these were formed by him of brass and iron. But as they are all sprung from a common stock, a golden parent may have a silver son, and a silver parent a golden son, and there must be change of rank; the son of the rich must descend and the child of the artisan rise, in the social scale; for an oracle says that the state will come to an end, if governed by a man of brass or iron."[1] We maintain that this was the very view of the ancient Rishis as regards the caste system in the best period of the Hindu history; although through the tendency to degeneracy inherent in all institutions, this system had to give way to the present one.

It is reasonable to maintain that colour was originally one of the grounds of differentiation between one caste and another or at least between the first three orders and the Shudras. The race prejudice and the colour bar are not peculiar to the early ages nor to the most recent ones; they are shared by all people at a certain stage of culture. No wonder then that the ancient Aryans tried to maintain their position of superiority by keeping aloof from the aboriginal elements. The caste system was a device to maintain rigid barriers between the pure Aryan elements and the non-Aryan ones; it was a device also to incorporate the non-Aryan elements without either giving way to them or exterminating them. The word *varna* has become itself one argument on behalf of this view of the division of early society on the basis of the difference of colours between different groups. "The complexion the Brahmins obtained was white; that which the Kshatriyas got was yellow; and that which was given to the Shudras was black."[2] The original unity of all the castes is frequently maintained; all differentiation was an after development. "There is really no distinction between the different orders. The whole world at first consisted of Brahmins. Created (equal) by Brahman, men have, in consequence of their acts, become distributed into different orders."[3] The Brihadaranyka Upanishad maintains that the Brahmins created other orders, because alone they were not sufficient for the work of socity. "Verily in the beginning this was the Brahman, one only. That being one was not strong enough. It created still further the most excellent Kshatra (power)......But Brahman is nevertheless the birth-place of Kshatra........He was not strong enough. He created the vish (people)......He was not strong enough. He created the Shudra colour."[4]

The fiction, therefore, that the different orders sprang from the different parts of God was only meant to represent the diversity of social functions of the four orders and not to lay any claim to historical turth. Historically there was one class at first, but owing to various causes, society divided itself into different classes. The story, therefore, of the creation of the different orders of society from the different parts of Godhead is not calculated to point to any rigid, absolute, eternal distinction between the four orders; but it definitely shows that there are four main aspects of social work which are represented in the world by four orders of men. "The Brahman was his mouth, of both his arms was the Rajanya made. His thighs became the Vaishya, from his feet the Shudra was produced."[5] The Brahmins represent the face of the Deity; that is, the head of the society; the Kshatriyas are the arms; that is, they form the military class; the Vaishyas are the belly and the thighs; that is the economic functions belong to them; and the Shudras are the leg; that is, they form the army of labourers. "One to high sway, one to exalted glory, one to pursue his gain, and one his labour : All to regard their different vocations, all moving creatures hath the dawn awakened."[6]

The Brahmins form the apex of society[6a]. Society should be governed by its Brahmins,-this is the root idea of the Hindu sociology. The Brahmins alone are born to rule; they alone are commissioned by God to govern mankind. The rule of the Brahmins is not, however, to be understood as the rule of a selfish bigoted priestcraft. Nothing could be more remote from the minds of the ancient seers than such an absurdity. The rule of the Brahmins was to be the rule of the best elements of society; it was to be the rule of intellect and character. The Hindus believed, above all, in aristocracy, the aristocracy not of birth, nor of wealth, nor of power, but the aristocracy of will and intellect. The Hindus believed in theocracy; the government of the society must be entrusted to those who are all of heaven, and none of earth, who have no private interests, but who are absolutely pure organs of divine truth, faithful messengers of

God. It is only when we grasp this cardinal fact, we can understand the apparently exaggerated way in which the claims of the Brahmins are marshalled in the ancient writings.

The duties of a Brahmin are : the maintenance of purity of descent, devotion of the duties of his caste, and the perfecting of people (by teaching).[7] "Study (of the Vedas), teaching, performance of sacrifies, officiating as priests at other men's sacrifies, gift making, and acceptance of gifts are the duties of Brahmins."[8] The foremost duty of a Brahmin, therefore, is to preserve intact the stores of intellectual wealth bequeathed by the past generation and to increase these by his own unsparing efforts.[9] But of greater importance to a Brahmin than the Vedic lore is character. It is frequently said that a learned Brahmin is worthless, if he fails to carry out the high principles which he has learnt. The Brahmins, therefore, have to embody in themselves not only the highest learning, but the highest virtues also. "The Brahmin has originated as the eternal embodiment of virtue. His origin is for the furtherance of virtue; he is the essence of Brahma. Born as a Brahmin, he wields the supremacy of the world, the ruler of all creatures, the custodian of the treasure of virtue."[10]

A Brahmin, however, has not to practise any and every virtue; he is, above all, for peace and not for sword. All the quietistic virtues find their most characteristic expression in this order of men. "Serenity, self-restraint, austerity, purity, forgiveness, and also uprightness, wisdom, knowledge, belief in God, are the duties of Brahmins, born of his own nature."[11] "The gods know him for a Brahmin who hath cast off anger and passion. The gods know him for a Brahmin who always speaketh the truth here, who always gratifieth his preceptors, and who, though injured himself, never returneth injury. The gods know him for a Brahmin who hath his senses under control, who is virtuous and pure and devoted to the study of the Vedas, and who hath mastery over anger and lust. The gods know him for a Brahmin who, congnisant of morals and endued with mental energy, is catholic in religion, and looketh upon all as equal unto himself."[12] An extreme tenderness of heart and kindness to all living creatures especially characterise a Brahmin soul. There are occasions, however, on which even a Brahmin is justified to take up arms. "The Brahmin, by taking up arms on these three occasions, does not incur sin, viz, for protecting himself, for compelling the other orders to betake themselves to their duties, and for chastising robbers."[13] "When robbers, breaking through all restraints, spread devastation around, all the orders may take up arms. By so doing they incur no sin, O Yudhishthira!"[14]

A life of poverty and renunciation is the one most appropriate for the Brahmins. Theirs is not the kingdom of this world; theirs is the kingdom of heaven. Neither worldly honour, nor worldly wealth are the objects of their ambition. A Brahmin is not a flatterer of any persons; he is sufficient unto himself. "The gods know him for a Brahmin who has given up all desire of fruit who hath no exertion in respect of worldly acts, who never bows down his head unto any one, who never utters the praises of others, and who is endued with strength though his acts have all been weakened."[15] "A Brahmin should avoid service of the king, wealth obtained by agriculture, sustenance derived from trade, all kinds of crooked behaviour, companionship with any but his wedded wives, and usury."[16] There are strict limitations to a Brahmins' accepting a life of mendicancy. "A Snataka (one who has duly fimished his studies) householder, famished with hunger, shall ask money of the king, or of this pupils and disciples, but of no other man."[17] "The firmness of a Brahmin consists in his refusal to solicit. The Brahmin, possessed of steadiness and learning and contentment gladdens the deities. The wise have said that an act of solicitation on the part of a poor man is a great reproach. Those persons that solicit others are said to annoy the world like thieves and robbers. The person who solicits is said to meet death."[18]

Great as are the duties of a Brahmin, equally a great are his privileges. The position of a Brahmin is entirely exceptional in society. The Shatapatha Brahmana mentions the following four prerogatives of the Brahmin; honour, gifts, freedom from oppression, and freedom from being killed.[19] "The Brahmins are the holiest of the holies on earth, a holier thing than they is not, nor ever will be."[20] They are considered almost gods on earth.[21] "Whatever property is in this world belongs to the Brahmin."[22] The sovereignty of the world, of right belongs to the Brahmin; it is by sufferance that the Kshatriyas rule.[23] The Brahmin's claims to reverence are superior to those of the king himself. "There are two persons whose lives are perpetual vows. The one is the king, the other is a Brahmin. Of these, one having the higher knowledge is the greater."[24]

The Brahmin enjoys an exceptional position in Law. A person draws down upon himself the most terrible consequences, if he wantonly approaches a Brahmin's wife or his property. "Dire is a Brahmin's wife led home by others; in the supremest heaven, she plants confusion."[25] 'One can digest iron, powdered stone, and even poison. What man, in three regions can digest a Brahmin's property?"[26] The sanctity of a Brahmin's own person is still more inviolable. The murder of a Brahmin is the only real murder.[27] "A Brahmin of all creatures must not be slain! He is, indeed, like fire....Hostility with Brahmins, would not, therefore, be proper under any circumstances. O sinless one, neither Agni nor Surya truly consumeth so, as doth a Brahmin of rigid vows when angry!"[28] The maintenance of Brahmins is a duty of the wealthy classes. Under certain circumstances, a Brahmin can appropriate to himself the things that he wants, from other's property.[29]

The position of the Kshatriya (or warrior) class forms, in many respects, a great contrast to the position of the Brahmins. The duties of the two classes vary accordingly. To the Brahmins belong all spiritual power; the Kshatriyas are the representatives of physical power. The former are passive, quietistic, forgiving; the latter are active, aggressive and unforgiving. The essence of the Brahminhood is non-resistance; the essence of the Kshatriya position is active resistance. "The Kshatriya's might has in physical strength; the Brahmin's in forgiveness."[30]

"The Brahmin shines by self restraint, the Kshatriya, by victory."[31] There is conflict, therefore, of methods between the two orders; the Brahmins want to achieve their aims through spiritual power; the Kshatriyas have to achieve their aim through physical force. But there is no conflict of ends; both the orders have to secure the triumph of right. Hence no divorce between the two is desirable; there should be healthy co-operation between the two orders.[32] The real power is the power of the spirit; the intellectual classes must guide and govern the actions of the military classes. The brute force is inferior to the higher force of the spirit; hence it must be guided and controlled by the latter. "O fie on Kshatriya prowess! Brahma prowess is true prowess! In judging of strength and weakness, I see that asceticism is true strength!"[33] "The Brahmin and the Kshatriya are connected with each other naturally, and each protects the other. The Kshatriya is the cause of the Brahmin's growth, and the Brahmin is the cause of Kshatriya's growth. When each helps the other, both attain to great prosperity. If their friendship, existing from days of old breaks, a confusion sets over everything."[34]

Protection of the people, gift-making, performance of sacrifices, study of the Vedas, and abstention from luxury are, in general, the duties of Kshatriyas.[35] The Kshatriyas are known to have taught the Vedas to Brahmins; and some of them like Janaka were very clever metaphysicians; but in general, this was not their business. "In word only have former sages (though Brahmins) come as pupils (to people of lower rank); but Gautama actually dwelt as a pupil (of Pravahana, who was a Rajanya) in order to obtain the fame of having respectfully served his master."[36] The fundamental function of the Kshatriyas was the protection of people. The role of the Brahmins was very exalted; but, in this matter-of-fact world it is the Kshatriyas who uphold the organization of society. "Amongst men, the highest duties are those which are practised by Kshatriyas. The whole world is subject to the might of their arms. All the duties, principal and subordinate, of the three other orders, are dependent (for their observance) upon the duties of the Kshatriya."[37]

A Kshatriya, therefore, has to practise all the active virtues, as a Brahmin is the soul of peaceful qualities. He has to achieve his objects by his own manliness; it is not for him to adopt a meek or servile attitude. "In thy case, O king, begging which is successful with Brahmins, hath been forbidden. Therefore, strive for the acquisition of wealth by exerting they might and energy. Neither mendicancy, nor the life of a Shudra is what is proper for thee. Might and energy constitute the virtue of the Kshatriya especially....They that are learned and wise say that sovereignty is virtue. Acquire sovereignty, therefore, is behoveth thee not, to live in a state of inferiority."[38] The third and fourth stage of life are not compulsory for the Kshatriyas; nor should they be resorted to till their life mission is accomplished. "A life of mendicancy is not obligatory upon the three orders (viz, Kshatriyas, Vaishyas and Shudras.)"[39]

Such qualities as contentment, forgiveness, humility, tenderness for life are not appropriate for a Kshatriya. 'असंतुष्टा द्विजाः नष्टाः संतुष्टाश्च महीभुजः' Discontent is the ruin of the Brahmins; while contentment is the ruin of the kings. Acquiescence in the *status quo* is not a praise worthy characteristic of the Kshatriyas, "Little streams are filled with only a small quantity of water. The palms of a mouse are filled with only a small quantity. A coward is soon gratified with acquisitions that are small."[40] "Never occupy the intermediate, the low, or the lowest station! Blaze up (like a well-fed fire)! Like a brand of *Tindooka* wood, blaze up even for a moment, but never smoulder, from desire of life, like a flameless fire of paddy chaff! It is better to blaze up for a moment than smoke for ever and ever![41] A life of excitement, in which there are keen pleasures and poignant pains, is to be preferred to a life of dullness, quiet, peace. "Overcoming sleep, and languor and wrath and joy, and hunger and thirst, and cold and heat, thy children are always in the enjoyment of that happiness which, as heroes, should be theirs!......Indeed, ordinary persons, caring only for comforts that satisfy the low and the mean, desire an equable state of dullness, without excitement of any kind. They, however, that possess superior stuff, desire either the acutest of human sufferings, or the highest of all enjoyments, that are given to man. The wise always delight in extremes, they find no pleasure in the mean; they regard the extremes as happiness; while that which lies between, is regarded by them as misery."[42] Such soldierly qualities as hot temper, intolerance, revengefulness are positive qualifications in a Kshatriya. "He is a man who cherisheth wrath and for giveth not; he on the other hand, who is forgiving, and without wrath, is neither a man nor a women.... A man is called Purusha because he is competent to trouble his foe.[43] A Kshatriya may justly cherish a high sense of honour, and stern and unbending pride. Humility and self-surrender are out of place in him. Self-assertion, and not self-denial is his characteristic virtue. "He that hath, in this world, been born as a Kshatriya in any high race and hath acquired a knowledge of the duties of that order, will never from fear, or for the sake of sustenance, bow down to any body on earth. One should stand erect with courage, and not bow down, for exertion is manliness; One should rather break in the joints than yield in this world to any body."[44]

Heroism is the prime virtue of a Kshatriya. "Prowess, splendour, firmness, dexterity, and also not flying from battle, generosity, the nature of a ruler, are the Kshatriya duties, born of his own nature."[45] "More than life itself, strive ye to win objects of enjoyment procurable by prowess, since objects won by prowess alone can please the heart of a person desirous of living according to Kshatriya practices."[46] Fighting on the battle-field is, therefore, the very highest duty ad pleasure to a Kshatriya. He should not deprecate wars but rather seek them. "Indra himself, though a Brahmin, became Kshatriya in his acts, and battled with his sinful kinsfolk for eight hundred and ten times. Those acts of his, O monarch, are adorable and worthy of praise. Through them, he obtained, as we have heard the chiefship of the gods."[47]

But the Kshatriya class has to remember that though it is admirable to have a giant's strength, it is not so good to use it like a giant. It is not the heroism of a brute that is glorified. A Kshatriya is not to be a worshipper of naked physical force. It is not the installation of might, but of right which is aimed at. But the might is to be harnessed in the service of right. Might is to make the world safe for right. The ultimate end of this military order is quite clear; it is the triumph of the forces of right. The method of ensuring this triumph, however, is blood and iron. "A Kshatriya should slay sires and grandsires, and brothers, and preceptors, and relatives, and kinsmen that may engage with him, *in a just battle*. This is their declared duty. That Kshatriya, O Keshava, is said to be acquainted with his duty who slays in battle his very preceptors, if they happen to be sinful, and covetous, and disregardful of restraints and vows."[48] Kalidas says that the real justification for a warrior's weapons lies in the protection they afford to the distressed, and not in injuring the innocent. आर्तत्राणाय वः शस्त्रं न प्रहर्तुमनागसि। The derivation of the word क्षत्रिय (Kshatriya) is highly significant. क्षतात्किलत्रायतित्युदग्रः क्षत्रस्य शब्दः भुवनेषु रूढः। (Raghuvansha). "And because he protecteth all people from wounds and injuries, for this he became a true Kshatriya."[49]

The duties of the last two orders may be briefly described. "Ploughing, protection of kine, and trade are the Vaishya's duty, born of his own nature. Action of the nature of service is the Shudra duty born of his own nature"[50] Not that these classes are unimprotant. Far from it. They are the real basis of the whole economic structure of the state; they are respectively the capitalists and labourers of the Hindu society. "A Vaishya, initiated with the holy thread, shall marry and daily attend to agriculture and cattle-rearing. *Prajapati* (the creator) created the beasts and gave them to the Vaishya; and all the creatures he gave to the king and the Brahmins. The Vaishya must not desire to keep no beasts; if the Vaishya desires to keep beasts (i.e. to rear animals), let none else do that. Let the Vaishya appraise the prices and qualities of gems, pearls, corals, metals, woven stuffs, scented things, and salts. Likewise he must possess the knowledge of sowing seeds, of the specific traits of the soil, of the measures of lands, and the rules of weighing articles, (as well as) defects or excellencies of articles, the good and evil traits of countries, profits or losses in manufactured articles and the increase of animals. He must know the wages of artisans and workmen, and languages of different races of men; he shall be able to forecast the increase or decrease in the prices, and amelioration or deterioratoin in the quality of an article at a particular place and time, as well as the mode of selling or buying. He shall constantly try to multiply his riches by honest means and give food to animals out of all creatures"[51]

The Shudras were the helots of the Hindu society. They were regarded as born servants. They could be 'expelled at will' and 'slain at will'.[52] They were unclean and unfit for sacrifice.[53] Manu considers them as slaves, and hence they have no right of property. "A Shudra whether a slave purchased or otherwise, must be employed in service. Even when set at liberty by his own master, a Shudra cannot be liberated from service : service is his vocation by nature: who shall emancipate him from that?.........A wife, a son, and a slave can never acquire any property for themselves: whatever they earn go to him to whom they belong."[54] The Shudras are disqualified for the study of the sacred literature. The Shudras are denied all access to the high offices. "The realm of a king, wherein a Shudra official administers justice, is destroyed under his very eyes."[55] The Shudras are not to amass wealth, nor try to be equal to the higher castes. "A fine of a hundred *Panas* should be realised from a Shudra striving to be equal to a Brahmin in a bed or seat or treating a Brahmin on the road as his equal."[56] No Brahmin is justified in treating Shudras as his equals or superiors.[57]

The higher classes, however, did not entirely forget the basis of common humanity that the Shudras shared with them. We hear of rich Shudras[58] of the Shudra kingdoms[59] of Shudra ministers,[60] of prayers for Shudra,[61] and of popularity with

Shudra,[62] in the early literature. Their competency to perform various ceremonies and the obligations of the other classes towards them are also referred to. "The fourth order of society is Shudra; and Shudras are all of one caste. Even Shudras should practise forbearance, toleration, and truthfulness, and wash their hands and feet for the purposes of *Achamanam* (sipping water as a religious ceremony). A Shudra is competent to celebrate the Shraddha ceremonies in honour of his departed manes. A Shudra shall support his own servants, and devote himself to the services of the three superior social orders ;... otherwise a Shudra may earn his livelihood by any kind of handicraft. The person, whom a Shudra might serve as his master, is bound to support him in his old age, even if he becomes incapable of doing further service. Likewise, a Shudra is bound to support his master in his old age, or if fallen on evil days. *'Namas'* is the only *mantra* which a Shudra is competent to utter. According to several authorities, a Shudra is competent to do the *Pakayajna*."[63] The prejudices against lower castes were at first not so strong as at present. The Shudras were able to serve as cooks to the members of the higher castes. Bhima called himself a Shudra; yet he was taken up in the service of the king Virata as a cook.[64] The Brahmins could take the food from the Shudra under certain circumstances. A Shudra woman could be accepted as a wife by all the three orders.[65] A Shudra who took to righteous courses of action came very near to the other orders. "For a Shudra who is desirous of hearing (Such scriptures as are not fobidden in his caste); who has accomplished his duties, who has begotten a son, between whom and the superior orders there is not much difference in consequence of the purity of his conduct, all the modes of life have been laid down except the observance of universal peacefulness, and selfrestraint (which are not necessary for him). For a Shudra, practising all these duties, as also for a Vaishya, and a Kshatriya, the *Bhikshu* (mendicancy) mode of life has been laid down."[66] A Shudra could take to commerce, as well as the practice of either mechanical or fine arts. "When the Shudra is unable to obtain his living by service of the three other orders, then trade, rearing of cattle, and the practice of the mechanical arts are lawful for him to follow."[67] "For a Shudra, all branches of art (such as painting and the other fine arts) can be resorted to for livelihood."[68]

There was equality with regard to all the castes as regards certain fundamentals of life. Practice of rites was often denied to the lower orders; yet the highest morality could be practised by them as well as others. "Forbearance, veracity, restraint, purity, liberality, self-control, abstention of injury to any living creature obedience towards one's Gurus, visiting places of pilgrimage, sympathy (with the affiliated); straight forwardness, freedom from covetousness, reverence towards gods, and Brahmins, and freedom from anger, are duties common (to all the castes)."[69] There is not only equality with reference to practice to the highest morality; there is equality with reference to the highest spiritual qualities. All castes have equal access of God. Indeed God looks to love and devotion and purity of heart of the devotees and not their caste. "Even the despised classes have a right to it."[70] Rama eats fruits previously tasted by Shabarya Chandala girl.[71] He says with regard to Guhaka : "It is through deep love that he uses 'thou' and 'thee' to me, and this makes me love him very dearly indeed. With love, the Chandala makes me his own, while without it the Brahmin is nothing to me." "These eight kinds of *Bhakti* (devotion) even if they exist in a Mlechha (a non-Hindu), turn him into a prince of Brahmins, a sage, an ascetic, a truly wise man."[72]

Now as regards caste, there are two main currents of opinion : the one view is that caste is based on birth, that a person takes the caste of a family into which he or she is born. The other view would make the caste of a person dependent upon his character. It is futile to deny that the former view has prevailed, and the other one has now vanished. But at one time the latter view was held by many persons. According to the former view, a man of lower caste can get a birth in the higher caste only by a life of hard penances in many successive births; in one and the same existence one cannot pass from one group into a higher one.

There is no doubt that a certain importance is always justly attached to purity of birth or descent. A man inherits from his parents, and grand-father and grand-mother, many of his intellectual and moral traits. Much stress was laid on being a descendant of a Rishi.[73] "The (racial) lives of men of all the four orders of society are subject to change aberrations, and hybridization. Virtue consists in preserving the purity of one's native stock."[74] But a far saner position is that it is one's qualities, acts, and character that alone can determine his status in life. If it is maintained that persons are born Brahmins not made, it means that to a great extent a man's character is determined by the congenital traits which he had received at his birth; and very substantial changes in it are possible, but not easy. It simply means that those who are born lovers of knowledge and peace and Brahmins; those who have inborn disposition to aggression are Kshatriyas and so on. Vishwamitra's story carries a plain moral. As long as he could not suppress his lust and wrath, he was not allowed to rise to the higher order. Again and again he resorts to penances and again and again he is thrown back by some impulsive action of his. It was only when he mastered his self completely that he naturally became a Brahmin.[75]

It is frequently asserted that a Brahmin is he who possesses the highest learning and character, whether he has acquired these through birth or education or borth.[76] Pupils were often accepted without their parentage being known.[77] It is said in a commentary on Shrauta sutras that "whoever studies the Stome-bhagas (a peculiarity of the Vasishthas) is a Vasishtha." The degradation of the character of a Brahmin carries with it a corresponding degradation in his status. His titles to reverence entirely depend upon his moral and intellectual status. "Those names which are applied among men to slaves and dogs and wolves, and (other) beasts, are applied to the Brahmin, who is engaged in pursuits that are improper for him."[78] "That wretched Brahmin, who falls away from his duties, and whose behaviour becomes wicked, becomes a Shudra. The Brahmin, who weds a Shudra woman, who becomes vile in conduct, or a dancer or a village servant, or does other improper acts, becomes a Shudra. Whether he recites the Vedas or not, O king, if he does such improper acts, he becomes equal to a Shudra, and on occasions of feeding, he should be assigned a place amongst Shudras."[79] The generic title of a Brahmin, therefore, does not carry much weight. The essentials of his self are to be fully looked to before his claims to pure Brahminhood can be made out. The sham Brahmins, well-known as *Brahma bandhus*, are no Brahmins at all.

The theory, therefore, which is very often set forth and which expresses the better opinion of the ancient Hindu seers, is that it is not birth, nor any other accident which determines a man's class, but his actions, habits, and character are the deciding factors. "My birth has been low. It is conduct, however, that determines the race."[80] "Man attains to a superior colour by righteous acts."[81] "Listen, O Yaksha! It is neither birth, nor study, nor learning, that is the cause of Brahminhood. Without doubt, it is behaviour that constitutes it."[82] "It is with the aid of these acts that a person who has sprung from a degraded order, viz, a Shudra may become a Brahmin, with all his stains removed and possesed of Vedic lore. One that is a Brahmin, when he becomes wicked in conduct and observes no distinction in respect of food, falls away from the status of Brahminhood, and becomes a Shudra. Even a Shudra, O goddess, that has purified his soul by pure deeds, and that has subjugated all his senses, deserves to be waited upon and served with reverence as a Brahmin. This has been said by the self-born Brahma himself. When a pious nature and pious deeds are noticeable even in a Shudra, he should, according to my opinion, be held superior to a person of the three regenerate classes. Neither birth, nor the purificatory rites, nor learning, nor offspring, can be regarded as grounds for conferring upon one the status of regeneracy (द्विजत्व). Verily, conduct is the only ground. All Brahmins in this world are Brahmins in consequence of conduct. The boon-giving Brahman while he created all creatures, himself said that the distribution of human beings into the four orders as dependent on birth is only for purposes of classification."[83] "O ruler of the Videhas, Brahmins learned in the Vedas, O monarch, regard a (virtuous) Shudra as equal to a Brahmin himself. I, however, O king, look upon such a Shudra as effulgent Vishnu of the universe, the foremost one in all the worlds."[84]

The following dialogue between the serpent and Yudhishthira throws an interesting light on the state of opinion on this controversy, at that period. "Yudhishthira said, Those characteristics that are present in a Shudra, do not exist in a Brahmin; nor do those that are in a Brahmin exist in a Shudra. And a Shudra is not a Shudra by birth alone,–nor a Brahmin, a Brahmin by birth alone. He, it is said by the wise, in whom are seen those virtues, is a Brahmin. And people term him a Shudra, in whom those qualities do not exist." "O king, if thou recognise a Brahmin by characteristics, then the distinction of castes becomes futile, as long as conduct does not come into play." Yudhishthira said, In human society, it is difficult to asceratin one's caste, because of the promiscuous intercourse among the four orders. This is my opinion. Men belonging to all the orders (promiscuously) begot offsprings upon women of all the orders...And to this the Rishis have borne testimony, by using at the beginning of a sacrifice, such expressions as, *–of whatsoever caste we may be, we celebrate the sacrifice.* Therefore, those that are wise have asserted that character is the chief requisite and needful. The natal ceremony of a person is performed, before division of the umbilical cord. His mother then acts as Savitri and his father officiates as priest. He is considered a Shudra as long as he is not initiated in the Vedas. Doubts having arisen on this point, the self-origined Manu has declared that the mixed castes are to be regarded as better than the (other) classes, if, having gone through the ceremonies of purification, the latter do not conform to the rules of good conduct, O excellent snake! Whosoever now conforms to the rules of pure and virtuous conduct, him have I, are now, designated as a Brahmin.[85]

It is interesting to compare how the Buddhist view of caste so well corresponds with the above view. "A man does not become a Brahmin by his platted hair, by his family, or by birth : in whom there is truth and righteousness, he is blessed, he is a Brahmin."[86] The following passage from Ashwaghosha is very instructive. "Tell me first of all what is Brahminhood? ....If you say Brahminhood depends on parentage or birth,– this notion is at variance with the known passage of the Smriti, that Achala Muni was born of an elephant, and Kesha Pingala of an owl, and Agastya Muni from the Agasti flower, and Kaushika Muni from the Kusha grass, and Kapila Muni from a monkey, and Gautama Rishi from a creeper that entwined a Shala tree, and Drona Acharya from an earthen pot, and Taittiri rishi from a partridge, and (Parashu) Ram from dust, and Shringa Rishi from a deer, and Vyasa Muni from a fisher-woman, and Kaushika Muni from a female Shudra, and Vishwamitra from a Chandali, and Vasishtha Muni from a strumpet, and yet all were notoriously called Brahmins.......

Say you that wisdom constitutes the Brahmin? This too is incorrect. Why? Because if it were true, many Shudras must have become Brahmins from the great wisdom they acquired. I myself know many Shudras who are masters of the four Vedas, and of Philology, and of the Mimamsa, and Samkhya, and Vaisheshika, and Jyotishika philosophies; yet not one of them is or ever was called a Brahmin....

What, then is the creature called a Brahmin?......That which removes sin is Brahminhood. It consists of Vrata (vows), and Tapa (penances), and Niyama (Self-control), and Upavasa (fasting), and Dana (charity), and Dama and Shama (mental equipoise)."[87]

Some of the most characteristic excellences and defects

of Hindu culture spring from the ideal of Caste organization. The system is one of the fundamentals of our ancient civilisation; and to part with it is to part with the most distinctive part of our work. The greatest service it has rendered to us is the *organization of society on a spiritual basis.* The western society rests upon purely economic foundations; its division of society is regulated by the consideration of money. Status in the West is determined by the measure of what a man *has;* status of man in the East is determined by what a man *is.* Individual exceptions apart, such is the consequence of the existing orders. In very few societies, culture and character are assigned such a sovereignty. Another great service rendered by the system is the excellent organization it provided by a systematic distribution of functions amoung various classes. Our caste-system was a great safeguard against all foreign governments. It rendered society here independent of the state to a great extent. But the ties became too rigid in course of time; and what were meant as distinctions became impassable barriers. The Hindus began to think in terms of the castes they belonged to and began to be oblivious of the larger whole to which they belonged. The obligations the higher castes owed to the lower castes were forgotten: and the tyranny of the priest actually became one of the worst tyrannies. "When the Shudra joined his palms in submission to the Brahmanical decree of inferiority, on that very day was dug the pit for the fall of the Brahmins." (Dr. Tagore). Caste-system can survive only if the four large groupings may again take to the performance of their obligations and not think too much of their rights. Every one must consult the heritage which he has received from the past, and build upon that foundation. The distinctions between culture classes, and money-classes, between the fighting temperaments and the quietistic souls, between those capable of splendid muscle-work, and those capable of the higher work of soul are not likely to vanish; and the old caste-system was nothing more than a registration of this fact.

References

1. Republic Book III. Tr. Jowett
2. Shanti. 186.5
3. Shanti. 186. 10-14
4. Br. U. I. 4. 11-13
5. Rg. X, 90. 12
6. Rg. I. 113. 6.
6a. M. I. 96.
7. S. Br. XI. 5, 7, 1
8. M. I. 88
9. M. I. 93
10. M. I. 98-99
11. Bg. XVIII. 42
12. Vana. 209, 34-39
13. Shanti. 78-34
14. Shanti. 78. 18.
15. Shanti. 209. 34
16. Shanti. 62. 3
17. M. IV. 33
18. Anu. 92. 3-5
19. S. Br. XI. 5.7.1
20. Vyasa IV. 12.
21. AV. V. 3.2. Vishnu. XIX. 20-22
22. M.I. 100-101
23. Shanti. 72. 14-15
24. Gautama. VIII
25. Rg. X. 109, 4. Br. Up. VI. 4, 12
26. Brihaspati. 48
27. S. Br. XIII. 3, 5, 3
28. Adi. 28, 4-7
29. Shanti. 163, 11-12
30. Adi. 191, 31.
31. Shanti. 299, 22.
32. S. Br. IV. 1, 4, 6, etc.
33. Adi. 191, 57-58
34. Shanti. 73, 49-51
35. M. I. 89
36. Br. Up. VI. 2, 7.
37. Shanti. 62, 24-32.

38. Vana. 33, 49-64
39. Shanti. 62, 23.
40. Udyoga. 133, 9
41. Udyoga. 133, 13-15
42. Udyoga. 90.94-100
43. Udyoga. 133. 33-35.
44. Udyoga. 134- 38-41
45. Bg. XVIII. 43
46. Udyoga. 90. 78
47. Shanti. 22. 11-12
48. Shanti. 64. 15-19
49. Drona. 69.2
50. Bg. XVIII. 44.
51. M. IX. 326-333
52. Ai. Br. VII. 29.4
53. S. Br. III. 1. 1. 10
54. M. VIII. 413-414, 416
55. M. VIII. 21
56. Gautama. XII
57. Shanti. 163, 28-29
58. Mai. S. IV. 2, 7, 10
59. M. IV. 61
60. S. Br. V. 3, 2, 2
61. Vaj. S. XVIII. 48
62. Av. XIX. 32. 8; 62. 1
63. Gautama. X
64. Virata. 10.13
65. M. III. 13
66. Shanti. 62. 12-14
67. Shanti. 300.4
68. Vishnu. II. 14
69. Vishnu. II. 16-17
70. Shandilya-sutras II. 78
71. Aranya-Kanda 78
72. Garuda Purana, I. 231. 9-10
73. S. Br. IV. 3.9.
74. Gautama VIII
75. Udyoga. 106. 7-18
76. Tai. S. VI. 6. 1. 4. Mai. IV. 8. 1
77. Ch. Up. VI. 4. 4; S. Br. XI. 5. 4. 1

78. Shanti. 61. 5
79. Shanti. 62. 4-5
80. Shanti. 111, 13
81. Shanti. 297, 5.
82. Vana. 314, 110
83. Anu. 217, 12-17
84. Shanti. 302, 12-18
85. Vana. 182, 21-26, 30-37, etc.
86. Dhammapada XXVI 393.
87. Quoted in Wilson's 'Caste' Vol. I.

Chapter - XV

FRIENDSHIP

Hindus very clearly recognised the possibilities of the sentiment of innate kinship which springs up between different souls under different influences. The fact that some persons are more closely adapted to our natures than the remaining world owing to either our respective positions, or common interests, or joint purposes, or spiritual affinities is a fact of considerable sociological significance. A special set of obligations is created towards these people; and it is for ethics to enter into minutiae regarding these. One of the images often put forth to picture the attitude of God to man is the image of friendship. "A Friend for friend, be thou (Indra), best finder of success."[1] "As father with the son, as friend with friends, with the beloved as lover, bear with me."[2]

Many are the causes leading to friendship. But the classical Sanskrit writers always grasped one fact about the highest friendship. It springs up of itself. The soul draws soul as magnet draws iron. There is a fine naivete, a certain artlessness, or spontaneity about all true friendships. The highest affection is essentially disinterested. It is called निष्कारणस्नेह. Bhavabhuti says : "That love is dependent upon causes is contradictory." It is a pariality which has no apparent explicable reasons behind it and which flows irresistibly towards its object. Love is, indeed, a transcendental phenomenon not easily explained by the categories of the utilitarian philosophers.

The role of friendship is appreciated to a considerable extent in the Ramayana. Sugriva says to Rama : "O free one, the felicity of high souled and self-governed friends like thee abounds and is enduring. Pious friends look upon the silver, and gold, and the elegant ornaments of pious friends as common property. Whether rich or poor, happy or miserable, good or bad, a friend is the greatest refuge (of his friend). Witnessing such affection, people can forsake wealth, comfort, and even their native land for the sake of their friends."[3] Here is a glimpse of a very high type of friendship based on pure love. Friendship was considered a solemn act, sealed by means of certain forms which were calculated to invest it with sacred significance. Sugriva says to Rama : "If you relish friendship with me, do you take this stretched arm and hand with yours, and bind your-self fast with a vow." Then they press each other's hands, and kindle a fire, and go round it; thus friendship was sealed.[4] It is very necessary to preserve one's friendship will all one's tact. "It is easy to contract friendship, but bery difficult to sustain it; for owing to the fickleness of our minds, a very slight casue brings about separation."[5] "He who loseth friendship with a qualified friend loses wealth."[6] Jatayu's act of self-sacrifice for the sake of his friendship with Dasharatha illustrates the nature of pure friends who die for the sake of their departed friends.[7] Inconstancy of friends is well exposed. "As the drops of water do not last long, so the friendship with unworthy persons. As the autumnal clouds, albeit muttering, do not pour forth water, so is the friendship with unworthy persons. As a bee flies away after sucking up the honey, so is the friendship with unworthy persons. As a bee, after feeding upon the Kasha flowers does not get honey, so (fruitless) is the friendship with unworthy persons."[8]

The Mahabharata is specially full of details regarding all sorts of friendship. Friendship is of various grades, ranging from the purest affection which no earthly taint about it to all worldly combinations. "Friendship is formed among people by reason of obligations (mutually conferred), among beasts and birds for some motive, among fools through fear and greed, and between the good at the very sight" (Panchatantra). This conception that true love is always more or less spontaneous is frequently emphasised. "It has been declared by wise men endued with true knowledge that by walking only seven paces with another, one contracteth a friendship with one's companion."[9] 'Friendship among righteous persons happens at a single meeting. It is a desirable object."[10] This is, however, comparatively a rare fact. All ordinary instances of friendship can be duly accounted for. "One becomes another's friend or enemy from some cause; therefore, a prudent man should form friendship and not enmity with others" (Panchatantra). Common pursuits often lead to friendship. No man is a born friend or a foe.[11] In a passage, the reasoning of which reminds us of the reasoning of utilitarian philosophers, self-interest is said to be the one emphatic root of all kinships and antagonisms. "This whole world of creatures is moved by the desire of gain. One never becomes dear to another (without any cause). The friendship between two uterine brothers, the love between husband and wife, depends upon interest. I do not know any kind of affection between any persons that does not rest upon some motive of self-interest....One becomes dear for one's liberality. Another becomes dear for his sweet words. A third becomes so in consequence of his religious acts. Generally, a person becomes dear for the purpose he serves."[12]

The fundamental feature of all genuine friendship is the existence of the identity of souls-of the highest spiritual and intellectual affinities between two persons. "He that hateth them, hateth me; he that loveth them loveth me! Know that virtuous Pandavas and my own self have but a common soul."[13] "Indeed Krishna is the soul of Arjuna, and Arjuna is the soul of Krishna, and whatever Arjuna may say Krishna is certain to accomplish. And Krishna is capable of abandoning heaven itself for the sake of Arjuna, and Arjuna also is capable of sacrificing his life for the sake of Krishna."[14] There are certain typical features characterising all true friendship. It is said to possess six indications. "First, friends delight in the prosperity of friends, and secondly, are distressed at their adversity. If any one asketh for anything which is dear to his heart but should not be asked for, a true friend surely giveth away even that. Fourthly, a true friend, who is of a righteous disposition, when asked, can give away his very prosperity, his beloved sons, and even his own wife. Fifthly, a friend should not dwell in the house of a friend on whom he may have bestowed everything, but should enjoy what he earneth himself. Sixthly, a friend stoppeth not to sacrifice his own good (for his friend)."[15] A true friend is one's centre of affections, the true seat of confidence the unfailing partner in one's joys and sorrows and the due helper in all difficulties. "The learned say that by these unmistakable signs, friends should be known, just as the examination of the fire of sacrifice is prescribed by those versed in it. He, who is our friend when adversity befalls is a real friend; when the time of prosperity comes even a wiched man becomes our friend."[16] "These three are the fruits derived from a friend viz a great benefit in adversity, the confiding of a secret, and freedom from calamity...who has created this jewel, viz. the two letters मित्र, which protects when a danger arises and which is a receptacle for affection and confidence?"[17]

The essence, therefore, of true kinship of hearts is mutual love, mutual fidelity, and mutual service. It is upon such foundations that the noble and lasting fabric of friendship is very well reared. "No part in Vak hath he who hath abandoned his own dear friend who knows the truth of friendship."[18] "O wealthy God, ne'er may I live to see my friend or son in need."[19] "May I not live to witness my wealthy, liberal, dear friend's destitution."[20] Partnership in joy and sorrow, comradeship in all dangers and calamities is the general characteristic of friendship. "Sorrowing on occasions of sorrow, and rejoicing on occasions of joy, are the indications of a friend, and opposite behaviour furnishes the indications of an enemy."[21] "It is friends and not others that wait by the side of him that is weak, of him that is prosecuted in a court of law, and of him that is borne towards the crematorium."[22]

Treason towards one's friend bears a peculiarly hateful look, because it is the very thing that is least expected from that quarter. All morality is ultimately reciprocal; and when a man instead of rising to respond to the calls of his friend in gratitude and affection, proves treacherous to him, he very naturally becomes the object of the greatest moral censure. Loyalty to one's friends and serviceableness with regard to him is the most natural attitude; hence disloyalty to him and injuries rendered to him become proportionately unnatural. "The very birds of prey abstain from touching the dead bodies of those who, having been served and benefited by friends, show ingratitude to the latter. Beest thou poor, or beest thou rich, thou shouldst worship thy friends. Until also some service is aksed, the sincerity or otherwise of friends cannot be known."[23]

It should be here borne in mind that a friend is the reverse of a flatterer, that his office does not consist in keeping an atmosphere of artificial sweetness round his friend, but to keep him in close touch with facts and views which tend to his well-being, however, repellent they may be. Hence friends should be capable both of offering and of resuing advice freely and frankly. "O king, such persons as always speak sweetly are easy to find, but he, who says what is unpleasant but beneficial is hard to get. Those alone are said to be friends who speak what is unpleasant but beneficial to men; others are friends only in name."[24]

It is recognised that however self-sufficient a man may be, it is necessary, if possible, to have congenial associates for the proper development of one's self. "Wise men, though endowed with plenty, should make friends; the lord of rivers though full of water expects the rise of the moon (to rise higher still)."[25] Friends are necessary for various reasons: to break up our mental isolation and solitude, to aid us by their sympathies, to warn us against evil paths by their advice, to share with us all joys and sorrows, to render us services in times of difficulty and need, and above all, to render possible the fulfilment of objects which require the co-ordination of many minds working for a common purpose and animated by a common spirit. "Since a man who has friends accomplishes objects difficult of accomplishment, one should make such friends as are equal to one (in disposition)".[26]

Great care is necessary in making a proper selection of one's friends. Various factors are to be taken into account in the exercise of this choice. Character, the mental likes and dislikes, the professional pursuits, social position, age : all these considerations are to be taken into due account in building up solid friendships. "Friendship and marriage are fit between those only whose wealth and family are equal, and not between those who are rich and poor, or fat and lean."[27] These extraneous circumstances often play a decisive part in one's alliances. Drupada says to Drona : "O thou of dull apprehension, great kings can never be friends with such luckless and indigent wights as thou! Friendship can never subsist between a poor man and a rich man, between a man of letters and an unlettered man, between a hero and a coward..... There may be friendship or hostility between persons equally situtated as to wealth or might."[28] There should be similarity of mental attitudes towards life between two persons wishing to unite. समानशीलव्यसनेषुसंख्या। "The friendship of those two persons never cooleth whose hearts, secret pursuits, and pleasures, and acquirements, accord in every respect."[29] Above all, character and wisdom of friends should be carefully looked into. These are very vital considerations, for it is not the gratification of one's fancy, or even one's mental longings or other pleasures which is fundamental here; but the influence of soul on soul is such a fact that the one all-important qualification of a friend is that he must possess a lofty character. "The opportunity of forming friendship with a righteous person should not be sacrificed. Therefore, the friendship of the righteous is to be sought."[30] "He that is intelligent should avoid ignorant person of wicked soul like a pit whose mouth is covered with grass, for friendship with such a person can never last. The man of wisdom should never contract friendship with those that are proud, ignorant, fierce, rash, and fallen off from righteousness. He that is grateful, virtuous, truthful, large-hearted, and devoted, and he that hath his senses under control, preserveth his dignity, and never forsaketh a friend, should be desired for a friend."[31]

References

1. Rg. IX. 104.5
2. Bg. XI. 44.
3. R. IV. 8. 6-9
4. R. IV. 5. 10-16.
5. R. IV. 32. 7.
6. R. IV. 33. 47.
7. R. III. 50. 6-10.
8. R. VI. 16. 11-14
9. Vana. 298. 24
10. Udyoga. 10.
11. Sabha. 81.
12. Shanti. 138. 140-156.
13. Udyoga. 91. 30.
14. Sabha. 78. 111. 112.
15. Udyoga. 46. 12. 13
16. Panchatantra.
17. Panchatantra.
18. Rg. X. 71.6
19. Rg. VIII. 115. 36.
20. Rg. II. 28. 11
21. Shanti. 103, 50.
22. Shanti. 152,. 28.
23. Udyoga. 36, 37-43.
24. Panchatantra.
25. Panchatantra.
26. Panchatantra
27. Panchatantra
28. Adi. 141. 5-11
29. Udyoga. 39.
30. Udyoga. 10. 23
31. Udyoga. 39.48-51.

Chapter - XVI

HOSPITALITY

Hindus held undoubtedly very generous ideas about the duties which one owes to one's guests. They are second to none in the magnificence of their conception of hospitality. The guest-worship was a regular institution; it was an integral part of the duties of both house-holders and non house-holders alike. "In men's houses, their well-loved guest was glorified."[1] The best room was reserved for him.[2] The Atharva-Veda has a hymn in which kind treatment of guests is considered equal to a sacrifice in point of merit. "When in truth the lord of guests meets with his eyes the guests, he looks at a sacrificing to the gods. When he greets them, he enters upon consecration; when he offers water, he brings forward the (sacrificial) waters. ...When they fetch a gratification-that is just the same as an animal for Agni and Soma that is boud (for a sacrifice.) In that they prepare lodgings, they so prepare the seat and oblation-holders."[3] The Upanishads are more emphatic. "Let the guest be to you a deity!"

Hospitality to strangers was a universal and laudable practice in the time of the Ramayana. The mountain-chief says to Hanumana : "Even an ordinary guest should be adored by him who abides by virtue, what of thee great as thou art?"[4] Here are some typical incidents illustrating the way of hospitality. The arrival of the sage Vishwamitra is announced. Dasharatha goes out to receive him. He then offers Arghya (a sort of worship) to him and says : "Like unto the obtaining of ambrosia, like unto a shower in a land suffering from draught, like unto the birth of sons of worthy wives to him without issue, like unto the recovery of a lost thing, yea, like unto the dawning of a mighty joy, I consider this thy arrival. O illustrious ascetic, art thou well? What is even that which is nearest thy heart? What shall I do for thee, experiencing sincere pleasure? Thou art worthy of my best services.[5] Even the ascetics were required to entertain their guests. When Rama goes to sage Agastya, he says, "Welcome!' "Offering oblation unto the fire, and presenting Arghya unto the guests, and paying them homage, that ascetic entertained them with food according to Vanprastha mode of life, and then first sitting down, he addressed Rama with joined hands : O Rama, if an ascetic acts otherwise (in respect of a guest) he in the next world feeds on his own flesh, like a false witness."[6]

Guests are to be objects of greater attention to a householder than himself or his wife. "As the Brahmins are the lords over all other castes, and as a husband is lord over his wives, a guest is the lord of a householder."[7] "Let the master and mistress of the house eat what remains after feeding the Brahmins (guests), relations, and servants."[8] "Fire alone hath power to give heat. The earth alone hath power to infuse life into the seed. The sun alone hath power to illuminate everything. So the guest alone hath power to command the virtuous and wise."[9]

Hospitality to one's guests becomes an act of great merit; and any neglect shown to one's guests brings proportionately serious evil consequences. "It is said by the learned that the blessings of an honoured guest are more efficacious than the merit of a hundred sacrifices."[10] "Let not (a householder) eat that himself which his Atithi (guest) has not partaken of; hospitality to an Atithi brings on wealth, fame, and longevity, and ensures heaven to him who practises it."[11] By the daily recitation of the Vedas, by the Agnihotra, by sacrificing, and by austerity, a householder does not obtain such excellent place of abode (after death) as by honouring a guest."[12] If a guest is turned back, he takes away with him all the religious merit of the repudiator and burns him up. "(The fire of) the Agnihotra, bulls, and a guest that has come in at the right time, children and persons of noble family : these burn up him who neglects them"[13]

There are more or less set ways of entertaining a guest. The first essential is the feeling of elation that comes over a kind host. All the other formalities follow. "The heart of a young man, when an aged and venerable person cometh to his house (as a guest), soareth aloft. By advancing forward and saluting him he getteth it back. He that is self-controlled, first offering a seat, and bringing water and causing his guest's feet to be washed and making the usual inquiries of welcome, should then speak of his own affairs, and taking everything into consideration, offer him food."[14] "If the guest is welcomed, the deities of fire become glade; and if he is offered a seat, it is the god of an hundred sacrifices, who is gratified. It his feet are washed it is the Pitris who are delighted, and if he is fed, it is Prajapti that is pleased."[15] Daksha also gives details of hospitality. "When any distinguished person comes to the house, one should gently offer these four,–the mind, the eye, the face, and the words. One should rise up and say–'Come here,' carry on a pleasant conversation, saying–'Welcome,' treat him with food, and follow him. (All) these works should be carefully (performed)."[16] The satisfaction of a guest is generally the criterion of successful hospitality. "When giving edibles to another, one should say-Is it sufficient ?-When presenting drink, one should ask-Will it gratify? and when giving sweetened milk and rice, or sugared gruel of barley, or milk with sesame, one should ask–Has it fallen!"[17] The precise wants of a guest should be looked to. But hospitality of a very simple sort is within the reach of all. "Grass (for seat), space (for rest), water (to wash and assuage thinst), and fourthly, sweet words-of these the houses of the good can never be in want. To the weary a bed, to one fatigued with standing, a seat, -to the thirsty, water, and to the hungry, food should ever be given. To a guest are due pleasant looks and a cheerful heart and sweet words."[18]

It remains to inquire as to what persons are specially deserving of hospitable treatment. The word Atithi (guest) is significant. " A Brahmin, who resides for a single night in the house of (another) is called Atithi; since there is no certainty of his staying (there, the next day) he is called an Atithi."[19] Much depends upon the time when a guest comes. "Any person, happening to call at one's house during the performance of the Vaishwadeva. Homa, should be regarded as an Atithi, whether he be erudite or ignorant, pleasant or undesirable guest; inasmuch as an Atithi leads his host to heaven."[20] Opinion is rather divided as to whether certain vices absolutely disqualify a man for the right of hospitality or not. Manu expresses hismelf against extending to undersirables the courtesy of hospitality. "Let him not welcome with even speech (guests) who go contrary to the Vedas, or live by professions other than peculiar to their order, or are cat-natured, or dispute the doctrines of the Vedas by false logic, or have no faith in the Vedas, or are crane-natured."[21] The Mahabharata, however, lays down that a guest is a guest, whatever his private character may be. "A physician, a maker of arrows, one that hath given up the vow of Brahmacharya before it is complete, a thief, a crooked-minded man, a Brahmin that drinks, one that causeth miscarriage, one that liveth by serving in the army, and one that selleth the Vedas when arrived as a guest, however undeserving he may be of even the offer of water, should be regarded (by a householder) as exceedingly dear."[22]

The treatment of guests must be appropriate to their social status. "There are six persons to whom the Arghya reception is due, (namely) a teacher, an officiating priest, a Snataka, a king, the father-in-law a friend coming as a guest."[23] However, if these appear again within a year, they need not be entertained in the way of Madhuparkam; except when a king, or a Snataka calls at one's house on the occasion of a sacrificial ceremony.[24] Reception varies with the social status of the guest, or his caste, or the degree of familarity he enjoys with the host. "Cushions, bedsteads, beddings, following, and worship, should differ according to the status of the Atithis. Better cushions etc., should be given to Atithis of better status, ordinary ones to Atithis of equal rank with the host, and inferior ones to Atithis of inferior rank."[25]

The habit of visiting other persons' houses, in order to partake of their hospitality is not looked upon with partiality. Unless there is some justifiable occasion, or unless the invitation or acceptance is inspired by love, the entertainment which one wishes to receive at another's house is more or less condemnable. "Householders, who, ignorant of the demerit of eating food given by others, stroll about in a village other than their own, out of a greed for sharing other men's hospitalities, become the domestic beasts of those whose hospitalities they then partake of."[26] "His life is in vain who hath no son; and his also who is out of the pale of virtue; and his too who liveth on the food of others; and lastly, his who cocketh for himself without giving therefrom unto the Pitris, the gods, and the guests, and who eateth of it before these all."[27] "Earned by his own efforts, without having to depend upon any one, he that eateth even fruits and vegetables in his own house is entitled to respect. He that eateth in another's house the food given to him in contempt, even if that food be rich and sweet, doth what is despicable. This, therefore, is the opinion of the wise that fie on the food of that mean wretch, who, like a god or Rakshasa, eateth at another's house."[28] Affection or necessity alone, can justify this procedure. "One taketh another's food when that other inspireth love. One may also take another's food when one is in distress."[29]

References

1. Rg. VI. 2.7.
2. Rg. I. 73, 1.
3. Av. IX. 6, 3-6, etc.
4. R. V. 1, 112.
5. R. I. 18, 43-58.
6. R. III. 12, 25-29.
7. Vishnu. LXVII. 31.

8. Manu. III. 116.
9. Adi. 82, 13.
10. Anu. 2. 106.
11. M. III, 106.
12. Vishnu. LXVII. 45
13. Sam. Gr. S. II, 16. 4, M. III. 100
14. Udyoga. 38. 1-3
15. Vana. 203. 68
16. Daksha III. 4-5
17. Shanti. 191. 22.
18. V. 2. 52.
19. M. III. 102
20. Parashara. I. 39-40.
21. M. IV. 30.
22. Udyoga. 39. 1-4., Shanti 145. 5-6.
23. Gr. G. IV. 10. 21-25.
24. M. III. 119.120
25. M. III. 109., M. III. 110.113.
26. M. III. 104.
27. Vana. 203. 5.
28. Vana. 196. 28. 30.
29. Udyoga. 91. 26.

Chapter - XVII

CHARITY

Hindu tradition of liberality towards the poor and destitute goes back to the time of the Rig-Veda. The distinction of the rich and the poor is as old as the Hindu civilisation; and the moralists always tried to modify the rigidity of the barrier of inequality by prescribing an attitude of complete munificence by those who have to those who have not. "Bounteous is he who gives unto the beggar, who comes to him in want of food and feeble; success attends him in the shout of battle. He makes a friend of him in future troubles."[1] Charity is so much emphasised in the Rig-Veda that we may well consider it the central virtue of the Vedic ethics.

High in heaven abide the Guerdon-givers; they who give steeds dwell with the sun for ever;

They who give gold are blest with life eternal; they who give robes prolong their lives, O Soma.....

Him I account the ruler of the people, who was the first to introduce the Guerdon.

Guerdon bestows the horse, bestows the bullock; Guerdon bestows, moreover, gold that glitters.

Guerdon gives food which is our life and spirit. He who is wise takes Guerdon for his armour.

The liberal die not; never are they ruined; the liberal suffer neither harm nor trouble.

The light of heaven, the universe about us, all this doth sacrificial Guerdon give them.[2]

These sentiments are frequently repeated.[3]

Mere negative virtues are not enough; self-control and other ascetic virtues may carry a man far; but they are useful only in so far as they prepare the way for more constructive activities. A king named Sweta performs penances for a long time and as the consequence of that he attains the region of Brahma. But he was still suffering from hunger and thirst. He inquires of Brahma as to the causes of his suffering. The patriarch replies; "O Sweta, thou didst only look to the growth of thy person, when thou didst perform rigid penances. O thou of great mind, nothing grows, when nothing is sown. Thou didst only perform ascetic penances, but thou didst not make any gift of charity. It is for that reason, that thou art in heaven, assailed by hunger and thirst."[4] Another story is given in the Mahabharata. "And the Grandsire said : "What is this that thou doest, O Shesa! Let the welfare of the creatures of the worlds also engage thy thought! O sinless one, thou art afflicting all creatures by thy hard penances."[5]

The main feature of most of the ceremonials was the donation of various gifts to Brahmins and others. Numerous gifts were given and dinners served to thousands of people at the time of Ashwamedha sacrifice. "Brahmins, Shudras, and ascetics, and Buddhist priests, and the aged, and the infirm and women, and children were continually fed. And although they had their fill, they knew no repletion. And 'give food, and clothes of various kinds' (was heard all round)."[6] Dilipa also made similar sacrifices. "In the abode of Dilipa, these five sounds were always to be heard, viz., the sound of Vedic recitations, the twang of bows, and Drink, Enjoy and Eat!"[7]

An interesting account is given of various historic charities in the Mahabharata. "Unto the deserving person there is nothing that cannot be given. They that are good and wise deserve to have even prince of steeds called Uchchaishravas, belonging to Indra himself. Satyasandh, having, with due humility, offered his own life–breaths for saving those of a Brahmin, ascended to heaven.....Shivi, having given away his own limbs and the dear son of his loins for the sake of a Brahmin, ascended to heaven from this world. Pratardana, the ruler of Kashi, having given away his very eyes to a Brahmin, obtained great fame both here and hereafter..... Sanskriti of Atri's race, having given instruction to his disciples on the subject of Impersonal Brahma, proceeded to regions of great felicity..... Nimi, the ruler of Videhas, gave away his kingdom. Jamadagni's son gave away the whole earth.....King Mitrasaha, having given away his own dear wife Mayadanti unto the high-souled Vasishtha, ascended to heaven, with the wife of his..... The royal sage Lomapada, by giving away his daughter Shanta to Rishyashringa, obtained the fruition of all his wishes."[8]

Charity is thus defined : "Even from a limited income, something should be given away daily with care and liberal spirit. This is called Dana or charity."[9] The spirit of charity exhibits itself in diverse ways. The underlying principle is that of helpfulness to those who need it. "To remove the fatigue of a fatigued person, to attend the sick, to worship the celestials, to adore the feet (of a worshipful person) and to clear the residue of the food (partaken by) a twice-born, is tantamount to the gift of a cow."[10] The following are the principal types of charity. "The deities and all the Rishis applaud food. The course of the world and the intellectual faculties have all been established on food. There has never been, nor will be, any gift that is equal to the gift of food."[11] The gift of earth is said to be superior to all other gifts, in one place and that of life, in another place.[12] "The fruits of all the (other) gifts, follow one birth, but those of the gifts of gold, land, and a seven years' old maiden, follow seven births."[13] "The virtue of a person, who establishes an orphan by performing the rite of investiture with the sacred thread, marriage, etc., for him, cannot be enumerated."[14] "Of all gifts.....a gift of the Vedas stands pre-eminently the most meritorious."[15]

There does not exist, however, an unlimited right to part with any and everything one has, in the name of charity. No doubt there are no limits to self-sacrifice so far as one's personal happiness is affected. "If you have but a morsel of food, why don't you give half of it to the poor?"[16] But no one has a right to involve other persons in misery for the sake of the "luxury of doing good." Hence certain things are held sacred. "A small property, what is gained by begging, what is kept as security, trust-money, a woman, a woman's personal property, what is inherited, the whole estate, and public property,–these nine articles should never be given away even in a calamity, if there is any living member in the family."[17] "One can give away his own property, if it does not interfere with the maintenance of his kinsmen, besides his wife and son; but not all, if son and grandson exist, nor what has been promised to another."[18] "The gift by one, who can find. Means to give to other indigent persons in the presence of his own people suffering from penury, may seem to him sweet and virtuous for the time being, but it will be like poison unto the end."[19] "We should, however, make gifts without afflicting those that depend upon us. By afflicting one's dependents one afflicts one's self."[20] Here is a fine illustration of how a king respects public property and does not make it an indiscriminate instrument for the gratification of his altruistic longing. "The king, then, representing unto the Rishi the equality of his expenditure and income, said,–O learned one, take thou from my possessions the wealth thou pleaseth!–Beholding, however, the equality of that monarch's expenditure with income, the Rishi who always saw both sides with equal eyes, thought that if he took anything under the circumstances, his acts would result in injury to creatures."[21]

Nothing is more remote from the spirit of Hindu ethics than indiscriminating charity. Enormous care has to be bestowed upon selecting the appropriate objects. "That gift is said to be good, which is given, because it ought to be given, to one who (can) do no service in return at a proper place and time, and to a (proper) person. But that gift, which is given with much difficulty, for a return of services, or even with an expectation of fruit is said to be Rajas. And that gift is described as dark, which is given to unfit persons at an improper place and time, without respect, and with contempt,"[22] Various lists of undeserving persons are given. "A virtuous man would not make gifts unto persons living by singing and dancing or unto those that are professional jesters, or unto a person that is intoxicated, or unto one that is insane, or unto a thief, or unto a slanderer, or unto an idiot, or unto one that is pale of hue, or unto one that is defective of limb, or unto a dwarf, or unto a wicked family, or unto one that has not been sanctified by the observance of vows. No gift should be made to a Brahmin destitute of the knowledge of the Vedas. Gifts should be made unto him only that is a Shrotriya. An improper gift and an improper acceptance produce evil consequences unto both the giver and the acceptor."[23] It is frequently emphasised that it is a positive sin to give anything to the unworthy. "A virtuous man must not make an insignificant gift to a Brahmin, who is cat-natured, or carries a cloak of religion, or is not read in the Vedas. By giving well-gotten wealth to any of these three kinds of Brahmins, both the donor and the receiver of the gift come to grief in the next world."[24]

The poor and the deserving should be the objects of special regard. "One should give unto a person of good lineage and conversant with the Vedas; unto a person that is poor; unto one leading a domestic mode of life, but burdened with wife and children; unto one that daily adoreth the sacred fire; and unto one that hath done him no service. Thou shouldst always give to such persons and not to those who are in affluence."[25] Charity should always begin at home, hence those who are near and dear should take precedence over those who are farther placed. "A gift made to one's father is hundred times more meritorious than the one made to an outsider, that made to one's mother and sister, being respectively ten times greater than the latter. A gift made to one's brother bears eternal fruit."[26]

Gifts vary as the givers. It is the concomitant feeling which gives its characteristic touch to an act of charity. "Through the difference of characters of the recipients and the variations of the feeling of sincerity with which it is offered, a gift acquires a greater or less merit in the next world."[27] "Give with faith. Give not without faith. Give in plenty. Give with bashfulness. Give with fear. Give with sympathy. This is the command. This is the teaching."[28] Sakalya said : "In what does the Dakshina abide?" Yajnavalkya said : "In श्रद्धा (faith), for if a man believes, then he gives Dakshina and Dakshina truly abides in faith."[29] Ungenerous feelings if they accompany an act of charity-render it useless. "One should make gifts, casting off anger; and having made gifts, should never give way to sorrow nor proclaim those gifts with one's own mouth."[30] "It is easy to fight in battle, but not to make a gift without pride or vanity."[31] "From desire of merit, from desire of profit, from fear, from free choice, and from pity gifts are made. Gifts, therefore, should be known to be of five kinds......With mind freed from malice one should make gifts unto Brahmins, for by making gifts unto them one acquires fame here and great felicity hereafter. (Such gifts are regarded as made from desire of merit.) He is in the habit of making gifts; or he will make gifts; or he had already made gifts unto me. Hearing such words from solicitors, one gives away all kinds of wealth unto a particular solicitor. (Such gifts are regarded as made from desire of profit). I am not his, nor is he mine. If disregarded be may injure me. From such motives of fear even a man of learning and wisdom may make gifts unto an ignorant wretch. (Such gifts are regarded as made from fear). This one is dear to me. I also am dear to him. Influenced by considerations like these, a person of intelligence, freely and with alacrity, makes gifts unto a friend. (Such gifts are regarded as made from free choice) The person that solicits me is poor. He is, again, gratified with little. From considerations such as these, one should always make gifts unto the poor, moved by pity. (Gifts made from such considerations are regarded as made from pity). These are the five kinds of gifts."[32] There should be mutual reverence between the giver and receiver. "Of a hundred, one is born a hero; of a thousand, a wise man; and of a hundred thousand, an orator. I doubt whether a really charitable person will ever take his birth or not. Conquest does not make a hero; nor studies a wise man. Eloquence does not make a man an orator; nor gifts, a charitable man. He who has conquered his senses is the real hero; he who practises virtues is really wise; a speaker is he who discusses pleasant and beneficial topics; and he who gives with reverence, is the maker of true gifts."[33] "He, who, being duly honoured, makes the gift, as well as he, who, being duly honoured accepts the gift, both of them go to heaven; if otherwise, they go to hell."[34] It is of no use to make property which is dishonestly earned a matter of charity. "The bestowal of the ill-gotten gains can never rescue the giver from the evil of re-birth."[35] Spontaneous gifts are always better than those given on solicitations. "Even space and time will die one day; but the merit of a spontaneous and voluntary gift will never suffer any death."[36] "That gift is highly prized which donor makes after seeking out the donee, and honouring him properly. That gift is middling which the donor makes upon solicitation. That gift, however, which is made contemptuously and without reverence, is said to be very inferior."[37] Gifts rendered to a person in return for the service are no gifts. "A reciprocity of gifts may be a social function, but is no virtue."[38]

Acceptance of gifts is justified only under certain circumstances. Generally speaking, only the Brahmins, who devote themselves absolutely to higher ideals, are entitled to accept anything in charity. "For a Brahmin leading a life of domesticity there is no means save the acceptance of gift for the sake of deities, or Rishis, or Pitris, a preceptor, or the aged, or the diseased, or the hungry."[39] Gifts from certain persons are unworthy of acceptance. "He (a Brahmin) must not accept the gift of a king, who is not the son of a Kshatriya, nor of him who lives by selling meat, nor of an oil-presser, nor of a wine-seller, nor of him, who lives upon the income of prostitution."[49] "If a Brahmin accepts the gifts made to him by the king, he loses by such acceptance, the merit that he would otherwise acquire by his penances that day."[41] "Articles brought unsolicited, may be accepted even from the perpetrators of iniquitous deeds, but not from unchaste women, eunuchs, outcastes, and enemies."[42] It is allowable to accept gifts for the pursuit of one's higher ideals or for the most essential wants, from all. "For the adoration of the celestials and guests, for the maintenance of elders and servants, and for the maintenance of one's own self, (one can accept presents from all."[43] Non-acceptance of gifts, however, remains the best thing. "Even if capable of accepting a gift, he must give up all attachment to gift-taking; gift-taking speedily extinguishes the energy of the supreme self, which is in a Brahmin."[44]

References

1. Rg. X. 117.3.
2. Rg. X. 107.
3. Rg. I.125, 6. VIII. 60.6. VIII. 86.2, etc.
4. R. VII. 78, 15-16.
5. Adi. 36. 6-7.
6. R.I. 14. 12-14.
7. Drona. 61. 3-10.
8. Shanti 240. 13-34.
9. Atri. 40.
10. Yaj. I. 209.
11. Anu. 98. 5-9.
12. Anu. 97. 96. 102.5.
13. Brihaspati. I.34.
14. Daksha. III.29.
15. M. IV.233.
16. Vyasa. IV.23.
17. Daksha. III.17-18.
18. Yaj. II. 178.
19. M.XI. 9.
20. Anu. 72.3.
21. Vana. 96.6.
22. Bg. XVII.
23. Shanti. 35.36-39.
24. M.IV. 192.193.
25. Vana. 203. 27-28.
26. Vyasa. IV.30.

27. M.VII.86.
28. Tait. Up.
29. Br. U. III. 9, 21.
30. Shanti. 314, 13.
31. Anu. 12, 11.
32. Anu. 138, Pratap Ray's Tr.
33. Vyasa. IV. 58-60.
34. M.IV. 235.
35. Vana. 260.
36. Vyasa. IV. 26.
37. Shanti. 299. 19-20.
38. Vyasa. IV.27.
39. Shanti. 240. 13-34.
40. M.IV.84.
41. Anu. 141. 18-22.
42. Yaj. I. 215.
43. Yaj. I. 216.
44. M.IV. 186; Yaj. I. 213.

Chapter - XVIII

AHIMSA

In the Vedic period the sanctity of human life in general was recognised. The institution of wergeld (वैर or वैरदेय) was in vogue as a means of self-protection on the part of society. A man's wergeld was a hundred cows.[1] In the Sutras we find that the wergeld for a Kshatriya was 1,000 cows, for a Vaishya 100 cows, and 10 for a Shudra, over and above a bull in each case.[2] The wergeld for women was the same according to apastamba; or according to Gautama, they were on a level with the Shudras.[3] The crime of slaying a Brahmin was too heinous for a wergeld.[4] The sin of killing a boy by careless driving required expiation.[5] The fact that foeticide (भ्रूणहत्या) was regarded as the greatest of all crimes is a crushig refutation of all loose charges levelled against the Vedic morality in its treatment of old men and daughters.[6]

Some controversy has raged round the place of human sacrifice in the Hindu theology. The story of Shunahshepa has given rise to much speculation. Harischandra got a son called Rohita but had promised to sacrifice him to Varuna. Rohita gives a hundred cows to one starving Rishi Ajigarta and gets in return his middle son Shunahshepa. He was to be sacrificed to Varuna. Nobody was ready to kill him. But his father was further bribed and he prepared himself to kill his son. But Shunahshepa prays to various deities and is at last saved.[7] It does not follow from this story that human sacrifices prevailed in the Vedic period. But it is not altogether impossible that at one time such an institution did exist, among the aborigines, if not among the very early Aryans. Max Muller says : "Human sacrifices are not incompatible with a higher stage of civilization, particularly among people who never doubted the immortality of the soul, and at the same time felt a craving to offer whatever seemed most valuable on earth to the gods in whom they believed. There are few nations in the history of the world whose early traditions do not exhibit some traces of human sacrifices."[8] In the Kalika-purana human sacrifices are lauded. (Ch. 55) A passage in the Aitareya Brahmana gives in brief the evolution of the ideas of the Aryans on the subject of sacrifice. "At first, the gods took man for their victim. As he was taken, medha (the sacrifice or the spirit) went out of him. It entered the horse. Therefore the horse became the sacrificial animal. Then the gods took the horse, but as it was taken, the medha went out of him. It entered the ox. Therefore the ox became the sacrificial animal. The same happened with the ox. Afterwards the sheep, then the goat and at last the earth became the victim. From the earth rice was produced and rice was offered in the form of purodasha, in lieu of the sacrificial animal. The other beings which had formerly been offered and then been dismissed, are supposed to have been changed into animals unfit for sacrifice, man into a savage, the horse into a Bos Gaurus, the ox into a Gayalox, the sheep into a camel, the goat into a Sharabha. All these animals are amedhya or unclean and should not be eaten."[9]

In the epic age the sacrifices were very popular institutions. Kaushalya kills a horse with her own hands.[10] King Ambarisha was going to sacrifice a boy, when his horse was stolen, in order to complete the ceremony.[11] But there is a passage–it may be an interpolation of a later age–which sees in a sacrifice, useless bloodshed. When Rama proposes to perform the Rajasuya sacrifice, Bharata says : "Thou art the refuge of all animals and the universe. Therefore, of what use is such a sacrifice unto thee? In such a sacrifice all the royal families meet with ruin."[12]

The Mahabharata contains many discussions concerning the nature of sacrifice. The Buddhist ideas were already in the air; and the bloodiness of sacrifices was fast becoming unpopular. "The time came for slaughtering the animals. When the animals selected for sacrifice were seized, the great Rishis, O king, felt compassion for them. Beholding that the animals had all become cheerless, those Rishis approached Shakra and said unto him :–This method of sacrifice is not auspicious..... This sacrifice is not consistent with righteousness. The destruction of creatures can never be an act of righteousness. Do thou perform the sacrifice with seeds of grain." Then a great dispute arose in the sacrifice of Shakra between the ascetics as to how sacrifices should be performed, that is, should they be performed with mobile or immobile creatures? The case is then referred to a king who decides that either way is good. The result was that the king had to go to hell for his false decision.[13] Another story is equally significant. Beholding the mangled body of a bull and hearing the exceedingly painful groans of the kine in a cow-slaying sacrifice, and observing the cruel Brahmins gathered there for assisting at the ceremonies, the king uttered these words :–Prosperity to all the kine in the world.....And the monarch said, only those that are transgressors of defined limits, that are destitute of intelligence, that are atheists and that desire the acquisition of celebrity through sacrifices and religious rites, speak highly of the slaughter of animals in sacrifices. Manu has applauded harmlessness in all acts. Indeed, men slaughter animals in sacrifices, urged only by the desire of fruit.....Urine, flesh, honey, meat, alcohol, and preparations of rice and sesame seeds, have been introduced by knaves. The use of these (in sacrifices) is not laid down in the Vedas. The hankering after these arises from pride, error of judgment, and cupidity. They that are true Brahmins realise the presence of Vishnu in every sacrifice."[14] The idea of Ahimsa thus gained ground; and sacrifices became more and more spiritual in their meaning and purpose. "They do not adore Brahma in costly sacrifices. They walk along the path of the righteous. The sacrifices they perform are perform-ed without injury to any creature. These men know trees and herbs and fruits and roots as the only sacrificial offerings..... These regenerate men, although all their acts have been completed, still perform sacrifices from desire of doing good to all creatures and constituting their own selves as sacrificial offerings."[15]

The idea of sacrifice has had thus a beautiful evolution. But from the very first it was the idea of real sacrifice, real crucifixion. Its entire form went on changing from human sacrifice to animal sacrifice, from animal sacrifice to rice sacrifice, and from rice sacrifice to sacrifice of one's own gross self. In the Rig-Veda, we find that the horse was sacrificed; but the horse who was the victim was considered blessed, for paradise was reserved for the creature. The horse was to be killed in such a way that it may not suffer unduly. The whole ceremony was a mixture of selfishness, pity and sacrifice. "Let not thy dear soul burn thee (make thee sad) as thou comest, let not the hatchet linger in thy body. Let not a greedy clumsy immolator missing the joints mangle thy limbs unduly. No, here thou diest not, thou art not injured : by easy paths unto the gods thou goest. May this steed bring us all sustaining riches, wealth in good kine, good horses, manly offspring."[16] The same idea contained in germ the highly ethical notion of self-sacrifice we meet with in the Gita. From the first to the last it was virtually the idea of the sacrifice of the flesh to the spirit. Death of body for higher purposes meant rebirth in the spiritual sphere. But its grossly selfish character, its unpitying bloodiness, its confusion of ideas gradually dropped away and with the dawn of a higher morality, the idea became to us full of pure unselfishness, full of higher and nobler enthusiasm for humanity. "Some pour as sacrifice, hearing and the other senses into the fire of restraint; some pour sound and the other objects of sense into the fire of the senses as sacrifice. Others again into the wisdom-kindled fire of union attained by self-control, pour as sacrifice all the functions of the senses and the functions of life : yet others the sacrifice of wealth, the sacrifice of austerity, the sacrifice of wealth, the sacrifice of silent reading and wisdom; yet others pour as sacrifice the outgoing breath in the incoming, and the incoming in the outgoing, restraining the flow of the outgoing and the incoming breaths, solely absorbed in the control of breathing. Others regular in food, pour as sacrifice their life breaths. All these are knowers of sacrifice, and by sacrifice have destroyed their sins. The eaters of the life-giving remains of sacrifice go to the changeless Eternal. This world is not for the non-sacrificer, much less the other."[17] The best and supreme sacrifice is ज्ञानयज्ञ in which the highest philosophy completely transmutes a man's personality and the great transvaluation of values takes place. सर्वं कर्माखिलं पार्थ ज्ञाने परिसमाप्यते. "The Eternal the oblation, the Eternal the clarified butter, are offered in the Eternal fire by the Eternal; unto the Eternal verily shall he go who in his action meditateth upon the Eternal."[18]

The ideal of Ahimsa gets full expression in the Mahabharata. "That person, O monarch, who gives unto all creatures an assurance of his harmlessness, goes to the highest of regions. The fruit that one obtains by giving an assurance unto all creatures of his harmlessness cannot be obtained by a thousand sacrifices or by daily fasts. Amongst all things there is nothing dearer than self. Death is certainly disliked by all creatures. Therefore compassion should certainly be shown unto all."[19] Harmlessness towards others assures complete harmlessness towards one's self in return. "That man who is devoted to compassion and who behaves with compassion towards others has no fear to entertain from any creature. It is heard that all creatures abstain from causing any fear unto such a creature. Whether he is wounded or fallen down, or prostrated, or weakened or bruised in whatever state he may be, all creatures protect him. Neither snakes nor wild animals, neither Pishachas nor Rakshasas ever slay him. When circumstances of fear arise, he becomes freed from fear who frees others from situations of fear. There has never been nor will there ever be a gift that is superior to the gift of life."[20]

All lives have value, but not equal value. Brahmanicide is always regarded with peculiar abhorrence, because a Brahmin is essentially a friend of truth, culture, and humanity. "By slandering Brahmins or by striking them one sinks in infamy for a thousand years."[21] Killing a Brahmin is a maha-pataka, a heinous sin.[22] No expiation exists for the sin of wilfully killing a Brahmin.[23] The killing of a Kshatriya brings on a quarter of the sin of Brahminicide.[24] "Having slain a Vaishya, one should perform a sacrifice for two years and make a present of a hundred kine with one bull. Having slain a Shudra, one should perform such a sacrifice for one year and make a present of a hundred kine with one bull."[25]

A special sanctity attaches to the lives of relatives, friends, preceptors, women, children, envoys. "These must never be slain, viz. Brahmins, kine, relatives, children, women; those whose food is eaten, and those also that yield asking for protection."[26] In most of these cases the sin is equal to Brahminicide.[27] "We have never heard these four, viz. he who injures a friend, he who is ungrateful, he who slays a woman, and he who slays a preceptor, ever succeed in cleansing themselves."[28] "Even such is the expiation provided for one who slays a woman quick with child. The man that knowingly slays such a woman incurs double the sin of what follows from Brahminicide."[29] "The perpetrator of sinful deeds, he who kills a Brahmin, who kills a woman, who kills his father, who kills a hundred or a thousand kine, who seizes land given by his own self or by another, rots with his departed manes by becoming a vermin in his own excreta."[30] Respect for the lives of ambassadors shows the development of international or inter-tribal relationships. "Envoys are not to be slain.....Disfigurement of the body, stripes, shaving of the head, one of these or all combined, these are said to be the punishments that should be inflicted upon the envoys.....Whether honest or otherwise, an envoy has been commissioned by others. Advocating interest not his own and identifying himself with another, an envoy does not merit being put to death."[31]

Tenderness to life extends to the animal and even vegetable kingdom. "Killing a dog, a bear, or a camel, one should perform the same penance that is laid down for the slaughter of a Shudra. For slaying a cat, a chasa, a frog, a crow, a reptile, a rat, it has been said one incurs the sin of animal slaughter."[32] "For having killed one thousand of vertebrate animals, one should do the penance for an act of Shudra–killing; the same penance should be practised for having killed a cart-load of invertebrate animals. For having killed a blossoming fruit-yielding tree, creeper, shrub, or plant one shall mutter a hundred Rik mantras. For killing parasites which germinate in food-grains, or in sweet saps, or in fruits and flowers, drinking of clarified butter should be known as the expiation. For having cut down corals, growing on a cultivated soil, as well as those which spontaneously grow on uncultivated fields, one shall regain his purity by living on a milk diet for a day, and by following the cows to the pasture-ground."[33]

There are important modifications and exceptions to this general attitude. It is quite justifiable to take up arms in self-defence. "An incendiary, a prisoner, one holding a weapon in one's hands, a robber, the taker away of lands, the seducer of another man's wife, these six are called assasins. They say that by killing an assasin for personal safety, one commits no sin."[34] "A preceptor, an old man, infant, Brahmin, or vastly erudite person, coming as an assasin, must be killed without the least hesitation. By killing an assasin, the killer acquires no demerit, in as much as it is anger that kills anger, in fact, in such a case."[35] Grounds of public safety and interest always fully justify resort to the violent methods of destruction. There is no ambiguity about this in Hindu Ethics. "When (the practice of) virtue is obstructed (by tyranny), when the eternal division of caste is in any wise jeopardised, Brahmins may resort to arms."[36] In the Ramayana there is a dramatic controversy about pacifism vs. legitimate destruction. Sita's feminine nature shrinks from the destruction of the Rakshasas. She says to Rama that it was not justifiable to bear hostility towards others, without the cause of hostility. She quotes the story of an ascetic, who was entrusted with a sword to protect himself. "Constantly carrying the sword, by degrees, the ascetic, foregoing all thoughts about asceticism, had his mind involved in fierce sentiments..... This ancient story asserts that even as fire works change in a piece of wood, the presence of arms works alteration in the mind of a person bearing them.....From following arms, one's senses get befouled and deformed."[37] This illustration of Sita shows that she had a wonderful insight into the inherent vice of all military policy which begins by taking to war measures as a pure means towards defence, but ends in making them ends in themselves. Rama virtually replies that it is justifiable to destroy life in the interests of society. "Kshatriyas wear bows in order that the word 'distressed' may not exist on earth."[38] Hence it is allowable to kill women also if they are baneful to society. "Do thou O Rama, for the welfare of kine and Brahmins, slay this exceedingly terrible Yakshi of wicked ways and vile prowess. Nor shouldst thou shrink from slaying a woman; for even this should be accomplished by a prince in the interest of four orders. And whether an act be cruel or otherwise, slightly or highly sinful, it should, for protecting the subjects, be performed by a ruler.....We hear that in days of yore Shakra slew Virochan's daughter, Manthara who had intended to destroy the earth."[39] Rama cuts off the head of Shambuka, the Shudra ascetic, because his asceticism was a source of trouble to the subjects.[40]

The Mahabharata goes further in emphasizing both the inevitableness of slaughter, and its enormous usefulness. "Without slaughter no man has been able to achieve fame in this world, or acquire wealth, or subjects. Indra himself, by the slaughter of Vritra, became the great Indra. Those amongst the gods that are given to slaughtering are adored much more by men. Rudra, Skanda, Shakra, Agni, Varuna are all slaughterers.....Humbled by their prowess all people lead to these gods, but not to Brahman or Dhatri at any time."[41] Destruction of life, again, is a part of the processes of nature; and whether we will it or not it will go on. "I do not behold the creature in this world that supports life without doing any act of injury to others. Animals live upon animals, the stronger upon the weaker. The mongoose devours the mice; the cat devours the mongoose; the dog devours the cat; the dog again is devoured by the spotted leopard. Behold, all things are destroyed by the destroyer when he comes. This mobile and immobile universe is food for living creatures. The very ascetics themselves cannot support their lives without killing creatures. In water, on earth, and in fruits, there are innumerable creatures. There are many creatures that are so minute that their existence can only be inferred. With the falling of the eyelids alone they are destroyed."[42] At times, destructive action is alone a true prelude to fresh construction. It then becomes a positive act of righteousness to do away with those who block the progress of humanity. "The sin that attaches to killing a person that should not be killed is equal to that which is incurred by not killing one who deserves to be killed."[43] "A Kshatriya should slay sires and grandsires, and brothers and preceptors, and relatives and kinsmen that may engage with him in a just battle. That Kshatriya is said to be acquainted with his duty, who slays in battles his very preceptors, if they happen to be sinful, covetous, and disregardful of restraints and vows."[44] "If by slaying a single individual, a family may be saved, or if by slaying a single family, the whole kingdom may be saved, such an act of slaughter will not be a transgression."

The question of flesh-eating is partly a question of humanity in as much as it involves the destruction of animal lives. The doctrine of Ahimsa is a late growth in the history of Hindu thought. The flesh of the sheep, the goat, and the ox was of common use. These were offered as victims in the sacrifices and the Brahmins ate the offerings.[45] The great sage Yajnavalkya had no objection to eating the meat of milch-cows and bullocks provided it was tender (amsala).[46] The guests were entertained with the flesh of a great ox or a great goat.[47] or a cow. The word *Atithigva* probably means slaying cows for guests.[48] "These are the occasions for killing a cow : (the arrival of) a guest, (the Ashtaka sacrifice offered to) the Fathers, and marriage."[49] Oxen were sacrificed at the time of marriage for food.[50] A child is given in the sixth month, goat's flesh if nourishment is desired, the flesh of fish if swiftness is required, partridge's flesh if holy lustre is desired and rice with ghee if splendour is an object of desire.[51]

Even in the Vedic period the doctrine of Ahimsa was gradually manifesting itself. The use of meat is forbidden when a man is performing a vow. It is classed with intoxicating liquors as a bad thing.[52] The use of certain types of flesh was forbidden emphatically in the Rig-veda. "The friend who smears himself with flesh of cattle, with flesh of horses, and of human bodies.....tear of the heads of such with fiery fury."[53] "Rend, O Agni, and put within thy mouth raw flesh-eaters."[54] "In deep distress, I cooked a dog's intestines."[55] The Brahamanas contain the doctrine of the eater in this world, being eaten in the next.

Flesh-eating within set limits was allowed to the Brahmins as well as the Kshatriyas in the Ramayana. Sita says to Ravaṇa who had gone as a Brahmin guest to her hermitage : "Instantly shall my husband return with good many wild fruits and roots and with sufficient meat after killing many a deer, hog, and Gasanop."[56] "A hedgehog, a porcupine, an iguana, a hare, and a tortoise-these five animals only having five toes, are unworthy of being eaten by Kshatriyas and Brahmins."[57]

Manu allows the use of flesh under certain limitations. "He must not eat the flesh of animals that move about alone (like a snake); nor of those beasts and birds, whose name and nature are not known, nor of those whose flesh is forbidden, nor of those which are possessed of five nails."[58] There is no radical and wholesale condemnation of all meat-food. Nature allows the use of meat. "Whatever exists in the world, all that *Prajapati* has ordained to be the food of living beings; all creation, both mobile and immobile, is the food of creatures. The immobile are the food of the mobile creatures; the handless are those of the persons with hands; and the timid those of the brave."[59]

In practice, Manu allows the use of animal food, only on limited occasions. "For the purpose of religious sacrifices, the beasts were created by the self-existent; the sacrifice is for the elevation of the whole universe, hence killing is not killing in a religious sacrifice. A *Madhuparka*, a Shraddha offered to the manes and deities, and a religious sacrifice are the occasions on which a beast should be sacrificed and on no other occasions."[60] To eat flesh for any other purpose is a monstrous practice.[61]

Manu is, therefore, on the whole, for the ideal of Ahimsa. "Flesh cannot be obtained without killing a beast; animal-killing does not lead to heaven; hence a man must forswear eating flesh. Considering the origin of flesh (which is a kind of transformed menstrual blood) and the pangs of death and incarceration the beast suffers, he must forswear eating all kinds of flesh. He, who sanctions the killing of an animal, he who quarters the slaughtered body, the actual immolator, the seller and the buyer of its flesh, the man who cooks the flesh, he who serves that cooked flesh to the eaters, and he who eats it are all called the killers. He, who, otherwise than for the purposes of Shraddhas offered to the manes and deities, tries to augment the flesh of his body with the flesh of a beast, is the greatest of all sinners. The merit of him, who forswears the use of meat, is equal to that of one who performs the Ashwamedha sacrifice, each year, for a century. He, whose flesh I eat in this life, shall eat my flesh in the next; this is the essential attribute of flesh, as disclosed by its etymological signification according to the wise."[62] The last verse contains the argument, first expressed in the Brahmanas from which the scholars inter the dependence of the Ahimsa doctrine upon the belief in the transmigration of the souls.

The Mahabharata bristles with lively discussions of the question in which one finds all the most significant *pros* and *cons* of the case. The usual arguments in favour of the case are : that animals acquire paradise through being offered at sacrifices; that nature prescribes all beings as food for living creatures; that the Vedic declarations enjoin animal sacrifices : that persons of historic reputation were devoted to the practice; that even vegetables have life; that consciously or unconsciously we do destroy numberless lives. "Those animals that are slain by me, and whose meat I sell, also acquire *Karma*; because (with their meat) gods and guests and servants are regaled with daily food, and the manes of our ancestors are propitiated. It is said authoritatively that herbs and vegetables, deer, birds, and wild animals constitute the food of all creatures. And king Shibi of great forbearance attained heaven by giving away his own flesh. And in days of yore, two thousand animals used to be killed everyday in the kitchen of king Rantideva; and in the same manner two thousand cows were killed everyday; and king Rantideva acquired unrivalled reputation by distributing food with meat everyday.....'The Sacred Fire is fond of animal food'–this saying has come down to us."[63] "Agriculture is considered to be a praiseworthy occupation, but it is well-known that even there, great harm is done to animal life; and in the operation of digging the earth with the plough, numberless creatures lurking in the ground, as also various other forms of animal life are destroyed. Dost thou not think so? Vrihi and other so-called seeds of rice are all living organisms. What is thy opinion?.....The earth and the air are all swarming with living organisms, which are unconsciously destroyed by men from mere ignorance. Is not this so? The commandment that people should not do harm to any creature was ordained of old, by men, who were ignorant of the true facts of the case. For there is not one man on the face of the earth, who is free from the sin of doing injury to any creature."[64] Flesh again, is very tasteful and nutritious. "There is nothing on earth that is superior to flesh in point of taste. There is nothing that is more beneficial than flesh to persons that are lean, or weak, afflicted with disease, or addicted to sexual congress, or exhausted with travel. Flesh speedily increases strength.....There is no food that is superior to flesh."[65] "Meat prevaileth in the food of the opulent, clarified butter in that of the middle classes; and oil in that of the poor."[66]

All the above arguments show that the Hindus were not blind to the advantages or even the morality of meat-eating. But their significance on the whole is limited to the fact that they are meant to show that too much must not be made of the Ahimsa doctrine, and that the use of animal food is not altogether an abominable practice. It has full justification in a scheme of naturalistic ethics; its value also from the utilitarian point of view is considerable. But man is above all a moral being. The standards by which he should be judged are altogether different from those which dictate the behaviour of other creatures. Hence, the general conclusion is that meat was allowable to the Brahmins only in sacrifices, so long as sacrifices required the offering of animals. The Kshatriyas required martial spirit; and they are allowed the use of meat which they obtained from hunting. "Listen to me as I tell thee what the ordinance is that has been laid down for the Kshatriyas. They do not incur any fault by eating flesh that has been acquired by the use of their strength. All deer of the wilderness have been dedicated to the deities and the pitris in days of old by Agastya. Hence, the hunting of deer is not censured. There can be no hunting without risk of one's own life. There is equality of risk between the slayer and the slain. Either the killer is killed or he kills the prey. Hence even royal sages betake themselves to the practice of hunting."[67]

All these modifications do not affect the general position laid down that all life is supremely valuable, and any wanton, selfish destruction of it is self-condemned. "That learned person who giveth to all living creatures the Dakshina of complete assurance comes to be regarded without doubt, as the giver of life-breaths in the world.....The life-breaths of other creatures are as dear to them as those of one's own to himself. Men of intelligence and purity should always behave towards other creatures in the same way as they would wish that others should behave towards them. Even persons of learning and candidates for Emancipation are not free from the fear of death. What need then, be said of those innocent and healthy creatures endued with love of life, when they are sought to be slain by sinful wretches subsisting by slaughter? For this reason discarding of meat is the highest refuge of religion, of heaven, and of happiness. Abstention from injury is the highest religion, abstention from injury is the highest penance; abstention from injury is the highest truth."[68]

References

1. Rg. II.32.4. Ai. Br. VII. 15.7.
2. Ap.I. 9, 24, 1-4; Baud. i, 10, 19, 1.2.
3. Ap. I. 9, 24-5, Gau. i. 10, 19, 3.
4. Ap. I, 9, 24, 7.
5. Panch. Br. XIII, 3, 12.
6. Av. VI. 112, 3. 113, 2.
7. Ai. Br. VII. 15, 7.
8. History of Ancient Sanskrit Literature, p. 216.
9. Ai. Br. 6.8.
10. R.I. 14.33.
11. R.I. 61. 5-24.
12. R.VII. 83.7-20.
13. Ashwa. 93. 11-25.
14. Shanti. 271. 1-13.
15. Shanti. 269, 25-26.
16. Rg. I. 162, 20-21-22.
17. Bg. IV. 26-31.
18. Bg. IV. 24.
19. Stri. 7.25-28.
20. Anu. 178. 7-43.
21. Shanti. 163. 44-46.
22. M.XI.55.
23. M.XI.90.
24. M.XI.127.

25. Shanti. 163. 57-58.
26. Udyoga. 36.66.
27. M.XI. 88-89.
28. Shanti. 108.32.
29. Shanti. 163.52.
30. Brihaspati. 27-28.
31. R.V. 52.14-18. VI.20.18-19.
32. Shanti. 163. 57-58.
33. M.XI. 141. 145.
34. Vasistha. III.
35. M.VIII. 351.
36. M.VIII.348.
37. R.III. 9, 9-32.
38. R.III. 10.3.
39. R.I. 25. 15-22.
40. R.VII. 76.4.
41. Shanti. 15, 14-17.
42. Shanti. 15. 20-28.
43. Shanti. 142, 27.
44. Shanti. 64. 15-19.
45. Rg. VIII. 43.
46. S.Br. III. 1, 2, 21.
47. S.Br. III. 4, 1, 2.
48. Rg. X. 68.3.
49. Gr. Ap. I.3.9.
50. Rg.X. 85. 13.
51. Sam. Gr.S.I. 27. 1-6.
52. Av. VI. 70-1.
53. Rg. X.87.16.
54. Rg.X.87.2.
55. Rg.IV. 18, 13.
56. R.III. 47.23.
57. R.IV. 17.39.
58. M.V. 11-16.
59. M.V. 27-29.
60. M.V. 39.41.

61. M.V.31.
62. M.V. 48-55.
63. Vana. 212. 4-16.
64. Vana. 212.
65. Anu. 178. 7.43.
66. Udyoga. 34.50.
67. Anu. 198. 7-43.
68. Anu. 177. 12-64.

Chapter - XIX

HUMANITY

The Aryan humanity is the greatest asset of the East, its most characteristic contribution to the culture of the world. It is not a refined product of a later age; it was born with the very birth of the Aryan civilization. Indra is the "stirrer to action of the poor and lowly, of priest, of suppliant."[1] He raises "the outcast from the depths and gives fame unto the halt and the blind."[2] He makes the cripple and the blind seeing.[3] Agni is full of benevolence and scorns no living man.[4] The deities accept the poor man's prayer, care even for the weak, and teach wisdom to the simplest.[5] The dawn does not withdraw her light from either the kinsmen, or the strangers, either from the high or the humble.[6] "If we have sinned against the man who loves us, have wronged a brother, friend, or comrade the neighbour with us, or a stranger, O Varuna, remove from us the trespass."[7]

The Vedic morality, however, is uncompromising in its attitude towards the enemies of civilization. "O Indra, beat our foes away, humble the men who challenge us; send down to nether darkness, him who seeks to do us injury."[8] "Slay thou (Soma) the enemy both near and far away; grant us security and ample pasturage."[9] All persons who are of a different faith, all non-Aryans were to be ruthlessly treated. "With these chase all our foes into every quarter : Subdue the tribes of Dasas to the Arya."[10] "Stir up, (O Agni), the wrath and hatred due to one who holds an alien creed."[11]

Man is born a debtor in this world; all that he has, all that he is, he owes to powers other than himself. A Hindu whenever he spends or is spent in the cause of society or family, he will not say 'he is serving the society;' he will say : "he is fulfilling his debts." A dutiful, conscientious life devoted to higher ideals is merely a systematic fulfilment of one's debts.[12] "All men, taking birth, incur debts to gods, guests, servants, Pitris and their own selves. Every one should, therefore, do his best for freeing himself from those debts. One frees oneself from one's debt to the great Rishis by studying the Vedas. One pays off one's debts to the gods by performing sacrifices. By performing the rites of the Shraddhas one is freed from one's debts to the Pitris. One pays off one's debt to one's fellow men by doing good offices to them. One pays off the debt one owes to one's self by listening to Vedic recitations and reflecting on their import, by eating the remnants of sacrifices, and by supporting one's body. One should discharge all the acts that one owes to one's servants."[13] It is incumbent upon a Hindu to offer food to dogs, to the degraded, to the Chandalas, to the persons afflicted with diseases, to crows and worms.[14]

It cannot be too often repeated that no man lives unto himself alone. A thoughtless, heartless, selfishness is a veritable perversity of souls. "Truly realised is the end of his life on whom depends the livelihood of friends, relations, and Brahmins. Who does not live for his own ends in this world? Even the beasts live and pamper their own bellies. Of what use is the strength, health, and longevity of him who does not do any public good?"[15] Bhartrihari well says : "I call those men best who, not caring for their own good, do good to others, those are medicare, who do good to others, but are careful for their own welfare. I consider, however, those as Rakshasas–demons–who mar the prospects of others, simply to benefit themselves–but I do not know, by what name to call those that ruin their own cause with a view to ruin others."[16] A householder has first to feed guests, relations, and servants and then alone he is entitled to take food.[17] "He who cooks food for his own sole use, eats sin; food, which is the residue of sacrificial oblations, is recommended by the virtuous."[18] The idea of humanity as a vast family is indicated. 'वसुधैव कुटुम्बकम्'[19].

The strongest point in the Hindu view of humanity is the philosophical basis upon which it is most securely based. It is the unity of the Self upon which hinges the whole Hindu view of life. "For him who views all beings as his own soul there can be no illusion or misery. Love all."[20] "The Self, harmonised by Yoga, seeth the Self abiding in all beings, all beings in the Self; everywhere he seeth the same. He seeth Me, everywhere, and seeth everything in Me, of him I will never lose hold, and he shall never lose hold of Me."[21] God is, therefore, best worshipped in humanity. It is a philosophic endorsement of the dictum of Coleridge that "he prayeth well, who loveth well both man and bird, and beast." Another consequence of this view is the philosophic basis of certainty it affords to the golden view of Jesus Christ. If the soul is one, there is fundamental identity of the highest interests of humanity. The Gita draws this corollary from the fundamental position of the Adwaita. "He who, through the likeness of the Self, seeth equality in everything, whether pleasant or painful, he is considered a perfect Yogi."[22] The very acme of moral perfection is reached when one seriously acts upon this theory. "The very deities, become stupefied in ascertaining the track of that person, who constitutes himself the soul of all creatures, and looks upon them as his own self, for such a person leaves no track behind. This, in brief, is the rule of righteousness. One by acting in a different way by yielding to desire, becomes guilty of unrighteousness. In refusals and gifts, in happiness and misery, in the agreeable and the disagreeable, one should judge of their effects by a reference to one's own self."[23] In this way, morality becomes identical with the greatest good of the greatest number, or the well-being and perfection of humanity. "Righteousness was declared for the advancement and growth of all creatures. Therefore, that which leads to advancement and growth is righteousness. Righteousness (धर्म) is so called because it holds all creatures."[24]

Humanity has two aspects–the internal and the external aspect. Its external aspect is concerned with the active service of our species in all possible ways. Its internal aspect is concerned with the feeling of kindness, the tenderness of soul. The former is Dana; the latter is Daya. Now Dana without Daya has very little meaning. Hence the feeling which the Christians call charity or goodwill is what we call Daya. The great sage Tulsidas says : दया धर्म को मूल है. All duty, all faith has its root in this innate sentiment of humanity. It is threefold : it connotes pity for the lowly, affection for the equal, and devotion to the great. Rama is described by Bhavabhuti as "आश्वासस्नेह-भक्तीनामेकमालम्बनं महत्।" Hence this sentiment is not mere pity. It is *Reverence* as Tennyson calls It; *charity* as defined by Christianity; it is tenderness of soul or refinement of feelings and sensibilities or love, true, genuine, broad, and catholic for all beings. "One should behave, like his own self towards others, his own relations and friends, him who envies him, and an enemy. This is called Daya (mercy)."[25] A man of Daya is truly a Vishwamitra. "The deities of the universe are my friends. I am also the friend of the Universe. Hence know that I am called Vishwamitra."[26]

There is a story in the Upanishads which may be cited here. Prajapati is visited by the Asuras, gods, and men. They asked : tell us something. He told them the syllable Da. Then he said 'Did you understand?' The Asuras said : 'We did understand. You told us : Dayadhwam' 'Be merciful' 'Yes' he said 'you have understood.' Similarly gods understood Damyata–Be subdued. Men understood Datta–Give. The story signifies that the Asuras must have kindness; gods, discipline, and men, active philanthropy. What is required above all here, is therefore, अद्रोह–complete good–will towards all living creatures, in mind, and deeds. "Abstention from injury as regards all creatures in thought, word, and deed, kindness, and gift, are the eternal duties of those who are good."[27] "In the same manner, every other duty and observance is supposed to be engulfed within the one duty of abstention from injury (to all creatures). He lives an everlasting life of felicity, who avoids injuring other creatures. One who abstains from injury, who casts an equal eye upon all creatures, who is devoted to truth, who is endued with fortitude, who has his senses under control, and who grants protection to all beings, attains to an end that is beyond compare."[28]

The poor, the diseased, the weak, the suffering, and the humble are the special objects of the sentiment of humanity. "Satisfied old men, infants, weaklings, and sick folk lead him to the region of the firmament; he shall respect his brother as his own father, and consider his wife and children as parts and parcels of his own self. He shall look upon his slaves as his own shadow, and his daughter as the receptacle of the highest affection; worried by them, he must patiently bear such a worry."[29] "He that is graced with humility, is never indifferent to the minutest sufferings of living creatures."[30] "Be he a Shudra or be he the member of any other order, he that becomes a raft on a raftless current, or a means of crossing where means there are none, certainly deserves respect in every way. That person, relying upon whom helpless men oppressed and made miserable by robbers, live happy, deserves to be lovingly worshipped by all as if he were a near kinsman."[31] The Shudras are not outcastes from the point of view of humanity. "Make thou me dear to Shudra and to Aryan!"[32] "Sages look equally on a Brahmin adorned with learning and humanity, a cow, an elephant, and even a dog, and an outcaste."[33]

It may be inferred from various passages that some institution like slavery did exist in the ancient times in India. "A hundred asses hath he given, a hundred head of fleecy sheep, a hundred slaves and wreathes besides."[34] "A captive of war, a slave for maintenance, the son of a female slave, one purchased for money, a slave obtained as a present, a hereditary one, and one condemned to slavery for any offence : these are the seven kinds of slaves."[35] Slaves were not entitled to have any property.[36] The moral conscience, however, was not quite deaf to the cause of these people. Here is a passage which lays down the sanctity of every life and exposes the inhumanity of all trafficking in flesh. "Men are seen to own men as slaves, and by beating, by binding, and by otherwise subjecting them to restraint, cause them to labour day and night.....In every creature that is endued with the five senses, live all the deities, the Sun, the Moon, the god of mind, Brahman, Prana, Kratu, and Yama."[37]

A life of active charity and not one of mere passive benevolence is preached. (सर्वभूतहिते रतिः) "One should devote one's eyes (to the service of others); one should devote one's heart (to the same); one should utter words that are agreeable; one should also follow and worship (one's guests). This is called the sacrifice with five gifts."[38] Ishta and Purta should be practised by all. "(The excavation of) tanks, wells, and other watery expanses; (the construction of) temples, (the distribution of) food, and the (laying out of) pleasure-gardens are called Purta."[39] "The man who causes a tank to be dug becomes entitled to the respect and worship of the three worlds."[40] The man who plants trees is highly applauded.[41] The Gita approves of लोकसंग्रह even for the perfected souls. "Janaka and others indeed attained to perfection by action; then having eye to the welfare of the world also, thou shouldst perform action."[42]

The comprehensive range of Aryan humanity includes within it even beasts, birds, and trees. "Bring by thy flowing, weal to kine, weal to the people, weal to steeds, weal, O thou king (Soma) to growing plants."[43] A sage was called Pashusakha. "I protect and tend all animals that I see, and I am always a friend to all animals. Hence am I called Pashusakha."[44] "They who set bullocks to work when the animals have not attained to sufficient age, they who bore the noses of bullocks and other animals for controlling them better when employed in work, and they who keep animals always tethered, have to sink in hell."[45] "There are many animals that grow up in ease and comfort in places free from gnats and biting insects. Knowing that they are loved dearly by their mothers, men prosecute them in various ways, and lead them into miny spots, abounding with biting insects. Many draft animals are oppressed with heavy burthens. Such acts of injury done to animals are in no way distinguishable from foeticide."[46] Even the sale of animals is not approved of. "The goat is Agni. The sheep is Varuna. The horse is Surya. Earth is the deity Virat. The cow and calf are Soma. The man who sells these can never obtain success."[47] Questions were always asked by visitors in hermitages as regards the welfare of even the trees, beasts, and birds.[48] A parrot was attached to a tree, and was asked to leave it. It says : "When it was capable of good, it supported my life. How can I forsake it?" Indra was quite pleased with this act and rewarded the parrot.[49]

Worship of the Cow is a normal feature of Hindu religious life at all times. Cow is thè main source of nourishment to the whole race, and how can it afford to neglect the very basis of its economic and spiritual life? Kings are called by Hindus गोब्राह्मणप्रतिपाल–protectors of cows and Brahmins. All wars waged on behalf of cows and Brahmins should inspire all sections of society, including the non-warrior classes. A cow was also one of the best objects of charity. The wealth of Hindus mostly lies in their cattle–especially of the Vedic Hindus. "May he (Indra) guard our wealth in kine and heroes."[50] "Bhaga, augment our store of kine and horses."[51] "To me the cows seem Bhaga (good luck), they seem Indra, they seem portion of the first poured Soma."[52] "The cow, the famous mother of the wealthy Maruts, pours her milk."[53] "May the wind blow upon our cows with healing."[54]

The theory that vegetables have life was not unknown to the ancient sages. It was upon this principle that they prescribed kindness to the vegetable kingdom. This theory is as old as the Upanishads. "All that lives, all that walks, all that flies, all that is motionless is accompanied by consciousness."[55] (सर्वं तत्प्रज्ञानेत्रम्) Manu also refers to this theory. Owing to the excess of Tamas we are unable to see the workings of consciousness. "Variously enshrouded by the quality of Tamas, the effects of their own acts, they retain their consciousness inward, susceptible to pleasure and pain."[56] The Mahabharata amplifies these points. "Without doubt, though possessed of density, trees have space within them. The putting forth of flowers and fruits is always taking place in them. They have heat within them in conse-quence of which, leaf, bark, fruit, and flower, are seen to droop. They sicken and dry up. That shows that they have perception of touch. Through sound of wind and fire, and thunder, their fruits and flowers drop down. Sound is perceived through the ear. Trees have therefore, ears, and do hear. A creeper winds round a tree and goes about all its sides. A blind thing cannot find its way. For this reason it is evident that trees have vision. Then again trees recover vigour and put forth flowers in conse-quence of odours good and bad, of the sacred perfume of diverse kinds of Dhupas. It is plain that trees have scent. They drink water by their roots. They catch diseases of diverse kinds. Those diseases are again cured by different operations. From this it is evident that trees have perception of taste. As one can suck up water through a bent lotus stalk, trees also, with the aid of the wind, drink through their roots. They are susceptible of pleasure and pain, and grow when cut or lopped off. From these circumstances I see that trees have life. They are not inanimate. Fire and wind cause the water thus sucked up to be digested. According, again, to the quantity of water taken up, the tree advances in growth, and becomes humid."[57]

A spirit of universal benevolence begets corresponding love on the part of others. "Men are always well disposed towards him, who pleaseth all in four ways, viz. with heart, eyes, words, acts."[58] Gautama Buddha is said to have disarmed the opposition of such creatures as snakes, and others through his power of love. Hindu sages endorse this tradition. "Possessed of this great intelligence as he sat on his seat, the goodness of his behaviour having been known to the creatures that lived in that forest, they used to approach him with affection. Fierce lions and tigers, infuriated elephants of huge size, leopards, rhinoceroses, bears, and other animals of fierce aspect, subsisting upon blood, used to come to the Rishi and address him the usual questions of polite inquiry. Indeed, all of them behaved towards him like disciples and slaves and always did unto him what was agreeable."[59]

Protection is held to be the due of all who seek it. From the moment one seeks our help or becomes a शरणागत, his life becomes sacred. "He that giveth up an affrighted creature seeking protection, unto its foe, doth not obtain protection when he is in need of it himself. Indeed the very clouds do not shower rain seasonably for him, and the seeds he may scatter do not grow for him. He that giveth up an afflicted creature seeking protection, unto its foe, hath to see his offspring die in childhood."[60] A pigeon went to king Shibi and sought his protection from a hawk. The king, in order to save the pigeon, begins to cut off flesh from his body, equal in weight to that pigeon. But the pigeon is so heavy that all his flesh was to be put in the scale, and so he mounted the scale himself.[61]

The natural outcome of a feeling of humanity, would be peace and good-will amongst mankind. It is a pleasant sight to see the brethren and sisters living together in peace and friendship. The result is not merely a union of hearts, but a co-ordination of efforts which is an essential condition of progress. "Like-heartedness, like-mindedness, non-hostility do I make for you; do ye show affection the one towards the other, as the inviolable (cow) towards her calf when born. Be the son submissive to the father, like-minded with the mother; let the wife to the husband speak words full of honey, wealful. Let not brother hate brother, nor sister, sister; becoming accordant of like courses, speak ye words auspiciously.....Having superiors, intentful, be ye not divided, accomplishing together, moving on with joint labour; come hither speaking what is agreeable to one another; I make you united, like minded. Your drinking (be) the same, in common your share of food; in the same harness do I join you together; worship ye Agni united, like spokes about a nave."[62]

This feeling of harmony is specially necessary in a community connected with blood ties. "He that succoureth his poor and wretched and helpless relatives,.....enjoyeth prosperity that hath no end.....Happiness should ever be enjoyed with one's relatives and not without them! To eat with one another, to talk with one another, and to love one another, are what relatives should always do. They should never quarrel."[63] In co-operation alone lies safety; in isolation and division there is death. "As milk is possible in kine, asceticism in Brahmins, and inconstancy in women, so fear is possible from relatives. Numerous thin threads of equal length, collected together, are competent to bear, from strength of numbers, the constant rolling of the shuttlecock over them. The case is even so with relatives that are good. O bull of the Bharata race, separated from one another, burning brands produce only smoke; but brought together they blaze forth into a powerful flame. The case is even so with relatives. They, O Dhritarashtra, who tyrannise over Brahmins, women, relatives, and kine, soon fall off their stalks like fruits that are ripe. And a tree that stands singly, though gigantic and strong and deep-rooted, hath its trunk soon smashed and twisted by a mighty wind. Those trees, however, that stand erect, growing close together are competent to resist winds more violent still, owing to mutual dependence. Thus he that is single, however endowed with all the virtues, is regarded by foes as capable of being vanquished like an isolated tree by the wind. Relatives again, in consequence of mutual dependence and mutual aid, grow together, like lotus-stalks in a lake."[64] Manu also deprecates all quarrels with near relatives; and man's ultimate happiness lies in their satisfaction.[65]

The importance of being polite in speech becomes quite evident. The Hindu view here is that : Speak Pleasant things; do not utter unpleasant truths; nor sweet lies.[66] A clever speaker must not utter truth in all its naked brutality, but if necessary soften down his language so as to unite these two ends. Such language is called सूनृता वाक्. "Agreeableness of speech, O Shakra, is the one thing by practising which a person may become an object of regard with all creatures and acquire great celebrity. This is the one thing, O Shakra, which gives happiness to all. By practising it, one may always obtain the love of all creatures. The person who does not speak a word and whose face is always furrowed with frowns, becomes an object of hatred unto all creatures. Abstention from agreeable speech makes him so. That person, who, upon beholding others, addresses them first with smiles succeeds in making friends of all. Even gifts, if not made with agreeable speeches, do not delight the recipients, like rice without curry."[67] "There is no such art of subjugation in the three worlds as Mercy, Friendship, charity, and sweet words."[68] It is interesting to note how far the sympathies of the princes extended and the polite forms of enquiry in which they found expression. "Thou must also represent unto the maidservants and man-servants there may be of the Kurus, and also many hump-backed and lame ones among them that I am doing well, and thou then ask them about their welfare. Thou must tell them, I hope Dhritarashtra's son still vouchsafes the same kindly treatment to you. I hope he gives you the comforts of life.....Thou should also, O sire, at our request, inquire after the welfare of those that are masterless and weak, and of those that are ignorant, in fact, of all those persons that are in pitiable circumstances."[69]

Malice or ill-will, in all its varied manifestations is severely condemned. "Slay ye the wicked man whose thought is evil, of the demonkind."[70] "On every side dispel all sin, Adityas, all hostility, indigence, and combined attack."[71] A truly imperial disposition disdains to despise or injure any creature. "One that hath his soul under control never disregards anybody in the three worlds,–no, not even the commonest creature."[72] A king who becomes a source of comfort to the very inmates of hell, said to the envoys of god of death : "Not in heaven, not in the very region of Brahma himself one attaineth that felicity one doth on relieving distress.....He is not a man, who, hard of heart, doth not feel kindly drawn towards infants, and old men, as well as those undergoing misery; verily such a one is a

Rakshasa."[73] Various causes account for the ill-will so rampant in the world. The root cause is absence of humanity, of love for the great human brotherhood. "Hostility springs from five causes. Those five causes are woman, land, harsh words, natural incompatibility, and injury."[74] One individual sees another and finds that "he is me over again." Another person sees a stranger and finds that "he is not me–an alien!" The former instinctively loves strangers; the latter feels hostilely inclined towards them. The result of the former mood is breadth of vision and a capacity of enjoying others' good. "They that are possessed of dexterity succeed in enjoying that prosperity which is vested in others."[75] The result of the latter mood is envy and rivalry. "Wicked individuals impute faults to even an honest person, moved by envy and rivalry. Enemies desirous of a quarrel cannot endure the elevation of an enemy brought about by his high feats. Faults are ascribed to even a pure soul engaged in penances. With respect to even an ascetic living in the woods, and employed in his own (harmless) acts, are raised three parties, viz. friends, neutrals, and foes. They that are rapacious hate them that are pure. The idle hate the active. The unlearned hate the learned. The poor hate the rich. The unrighteous hate the righteous. The ugly hate the beautiful, many amongst the learned, the unlearned; the rapacious, and the deceitful, would falsely accuse an innocent person even if the latter happens to be possessed of the virtues and intelligence of Brihaspati himself."[76] Slander and selfishness and such other qualities are the natural result of ill-will. "A wicked person is he who proclaims the faults of others at their back, who is inspired with envy at the accomplishments of others, and who remains silent when the merits of other people are proclaimed in his presence, feeling a reluctance to join in the chorus. Mere silence on such occasions is not an indication of wickedness. A wicked person, however, at such times breathes heavily, bites his lips, and shakes his head."[77] "Know him for a malevolent and a wicked person who quietly and alone takes edibles and drinks and other kinds of food that are regarded choice, even if persons are standing by with wishful eyes."[78]

Harshness of tongue is as much an object of censure as sweetness of speech is a subject of praise. "To control speech, O King, is said to be most difficult! It is not easy to hold a long conversation, uttering words full of meaning and delightful to the hearers. Well-spoken speech is productive of many beneficial results; and ill-spoken speech is the cause of evils. A forest pierced by arrows or cut down by hatchets may again grow, but one's heart wounded and censured by ill-spoken words never recovereth."[79] All forms of abusive language call forth punishment. "Whether truly or falsely or by way of joke, if one vilifies another as having a defective limb, or a defective organ, or suffering from a (vile) disease, he should be punished with a fine of thirteen Panas. A king should punish, with a fine of twenty-five Panas, (a person) vilifying another, by saying–I have known your mother and sister."[80]

The use of force in private quarrels is much deprecated. "A wife, son, servant, disciple, or uterine brother, found guilty of an offence should be punished with a cord or with bamboo-stick. They shall never be chastened on the lower part of the bodies, and never upon the upper limbs."[81] Spitting on a Brahmin brings on a person the cutting off of his lips; pulling him by his beard brings on the offender the cutting off of his hands and legs. If in an assault, skin or flesh is injured, fine is the penalty; if bones are broken, exile follows.[82] A driver is punished for rash driving ending in the loss of life.[83] Twigs should be used for goading cattle.[84]

Malevolence often results in large-scale destruction of public or private property, general warfare, incendiarism, and the like. "Drinking, quarrels, enmity with large numbers of men, connubial disputes, internecine quarrels, disloyalty to the king, sexual brawls, these and all paths that are sinful, should be avoided."[85] "They who rob others of their wealth, or destroy the wealth and possessions of other people, or proclaim the faults of other people, sink in hell. They who destroy water-works, who injure such buildings as are used for purposes of public meetings, break down bridges and causeways, and pull down houses used for purposes of habitation, have to sink in hell. They who destroy the means of other people's living, they who exterminate the habitations of other people, they who rob others of their spouses, they who sow dissensions among friends, and they who destroy the hopes of other people, sink into hell."[86]

The highest triumph of humanity is reached when evil is met by good and hatred by love. Evil may be met by evil to a certain extent. "One should behave towards another just as that other behaveth towards him. Even this is consistent with policy. One should behave deceitfully towards him that behaveth deceitfully and honestly towards him that is honest in his behaviour."[87] But a superior morality teaches that the saint need not condescend to devilish methods in encountering a devil, but his very saintliness will overcome all resistance. "He that is wicked behaveth wickedly even unto him that is humble; he also that is humble, behaveth with humility and honestly unto him that is wicked."[88] "The very gods desire his company who, stung with reproach, returneth it not himself nor causeth others to return it, or who, struck himself, doth not himself return the blow, nor causeth others to return it, and who wisheth not the slightest injury to him that injureth him."[89] "Anger must be conquered by forgiveness; the wicked must be conquered by honesty; the miser must be conquered by liberality, and falsehood must be conquered by truth." Bhartrihari well defines a saint :–

अपकारिषु यः साधुः स साधुः सद्भिरुच्यते।

References

1. Rg. II. 12.6.
2. Rg. II. 13.12.
3. Rg. II. 15.7.
4. Rg. X.91.2.

5. Rg. I. 31.13-14.
6. Rg. I.126.6.
7. Rg. V. 85.7.
8. Rg. X. 152.4.
9. Rg. IX.78.5.
10. Rg. VI.25.2.
11. Rg. V.20.2.
12. S.Br.I. 7, 2, 1-5.
13. Shanti. 298, 9-11.
14. M.II.92.
15. Vyasa. IV.21-22.
16. Niti-shataka 74.
17. M.II.116.
18. M.II.118.
19. Panchatantra.
20. Isha. Up.
21. Bg. VI. 29-31.
22. Bg. VI. 32.
23. Anu. 175, 7-10.
24. Shanti. 109, 11-21.
25. Atri. 41.
26. Anu. 142.35.
27. Shanti. 160.21.
28. Shanti. 251. 18-20; Shanti. 303. 35-36.
29. M.IV. 185.
30. Udyoga. 39.10.
31. Shanti. 78.37-41.
32. Av. XIX. 64.1.
33. Bg. V.18.
34. Rg. Val. VIII. 3; VIII.1.5; VIII; 19, 36.1.92.8.
35. M.VIII.415.
36. M.VIII. 416.
37. Shanti. 268, 37-49.
38. Anu. 10. 6-7.
39. Atri. 44.
40. Anu. 93. 4-5.
41. Anu. 93. 24.26.
42. Bg. III. 20.
43. Rg. IX. 11.3.
44. Anu. 142. 43.

45. Anu. 62. 35.
46. Shanti. 268. 37-49.
47. Shanti. 268, 37-49.
48. R.II. 90.8.
49. Anu. 11. 24-31.
50. Rg. VII. 23.6.
51. Rg. VII. 41. 3.
52. Rg. VI. 28.5.
53. Rg. VIII. 83.1.
54. Rg. X.169.1.
55. (सर्वं तत्प्रज्ञानेत्रम्) (Ai.Up. 5.3; Ch. Up. VI. 11.1. Katha Up. V.7.
56. M.I.49.
57. Shanti. 182, 10-18.
58. Udyoga. 34. 26.
59. Shanti. 116, 6-8. Yoga-sutra II. 35.
60. Vana. 200.12-14.
61. Vana. 133, 26-32.
62. Av. III. 30. Av. VII. 52, 1. VI. 64, 2-3.
63. Udyoga. 39, 17-27.
64. Udyoga. 36, 55-65.
65. M.IV. 179-181.
66. M.IV. 138.
67. Shanti. 84. 3-10.
68. S.N.I. 342.
69. Udyoga. 30. 40-43.
70. Rg. VII. 94. 12.
71. Rg. VIII. 56.21.
72. Udyoga. 124. 41-42.
73. Mk. P. XV.
74. Shanti. 139. 42-44.
75. Shanti. 104. 33.
76. Shanti. III. 60-63.
77. Shanti. 103. 46-47.
78. Shanti. 162. 11.
79. Udyoga. 34.77-81.
80. Yaj. II. 207-8.
81. M.XI. 299.300.
82. M.VIII. 282-284.
83. M.XI. 292-295.
84. P.IX.2.

85. Udyoga. 35.54.
86. Anu. 62. 18-22.
87. Udyoga. 37.7; Shanti. 109. 34.
88. Vana. 197. 4-6.
89. Udyoga. 36. 11.

Chapter - XX

QUIETISTIC VIRTUES

(1) Anger : Forbearance

Anger presupposes a disruption of the state of normal equilibrium which ought to exist between man and man; it is, therefore, an abnormal state of man due to man's weakness and want of self-control. Its suppression, therefore, under ordinary circumstances is supremely desirable. "Maruts, the man whose wrath is hard to master, he who would slay us ere we think, O Vasus, May he be tangled in the foils of mischief."[1] "Pass him who pours libations out in angry mood or after sin."[2] It is born of Kama or desire and leads to infatuation and ultimately extinction of reason in man and his consequent ruin.[3]

Control over anger is a necessary part of a course of discipline which every man must under-go. It is an essential constituent of that perfect self-mastery which alone effectively distinguishes man as a controller of circumstances from man as a mere tool of his surroundings. "I know that thou hast burnt a she crane with thy wrath! But, the anger which a person cherishes is the greatest of foes which a person hath! The gods know him for a Brahmin, who hath cast off anger and passion."[4] "He that suppresseth his anger, certainly acquireth the four objects for which we live. Between him that performeth without fatigue sacrifices every month for a hundred years, and him that never feeleth wrath in respect of anything, he that feeleth not wrath is certainly the higher."[5] "They that restrain their own wrath and pacify the wrath of others succeed in overcoming all difficulties."[6]

Anger is a fit of madness and consequently renders a man unfit for true discrimination between right and wrong. "Blessed are those high-souled ones who control their wrath by dint of their own good sense, like unto fire quenched by water. What iniquity is there which cannot be perpetrated by the angry?"[7] "The angry man committeth sin; the angry man killeth even his preceptors. The angry man insulteth even his superiors in harsh words."[8] It shows not strength but weakness of a man who yields to it. "The man that is overwhelmed with wrath acquireth not with ease generosity, dignity, courage, skill, and other attributes belonging to real force of character. A man by forsaking anger cannot exhibit proper energy, whereas it is highly difficult for the angry man to exhibit his energy at the proper time!"[9] Anger is a manifestation of our ill-will; and if it is allowed to become universal, all social intercourse, all amenities of domestic life would cease. "If the man, who heareth ill speeches of another, returneth those speeches afterwards; if the injured man returneth his injuries; if the chastised person chastiseth in return; if fathers slay sons, and sons fathers; and if husbands slay wives, and wives husbands, then, O Krishna, how can birth take place in a world where anger prevaileth so! .....Wrath, therefore, hath for its consequence, the destruction and distress of the people."[10] Sweetness of temper behind an action lends it its fragrance; but otherwise acts, however beneficent in outer aspects, lose their characteristic colour, when done in anger. "The sacrifice that one performs in anger, the gifts one makes in anger, the penances one undergoes in anger, and the offerings and libations one makes to the sacred fire in anger, are such that their merits are robbed by Yama. The toil of an angry man becomes entirely fruitless."[11]

Righteous indignation, however, has its legitimate place in a healthy life. "He is a man who cherisheth wrath and forgiveth not! He, on the other hand, who is forgiving and without wrath, is neither a man nor a woman. Contentment and softness of heart; and these two, want of exertion, and fear, are destructive of prosperity."[12] The incapacity of feeling anger on right occasions is often another name for sheer importence. "O let no woman bring forth such a son (as thou) that art without wrath, without exertion, without energy."[13] It is righteous indignation which is a great check on the wicked. "The man that represseth his wrath that has been excited by (adequate) cause becometh incapable of duly compassing the three ends of life. The wrath that kings desirous of subjugating the whole earth exhibit, is not without its uses. It serveth to restrain the wicked and to protect the honest."[14]

Its counterpart is forbearance–a capacity of broadly tolerating all offence. A touch of sympathetic tolerance, of sweet feeling renders possible all social relationships. "And because it is seen that there are in the world men, who are forgiving like the Earth, it is, therefore, that creatures sustain their life and enjoy prosperity. O beautiful one, one should forgive, under every injury. It hath been said that the continuation of species is due to man being forgiving."[15] Forgiveness, as a manifestation of the spirit of charity, is a virtue of virtues. "Forgiveness is the Vedas. He, that knoweth this, is capable of forgiving everything."[16] "O sire, there is nothing more conducive to happiness, and nothing more proper for a man of power and energy as forgiveness at every place and at all times. He that is weak should forgive under all circumstances. He that is possessed of power should show forgiveness from motives of virtue. And he, to whom the success or failure of his objects is the same, is naturally forgiving."[17]

Forgiveness is truly inward; it has nothing to do with the possession of the capacity to harm others or not. However, if there is no power behind it, it is often taken for mere pusillanimity. The virtue rises to its height when injuries, however grave, are allowed to pass into quiet oblivion, in spite of one's having the unmistakeable power to punish them. Under such circumstances, it becomes truly divine and disarms all thoughtless opposition. Its victories are the victories of love; its trophies are the trophies of higher morality. True forbearance, therefore, is not a weakness, but a power. "There is only one defect in forgiving persons, and not another; that defect is that people take a forgiving person to be weak. That defect, however, should not be taken into consideration, for forgiveness is a great power. Forgiveness is a virtue of the weak, and an ornament of the strong. Forgiveness subdueth (all) in the world; what is there that forgiveness cannot achieve? What can wicked person do unto him who carrieth the sabre of forgiveness in his hand? Fire falling on a grassless ground is extinguished of itself."[18]

Here also the true attitude is the middle path, the Aristotelian mean, avoiding too much meekness on the one hand, and too much intolerance on the other. The following passage gives all the details as regards the application of the general maxims. "Know, O child, these two truths with certainty, viz. that might is not always meritorious and forgiveness also is not always meritorious! He that forgiveth always suffereth many evils, and strangers and enemies always disregard him. No creature ever bendeth down unto him.....Vile-souled servants also themselves appropriate his vehicles and clothes and ornaments and apparel and beds and seats and food and drink and other articles of use.....O child, sons and servants and attendants and even strangers speak harsh words unto the man who always forgiveth. Persons, disregarding the man of ever forgiving temper, even desire his wife, and his wife also becometh ready to act as she willeth.....Listen now to the demerits of those that are never forgiving. The man of wrath, who, surrounded by darkness, always inflicteth, by help of his own energy, various kinds of punishments on persons whether they deserve them or not, is necessarily separated from his friends. Such a man is hated by both relatives and strangers. Such a man, because he insulteh others, suffereth loss of wealth, and reapeth disregard, and sorrow, and hatred, and confusion, and enemies.....He, that becometh forgiving at the proper time, obtaineth happiness, both in this world and the other. I shall now indicate the occasions in detail of forgiveness. He that hath done thee a service, even if he is guilty of a great wrong unto thee, recollecting his former service, shouldst thou forgive that offender. Those also that have become offenders from ignorance and folly should be forgiven, for learning and wisdom are not always attainable by man. They, that, having offended thee knowingly, plead ignorance, should be punished, even if their offences be trivial. Such crooked men should never be pardoned. The first offence of every creature should be forgiven. The second offence, however, should be punished, even if it be trivial.....Nothing can succeed that hath been undertaken without reference to place and time. Sometimes offenders should be forgiven from fear of the people. And it hath been said that on occasions besides these, might shall be put forth against transgressors."[19]

(2) **Pride : Humility**

Egotism in all its shapes and forms is an object of supreme moral aversion to a Hindu. An undue self-consciousness, naturally takes an aggressive shape and is rooted in ill-will. It is a form of self-love, so narrowly conceived as to rule out all social love. It is, therefore, a symptom of diseased state of things. "Give up the people who are high and haughty to these men and to me, O Thunder-Wielder!"[20] "O Indra-Varuna, grant to the worshippers cheerfulness, void of pride."[21] "Give us not Indra, as a prey unto the scornful or the proud."[22]

Pride is the result of a want of sense of proportion in one's appreciation of the things of this world. Hence there ensues intoxication to a person who takes a highly exaggerated view of some quality or attainment of his. "Pride of learning, of wealth, and of alliances, these intoxicate men of little sense, while they that are wise always restrain it."[23] "Intoxication of wealth is much more censurable than wine, for a man intoxicated with prosperity can never be brought to his senses unless he meeteth with a fall."[24] True self-consciousness never commits itself to exaggeration of words or feelings; it is always accompanied with sobriety. Caesar Truly said : "It is easier for me to punish you, than to say that I shall punish you." That is the reason why really clever people prove their mettle by deeds, not by empty words. ब्रुवते हि फलेन साधवो न तु कंठेन निजोपयोगिताम्।

Vanity brings in its train numerous other vices. "And at first the sinful Asuras were possessed with pride. And pride begat wrath. And from wrath arose every kind of evil propensity, and from the latter sprang shamelessness. And in consequence of shamelessness good behaviour disappeared from among them. And because they had become shameless and destitute of virtuous propensities and good conduct and virtuous vows, forgiveness and prosperity and morality forsook them in no time. And prosperity then, O king, sought the gods, while adversity sought the Asuras."[25] "Mada (vanity) hath eighteen faults. They are ill-will towards others, throwing obstacles in the way of virtuous acts, detraction, falsehood in speech, lust, anger, dependence, speaking ill of others, finding out the faults of others for report, waste of wealth, quarrel, insolence, cruelty of living creatures, malice, ignorance, disregard of those that are worthy of regard, loss of the sense of right and wrong, and always seeking to injure others."[26]

The practice of the highest virtues, and the possession of the highest attainments, becomes generally vitiated by an element of vanity in men. It is the weakness of the greatest souls, and is found in company with very noble qualities. But once conceit enters into a man's nature, it destroys the blissfulness of all the other virtues possessed by a man. The dominance of pride makes the most self-less and exalted act mean and selfish and thus takes away its virtuous character. "An Agnihotra performed from motives of pride, abstention from speech practised from similar motives, study, and sacrifice, from the same motives,–these four, of themselves innocent, become terrible when practised unduly."[27] Yayati similarly falls from his position through conceit. He says : "O Indra, I do not in ascetic austerities, behold my equal among men, the celestials, the Gandharvas, and the great Rishis. Indra said–O monarch, because thou disregardest those that are thy superiors, thy equals, and even thy inferiors, without, in fact, knowing their real merits, therefore, thy virtues have suffered a diminu-tion and thou must fall from heaven."[28]

Self-conceit issues, thus, in un-social acts and words. It renders us incapable of doing justice to others. It makes ourselves the constant centre of all talk. Self-praise and slander of others are the two inevitable concomitants of a boisterous vanity. "O royal sage, this region can never be made eternal by vanity, or pride of strength, or malice, or deceitfulness! Never disregard those that are inferior or superior or those who occupy the middle station!"[29] "That man, who, having acquired knowledge, regardeth himself as learned, and with his learning destroyeth the reputation of others, never attains to regions of indestructible felicity. That knowledge also doth not make its possessor competent to attain to Brahma. Study, taciturnity, worship before fire, and sacrifices, these four remove all fear. When, however, these are mixed with vanity, instead of removing, they cause fear. The wise should never exult on receiving honours; nor should they grieve at insults. For it is the wise alone that honour the wise; the wicked never act like the virtuous. I have given away so much, I have studied so much, I have observed these vows, such vanity is the root of fear."[30] A wise and saintly person is, therefore, expected to wrap himself in complete obscurity. "As a dog often times devoureth its own evacuations to its injury, so those Yogis devour their own vomiting, who procure their own livelihood by disclosing their preeminence. The wise know him for a Brahmin, who, living in the midst of kindred, wishes his religi-ous practices to remain always unknown to them."[31] A true saint is always eager to hear criticisms about himself and not praises. "The man who is pleased and not angry with hearing of his own defects, and who exerts to discover his weak points and abandons them when told by others, who after hearing his own merits remains the same and does not display vanity, who considers 'I am the mine of all defects–why attribute merits to me? Ignorance also is in me,' is superior to all. He is a Sadhu. The gods do not attain a portion of his sixteenth part."[32]

The Shukra-niti points out how each type of pride leads to certain special evils. "One should never be mad or vain with learning, valour, wealth, birth, or strength. The man who is proud of his learning does not care for the advice of the authorities.....The man, who, proud of his valour, abandons the path followed by the people, loses his life by rashly undertaking warfare, and though armed, by giving up the recognized military tactics. The man who is proud of his wealth does not know of his own infamy. So also the man who is proud of his distinction looks upon the whole world as a piece of straw."[33]

As has been said already, the head and front of offending of pride lies in the incapacity which it creates in us of giving the other people their due. All expressions of contempt of others are to be deprecated. "One should never address an eminent person familiarly (by using the word Twam-thou). To address such a person as *Twam* and to slay him are equal."[34] "One should not seek self-elevation by depreciating others. Indeed, one should, by one's merits alone, seek distinction over persons that are distinguished but never over those that are inferior..... One possessed of real wisdom and endued with real merits, acquires great fame by abstaining from speaking ill of others and from indulging in self-praise. Flowers shed their pure and sweet fragrance without trumpeting forth their own excellence. Similarly, the effulgent sun scatters his splendour in the firmament in perfect silence. After the same manner, those men blaze in the world with celebrity, who by the aid of their intelligence, cast off these and similar other faults and who do not blaze forth their own virtues. The fool can never shine in the world by bruiting about his own praise. The man, however, of real merit and learning, obtains celebrity even if he be concealed in a pit."[35] One undesirable result of an undue development of self-consciousness is the breakdown of one's power of introspection. "Thou, O king, seest the faults of others, even though they be as small as a mustard seed. But seeing, thou noticest not thy own faults even though they be as large as the Bilwa fruit."[36]

The proudest of us have our own limitations, weaknesses, and imperfections. An all-round perfection is not given to man. Hence a certain amount of humility in one's character is nothing but an acceptance of this fact. "One should remember that there is the animal which devours the devourer of whales. Raghava (a kind of animal) is the devourer of that even, and there is the destroyer of Raghava."[37] "The illustrions Rama was equal unto Indra in prowess, and yet he had to range the forest renouncing all pleasures! Therefore should no one act unrighteously, saying–I am mighty."[38]

Humble behaviour has much to recommend it on the ground of expediency. Intractableness of nature is often the cause of our ruin. "The cow that is difficult to milk is greatly tormented; whereas that one which is easy to milk hath nothing to suffer. Anything that bendeth without being heated, is never heated; the wood that bendeth of itself is never bent with force. A wise man following this example humbleth himself before one stronger than himself; and he that bendeth down before a stronger person boweth down, in fact, unto Indra."[39] "Trees stand in one and the same place and are unyielding in respect of the spot where they stand. In consequence of this disposition of theirs to resist currents, they are obliged to leave the place of their growth. Canes, however, act differently. The cane beholding the advancing current, bends to it. After the current has passed away, the cane resumes its former posture. The cane knows the virtues of time and opportunity. It is docile and obedient. It is yielding without being stiff."[40]

The Gita attacks the last and most ultimate type of vanity in us. It is the presence of self-consciousness within us, which is called Ahamkara. Ego is not the centre of things. This consciousness that I am doing this or that, is fundamentally vicious. It is the root of most of our narrow virtues and vices.

The abandonment of this egoism is the first condition for entrance into higher, spiritual life. The आधिभौतिक I within us must be supplanted by the आध्यात्मिक I. A man is not to act as a resident here and now, but as a spectator of all time and existence, as a citizen of the kingdom of God. He is not an isolated, atomic individuality, pitted against other rival individualities. There is no I as opposed to *You* ; there is the intellectual and emotional submergence of the narrower I at each step of progress in a broader I, until there remains one I, call it what we will. Pride, in this sense, is defined as "a consciousness of one's being himself an actor or sufferer in life."[41] "Egoism (अस्मिता) is defined as the identification of the power that sees with the power of seeing."[42] An exalted, spiritual self-consciousness, however, survives this last surrender, which views things broadly, inclusively, comprehensively *sub specie eternitatis.*

(3) Cheerfulness : Grief

Such weaknesses as fear and grief merely lead to depression. The Upanishads clearly say that "Knowing that Brahman is joy, a wise man does not near anything." "He who knows his self overcomes all grief." A true philosophy of life enables a man to view existence and its incidents in a true perspective. Temporary sorrows therefore lose their burning sting in such a man. "Sorrow can never touch the man that is possessed of intelligence, that has acquired wisdom, that is mindful of listening to the instructions of his betters, that is destitute of envy, and that has self-restraint."[43] Nothing flourishes in an atmosphere of depression; it kills a man, body, and soul, "Sorrow killeth beauty, sorrow killeth strength, sorrow killeth the understanding, and sorrow bringeth disease. Grief instead of helping acquisition of its object, drieth up the body, and maketh one's foes glad. Men repeatedly die and are reborn; repeatedly wither and grow.....Happiness and misery, plenty and want, gain and loss, life and death are shared by all in due order. Therefore, he that is self-controlled, should neither joy nor repine."[44] Krishna says : "Do not give way to womanliness. It is a weakness of the soul. Cast it off and rise."[45] It is a characteristic of a truly self-poised soul to offer the same front to prosperity and adversity. संपत्तौ च विपत्तौ च महतामेकरुपता। The royal swan plunges into white as well as dark waters; but its whiteness does not increase nor diminish.[46]

(4) Gratitude

It is the mark of a magnanimous soul to have lively remembrance only of services rendered to oneself and to be oblivious of all evil acts or words one receives. "They that are good, they that are distinguished above the common level, remember not the wrongs done to them but only the benefits they have received."[47] "He, indeed, is a man upon whom good offices are never lost. The measure of his requital becometh greater than the measure of the services he receiveth."[48] "Whence can an ungrateful person derive fame? Where is his place? Whence can he have happiness?.....He that injureth a friend sinks into terrible and everlasting hell. Every one should be grateful, and every one should seek to benefit his friends. Every thing may be obtained from a friend. Honours may be obtained from friends. In consequence of friends, one may enjoy various objects of enjoyment. Through the exertions of friends, one may escape from various dangers and distresses. He that is wise would honour his friends with his best attention."[49] "The very birds of prey abstain from touching the dead bodies of those who, having been served and benefited by friends, show ingratitude to the latter."[50] Ingratitude is regarded as the vilest of sins; because it is a symptom of a highly selfish and treacherous state of mind. "For one that slays a Brahmin, for one that drinketh alcohol, for one that steals, for one that has fallen away from a vow, there is expiation, O king. But there is no expiation for an ungrateful person! That cruel and vile man who injures a friend and becomes ungrateful is not eaten by the very cannibals, nor by the worms that feed on carrion."[51]

(5) Ambition : Modesty

Hindus valued highly the importance of the social self of man; and from that point of view, they considered pure glory as a legitimate object of ambition to every man. The sentiment as regards fame was quite a healthy one amongst the heroes of the Rig-veda. "Bestow upon us splendid fame and riches."[52] "Give us trimmed grass and fame among the living."[53] Immortality which a person receives through his surviving reputation was highly prized. "For glory is he born, he (Soma) hath come forth to glory, he giveth life and glory to the singers. They, clothed in glory, have become immortal."[54] The Upanishads recognise लोकैषणा (desire for fame) as one of the powerful springs of action.

Pure renown is never considered idle; it is not a mere vanity of the world. Even the very highest saints are not above its influence. Hindu view is powerfully expressed in such lines as these : संभावितस्य चाकीर्तिर्मरणादतिरिच्यते। अथ मरणमवश्यमेव जन्तोः किमिति मुधा मलिनं यज्ञः कुरुध्वे। Death is considered infinitely superior to disgrace. That is why Rama gives up Sita; that is why a king in the Raghuvansha is ready to give up his life, to save his reputation. Good name is indeed a precious jewel of our souls. "The report of virtuous deeds spreadeth on the Earth and ascendeth to heaven. As long as that report lasts so long is the doer said to be in heaven. The man whose evil deeds are bruited about, is said to fall down and live, as long as that evil report lasts, in the lower regions. Therefore, should a man be virtuous in his acts if he is to gain Heaven."[55] Karna expresses the voice of all heroes when he says : "For persons like us, it is not fit to save life by a blameworthy act. On the contrary, it is even proper for us to meet death with the approbation of the world and under circumstances bringing fame.....Fame keepeth people alive in this world even like a mother, while infamy killeth men even though they may move about with bodies undestroyed. That fame is the life of men is evidenced by this ancient Shloka sung by the Creator Himself, in the next world it is fame that is the chief support of a person, while in this world pure fame lengthens life."[56] A high sense of honour is a mark of a high-minded man. "Men of the lower orders are afraid of injury to their lives; those of middle classes, of death; and good men of insult."[57] "Hostilities such as these do go on. But the honour of the family is never suffered to be interfered with. If any stranger seeketh to insult the honour of a family, they that are good never tolerate such insult coming from the stranger."[58]

Tennyson says : Better fifty years of Europe than a cycle in Cathay. Scott also proclaims to all the sensual world that one crowded hour of glorious life is worth an age without a name. The Mahabharata echoes the same sentiment : मुहूर्तमपि ज्वलितं श्रेयः न तु धूमायितं चिरं। "It is better that a king should blaze up for a moment like a charcoal of ebony wood than that he should smoulder and smoke like chaff for many years."[59] However, the value of ambition lies in its enabling us to scorn delights and live laborious days. "Behold, Indra, even though he hath obtained the sovereignty of the celestials, both yet, for fame alone, perform sacrifices.....All royal sages and Brahmins possessed of ascetic wealth have achieved, for fame alone, the most difficult of ascetic feats."[60]

It is clearly recognised that a desire for pure glory should not be confounded with a vulgar love for notoriety. True honour lives only in the estimation of the worthy. Appreciation at the hands of fools is worth nothing. The Greek orator, when he was applauded by his people, at once exclaimed : "Have I said anything foolish?" It is Bhavabhuti's idea to appeal from the ignorant many to the wise few. "That man who is highly spoken of by swindlers, mimes and women of ill fame, is more dead than alive."[61] "He should never regard himself as honoured by others. One should not, therefore, grieve when one is not honoured by others. People act according to their nature just as they open and shut their eyelids; and it is only the learned that pay respect to others. They, again, in this world, that are foolish, apt to sin, and adept in deceit, never pay respect to those that are candidates for esteem, while the other world is for those that are devoted to asceticism."[62]

A feeling of modesty implies a general respect for the customs, traditions, sentiments of the mass-mind. It is an instinctive regard for the ethos of a country. It generally keeps people on the right track. "He that hath shame hath an aversion from sin, and his prosperity also increaseth; and he that hath prosperity truly be cometh a man.....He that is without shame is neither man nor woman. He is incapable of earning religious merit; and is like a Shudra. He that hath shame gratifieth the gods, the Pitris, and even his own self; and by this he obtaineth emancipation, which, indeed, is the highest aim of all righteous persons."[63]

(6) Contentment

The one essential thing to be borne in mind here is that discontent is held up as a virtue for the classes other than Brahmins, while contentment is quite suited to the quietistic life of the Brahmins. "The discontented Brahmins perish; so also the contented kings." "Little streams are filled with only a small quantity of water. The palms of a mouse are filled with only a small quantity. A coward is soon gratified with acquisitions that are small."[64] "Never occupy the intermediate, the low, or the lowest station! Blaze up! It is better to blase up for a moment than to smoke for ever and ever!"[65]

It is clearly perceived that divine discontent is the first condition of all progress not only in worldly matters, but in the spiritual life as well. यो वै भूमा तत्सुखं। नाल्पे सुखमस्ति। The infinite alone can make us happy; there is no happiness in the finite. A distinction is drawn between things regarding which contentment is the most desirable attitude; and pursuits regarding which discontent is the best thing. A person should be supremely contented with regard to one's own wife, dinner, and wealth; but as regard penances, efforts, and studies an endless progress alone can be the ideal.[66]

The general attitude towards worldly wealth and ambition is that of disinterestedness. The oriental view is that a true philosopher should have as few wants as possible. The Hindus never confounded civilization with the multiplication of wants. "Whatever of paddy and wheat and gold and animals and women there are on earth, even the whole of these is not sufficient for one man. Thinking of this, one should cultivate contentment!"[67] Desire for the perishable commodities of the world is the root of all miseries; hence the centre of gravity of man's ambition should be shifted from this world and its vanities to the everlasting riches of the spirit. "And so should affection for one's own person be extinguished by knowledge. Like the lotus leaf that is never drenched by water, the souls of men capable of distinguishing between the ephemeral and the everlasting.....can never be moved by affection. The man that is influenced by affection is tortured by desire; and from the desire that springeth up in his heart, his thirst for worldly possessions increaseth. Verily, this thirst is sinful and is regarded as the source of all anxieties."[68]

(7) Temperance

One of the peculiarities of ancient Hindu thought was the enormous importance it attached to such matters as eating and drinking. All the intellectual apparatus was believed to be a transformation of food. The Gita says : अन्नाद्भवन्ति भूतानि। All beings are born out of food. The Upanishads say : अन्नमयं हि सौम्य मनः। "Mind is the outcome of food."[69] The Gita traces the dependence of the qualities which a man possesses upon the type of food he eats. "The foods that augment vitality, energy, vigour, health, joy and cheerfulness, that are delicious, bland, substantial and agreeable are dear to the pure. The passionate desire foods that are bitter, sour, saline, over-hot, pungent, dry and burning and which produce pain, grief, and sickness. That which is stale and flat, purified and corrupt, leavings also and unclean, is the food dear to the dark."[70] "When the food is pure, the whole nature becomes pure; when nature becomes pure, memory becomes firm; and when a man is in possession of a firm memory, all the bonds (which tie a man down to the world) become unloosed."[71]

Hence the importance of food in the eyes of Hindu writers is naturally very great. "In thee, O Food, is set the spirit of great gods, under thy flag brave deeds are done."[72] "From food is the origin of creatures. From food is the happiness and delight. Know that moral and material well-being depend upon food. The cure of disease or health also flows from food.....Food is Earth, Food is Heaven. Food is the Firmament. Everything is rooted in food. In the absence of food, the five elements that constitute the physical organism cease to exist in a state of union. From the absence of food, the strength of even the strongest man is seen to fail. Dinners and marriages and sacrifices all cease in the absence of food. The very Vedas disappear when food there is none."[73] The Hindus of transcendental theories fully realised the saying of Emerson that the whole effort of civilization is directed to put something between the two mandibles. सर्वारम्भाः तण्डुलप्रस्थमूलाः।

Elaborate regulations are laid down in order to ensure purity in the articles of food. Much depends upon the character of the person from whom food is taken. "Food given by a king robs its (partakers) of his spirit and energy; that given by a Shudra robs the Brahma energy (of its partaker); food given by a goldsmith impairs the vitality; and that offered by a cobbler destroys the good name."[74] Food from all unclean and immoral persons, from professional actors, mechanics, physicians, and such other persons is to be boycotted.[75] Certain articles of food such as garlic or onion are to be avoided by the highest castes.[76] Temperance in matters of eating is insisted on. "Over-eating brings on ill-health, shortens the duration of life, proves hostile to acts which lead to heaven. It is sinful and condemned by men. Hence let a man avoid over-eating."[77] "He that eateth sparingly winneth these viz. health, long life and ease, his progeny also becometh healthy."[78]

The soma-drinking was highly lauded in the Vedas. But the use of Sura was not altogether approved.[79] "The Soma is truth, prosperity, light : and the Sura untruth, misery, darkness."[80] Sura involves men in quarrels.[81] It was classed with dicing and meat as an evil.[82] In the age of the Ramayana, drinking was not unusual. "Let wine-drinkers drink wine; the hungry eat Payasha, and those who are inclined to it eat clean meat."[83] Its excess was deprecated. "For the attainment of piety and wealth, drinking is not a proper course. It is by drinking that people lose piety, wealth, and objects of desire."[84] In fact, two traditions are seen to exist side by side, one allowing the use of wine, the other classing it as a serious sin. Manu says : "No sin is attached to winching, flesh-eating, or wine drinking; these are the natural propulsions of man; but abstinence bears greater fruits."[85] Shukra-niti says : "Of the man who drinks wine excessively intelligence disappears. Wine drunk according to some measure, increases the talent, clears the intelligence, augments patience, and makes the mind steadfast; but otherwise it is ruinous."[86] The same is the view of Garuda Purana. "If taken in moderation it leads to salvation, otherwise to damnation. Wine gives strength, stimulates the natural faculties, prolongs life. If one drinks wine keeping these facts in mind, he drinks beauty, he drinks nectar."[87] The Mahabharata records a story which shows that at one time wine-drinking became unpopular, and the sages interdicted its use. The learned Shukra saw the state of unconsciousness which comes over a man under the influence of drink, and said : "That wretched Brahmin, who from this day, unable to resist the temptation, will drink wine, shall be regarded to have lost his virtue, shall be reckoned to have committed the sin of slaying a Brahmin, shall be hated both in this world and the next world. I set this limit to the conduct and dignity of Brahmins everywhere."[88] In the Chhandogya Upanishad drinking is considered a heinous sin. "The stealer of gold, the drinker of spirits, the violater of the bed of his teacher, the killer of a pious man, are the four who fall, and the fifth who associates with them."[89]

Manu says that wine must be renounced because it disables a man from seeing right or wrong, and because it is a refuse matter.[90] To get rid of its sin, one must die after drinking hot liquids.[91] Even its scent is to be avoided.[92] A wife may be superseded if she is given to wine-drinking.[93]

Hindu ethics always differentiated morality of the average man from morality of the superman. The Markandeya Puran mentions the instance of a sage who took to wine-drinking and such other practices in order to maintain his solitude; and he was not affected by the sin. "Nor did that foremost of the Yogis commit any fault, although he drank Varuni like air in the habitation of a Chandala."[94] "The Brahmin possessed of learning, becomes the subjugator of the food that he eats. Having eaten it, he begets other food. The ignorant man who eats the food offered to him, loses the right to the children he begets, for the latter become his whose food has enabled the progenitor to beget them. Even this is the subtle fault attached to persons eating other people's food, when they have not the puissance to conquer that food."[95]

References

1. Rg. VII. 59.8.
2. Rg. VIII. 32.21.
3. Bg. II.
4. Vana. 209, 33, 34, 36.
5. Adi. 73. 1-11.
6. Shanti. 110, 21.
7. R.V. 55. 2-6.
8. Vana. 29.3-37.
9. Vana. 29. 3-37.
10. Vana. 29. 3-37.
11. Shanti. 305. 27.
12. Udyoga. 133. 33-35.
13. Udyoga. 133.33.
14. Adi. 96. 2-3.
15. Vana. 29. 3-37.
16. Vana. 29. 38-47.

17. Udyoga. 39. 59-60.
18. Udyoga. 33. 55-59.
19. Vana. 28. 6-35.
20. Rg. VI. 19.12.
21. Rg. Valkh. 11.7.
22. Rg. VIII. 2.15.
23. Udyoga. 34. 45.
24. Udyoga. 34.54.
25. Vana. 92. 8-11.
26. Udyoga. 45. 9-11.
27. Udyoga. 35.56.
28. Adi. 82, 2-3.
29. Udyoga. 123. 15-17.
30. Adi. 84. 22-27.
31. Udyoga. 42. 32-33.
32. S.N. III.613-618.
33. S.N. III. 172-186.
34. Anu. 268.32.
35. Shanti. 293. 25-33.
36. Adi. 79.1.
37. S.N. III. 447.
38. Vana. 25. 10.
39. Udyoga. 34. 36-38.
40. Shanti. 113. 8-11.
41. Vana. 314. 58.
42. Yoga-sutras. II.6.
43. Shanti. 173. 43.
44. Udyoga. 36. 44-45.
45. Bg. II.
46. Quoted in Kavya-Prakash.
47. Ashram. 13.2.
48. Adi. 176. 17-18.
49. Shanti. 172. 17-24.
50. Udyoga. 36.42.
51. Shanti. 171. 25-27.
52. Rg. VII. 25.3.
53. Rg. VII. 46-4.
54. Rg. IX. 94.4.
55. Vana. 202. 13-15.
56. Vana. 301. 28-34.

57. Udyoga. 34.53.
58. Vana. 244.203.
59. Shanti. 140.19.
60. Adi.133.11-13.
61. Udyoga. 38, 45.
62. Udyoga. 42. 38-42.
63. Udyoga. 71. 44-47.
64. Udyoga. 733, 9.
65. Udyoga. 133. 13-15.
66. Panchatantra.
67. Drona. 63. 11.
68. Vana. 2. 46-50.
69. Ch. VI. 5.4.
70. Bg. XVII. 8-10.
71. Ch. VIII. 26.2.
72. Rg. I. 187.6.
73. Anu. 98. 30-33.
74. M.IV. 218.
75. M.IV. 223.
76. M.V. 5-10.
77. M.II. 57.
78. Udyoga. 37.34.
79. Rg.I. 116.7, X. 131. 4.5; S.Br.XII. 7.3.8; Rg. VII. 86. 6, VIII. 2.12.
80. S.Br. V.1.2.10.
81. Rg.VIII.2.12.
82. Av.XIV. 1,35, 36; Rg. VII. 86, 6.
83. R.II. 91.52.
84. R.IV. 33. 46-47.
85. M.V. 56.
86. S.N.I. 229.31.
87. Garuda-Purana I.Ch.160.
88. Adi.70.70.73.
89. Chh. V.X.9.
90. M.XI. 97. 94.
91. Yaj. III. 253.
92. Shanti. 163. 78-79.
93. Yaj. I.73.
94. Mk. P.XVII.
95. Anu. 183. 14-15.

Chapter - XXI

SANNYASA

(1)

An elaborate development of the idea of renunciation is a peculiar feature of the Hindu ideal of life. The Hindu view fully emphasises the claims of the present life in any rounded scheme of ethics. But human life remains very much dwarfed and stunted, if it is pinned down absolutely to the here and the now. Reality of time, space, and circumstance is relative only : man essentially transcends these limitations and takes a wider view of existence in which he becomes a spectator of all time and existence. The institution of Sannyasa is the expression of this transcendental view of life; it is the triumph of the claims of the eternity over the claims of the present world.

It is with great difficulty that a man evolves an independent existence unfettered by the worries of the world. 'To get and beget' is the law of life. But a higher morality asks man to enjoy by renunciation, to receive pleasure by transcending it. तेन त्यक्तेन भुंजीथा:। This movement of self is not a movement of contraction, but of expansion. It is not self-extinction, but self-realization which is the ideal dominating a Sannyasin. In the first stages of life, a man remains very much handicapped : the tyranny of time, space, and circumstance hangs heavy upon him at every step. Worldly proprieties or conventions smother his higher tendencies. He has to remain largely pinned down to the earth : he can seldom soar aloft. Compromise is the very stuff of worldly career; the triumph of pure principle is rare. Accommodation to world at every turn is considered the height of wisdom. Man is often obliged to give to family what may be meant for all mankind. This constant surrender of honour, of the higher principles necessitated by the very situation itself, makes the life of a man practical but intensifies its narrow exclusiveness. The soul is never free to do justice to the inner treasures of itself. Its higher tendencies which make a call upon in the name of justice or humanity have to be silenced : and the reign of expediency which supervenes renders man dwarfish and stunted.

Hindu view always allowed exceptional natures who have in them supreme strength of will or power of love to discard at once the ties of the world and to enter the final stage of life. Gautama Buddha, Shukadevaji, Shri Shankaracharya were born Sannyasins : they could, therefore, with ease shake off the petty tyranny of the world. यदहरह: विरजेत् तदहरह: प्रव्रजेत्। The very moment one inwardly rises superior to the world, he is free to move out as a Fakir. This law was meant for exceptionally powerful natures. Again, there was the institution of lifelong Brahmacharya (नैष्ठिकब्रह्मचर्य) for those who feel an irresistible call to devote their entire lives to the intellectual pursuits. But for ordinary men there were limits to their worldly ambitions. Old men in their very dotage concentrating their powers on worldly objects are not very attractive figures in society. Every man was asked to cry halt to his earthly ambitions at an advanced period of his life. Princes and paupers alike were to come out at sixty or seventy, on the noble mission of leading a life of perfect harmlessness, pure love. But not till all the worldly debts were fulfilled. A premature attempt to get at the Absolute by a short cut was held highly dangerous. "Having studied the Vedas according to the rules of virtue, and performed the religious sacrifices to the best of his ability, let him turn his thought to self-emancipation. For seeking the emancipation of self, without having studied the Vedas, and procreated children and performed the sacrifices, a Brahmin shall obtain a very degraded status in the next world."[1]

A Sannyasin is often the most picturesque figure in Hindu

society, because he is largely free from the relativity of the ethics of the man of the world. He knows no law except that of love : he knows no limits to his goodwill except those of his vision. He is not a member of any family, not a constituent of any caste, nor a citizen of any Commonwealth, but a member of that great brotherhood of the noble living and the noble dead, and a citizen of the noble living and the noble dead, and a citizen of the kingdom of God. He does not belong to the East or the West; he transcends all geographical, all historical, all ethnological barriers. Even evil he conquers by good : hatred he conquers by love; he disarms opposition by his friendship. A wonderful being is he above pleasure and pain, above respect and insult, above good and evil, above attraction and aversion, above all party ties, provincial egotisms, racial jealousies. "Those Brahmins, who, declaring protection to all creatures, leave their homes and take to asceticism attain the effulgent regions. The soul of a Brahmin gives no cause of terror to any creature, nor is frightened by any creature in return.....Life or death he must not court; like a servant waiting for the receipt of his salary, he must bide the time of death. Every step that he takes should be sanctioned by his sight; he should drink water purified by filtration, speak the speech the truth of which has been guaranteed, and do whatever his conscience would approve of. Dispassionately he must bear with his revilers, nor offer affront to any one; let him not create any enmity whatsoever......Universal compassion, abstention from injury to all creatures, control of the senses, institution of religious rites enjoined in the Vedas, and practice of austere penances are the factors by which one can realise the supreme Self in life."[2]

Renunciation, however, does not mean renunciation of all activity. It means renunciation of our egoism, our narrow partialities and narrow aversions. Life of activity is central in a well-regulated life : but this activity is lifted to a higher plane, its character altogether altered. Even a Sannyasin has to do the work allotted to him by his own situation; he is not to aimlessly wander over the surface of the whole globe. स्वे स्वे कर्मण्यभिरत: ससिद्धिं लभते नर:। The poet-Sannyasin may write immortal verse : the artist-Sannyasin may put his soul in various forms of fine art; the politician-Sannyasin may try to elevate the status of his country. But behind this outward diversity there lies a profound unity in these. Every act every Karma has a twofold aspect : the outer and the inner. Its objective aspect varies with men; its subjective aspect should remain the same. The individual self may speak through the former; but the cosmic self should speak through the latter. These two moments of every activity are perfectly compatible with each other. A life without activity is no life : it is death. Activity with out one's interest in it is also a psychological impossibility. Interest must also relate to self : it cannot relate to anything else. Man is and must remain the measure of things. The Upanishads say : Everything is dear for the sake of Atman; nothing is dear for its own sake. Then how is it possible to transcend this fundamental fact of our being? Man cannot transcend a life of activity as long as he lives. 'न हि कश्चित्क्षणमपि जातु तिष्ठत्यकर्मकृत्"[3] Manu repeats the line of argument of the Upanishadic seers when he says : "No action is found, in this world, of a man without desire. Whatever act a person does is but the effort of his desire."[4] But all purposes or interests or desires have an inevitable ultimate reference to self. Shankara proves this too clearly in the introduction to his Bhashya on the Sutras. Hence the only point upon which the idea of Sannyasa can be brought to bear is this idea of self. The whole teaching of Gita is concentrated on this point. Its fundamental question is : what should be the consciousness behind our actions? The problem is not whether Pravritti or Nivritti should be the goal of life. Pravritti is absolutely inevitable; activity is the very law of our being. The question therefore relates to the psychology of our truly moral actions. No outward difference exists between an animal, an uncultured man, and a Tyagi. All these must act, and act with ultimate reference to their own selves. The fundamental criterion of a regenerate man lies in the standpoint of his actions, the basis of his moral life. The whole science of ethics ultimately turns upon the interpretation of self. Self means in a Sannyasin not Ahamkara, not the empirical I, but God-Atman, the pure ego or adhyatmik I. Islam asks men to act for the sake of Allah. Christianity does the same; Buddhism asks us to renounce our false individuali-ties; but Hinduism alone takes the bold step of identifying the self within and the self without, the Jivatman and Paramatman, the individual self and the cosmic self. Hence while each of these great faiths is right in its emphasis on love of man and love of God as the supreme basis of all life : only Hinduism enables us to see the irrefutable logic behind this attitude and enables us to see in God not an external agency, not a tertium quid, but the central presence abiding at the heart of all agitation. A man who realises this in words, deeds, and thoughts begins to move in an altogether different plane; his hands may be always at work; but his heart is always in God. Such is true Sannyasa : and when so understood it becomes the highest gospel ever preached to humanity.

(2)

Renunciation is said to be the characteristic attitude of the East. Hindu thought preaches certain indifference to the pleasures and pains of our life. All desire is radically vicious; it grows upon what it feeds. "Truly, one's appetites are never satiated with enjoyment. On the other hand, like sacrificial butter poured into the fire, they flame up with indulgence. Even if one enjoyed the whole Earth with its wealth, diamonds, and gold animals and women, one may not yet be satiated."[5] True renunciation, therefore, does not mean the adoption of the outward garb of a Sadhu, but the casting off of all attachment to earthly objects. "If men leading domestic mode of life be endued with self-control, they become the equals of Sannyasins. If, on the other hand, Sannyasins be endued with desire and aversion, and spouses, and honour, and pride and affection they become the equals of men, leading domestic modes of life. The wearing of brown clothes, shaving of the head bearing of the triple stick, and the Kamandalu, these are the outward signs of one's modes of life. These have no value in aiding one to the attainment of Emancipation.....Emancipation does not exist in poverty, nor is bondage to be found in affluence. One attains to Emancipation through knowledge along, whether one is indigent or affluent."[6] "The word mama (mine) consisting of two letters, is Death's self; while the opposite word na-mama (not mine), consisting of three letters is eternal Brahma."[7]

When once this fundamental condition is assured, a life of formal renunciation, too, becomes a veritable means to spiritual peace. It is said that things are often in the saddle and ride mankind. Renunciation assures us immunity from this tyranny of things. "I weighed poverty and sovereignty in a balance. Poverty weighed heavier than sovereignty and seemed to possess greater merits. Between poverty and sovereignty there is this great distinction, viz. that the sovereign, possessed of affluence, is always agitated by anxiety and seemed to be within the very jawas of death. As regards, however, the poor man, who in consequence of the divestment of all wealth has freed himself from hopes, and emancipated himself, neither fire, nor foe, nor death, nor robbers, can get the better of him. The very gods applaud such a man who wanders about according to his will, who lies down on the bare ground with his arm for a pillow, and who is possessed of tranquillity..... Without renunciation one can never attain to happiness. Without renunciation one can not obtain what is for one's highest good. Without renunciation one can never sleep at ease."[8]

A life of renunciation outward as well as inward belongs only to the last stage of a man's life. It is the consummation of an existence. A life of such severe discipline cannot be compulsory for all types of men. Only the Brahmins must resort to it.[9] And if it is resorted to at all, it should be done after doing one's duty fully. "Having studied the Vedas duly and the treatises on the duties of kings, having begotten children, and performed other acts of a like nature, having quaffed the Soma, and ruled over and protected all his subjects righteously, having performed the Rajasuya, the horse-sacrifice, and other great sacrifices, having invited the learned Brahmins for reciting the Scriptures, and made presents unto them according to their deserts, having obtained victories, small or great in battle, having placed on his throne, the son of his own loins, or some Kshatriya of good birth, for the protection of his subjects.....the Kshatriya, who, in old age, desires another mode of life, may, O king, adopt it."[10]

Self-control is absolutely essential to a life in which spiritual interests are predominant over worldly impulses. It is the first important step in the journey towards heaven. The Indian thinker, like Plato, compares the senses to horses, and wind to a charioteer; and realises that what is required is the discipline of these horses not their annihilation. "Heaven and hell are both dependent on our senses. When subdued, they lead to heaven; when indulged in they lead to perdition. This subjugation of the senses is the highest means of attaining spiritual light. Our senses are at the root of our spiritual advancement, as also at the root of our spiritual degradation. The self-restrained man, who acquires mastery over the six senses, inherent in our nature, is never tainted with sin, and consequently evil has no power over him. Man's corporeal self has been compared to a chariot, his soul to a charioteer, and his senses to horses. A dexterous man drives about without confusion, like a quiet charioteer, with well-broken horses."[11]

The definition of self-restraint is very comprehensive, as it includes, directly and indirectly, most moral qualities. "It has been said that in all the four modes of life, self restraint is the best of vows.....Forgiveness, patience, abstention, from injury, impartiality, truth, sincerity, conquest of the senses, cleverness, mildness, modesty, steadiness of speech, benevolence, freedom from malice, the union of all these is self-restraint. It also consists of veneration for the preceptors and universal compassion. The self-restrained man avoids both adulation and slander. Depravity, infamy, false speech, lust, covetousness, pride, arrogance, self-glorification, fear, envy, and disrespect, are all avoided by the self-restrained man. He never incurs obloquy. He is free from envy. He is never gratified with small acquisitions. He is even like the ocean which can never be filled. The man of self-restraint is never bound by the attachments that arise from earthly connections like to those involved in sentiments like these, I am thine.....There is only one fault in self-control. A person who has self-control is regarded by men as weak and imbecile. Its merits are many. By forgiveness (which is only another form of self-control), the man of self-control may easily acquire innumerable worlds. What need has a man of self-control for a forest? Similarly, of what use is the forest to him who has no self-control? That is a forest where the man of self-control dwells, and that is even a sacred asylum."[12]

Self-control only means that the highest and deepest principle within us should govern all the other principles of our nature. It is the first essential condition to a life of discipline and organization. "Speech and mind are to be subdued by the Understanding, which in its turn, is to be kept under control by the eye of knowledge."[13] Self-control is the triumph of reason within us. "That man, who abandoning Virtue and Wealth, pursues only Pleasure, reaps as the consequence of such conduct the destruction of his intelligence. The destruction of intelligence is followed by heedlessness that is at once destructive of virtue and wealth."[14]

Self-control, as Tennyson says, leads along with self-reverence and self-knowledge to sovereign power. All disciplined, organised life implies its possession. It is, therefore, absolutely necessary not only for spiritual peace, but worldly success as well. "He that hath his soul under control, and is endued with great indulgence, can rule a kingdom! Lust and wrath wean away a man from his possessions and enjoyments. Conquering these foes first, a king bringeth the earth under his subjection! Sovereignty over men is a great thing. Those that are of wicked souls may easily desire to win a kingdom, but they are not competent to retain a kingdom.....One that seeketh to conquer his counsellors without conquering his own self is soon vanquished himself, and is ruined."[15]

The value of penances is specially recognized by the Hindu faith. "They, that are possessed of knowledge, say that everything has penance for its root. The puissant Creator created all this universe with the aid of penances. Whatever things there are that are apparently unattainable, are sure to be won by the aid of penance. Without doubt, the Rishis obtained their six-fold divine attributes through penances. A person that drinks alcoholic liquors, one that appropriates the possession of others without their consent, one guilty of foeticide, one that violates one's preceptor's bed, are all cleansed by penances properly practised.....It was through penances that the gods acquired their superiority."[16]

There is the right type of penance, and there is the wrong kind of it. The Gita brings out the characteristics of both. "The men who perform severe austerities unenjoined by the scriptures, wedded to vanity and egoism, impelled by the forces of their desires and passions; Unintelligent, tormenting the aggregated elements forming the body, and Me also, seated in the inner body, know these domoniacal in their resolve."[17] Penances undertaken with a view to torture oneself or others are of the lowest type; those undertaken for ostentation are of the middle type; those inspired by faith and disinterestedness are of the highest type.[18] The test of a true penance is given : "The objects of sense, but not the relish for them, turn away from an abstemious dweller in the body; and even relish turneth away from him after the Supreme is seen."[19] There are three types of penances. "Worship given to gods, to twice-born, to the teachers, and to the wise, purity, straightforwardness, continence, and harmlessness, are called the austerity of the body. Speech causing no annoyance, truthful, pleasant and beneficial, the practice of the study of the scriptures, are called the austerity of the speech. Mental tranquillity, equilibrium, silence, self-control, purity of nature-this is called the austerity of the mind."[20]

The essence of all true mortification lies in the heart. "Abstention from injury, truthfulness of speech, benevolence, compassion, these are regarded as penances by the wise, and not the emaciation of the body. All kinds of crookedness mean death, and all kinds of sincerity are called Brahma."[21]

References

1. M.VI. 36-37.
2. M.VI. 39-75.
3. Bg. III.5.
4. M.II.4.
5. Adi. 69. 53-56.
6. Shanti. 325. 42-52.
7. Shanti. 13. 1-4.
8. Shanti. 175. 7-22.
9. Shanti. 62. 23.
10. Shanti. 62. 16-21.
11. Vana. 215. 19-27.
12. Shanti. 158. 6-36.
13. Shanti. 280. 12.
14. Shanti. 123. 15-16.
15. Udyoga. 129. 23-33.
16. Shanti. 159. 1-13.
17. Bg. XVII. 5-6.
18. Bg. XVII. 17-18.
19. Bg. II.59.
20. Bg. XVII. 14-16.
21. Shanti. 79. 18.

Chapter - XXII

FATE AND FREE WILL

(1)

A very early recognition of a Power other than ourselves over us is met with in the ancient Sanskrit literature. The gods control our very thoughts and hence govern our actions. "For over every thought thou (Agni) art the ruler; thou furtherest even the wisdom of the pious."[1] "Assist our holy thoughts, wake up our spirit."[2] "For ye are they who guard aright our bodies, ye are the rulers of our speech and vigour."[3] The gods send good thoughts to those who prosper and evil thoughts to those whom they set apart for destruction. "The gods do not protect men, taking up clubs in their hands after the manner of herdsmen. Unto them, however, they wish to protect, they grant intelligence. There is no doubt that one's objects meet with success in proportion to the attention he directs to righteousness and morality."[4] In the Atharva-veda, all causal power is attributed to Kala or Time or Destiny.[5] The all-powerful nature of Time is also brought out in the following passage : "Existence and non-existence, pleasure and pain, all have Time for their root. Time createth all things, and Time destroyeth all creatures. It is Time that burneth creatures and it is Time that extinguisheth fire. All states, the good and the evil, in the three worlds are caused by Time. Time cutteth short all things and createth them anew. Time alone is awake when all things are asleep; indeed Time is incapable of being overcome."[6]

A general recognition indeed is made of both the elements–the element of human effort, and of predestination.

The sense of the over-powering necessity making helpless creatures of us all, now and then breaks out. Rama, in reply to Bharata's insistence on his restoration, says that he is not the master of his wishes. All are driven hither and thither by destiny. Every collection is doomed to decay, every raised thing to fall, every union to separation, and every life to death.[7] Again, when he comes to know of Kaikeyi's boon, securing his banishment, he says that it was due to fate. Kaikeyi's nature was good; she could never mean harshness unless it was fate which guided her. The incomprehensible element in the situation is fate, to whose power all must bow down. No man can fight with fate; only our former deeds can regulate its working. Our life, our death, our happiness and our misery, our fear and our anger, our loss and our gain, are all due to fate. Even saints of powerful capacities for enduring pain give up their penances and fall victims to lust and anger, under the operation of destiny. Hence this unthought of and accidental stroke is due to fate. It is to be remembered that fate is the lord of all.[8] The operations of destiny are said to be as unavoidable as old age or death.[9] Sita takes her imprisonment quite philosophically as due to fate. In all states, in prosperity and in adversity, fate drags us like ropes.[10] "Like some brilliant body falling before the eyes, Fate depriveth us of reason; and man, tied as it were with a cord, submitteth to the sway of Providence."[11] This irresistible power of fate over all human affairs is one of the deepest convictions of Aryan consciousness. All beings from the most powerful to the feeble are alike subject to its sway.

This fatality does not work independently of God. There is nothing like a blind necessity over-ruling the human beings and turning and twisting their actions in any way it likes. No unconscious will, no blind chance governs our affairs in a mysterious way. The Hindu theology attributes ultimate agency to God. Fate is the name of the power which God wields over all beings, mortal and immortal. Man, however, is completely a creature of Fate or a mere agent of God. "There is one ordainer and no second; His control extends over the being that lies within the womb. Controlled by the great Ordainer, I go on as he sets me on, like water along a downward path. Knowing what is existence and what is emancipation, and understanding also that the latter is superior to the former, I do not, however, strive for attaining to it. Doing acts that tend towards the direction of virtue, and also those that tend towards the opposite direction, I go on as He sets me on. One gets those things that are ordained to be got. That which is to happen actually happens. One has to reside repeatedly in such wombs in which one is placed by the ordainer. One has no choice in the matter."[12] "The supreme Lord and Ordainer of all, ordaineth everything in respect of the weal and woe, the happiness and misery, of all creatures, even prior to their births guided by the acts of each, which are even like a seed. O hero, as a wooden doll is made to move its limbs by the wire-puller, so are creatures made to work by the Lord of all.....Like a pearl on its string, or a bull held fast by the cord passing through its nose, or a tree fallen from the bank into the middle of the stream, every creature followeth the command of the Creator, because imbued with his spirit, and established in Him."[13] "The Lord dwelleth in the hearts of all beings, O Arjuna, by His illusive power, causing all beings to revolve, as though mounted on a potter's wheel."[14] Man's impotence is well brought out by the following verse quoted in the Panchdashi : "I know what is right, yet I do not do it : I know what is wrong, yet I do not abstain from it. I merely follow the inner promptings of some mysterious Deity, working in my heart."[15]

If the element of necessity-be it fate or be it the Deity within the heart–is very much emphasised here, it is but meet to point out that the power of Karma, of human agency is equally well emphasised. Effort is no negligible factor in the constitution of the universe. It is equally fundamental. Here and now we see the causal efficiency, the fruitfulness of deeds : "Some say that success in the world to come depends upon work. Some declare that work should be shunned and that salvation is attainable by knowledge. The Brahmins know this that though one may have a knowledge of eatable things, yet his hunger will not be appeased unless he actually eats. Those branches of knowledge that help the doing of work, bear fruit, but not the others; for the fruit of work is of ocular demonstration. A thirsty person drinks water, and by that act, his thirst is allayed. This result proceeds, no doubt, from work. Therein lies the efficacy of work. If any one thinks that something else is better than work, I deem him weak, and his words meaningless. In other words, it is by virtue of work that the gods flourish; it is by work that wind blows. It is by virtue of work that the sleepless Surya (the sun) rises everyday, and becomes the cause of day and night; and Soma passes through the months and the fortnights, and the combinations of constellations. Fire is kindled of itself, and burns by virtue of work, doing good to mankind."[16]

Immediate success is not the uniform consequence of one's deeds; but one's own effort is a factor of considerable importance in it. Out of nothing will come nothing. "In all acts, the attainment of success is always uncertain. People still act, so that they sometimes succeed and sometimes do not. They, however, that abstain from action, never obtain success. In the absence of exertion, there is but one result, viz., the absence of success. There are, however, two results in the case of exertion, viz. the acquisition of success, or its non-acquisition."[17] Action is the law of our being and must be obeyed, whether it immediately promises results or not. "If a creature acteth not, its course of life is impossible. In the case of a creature, therefore, there must be action, and not inaction.....All the creatures in the world would be exterminated, if there were no action. If all acts bore no fruits, creatures would never have multiplied. It is even seen that creatures sometimes perform acts that have no fruits, for without acts, the course of life itself would be impossible."[18]

There is nothing like pure chance in the government of human affairs. A belief in the power of Destiny to the exclusion of all other agencies renders man impotent in the midst of his career. It is, therefore, regarded justly as a sign of great unmanliness to invoke the power of fate when we have capacity to influence events by our actions. "Those persons in the world who believe in destiny and those again who believe in chance, are both the worst among men. Those only that believe in the efficiency of acts are laudable. He that lieth at ease, without activity, believing in destiny alone, is soon destroyed like an unburnt earthen pot in water. So also he that believeth in chance and sitteth inactive though capable of activity, liveth not long, for his life is one of weakness and helplessness. For all this, however, a person should act."[19] "By devoted application, one acquires beauty, fortune, and riches of various kinds. Everything can be secured by exertion; but nothing can be gained through destiny alone, by a man that is wanting in personal exertion. "Even He the adorable Vishnu, who created three worlds, with the Daityas and all the gods, even He is engaged in austere penances in the bosom of the deep. If one's Karma bore no fruit, then all actions would become fruitless, and relying on Destiny men would become idlers."[20]

It follows that both the elements are equally necessary in bringing about the final consummation. Success is the result of the co-operation of many causes. A combination of destiny and effort is sufficient to ensure success. "Destiny does not help the man that is steeped in spiritual ignorance and advice. Even as a fire of small proportions, when fanned by the wind, becomes of mighty power, so does destiny, when joined with individual exertion, increase greatly in power. As by the diminution of oil in the lamp its light is extinguished, so does the influence of destiny, by the abatement of one's acts."[21] "Some (say that success originates) from divine grace; some, from nature; some, from time; and some from one's own efforts. But those, who are clever, desire fruits in the union of all these. As there can be no movement of a car with (only) one wheel, (even) so Daivam does not succeed without effort."[22] Man can, to a great extent, control his own actions, although of the success of those actions, he cannot be sure. As is well put, it is for man to *deserve* success, not to *command* it. Success is the outcome of many circumstances, some of which are under his control, and some are beyond it. Man's efforts are one important factor in the final result, but not the only factor. "How can one know beforehand what the consequences will be? Having exerted thyself, thou wilt know what the fruit of thy exertions will be. The tiller tilleth the soil with the plough, and soweth the seeds thereon. He, then, sitteth silent, for the clouds (atter that) are the causes that would help the seeds to grow into plants. If, however, the clouds favour him not, the tiller is absolved from all blame.....Whether there be success or failure there should be no despair, for success in acts dependeth upon the union of many circumstances. If one important element is wanting, success doth not become commensurate with our work, or doth not come at all. If, however, no exertion is made, there can be no success. Nor is there anything to applaud in the absence of all exertion. The intelligent, aided by their full might, bring means, place, time, auspicious rites, for the acquisition of prosperity. In fact, success in this world is said to depend upon acting according to time and circumstances."[23]

The expressions indicating the might of Circumstance, point unmistakably to a powerful current of opinion making for a theory of pure necessarianism. But here we must remember some essential points. In the first place, the belief in fate is invoked only in those situations where effort is unrighteous or impossible. Under such circumstances, a conviction that events are being ordered by a power above us, in a mysterious but perfectly rational way, becomes of very great value in reconciling us to our situations, and soothing our souls. In situations where effort appears both just and possible, it is always to be made. Secondly, the power alluded to as fate is nothing but the power of our own deeds done in previous existences. This is the unknown factor in every situation; it is not pure chance or divine caprice. Necessity takes a more reasonable form of one's own deeds influencing the events from behind. Even in this life we feel that every act we do, every habit we form means for us so much loss of liberty. It is the same with the deeds of our previous lives. "The success of a work lies in destiny and efforts; of them efforts of a pristine birth are manifested in destiny."[24] Karman is of three kinds : Samchit; Prarabdha; and Kriyamana. The accumulated result of previous deeds is called Samchit; that portion of which has begun to take effect under the influence of which our present life shapes itself is known as Prarabdha; and this is another name for destiny or fate; those actions which we are doing form Kriyamana. We have lost all liberty with regard to the two former types of works; but as regards Kriyamana, it is not so. The idea of fate, therefore, in the Hindu faith, is not an inexplicable idea; it does not stand for pure necessity or mere chance. Fate is the capital, while our present Karma is the income. If we merely centre our attention on enjoyment, our capital will be gradually lost. Fresh efforts are necessary to add to the capital of our good deeds. It is here that the usefulness of our own efforts, our Purushartha lies. We are governed by the past; but we can govern the future because our present deeds will be crystallised into destiny.

(2)

The factor of the greatest importance in human life is Karma. The possibility of Karma is a special characteristic of the human beings. Moral life is a prerogative of man. Moral responsibility does not exist in the animal kingdom. It is all unmoral. It is only the civilised human beings who are capable of leading a moral life. They are conscious of a better and a worse; they are also capable of selecting the former and rejecting the latter. This capacity constitutes the special privilege of man, although it is his special danger also. Man can hope to rise or fear to fall. Karma or moral law governs the entire realm of existence. All beings are alike subject to its laws. "Indeed all creatures live according to the inspiration of their former life; even the Creator and the ordainer of the universe."[25]

All the lower creatures are entirely dependent as regards

their birth and destiny on the law of Karma. Man also is subject to its laws; but it is his special glory to make that very law the instrument of his future rise. "Of all births, the status of humanity is preferable even if one has to become a Chandala. Indeed, O monarch, that order of birth (viz. humanity) is the foremost, since by becoming a human being, one succeeds in rescuing one's self by meritorious acts."[26] Shankara says in the Vivekachudamani that the birth in the kingdom of humanity is exceedingly difficult to obtain, still more difficult it is to be born as a male; then it is a further step to be born into the order of Brahmins; and lastly to be fired with thirst for emancipation is the most difficult of all acquisitions. Manu also fixes the hierarchy of beings on the principle of the capacity for moral life. "Of the created things the animate creatures, among these the intelligent ones are the highest; of the intelligent creatures men are the highest, and among men the Brahmins are the highest. Among Brahmins the erudite ones are the highest; among the erudite Brahmins, those who think it their duty to perform the Shastraic rites are the highest, among those, those who perform such rites are the highest, and among the performers of rites the knowers of Brahma are the highest."[27] All creatures are capable of activity; but man alone has the capacity of moral activity. He alone entertains the idea of good and thinks it desirable to shape his life under its influence. "Every conscious creature should certainly act in this world. It is only the immobile, and not other creatures, that may live without acting.- The calf, immediately after its birth, sucketh the mother's tear.....Amongst mobile creatures man differeth in this respect that he aspireth to affect his course of life in this and the other world by means of his acts."[28] Man is distinguished to advantage not only from the lower animals, but also from gods. The land of gods is known as Bhoga-bhumi–the place of enjoyment; the earth is called Karma-bhumi the theatre of moral life.[29] Other creatures can enjoy and suffer; gods can *enjoy*; but man alone can *act*.

The law of Karma is inexorable in its operation. It is the

application of the category of causality to the moral sphere. The whole moral life is securely based on the operation of this law. Man's good and evil deeds lead inevitably to corresponding good and evil consequences "Man's actions are either good or bad, and he undoubtedly reaps their fruits. The ignorant man having attained to an abject state, grossly abuses the gods, not knowing that it is the consequence of his own evil Karma."[30] "A sinful person, by committing sin, is over-taken by evil consequences. A virtuous man, by practising virtue, reapeth great happiness. Therefore, a man should, rigidly resolved, abstain from sin. Sin, repeatedly perpetrated destroyeth intelligence; and the man who hath lost intelligence repeatedly committeth sin. Virtue, repeatedly practised, enhanceth intelligence; and the man whose intelligence hath increased, repeatedly practiseth virtue."[31]

The law of the conservation of energy operates in the moral kingdom; no good act is ever lost nor an evil one. Nor does any individual suffer for other's evils nor enjoy for other's merits. "In the world of men, no man reaps the consequences of another man's Karma. Whatever one does, he is sure to reap the consequences thereof; for the consequences of the Karma that is once done, can never be obviated. The virtuous become endowed with great virtues, and sinful men become the perpetrators of wicked deeds. Men's actions follow them; and influenced by them they are born again."[32] No outward or apparent failure encountered in a course of righteousness takes away a man's share of merit in it. "If a man striving to the best of his abilities to perform a virtuous act meets with failure, I have not the least doubt that the merit of that act becomes his, not with standing such failure."[33] The Gita gives assurance that no one engaged in his duty ever suffers or is lost. "In this there is no loss of effort, nor is there any transgression. Even a little of this Dharma protects from great fear."[34] Arjuna asks Krishna as regards the destiny of the *Yoga-bhrishta* (Those who have fallen from high ascetic practices). "Fallen from both, is he lost like a separated cloud or not?" Krishna replies : "Neither here, nor hereafter, doth ruin exist for him, since none who performs good acts comes by an evil end."[35] The course of events is not always smooth; there are apparent set backs for the virtuous and apparent triumphs for the wicked. "Whether righteous or sinful, acts are never destroyed. Sometimes, the happiness due to good acts remains concealed and covered in such a way that it does not display itself in the case of the person who is sinking in life's ocean till his sorrows disappear. After sorrow has been exhausted (by endurance), one begins to enjoy (the fruits of) one's good acts."[36]

Man's dependence upon the past is very great. The acts of previous lives are instrumental in shaping his present destiny. The theory of transmigration is merely the extension of the doctrine of Karma. The doctrine of Karma requires that justice must hold indomitable sway over the destinies of all beings, and that no being should get an atom of happiness or misery except as a consequence of its own deeds. This fact requires that there should be no waste of actions done (कृत-प्रणाश:); nor should one suffer for what one has not done. (अकृता-भ्यागम:) This is frequently asserted. "One never has to enjoy or endure the good and bad acts of another. Indeed, one enjoys and endures the fruits of only those acts that one does oneself."[37] But if there is neither previous life, nor after life, it is evident that the law of Karma would be nowhere. It is only the hypothesis of transmigration that can establish completely the law of Karma. The fact that all the efforts of a man are not successful shows that the effect of former acts is not a myth.[38] "And if the fruits of our exertion were not dependent on anything else, people would attain the object of their desire, by simply striving to attain it. It is seen that able intelligent, and diligent persons are baffled in their efforts, and do not attain fruits of their actions. On the other hand, persons who are always active in injuring others and practising deception on the world, lead a happy life. There are some who attain prosperity without any exertion. And there are others, who with the utmost exertion, are unable to achieve their dues."[39] All the differences in moral and intellectual calibre of different persons are expli-cable on this hypothesis of pre-existence. In the Brihadaranyaka Upanishad, it is said that three factors accompany a soul in its journey : "his knowledge, his actions, and his previous experience."[40] Certain impressions are left in the soul by the former experiences; and these called *Vasanas* influence a man's actions. No man can start any action or enjoy the fruits of previous actions except under the influence of this factor. It is *Vasana* which renders differences among men as regards skill and talent and character possible.[41] No man attains cleverness in any subject without its study; yet some are born clever in some subjects. That is due to the previous experiences of the individual. The past deeds of a man take the form of an *Apurvam*. "It is clear that a deed cannot effect a result at some future time, unless, before passing away, it gives birth to some unseen result; we, therefore, assume that there exists some result which we call *Apurva,* and which may be reviewed either as an imperceptible after state of the deed or an antecedent state of the result."[42]

The transmigration of souls becomes, therefore, one of the fundamental beliefs of the Hindus. There is a very long chain of births and rebirths for each being, determined by its Karma. "By the performance of virtuous actions it attains to the state of the gods, and by a combination of good and evil, it acquires the human state, by indulgence in sensuality and similar demoralising practices, it is born in the lower species of animals; and by sinful acts, it goes to the infernal regions."[43]

The deeds of a man are followed by two-fold retribution; the one takes place in the other world, the other requires a rebirth here. "After the fruit of that set of works which is requited in the other world has been enjoyed, the remaining other set of works whose fruits are to be enjoyed in this world constitutes the so-called *Anushaya* (residue) with which the souls redescend."[44] The works whose operation is obstructed by other works leading to fruits of a contrary nature last for a long time. Again, some deeds like the murder of a Brahmin require more than one existence. Here a distinction is drawn between ritual and moral works.[45] Some are of opinion that moral works (चारित्र) condition a man's entry into another birth, and not *Anushaya* which is recompensed in the life beyond. Another teacher distinguishes between the two, but thinks that the two factors are closely connected with each other. For the practice of rites demands certain moral fitness. "The Vedas do not purify a man without character." And for good conduct a man will receive a certain surplus reward. Character, therefore, is included in the residue of works which conditions a man's rebirth. Badarayana, however, does not admit any substantial distinction between the two.

(3)

Now the question is : is man free? Or is he a mere helpless agent in the hands of other powers? There are three agencies : man, nature and God. "Indeed, like a wooden machine, man is not an agent (in all he does). In this respect three opinions are entertained. Some say that everything is ordained by God : some say that acts are the results of our own free will; and others say that our acts are the result of those of our past lives."[46] For all practical purposes, man is the author of his own actions, and hence responsible for them. "If it is Time that causes weal and woe and birth and death, why do physicians then seek to administer medicines to the sick? If it is Time that is moulding everything, what need is there of medicines? Why do people deprived of their senses by grief, indulge in such delirious rhapsodies? If Time, according to thee, be the cause of acts, how can religious merit be "acquired by persons performing religious merit be acquired by persons performing religious acts?"[47] "The man, who destitute of exertion tills his land disregarding the season of rain, never succeeds in obtaining a harvest. He, who takes every day food that is nutritive, be it bitter, or astringent, or sweet, or palatable, enjoys a long life. He, on the other hand, who disregards whole some food and takes that which is injurious without an eye to consequences, soon meets with death. Destiny and exertion exist, depending upon each other."[48] "Man, having first settled some purpose in his mind, accomplisheth it himself working with the aid of his intelligence. We, therefore, say that man himself is the cause (of what he doth). It is impossible to number the acts of men, for mansions and towns are the results of man's acts. Intelligent men know, by the help of their intellect, that oil may be had from sesame, curds from milk, and that food may be cooked by means of igniting fuel. They know also the means for accomplishing these. And knowing them, they afterwards set themselves, with proper appliances, to accomplish them. And creatures support their lives by the results achieved in these directions by their own acts. If a works is executed by a skilled workman, it is executed well. From differences (in characteristics) another work may be said to be that of an unskilful hand. If a person were not, in the matter of his acts, himself the cause thereof, then sacrifices would not bear any fruits in his case, nor would anybody be a disciple or a master. It is because a person is himself the cause of his work that he is applauded when he achieveth success, and censured if he fails. If a man were not the cause of his acts, how would all this be justified?"[49]

Man, indeed, determines what his actions will be, but he is not free in determining his acts. Man's past actions govern his present acts; and he is helplessly driven to do acts good or bad, as the past deeds behind him are good or bad. It would seem, at first, that man is not free as regards the results of his acts but he is free as regards the acts themselves. "Householders may, without any compunction, enjoy wealth and other possessions that are obtained without exertion. But the duties of their order, they should discharge with the aid of exertion."[50] But the acts of previous lives are all-powerful not only as regards what a man would enjoy and suffer, what order of existence he will belong to, what gifts and faculties he will possess, what sort of circumstances he will have in life; but also what actions he will initiate and what character he will form. "As vessels of white brass, when steeped in liquified gold or silver, catch the hue of these metals, even so a living creature, who is completely dependent upon the acts of his past lives, takes his colour from the character of those acts. Nothing can sprout forth without a seed."[51] There is no freedom for a man as long as he is within the realm of Prakriti or nature. The law of Karma is supreme in this sphere. "As the tree is evolved out of a seed, so also the world is evolved under the operation of the Karma of all creatures."[52] There is no independence for a man in the phenomenal world. Karma is frequently represented as a form of bondage. "The world is bound by the law of Karma." "A being is bound by Karma." "They (i.e., those who perform mere Karma) have to go and return, and never attain independence anywhere."[53] "There is no independence for a being led by the law of Karma."[54]

What is this Prakriti? It is not outward nature, the play of the outer forces which governs man. It is the peculiarity of man that Prakriti has to govern him from within, not without. It is defined as follows; "Nature (Prakriti) is the Samskara (the latent self-reproductive impression) of the past acts of Dharma and Adharma, manifesting itself at the commencement of the present birth."[55] To say that man is governed by Prakriti is to say that he is governed by his own past, by his own character, which is the result of his past deeds.

What we call freedom of will consists in attributing to our own agency the actions done by us. This consciousness of initiative itself is due to Prakriti. Far from leaving us passive and helpless, Prakriti creates a powerful sense of individuality in us through which we pose as authors of our own acts. Prakriti, therefore, dose not extinguish responsible life, but rather itself creates the possibility of responsible life. But for this Prakriti there will be no freedom of will, but for Prakriti there will be no moral life. This sense of individuality in us is called Ahamkara and this is the root of all action. "अहंकार एव हि सर्वस्य प्रवृत्तिबीजं दृष्टे लोके।" By creating within us this sense of self, Prakriti becomes the very basis of all life whatsoever. "That the primeval natural nescience (अविद्या) leaves room for all practical life or activity-whether ordinary or based on the Veda–we have explained more than once."[57]

The basis of our moral life, therefore, is egoistic. Ego is the root of morality; ego is the root of immorality. Prakriti acts on our ego through no outside pressure, but through its own attractions and repulsions (राग and द्वेष) या हि पुरुषस्य प्रकृतिः सा रागद्वेषपुरः सरैव स्वकार्ये पुरुषं प्रवर्तयति।[58] This ego with its Raga and Dwesha is fundamental in all activity. Ego is, therefore, the presupposition in all intellectual and moral activity. "The mutual superimposition of the Self and the Non-self, is the presupposition on which are based all the practical distinctions-those made in ordinary life as well as those laid down in the Veda, between means of knowledge, objects of knowledge (and knowing persons), and all scriptural texts, whether they are concerned with injunctions and prohibitions or with final release. "This is thus explained. The means of right knowledge cannot operate unless there be a knowing personality, and because the existence of the latter depends on the erroneous notion that the body, the senses, and so on, are identical with, or belong to, the Self of the knowing person. For without the employment of the senses, perception and the other means of right knowledge cannot operate. And without a basis (i.e., the body) the senses cannot act. Nor does anybody act by means of the body on which the nature of the Self is not superimposed. Nor can, in the absence of all that, the Self, which, in its own nature, is free from all contact, become a knowing agent. And if there is no knowing agent, the means of right knowledge cannot operate."[59]

Shankara realises the importance of freedom of action for responsible moral life. "If every being acts according to Prakriti only, and there is none which has no Prakriti of its own, then, there being possibly no scope of personal exertion. (पुरुषकारस्य विषयानुपपत्तेः) the teaching of the Shastras will be quite purposeless."[60] Morality requires that man's freedom of will must be preserved. Man's capacity for initiating actions, good or bad, is therefore fully granted. But there is no capacity in him to initiate any and every action at his sweet will. There can be no arbitrariness, entire indeterminism, complete lawlessness in his life. Man is determined in his choice of actions and his capacity of originating them by his birth, heredity, education, habit, circumstances, and character. But he is not determined from without as inert objects are; nor is he determined by any power and agency other than himself. He is himself the author of his destiny; he is the creator of his future and master of situation in every respect. In very few theories of life, the part played by man's efforts in making up his own character and destiny is so completely insisted on, as in the Hindu view of life. Man's actions are the result as is said of character and environment or rather the result of the mutual action and reaction of character and environment upon each other. But man's character is the result of his own past acts; and his environment is favourable to him or otherwise according as his own past deeds are good or bad. The Hindu view, therefore, regards Karma as the central factor, the basic foundation of a man's character and destiny. No blind fate, no mysterious necessity, no high-handed Providence predetermines man's actions arbitrarily. But his own past deeds, his own Karma regulates his character, and governs its future development.

Prakriti has paramount sway over the destinies of man; it rules all persons by its law of Karma. But neither Prakriti nor Karma, neither man's past nor his present Karma, is an autocratic entity. All ultimate power is lodged in God. सर्वास्वेव प्रवृतिष्वीश्वरो हेतुकर्तेति श्रुतेरवसीयते।[61] "And God, the Ordainer of the universe, judging according to the acts of former lives, distributeth among men their portions in this world. Whatever acts good or bad, a person performeth, know, that they are the results of God's arrangements agreeable to the acts of a former life. This body is only the instrument in the hands of God, for doing the acts that are done. Itself inert it doth as God urgeth it to do. It is the supreme Lord of all who maketh all creatures do what they do."[62]

Shankara attempts to reconcile the activity of the human beings with the omnipotence of God. "For although the soul has its own imperfections such as passion and so on for motives, and although ordinary experience does not show that the Lord is a cause in occupations such as ploughing and the like, yet we ascertain from Scripture that the Lord is a causal agent in all activity. For the Scripture says : 'He makes him whom He wishes to lead up from these worlds to do a good deed,' and again, 'He, who dwelling in the Self pulls the Self from within."[63] "Scripture represents the Lord not only as the giver of all fruits, but also as the causal agent with reference to all actions, whether good or bad."[64] But why is the soul responsible for its deeds? "The Lord makes the soul act, having regard to the efforts made by it, whether meritorious or non-meritorious./...He arranges favourable or unfavorable circumstances for the souls, with a view to their former efforts.....The Lord indeed causes the soul to act (करयति), but the soul acts (करोति) itself. Moreover, the Lord, in causing it to act now, has regard to its former efforts, and He caused acts in a former existence, having regard to efforts previous to that existence, a regresses, against which, considering the eternity of the Samsara, no objections can be raised. But how is it known that the Lord has regard to the efforts made (in former existences)? The Sutra replies, from the purportlessness etc. of injunctions and prohibitions.....On the other alternative, they would be without purport, and the Lord would in fact be enjoined in the place of injunctions and prohibitions, since the soul would be absolutely dependent. And then the Lord might requite with evil, those who act according to the injunctions, and with good, men, doing what is forbidden, which would subvert the authoritativeness of the Veda. Moreover, if the Lord were absolutely without any regard, it would follow that also the ordinary efforts of man are without any purport, and so likewise the special conditions of place, time, and cause."[65]

The Hindu view has very great regard for the law of causation and the ultimate agency of God. The former fact is the demand of science and ordinary life; the latter is the demand of religious life. The laws of Karma are supreme in the empirical sphere; man's present comes helplessly out of his past. Every act of man is severely determined by his own past acts; no act of man is free. The pure Ego or the free Self stands apart; and the empirical Ego or Ahamkara is merged in the power of Prakriti. The autonomy of Self is not denied; but it is explained away.

References

1. Rg. IV. 6.1.
2. Rg. IV. 50.1.
3. Rg. VI. 51.6.
4. Udyoga. 35.52.
5. XIX. 53-54.
6. Adi. I. 271-275.
7. R.II. 105. 15-17.
8. R.II. 22. 15-24. 30.
9. R.III. 64.75.
10. R.V. 3.
11. Sabha. 83. 18.
12. Shanti. 233. 9-12.
13. Vana. 30. 30-36.
14. Bg. XVIII. 61.
15. Panchadashi. 6.176.
16. Udyoga. 29. 5-16.
17. Udyoga. 35. 26-29.
18. Vana. 32. 3-20.
19. Vana. 32. 25-59.
20. Anu. 9. 13-31.
21. Anu. 9. 44-46.
22. Yaj. I. 350-351.
23. Vana. 32. 3-20.
24. Yaj. I. 349.
25. Vana. 32. 3-20.
26. Shanti. 303. 31-32.
27. M. I. 96-97.

28. Vana. 32. 3-20.
29. Adi. 64. 39.
30. Vana. 213. 5-12.
31. Udyoga. 35. 72-75.
32. Vana. 213. 22-23.
33. Udyoga. 93. 7.
34. Bg. II. 40.
35. Bg. VI. 40.
36. Shanti. 296. 11-19.
37. Shanti. 296. 21.
38. Vana. 32. 3-20.
39. Vana. 213. 5-12.
40. Br. Up. IV. 4.2.
41. Br. Up. IV. 4.2.
42. S.B. III. 2. 39.
43. Vana. 213. 22-33.
44. S.B.III. 1.8.
45. S.B.III, I.9-11.
46. Udyoga. 159. 14-15.
47. Shanti. 139. 56-57.
48. Shanti. 139. 80-85.
49. Vana. 32. 3-20.
50. Shanti. 301. 35.
51. Shanti. 296. 11.
52. Br. Up. Com. I. Introduction.
53. Bg. Com. VIII. 19.
54. Br. Up. Com. 4.4.2.
55. Bg. Com. III. 38.
56. Bg. Com. VIII.4.
57. S.B. III.2.15.
58. Bg.Com. III.34.
59. S.B.I. Introduction.
60. Bg. Com. III. 33.
61. S.B. II. 3.41.
62. Vana, 32. 21-24.
63. S.B.II. 3.4.
64. S.B.III.2.41.
65. S.B. II.3.42.

Chapter - XXIII

THEOLOGICAL AND METAPHYSICAL IDEAS

(1)

The Hindu teachings have an esoteric and an exoteric side. One fact that they expressed so well was the existing diversity of talents and temperaments. "न ह्यविकारेऽनन्ते ब्रह्मणि सर्वैः पुंभिः शक्या बुद्धिः स्थापयितुं मन्दमध्यमोत्तमबुद्धित्वात्पुंसामिति।"[1] It is not possible, says Shankara, for all persons to understand the Timeless and Changeless Absolute; because there is an infinite variety of grades of intellect. The doctrinal differences in Hindu theology are calculated to meet this psychological fact. Hindu sages did not want to create a structure of faith for the metaphysical few only; nor for the vulgar many. Hence we meet with the most abstract conceptions of the Deity along with the most concrete forms at the other level.

The fundamental unity of God beneath all the apparent diversities of His manifestations is a universally accepted fact of Hinduism. The Vedas say : एकं सद्विप्राः बहुधा वदन्ति। "Reality is one; sages call it by various names." "They call him Indra, Mitra, Varuna, Agni, and he is heavenly nobly-winged Garutman. To what is one sages give many a title : they call it Agni, Yama, Matarishwan."[2] "That which is one hath unto all developed."[3] "That which is earlier than this earth and heaven before the Asuras and Gods had being, what was the germ primeval which the waters received where all the gods were seen together."[4] The Upanishads centre round the unity of spiritual being. "He goes from death to death who sees any difference here."[5] The later epic and Pauranik ages never lost sight of this essential characteristic.[6]

Now there are two conceptions of God in the Vedic literature–one sets forth the metaphysical picture of Him as the absolute, the other sets forth the more concrete picture of a Personal God. God is both personal and impersonal; personal from the point of view of unregenerate man, yet clothed in human weaknesses and subject to human limitations; impersonal from the point of view of rigorous truth, from the point of view of purest and highest thought. There is no essential contradiction between these two; man gradually rises from the one to the other. "The difficulty of those whose minds are set on the Unmanifested is greater; for the path of the Unmanifested is hard for the embodied to reach."[7] This is the truth of imageworship. "Here in this way does Brahman become the object of worship, because He, as Brahman, is superimposed on the Pratikas, just as Vishnu etc. are superimposed upon images."[8] Impersonal Brahman, has been translated in the language of man for the purposes of meditation.

The prominent characteristics of Godhead are His infinity, omnipresence, omnipotence, essential timelessness, and spacelessness. He is the innermost fact, the soul of souls. "In the beginning Brahman was all this. He was one and infinite; infinite in the East, infinite in the south, infinite in the west, infinite in the North, above and below and every where infinite. East and other regions do not exist for Him, nor across, nor above, nor below. The highest Self is not to be fixed. He is unlimited, unborn, not to be reasoned about, not to be conceived."[9] "The wise who know the Self as bodiless within the bodies, as unchanging among changing, as great and omnipresent, do not grieve." "He who dwells in all beings and within all beings, whom all beings do not know, whose body all things are, and who pulls all beings within, is thy Self, the puller within, the immortal"[10]

Equally prominent is the conception of personal God who

is to us now a friend, now a Father, now a king. Above all, He is the Creator of the Universe. "That from whence these beings are born, that by which when born they live, that into which they enter at their death, try to know that. That is Brahman"[11] "For, gracious Shatakratu, thou hast ever been a Mother and a Sire to us."[12] "I am the Father of this universe, the Mother, the Supporter, the Grandsire, the Holy One to be known.....the Path, Husband, Lord, Witness, Abode, Shelter, Lover, Origin, Dissolution, Foundation, Treasure-house, Seed imperishable."[13]

(2)

The question is : what duties does a man owe to God? Man's progress is conceived in Hindu Scriptures as gradual approach to God and ultimate submergence in Him. Four broad paths are open to him : Yoga, Bhakti, Karma, and Jnana. Yoga is defined as mental concentration[14] Many exercises in self control are mentioned. Among these are Ahimsa or harmlessness-the result of which is that even the enemies begin to love a Yogi (तत्संनिधौ वैरत्याग:); Truthfulness, enabling him to secure fruits without work; abstinence from theft-the result is that all jewels are at his disposal; celibacy resulting in bodily and mental lustre; and non-covetousness enabling one to know of one's past. Purity gives him a right attitude towards the body; contentment gives him exquisite happiness; austerities enable him to perfect the vigour of the senses; Devotion to God gives one sight of God and so on.

The candidate for Yoga should avoid overeating, underfeeding, dreaminess, and too much wakefulness. All activities of his must have the stamp of moderation.[15] "Dissociated from all attachments, abstemious in diet, and subduing all the senses, one should fix one's mind on the soul. When one does not hear, and smell, and taste and see, when one is not conscious of any touch, when one's mind becomes perfectly free from every purpose, when one is not conscious of anything, when one becomes like a piece of wood, then is one called to be in Yoga."[16] There is perfect identification of the knower, the known, and knowledge.

Another great pathway to Reality is Bhakti or Devotion. It is defined as 'supreme love' (परमप्रेमरूपा) (Bhakti-sutras 2). It takes various forms : "It takes the course of attachment to the attributes and greatness of God, attachment to His beauty, attachment to His worship, attachment to His service, attachment to His friendship, attachment to parental affection towards Him, attachment to Him (as) of a beloved wife, attachment to self-consecration, attachment to permanent self-effacement. "[17] The devotee must not give up his business or the performance of his social duties, but all ideas of conse-quences must be left to God. All worship of women, of wealth, and association with unbelievers should be avoided. All forms of pride must be given up. All distinctions of birth, learning, appearance, family, wealth, observance, and the like cease to have any efficacy for the God-intoxicated man. The practice of such virtues as veracity, non-resistance should be looked to.[18] The Bhakta lays aside even the Vedas.[19] Supreme content-ment, perfect self-control, unbending will, surrender to God, freedom from joy, anger, grief; freedom from malice and partiality, equality with respect to praise and censures, friends and foes, varieties of temperature, are some of the characte-ristics of the God-intoxicated.[20] He never fears nor inspires others with fear. But above all, he is full of love for all beings. God is above all to be worshipped in humanity. "He who seeth Me everywhere, and seeth everything in Me, of him I will never lose hold, and he shall never lose hold of Me. He, who established in unity, worshippeth Me, *abiding in all beings,* that Yogi liveth in Me."[21] The supreme secret (सर्वगुह्यतमं) is thus revealed : "Merge thy mind in Me, be my devotee, sacrifice to Me, prostrate thyself before Me, thou shalt come even to Me; Abandoning all duties, come into Me alone for shelter; sorrow not, I will liberate thee from all sins."[22]

A third road leading to God is Karma. There is a conflict of opinions about the respective efficacy of morality and knowledge. Morality as well as ritualism may be the most as regards the attainment of the final objective. चित्तस्य शुद्धये कर्म न तु वस्तूपलब्धये। "But frail, in truth, are those boats, the sacrifices .....Fools who praise this as the highest good, are subject again and again to old age and death. Let a Brahmin, after he has examined all these worlds which are gained by works, acquire freedom from all desires Nothing that is eternal can be gained by what is not eternal."[23] By acts a living creature is destroyed. By knowledge, however, he becomes emancipated. "Through acts one is forced to take rebirth after death. Through knowledge one is transformed into that which is Eternal, Unmanifest, and Immutable.....The fruit that one obtains of acts consists of pleasure and pain, of existence and non-existence. By knowledge one attains to that whither there is no occasion for grief, whither one becomes freed from both birth and death, whither one is not subject to decrepitude.....Reaching that stage, they cast equal eyes on everything, become universal friends, and devoted to the good of all creatures."[24]

It is not meant that mere intellectual culture is sufficient to secure one an access to the kingdom of God. Character is equally necessary आचारहीनं न पुनन्ति वेदाः। But a rigorous moralist of the Kantian type who eschews all elements from his life except the consciousness of duty is very far from the goal. An element of Bhakti, of pure joy is equally necessary. The result is a synthesis of willing, thinking, and feeling. Yoga and Karma develop willing; knowledge develops thinking, and Bhakti develops feeling. "That Self cannot be gained by the Veda, nor by understanding, nor by much learning. He whom the Self chooses, by him the Self can be gained. The self chooses him as his own."[25] A life of Karma is despised because Karma is finite. It is its necessary limitation to a narrow ego and immediate consequences which renders it so circumscribed in its scope. The highest life assuredly is not a life of mere repose, or idleness : it is supremely active. But for actions to have any value, they must be done from the purest and highest motives. The whole mental mood, the fundamental psychology must be changed. Then a life of निष्कामकर्म selfless actions done in the name of God is the highest of all types of lives. Action is a veritable accident; the consciousness which inspires it, the character which stands behind it, is fundamental. Actions mechanically done, however high they may look, in obedience to external stimuli, in obedience to the call of the ego are of the earth, earthy. It is the personality behind them which lifts them up from the egocentric plane to cosmocentric plane. "कर्मण्येवाधिकारस्ते मा फलेषु कदाचन।" This sentence marks indeed the high water-mark of the development of our ethical consciousness. But it is not to be understood in Kantian sense merely; all reference to consequences so far as these concern the petty good and petty evil of our worldly self must be eschewed. Duty for duty's sake further means that it should proceed not from our Ahamkara, but it should be inspired with the consciousness that the Self of the universe speaks and acts through us, that God works through his instruments.

(3)

The one most essential virtue which religious consciousness requires is faith. तं यथा यथोपासते तदेव भवति। Man's convictions are the most dominant factor about him. "श्रद्धामयोऽयं पुरुष:।" "The faith of each is shaped to his own nature. The man consists of his faith; that which his faith is, he is even that."[26] "The man who is full of faith obtaineth wisdom, and he also who hath mastery over his senses; and, having obtained wisdom, he attains swiftly to the supreme peace. But the ignorant, faithless, doubting self goeth to destruction; neither this world, nor that beyond, nor happiness is there for the doubting self."[27] But belief that is idealised here is belief grounded in intelligence, not blind, uncritical belief. यदेव विद्यया करोति श्रद्धयोपनिषदा तदेव वीर्यवत्तरं भवति।[28]

Any scepticism with regard to the fundamentals of faith is in the highest degree unhealthy. It is called नास्तिकता—atheism. The passion for 'Nay' must not triumph ultimately over the passion for 'Yea.' Man must rise upon the ruins of negations to more positive affirmations. "Man winneth faith by the yearnings of the heart, and opulence by Faith. Faith in the early morning, Faith at noon-day we invocate. Faith at the setting of the Sun. Oh Faith endow us with belief."[29] "The foolish, faithless, rudely speaking niggards, without belief, or sacrifice, or worship. Far, far away hath Agni chased these Dasyus."[30] "The man who brings no sacrifice, inhuman, godless, infidel, Him let his friend the mountain cast to rapid death."[31]

The Mahabharata deprecates all doubts with regard to the foundations of belief. "The fool that doubteth religion and disregardeth virtue, proud of the proff derived from his own reasoning regardeth not other proofs and holdeth the Rishis who are capable of knowing the future as mad men. The fool regardeth only the external world capable of gratifying his senses and is blind to everything else."[32] "Disregard of the Vedas, disobedience to the dictates of the scriptures and violation of all wholesome restraints are productive of self-destruction."[33] It is clearly seen that society in those days tolerated the existence of other beliefs and faiths. There was no persecution for those who doubted or dissented from the normal track. Many renowned and respectable scholars used to wander about calling themselves Samkhyas and disbelieving in God. Constant discussions in assemblies were a normal feature of those times. Hence we find various types mentioned; materialists, utilitarians, scoffers, and sophisters. "In my former life I had much useless learning. I always sought for reasons and had very little faith. I was a slanderer of the Vedas. I was destitute of the (four-fold) objects of life and was devoted to that science of argumentation which is based upon ocular or tangible proofs. I used to utter words based on (Plausible) reasons. Indeed, in assemblies, I always spoke of reasons. I used to speak irreverently of the declarations of the Shrutis and address Brahmins in dominating tones. I was an unbeliever, sceptical of everything, proud of my learning. This status of jackal that I have obtained in this life is the consequence of those sins of mine!"[34] Selling the Vedas, criticizing them, reducing them to a written form are all sins.[35]

A desire to keep one's mind open when the gravest questions confront us is not a mark of intellectual or spiritual strength. It is a mark of spiritual poverty. The thing that counts in action, in the battle of life, that turns the scale is not cold, intellectual opinion but warm, impulsive belief. Belief is action, belief is life, belief is character, belief is man. To say that "much can be said on both sides" may argue a very clever mind, but it is positively sinful when decisions are to be taken with regard to the fundamentals of life or the essentials of immediate action. All other discrepancies can be atoned for; but scepticism on points the most clear or most vital goes to the root of the matter and vitiates the very springs of life, of action. Man is not a bloodless ballet of categories. He is not a logic-chopping machine. He is above all a force, capable of turning this way or that the tide of social progress. "Faith is superior to the merit born of (Vedic) recitations and meditation. An act vitiated by defect of speech is saved by Faith. An act vitiated by defect of mind is saved by Faith. But neither speech nor mind can save an act that is vitiated by want of faith. The offerings in sacrifices of a person that is pure, but wanting in Faith : and of another that is impure but endued with Faith, the deities had regarded equal.....Abstaining from all faults of behaviour, he who betakes himself to Faith, is sanctified. What need hath such a person of penances, or of conduct, or of endurance?"[36]

More things are wrought by prayers than the world dreams of. Prayers strengthen gods whose powers of doing good to man are limited by the latter's capacity for devotion and self-sacrifice. "As rivers swell the ocean, so, Hero, our prayers increase thy might."[37] "May our songs strengthen him who still hath strengthened us."[38] "Fulfil the wish and thought of him who sings thy praise."[39] "Bring splendid treasures to the man who lauds thee."[40] In fact, men and gods, are co-workers in forging the destinies of the universe. Each factor makes its own contribution to the culture of the world. "With this nourish ye the shining ones, and may the shining ones nourish you : thus nourishing one another ye shall reap the supremest good. For nourished by sacrifice, the shining ones shall bestow on you the enjoyments you desire. A thief verily is he who enjoyeth what is given by them without returning them aught."[41]

(4)

All violation of Dharma (duty) is sin. Every sin is an offence to man and to God. To remove the taint of these offences is necessary in order to establish the normal equilibrium between man and man, and man and God. Various ways are suggested by which this can be done. Hindu theory does not believe in the ruthless operation of the law of destiny. Not that the law of causation is suspended for a moment. But the evil after all is psychological; if the mentality can be changed, real evil vanishes. One way of its being exhausted is natural suffering, following in the wake of such infringements. Another is punishment at the hands of the secular agencies like the state. A third is punishment in after life in in future existences. A fourth is the consignment of hell to the sinner. a fifth way is the voluntary resort to penances, charities and so on. A sixth way is devotion to God and invoking his help. A seventh way is confession of sin, and remorse.

The Hindus believe in the concept of the grace of God. God is all-powerful, and all-merciful. All sins are expiated by a complete surrender to Him. He is (कर्तुमकर्तुमन्यथा कर्तुं समर्थः) able to do and undo everything. "Ye Gods, raise up once more the man whom ye have humbled and brought low, O Gods, restore to life again the man who hath committed sin."[42] "If by address, by blame, by imprecation, we have committed sin, awake or sleeping. All hateful acts of ours, all evil doings; may Agni bear away to distant places."[43] "Whatever sin is found in me, whatever evil I have wrought, If I have lied or falsely sworn, waters remove it from me."[44] "O bright and powerful God, through want of strength I erred and went astray. Have mercy, spare me mighty Lord."[45] "Not for one trespass, not for two, O Hero, slay us not for three, Nor yet for many trespasses."[46] The conception of ईश्वरकृपा or ईश्ववरप्रसाद (grace) finds frequent expression in the holy writings. मुख्यतस्तु महत् कृपयैव भगवद्कृपालेशाद्वा[47] "That (pure love of God) is obtained principally by the grace of the great ones, or in other words, from the touch of divine compassion." The Gita also supports this contention. "Through ever performing all actions, taking refuge in Me, *by my grace* he obtaineth the eternal indestructible abode."[48]

A distinction is established between sins committed unconsciously or through ignorance and folly and those committed deliberately. "All sins that are committed consciously are grave, while those that are committed unconsciously are trivial. There is expiation for both."[49] "That man who, having knowingly committed sin, acts righteously for expiating that sin, has to enjoy and endure the fruits of his good and bad acts separately. The utterers of Brahma maintain that all acts of injury committed in ignorance are cancelled by acts of righteousness. A sin, however, that is committed consciously, is never cancelled by righteousness. As regards myself, my view is that whatever acts are done, be they righteous or sinful, be they done knowingly or otherwise, remain.....Those acts, however, which are fraught with great injury, if done in ignorance, do without fail produce consequences and even consequences that would lead to hell, with this difference that those consequences are disproportionate in point of gravity to the acts that produce them."[50] A mild view is possible of a sin committed for the first time : but sin goes on being intensified by its repetition. "From a sinful act committed only once, one may cleanse one's self by repenting for it. From a sinful act committed twice, one may cleanse one's self by vowing never to commit it again. From such an act committed thrice, one may cleanse one's self by the resolution to bear one's self righteously ever afterwards. By committing such an act repeatedly, one may cleanse one's self by a sojourn to sacred places."[51]

One way of atonement for ordinary sins is confession.

"Thereupon the Pratiprasthatri returns to the place where the sacrificer's wife is seated. When he is about to lead the wife away, he asks her : 'With whom holdest thou intercourse?' Now when a woman who belongs to one man carries on intercourse with another, she undoubtedly commits a sin against Varuna. He therefore asks her lest she should sacrifice, with a secret pang in her mind; for when confessed the sin becomes less, since it becomes truth; this is why he thus asks her. And whatever connection she confesses not, that indeed will turn out injurious to her relatives"[52] "The heart of the sinful man proclaims the sins he has committed. Those men who have deliberately committed sins meet with destruction by seeking to conceal them from others."[53] The gods behold what one does, also the Being that is within every one.[54] Another step is repentance, the sincerity and inwardness of which is further attested, by its non-committal in future. "By confession, by repentance, by penitential austerities, and by study, a sinner is absolved of his sin.....Whenever his mind censures the misdeed his body becomes free from that sin. Having repented for his sins, he becomes absolved thereof; the mind becomes purified by the determination to desist from it in future..... Wishing to be free from the consequences of misdeeds, which he might have wilfully or unwilfully committed, let him refrain from doing it the second time."[55] The man seeking redemption looks pure and resplendent like the moon emerged from the clouds.[56] Intense repentance and complete confession in the presence of Brahmins are sufficient to remove the guilt of a sinner.[57]

There are other ways of purification, among which the practice of severe austerities is the chief. Hindu view emphasizes the powerful value of suffering as a purifying and invigorating force. "Whatever is insurmountable, whatever is inaccessible, whatever is impossible, and whatever is impossible to be performed, is easy of accomplishment by Tapasya alone; verily irresistible is the power of Tapasya. Mahapatakins (perpetrators of the heinous sins) and other miscreants become free from sins by means of severe penitential austerities."[58] Every man should choose his own way of purification suitable to his nature and capacities. "Knowledge is the Tapas of a Brahmin; protection of subjects forms the Tapas of a Kshatriya; agriculture, trade, and cattle-rearing form the Tapas of a Vaishya; and service forms the Tapas of a Shudra."[59]

Practice of virtues is also a great instrument of self-purification. Man's good and evil cancel each other; hence for every sin a man should practise more intensely the corresponding virtues. "If having committed a sin, one seeks to have it covered by righteousness, that sin becomes destroyed and leads to righteousness instead of other sins. If a quantity of water be poured upon salt the latter dissolves away."[60] "If having committed sin through folly, one does meritorious acts understanding their nature, one succeeds by such righteousness, in cleansing one's self from sin even as a piece of dirty cloth is washed clean by means of some saline substance."[61] "A slayer of creatures is cleansed of his sins by saving from imminent peril as many creatures of that particular species as have been slain by him."[62] "Sacrifice, gift, compassion, the Vedas, and Truth, these five are cleansing. The sixth is penance well-performed."[63]

The most powerful agency of expiation is knowledge. It means the most radical, the most fundamental change of one's mentality.[64] Confession, repentance, penances, and good deeds go a great way towards purifying the mind. But as long as man is not inwardly changed, he is still capable of doing future mischief. What is most essential is sincerity. This sincerity is likely to be verbal as long as it does not guarantee a man complete immunity from all weaknesses. Such a revolution in a man's mind becomes possible only when a man is converted; or in other words, when he undergoes spiritual rebirth. All actions culminate in knowledge, in realization. "And having known this, thou shalt not again fall into this confusion, O Pandava; for by this thou wilt see all things without exception in the Self, and thus in Me. Even if thou art the most sinful of all sinners, yet thou shalt cross over all sin by the raft of knowledge. As the burning fire reduces fuel to ashes, so doth the fire of knowledge reduce all actions to ashes. Verily there is no purifier in this world like knowledge."[65] क्षीयन्ते चास्य कर्माणि तस्मिन्दृष्टे परावरे।[66]

(5)

The cosmic view of existence presented to our imagination by ancient Rishis stretches out man's existence into the infinite past on one side and infinite future on the other. Mystery hangs over his beginnings, mystery hangs over his end; only the present is a bit clear.[67] The greatest step forward was taken when it was established beyond all possibility of doubt that man is essentially a soul, raised by the very nature of his position over all the accidents of a phenomenal life. "The knowing (Self) is not born, it dies not; it sprang from nothing, nothing sprang from it. The Ancient is unborn, eternal, everlasting; he is not killed though the body is killed."[68]

The necessity of postulating another world arises from the observation of an imperfect fulfilment of the divine end of justice. "The Earth holds the honest and the wicked. The sun warms the honest and the wicked. The wind blows equally for them. Water cleanses them equally." Kashyapa said, "Such indeed is the course of this world. It is not so hereafter. In the other world, there is great difference of condition between the person that acts righteously and him that acts sinfully. The regions that meritorious men acquire are full of honey. The region for the sinful is hell."[69]

These ideas have come down from the Vedic period. "Thy spirit that went far away, went to the waters and to the plants. We cause to come to thee again that thou mayst live and sojourn here."[70] "The sun receives thine eye, the wind thy spirit; go as thy merit is to earth or heaven. Go, if it be thine lot, unto the waters; go, make thine home in plants with all thy members."[71] Such passages show the rise of the doctrine of the transmigration of soul in the Vedic India. The idea of immortality also was specially connecting itself with a man's worth. "Looking on men, never slumbering, they by their deserts attained as Gods to immortality."[72] "Make me immortal in that realm where happiness and transports, where joy and felicities combine, and longing wishes are fulfilled."[73]

Hindus developed the idea of gradual emancipation (क्रम-मुक्ति), in which a man rises from personal to impersonal immortality. "As these flowing rivers that go towards the ocean, when they have reached the ocean, sink into it, their name and form vanish, and people speak of the ocean only, exactly thus these sixteen parts of the spectator that go towards the person, when they have reached the person, sink into him, their name and form vanish, and people speak of the one person only, and he becomes without parts and immortal."[74]

References

1. S.B. III. 2-33.
2. Rg. I. 164. 46.
3. Rg. Valk. X.2.
4. Rg. X.82.5.
5. Katha. Up. II. 4-11.
6. Vana. 192. 4.7.
7. Bg. XII. 3-5.
8. S.B.
9. Mait. B. Up. IV. 17.
10. Br. Up. III. 7.15.
11. Ta. Up. III. 1.
12. Rg. VIII. 87.10.
13. Bg. IX. 17-18.
14. वित्तवृत्तिनिरोध:; Sutras. 1. 2.
15. Bg. VI.
16. Shanti. 311. 13-20.
17. Shanti. 82.
18. Shanti. 62-68.
19. Shanti. 49.
20. Bg. XII.
21. Bg. VI. 30-31.

22. Bg. XVIII. 65-66.
23. Mu. U.I. 2.7-12.
24. Shanti. 247. 6-12.
25. Mu. Up.
26. Bg. XVII.3.
27. Bg. IV. 39-40.
28. Chh. Up. I.1.7.
29. Rg. X.151.
30. Rg. VII. 6.3.
31. Rg. VIII. 59. 11.
32. Vana. 31. 16-23.
33. Shanti. 75. 19.
34. Shanti. 178. 47-50.
35. Anu. 62. 28.
36. Shanti. 270. 8-17.
37. Rg. VIII. 87.8.
38. Rg. VIII. 13.18.
39. Rg. VIII. 24.6.
40. Rg. IX. 69. 10.
41. Bg. III. 11-12.
42. Rg. X. 137. 1.
43. Rg. X. 164. 3.
44. Rg. X. 9. 8.
45. Rg. VII. 89. 3.
46. Rg. VIII. 46. 34.
47. Bhakti-Sutras 38.
48. Bg. XVIII. 56 also 62.
49. Shanti. 34.45.
50. Shanti. 297. 11-16.
51. Shanti. 151. 23-26.
52. S.Br. II. 5, 2, 20.
53. Anu. 268. 36-38.
54. Vana. 210.
55. M.XI. 228-233.
56. Vana. 210. 53-60.
57. Anu. 194. 3-7.
58. M.XI. 239-240.
59. M. XI. 236.
60. Anu. 268. 33-38.
61. Shanti. 151. 34.

62. Shanti. 151. 23-26.
63. Shanti. 159. 7-9.
64. See the definition of–प्रायश्चित "तपोनिश्चयसंयोत्प्रायश्चित्तमितीर्यते।"
65. Bg. IV. 35-38.
66. Mu. Up. 2. 2.8.
67. Bg. II. 28.
68. Katha. Up. I.2.18.
69. Shanti. 73. 62-65.
70. Rg. X. 58. 461.
71. Rg. X. 16.3.
72. Rg. X. 63.4.
73. Rg. X. 113.7.
74. Pr. Up. VI. 5.

BIBLIOGRAPHY

Original Sources :

Aitareya Aranyaka with the comm. of Sayana ed. by R. Mitra, Bibliotheca Indica, Calcutta.

Aitareya Aranyaka, Ass. No. 38, Poona.

Aitareya Brahmana with the com. of Sayanacharya, Anandashrama Press, Poona.

Apastamba Paribhasa com. by Dhutraswami & Tr. by Bhattacharya, S.S., Calcutta.

Ashtangahridaya of Vagbhatta ed. by H.M. Patel, Sastu Sahitya Vardhaka Karyalaya, Bombay.

Atharvaveda com. by Sayana ed. by Vishvabandhu, Vishveshvarananda Vedic Research Institute, Hoshiarpur.

Atharvaveda Parishishta pub. by Chaukhamba Orientalia, Varanasi.

The Atharvaveda, W.D. Whitney, Part I and II, Hos. Vol. 7 and 8, Cambridge Massachusettes, Harvard University.

Baudhayana Dharmasutra, com. by Govindaswami, ed. by Shri Nivasacharya Government Branch Press, Mysore.

Bhagavadgita, Sastu Sahitya Vardhka Karyalaya, Bombay.

Bhagavad Mahapurana, ed., Shastri Rama Teja, Laxminarayana Press, Banaras.

Bhagavata Purana ed. by Shastri G.M., Sastu Sahitya Vardhaka Karyalaya, Princess Street, Bombay.

Black Yajurveda, A.B. Keith, Hos. Vols. 18 and 19, Cambridge, Massachusetts, The Harvard University Press.

Brahmanda Purana, ed. by Phanasikar Vasudeva, Nirnaya Sagara Press, Bombay.

Brahmasiddhanta by Oza Madhusudana, Banaras Hindu University.

Brahmasutrabhashya of Madhva Tr. by Rangacarya, B.R., Poona.

Brahmasutrabhashya of Nimbarka ed. Pandit Shri Dhundhiraj Shastri, Chawkhamba Sanskrit Series, Banaras.

Brahmasutrabhashya of Ramanuja Tr. by R.D. Karmarkar, University of Poona.

Brahmasutra Shankarabhashya, Nirnaya Sagar Press, Bombay.

Brahmasutranubhashya by Shri Vallabhacharya, Nirnaya Sagar Press.

Brihadaranyaka Upanishad, Madhava, SBH, Vol. XIV, The Panini Office, Bhuvaneshvari Ashrama, Allahabad.

Brihadaranyaka Upanishad com. by Sankara, Gita Press, Gorakhpur.

Brihad-Devata ed. by Mitra Rajendralala, The Asiatic Society of Bengal.

Caranavyuhaparishishtasutram by Shaunakamuni, Chaukhama Sanskrit Series, Varanasi.

Chandogya Upanishad, Madhava, SBH, Vol. XIV, The Panini Office, Bhuvaneshvari Ashrama, Allahabad.

Chandogya Upanishad, Ranga Ramanuja, Anandashrama, Ed. No. 63, Ass. No. 63, Poona.

Chandogya Upanishad, Gita Press, Gorakhpur.

Gautamasutra with the com. of Vatsyayana ed. by V.G. Apte, Anandashrama Sanskrit Series, Poona.

Gopath Brahmana, ed. by Dieuke Gaastra, Leiden.

Halayudhkosha ed. by Joshi Jayashankar, pub. by Prakashana Berau, Sachana Vibhaga, Lucknow, U.P., Jaimini Grihya-sutra, Tr. by Caland, W., Motilal Banarsidass, Delhi.

The History of Indian Literature, Albrecht Weber, Kegan Paul, Trench, Trubner & Co. Ltd., Broadway House, 68-74, Carter Lane, E.C. London.

A History of Indian Literature, M. Winternitz, Vol. I, University of Calcutta.

Jaiminiya Brahmana ed. Raghuvir and Lokesh Sharma, Sarasvati Vihara Series, Vol. 21.

Jaiminiya Upanishad com. by Upanishad Brahmayogin, Adyar Library, Madras.

Kathopanishad with the com. of Sankara, ed. by Apte, V.G., Anandashrama Printing Press, Poona.

Kaushikasutra com. by Dharila, Tilaka Vidyapitha, Poona.

Kaushitaki Brahmana text., ed. Heradsgegebenvon, E.K., Sreekrishna Sarma, Franz Steiner Verlag Gmbh, Uicsbaden.

Kapishthalakoshtha Samhita, ed. Raghuvir, Pub. Meherchand Lachhamandas Sanskrit Depot, Lahore.

Kaushitaki Kalpataru, Vol. 27.

Kaushitaki Upanishad, Sankaracharya, SBH, Vol. XXXI, Part 1, Allahabad.

Kenopanishad, pub. by Gita Press, Gorakhpur.

Kurmapurana ed. by Bhattacharya R.S., Indological Book House, Varanasi.

Kuvalayananda of Appaya Dikshita, ed. by Phanashikar, V.S., Bombay.

Mahabharata (Critical ed.), Bhandarkar Oriental Research Institute, Poona.

Mahabharata, Geeta Press, Gorakhpur.

Mahabharata, Tr. by Shastri, S.P., Sastu Sahitya Vardhaka Karyalaya, Princess Street, Bombay.

Maitri Upanishad, Sankarananda, SBH, Vol. XXXI, Part 2, Published by Major B.D. Basu, Bhuvaneswari Ashrama, Allahabad.

Manusmriti, Tr. by Shastri, G.M., Sastu Sahitya Vardhaka Karyalaya, Princess Street, Bombay.

Manusmriti with Kulluka's Commentary (6th ed.) Pub. Pandurang Jawaji, Nirnaya Sagara Press, Bombay.

Matsya Purana, ASS, No. 54, Poona.

Matsya Purana Vol. I and Vol. II. ed. Jamna Das Akhtar, The Sacred Books of the Aryans Series, Delhi.

Muktika Upanishad, ed. by Pandit Jibananda Vidyasagara, Sanskrit College of Calcutta.

Mundaka Upanishad, Gita Press, Gorakhpur.

Mandukya Upanishad, Gita Press, Gorakhpur.

Naradiya Purana, Delhi.

New World Dictionary, Webster, American Publishing Co. Pvt. Ltd., New Delhi.

Nirukta of Yaska, Anandashrama Press, Poona.

Panchavimsha Brahmana.

Patanjali Vyakarana Mahabhashya, ed. by Shastri Guruprasad, Rajasthan Sanskrit College Granthamala No. 30. Banaras.

Pranavavàda of Gargayana, Bhagavan Das, Banaras Hindu University.

Prashna Upanishad, Gita Press, Gorakhpur.

Rigveda with the com. of Sayana, Vedic Research Institute, Poona.

Rigvedadibhashyabhumika by Swami Dayananda, S., Pub. by Vaidika Yantralaya, Ajamer.

Rigveda Mandalas 1 to 10, with Sayana's Commentary, Pub. Tilak Maharashtra Vidyapitha, Vaidik Samsodhana Mandala, Poona.

Riktantram, A Pratishakhya of the SV, ed. by Shastri Suryakanta, Meharchanda Lachhamandas Sanskrit Book Depot, Lahore.

Sahityadarpana of Vishvanatha, Chaukhamba Sanskrit Series.

The Samnyasa Upanishads, with the Upanishad Brahmayogin Commentary ed. by Dikshitar, T.R.C., The Adyar Library and Research Centre, Vol. 12, Madras.

The Shakta Upanishads with Brahmayogin's Comm. ed. Mahadeva Shastri, The Adyar Library Series, No. 9, Madras.

Satapatha Brahmana with Sayana, Kaviraj Saraswati & Hariswami's Commentary, Laxmivyamkateshvar Stream Press, Kalyana, Bombay.

Satapatha Brahmana, Tr. by Pandita Gangaprasad Upadhyaya, pub. by The Research Institute of Ancient Scientific Studies, New Delhi.

Svetasvatara Upanishad, Gita Press, Gorakhpur.

Taittiriya Aranyaka, Commented by Bhatta Bhaskar Mishra, Pub. by Govt. Press, Mysore.

Taittiriya Aranyaka, com. by Sayana, Ananda Ashram Press, Poona.

Taittiriya Brahmana, com. by Bhatta Bhaskara, ed. by Shastri R.S., The Govt. Branch Press, Mysore.

Taittiriya Brahmana, ASS. No. 36, Poona.

Taittiriya Brahmana, ASS. No. 37, Poona.

Taittiriya Brahmana, ASS. No. 42, Poona.

Taittiriyasamhita, with the coms. of Bhatta Bhaskara Mishra and Sayanacharya, ed. by N.S. Sontakke & T.N. Dharmadhikari, Pub. by Vaidika Samsodhana Mandala, Poona.

Taittiriya Upanishad, with the com. of Sankara, Ananda Ashrama Press, Poona.

Taittiriyopanishadbhashyavartikam by Sureshacharya, Anandashrama Printing Press, Poona.

Tandyamahabrahmana, Kashi Sanskrit Series No. 105, Banaras.

Tarkasamgraha of Annambhatta, ed. by Athalye, Y.S., Bhandarkar Oriental Research Institute, Poona.

The Ten Principal Upanishads with Sankarbhashya, Pub. by SBE Vol. 25, Part I & Part II, Delhi.

Vachaspatyam Brihat Samskritabhidhanam, Chaukhamba Sanskrit Series, Varanasi.

Vaidika Padanukramakosha, VVRI, S.V. Series, Vol. XIII, Hoshiarpur.

Vaikhanasa Grihyasutras, ed. by S. Shastri, Baroda.

Vaiyakarana Siddhanakaumudi, ed. by Pandit Gopalashastri Nene, Chaukhamba Sanskrit Series Office, Varanasi.

Varaha Purana, All India Kashiraj Trust, Varanasi.

Vayupurana, ed. by Mitra Rajendralal, The Asiatic Society of Bengal, Culcutta.

Vishnu Purana, Gita Press, Gorakhpur.

Vishnu Purana, Oriental Press, Bombay.

INDEX

C

L

M

N

O

P

Q

R

S

T

U

V

W

Y